New Proficiency Testbuilder

Mark Harrison

◆

Macmillan Education
Between Towns Road, Oxford OX4 3PP
A division of Macmillan Publishers Limited
Companies and representatives throughout the world

ISBN 0 333 95498 X (with key)
0 333 95497 1 (without key)

First published 2002

Designed by Xen Media Ltd
Cover design by Xen Media Ltd

The author would like to thank Lena Hauberg, Denisa Coufalova, Anja Ferstl, Charlotte Hanstrom, Andrea Zs Toth, Eva Orieskova and Luise Kloss for providing the sample answers for Papers 2 and 3.

The publishers would like to thank the staff and students of East Finchley School of English for their help, and Mike Gutteridge and Lynn Gold for their input.

The author and publishers would like to thank the following for permission to reproduce their material: Halifax plc for an extract from 'No place like home' by Christine Webb in *Homes and Savings*, Summer 1995 (p8); Telegraph Group Ltd for an extract from 'Turning Points Number 19, Pennsylvania Station, New York' by Giles Worsley in *The Daily Telegraph Arts & Books*, 8 May 1999, © Telegraph Group Limited (1999) (14); PFD for an extract from *The Steps of the Sun* by Caroline Harvey reprinted by permission of PFD on behalf of Joanna Trollope, © Caroline Harvey, 1983 (p14); the Harvill Press for excerpts from *Soft City* © Jonathan Raban, 1974. Reproduced by permission of the Harvill Press (pp15, 132); Pan Macmillan for an extract from *The Dead of Jericho* by Colin Dexter, Sidgwick & Jackson, Macmillan, London, UK (p15); David Higham Associates on behalf of the author for extracts from *Inspector Thanet Omnibus* by Dorothy Simpson, Warner Books (1994) (p16); Pearson Education Ltd for extracts from *The Penguin History of the United States of America* by Hugh Brogan, Penguin (1990), © Pearson Education Limited 1985, 1999, reprinted by permission of Pearson Education Limited (pp18, 88); News International Syndication for an extract from 'Why advertising matters' by Stephen Armstrong in *The Sunday Times Arts Supplement*, 30 April 2000, © Stephen Armstrong/Times Newspapers Limited, 2000 (p25); *The Hendon and Finchley Press* for an extract from 'Tube inspired a book', *The Press* 27 April 2000 (p28); Abner Stein on behalf of the author for an extract from the Foreword by Dr Anthony Clare to *You and Your Adolescent* by Laurence Steinberg and Ann Levine, Ebury Press (1992) (p31); Mic Cheetham Literary Agency on behalf of the author for an extract from *Teenagers – A Family Survival Guide* by Laurie Graham, Chatto & Windus (1992) (p32); Pan Macmillan for an extract from *Spencer Tracy* by Bill Davidson, Sidgwick & Jackson, Macmillan, London, UK (p50); Penguin Books (UK) for an extract from *Peerless Flats* by Esther Freud (Hamish Hamilton, 1993) Copyright © Esther Freud, 1993 (p50); Jane Furnival for an extract from 'The most liberating gadget ever?' in *Weekend Telegraph*, 5 September 1998; News International Syndication for an extract from 'Game for a laugh' by Simon Barnes in *The Times MM Supplement*, 9 October 1999, © Simon Barnes/Times Newspapers Limited (1999) (p52); Little, Brown and Company (UK) for an extract from *Staying Up* by Rick Gekoski, (1998) (p52); Mainstream Publishing Co. Ltd for an extract from *The Red and the Black* by Michael Aylwin with Matt Singer (1999) (p53); Macmillan for an extract from *All the Rage* by Ian McLagen, Sidgwick & Jackson, Macmillan Ltd, London (p57); Blake Friedmann Literary Agency on behalf of the author and The Random House Group for an extract from *Free to Trade* by Michael Ridpath, published by William Heinemann. Reprinted by permission of The Random House Group Ltd (p59); Coventry *Evening Telegraph* for an extract from 'King of the watchmakers' by Mark Forster, 12 February 2000 (p67); International Thomson Publishing Services Ltd for an extract from *Understanding Popular Culture* by John Fiske, Unwin Hyman (1989) (p72); News International Syndication for an extract from 'The Horse's Tale' by Rachel Campbell-Johnston in *The Times Magazine*, 21 June 1997, © Times Newspapers Ltd (p86); Penguin Books (UK) for an extract from *Gossip from Thrush Green* by Miss Read (Michael Joseph, 1981) © 1981 by Miss Read (p87); The Orion Publishing Group Ltd for an extract from *Kenneth Williams* by Michael Freedland, Weidenfeld & Nicolson (1990) (p88); Transworld Publishers, © Kate Atkinson. Extracted from *Human Croquet*, published by Black Swan, a division of Transworld Publishers. All rights reserved (p89); The Orion Publishing Group Ltd for an extract from 'The Pawn King' by Dominic Lawson in *More Than a Game, GQ on Sport* ed. Philip Watson, The Orion Publishing Group Ltd (p97); Telegraph Group Ltd for an extract from 'Celebrity crossover' by Tim Dowling in *Telegraph magazine*, 26 February 2000, © Telegraph Group Limited (p107); Atlantic Syndication for an extract from 'Hero sunk by a lust for stardom' by Roger Deakin in *Mail on Sunday Review*, 25 June 2000 (p108); HarperCollins Publishers for an extract from *Class: Image and Reality* by Arthur Marwick, HarperCollins Publishers Ltd (p114); The Random House Group for Extract from *Class* by Jilly Cooper, published by Methuen. Used by permission of The Random House Group Ltd (p115); News International Syndication for an extract from 'Getting the bird' by A. A. Gill in *The Sunday Times*, 15 June 1997, © A. A. Gill/Times Newspapers Limited (1997) (p131); The Random House Group for an extract from *Swing Hammer Swing!* by Jeff Torrington, published by Martin Secker & Warburg. Reprinted by permission of The Random House Group Ltd (p131); Penguin Books (UK) for an extract from *X-Ray* by Ray Davies (Viking, 1994) Copyright © Ray Davies, 1994 (p133) and for an extract from *Faithfull* by Marianne Faithfull with David Dalton, Michael Joseph (1994) Copyright © Marianne Faithfull, 1994 (p134); The Random House Group for an extract from *The Railway Man* by Eric Lomax, published by Jonathan Cape. Reprinted by permission of The Random House Group Ltd (p135); News International Syndication for an extract from 'Rainmaker with his head in the clouds' by Anjana Ahuja in *The Times*, 16 February 1998, © Times Newspapers Limited (1998) (p136); The Random House Group for an extract from *Over the Limit* by Bob Monkhouse, published by Century. Reprinted by permission of The Random House Group Ltd (p138); Dyson Appliances Ltd for an extract from 'The slow arrival of the wheel' by James Dyson, *James Dyson's History of Great Inventions*, Part 1, 2000 in *Telegraph magazine* (p151); Telegraph Group Ltd for an extract from 'Frantic Semantics: Bogus' by John Morrish in *Telegraph magazine*, 4 March 2000 (p152); Thames & Hudson Ltd for an extract from *Design Since 1945* by Peter Dormer (1993) (p157).

The author and publishers would like to thank the University of Cambridge Local Examinations Syndicate for the assessment criteria and sample answer sheets.

The author and publishers would like to thank the following for permission to reproduce their material on cassette: Telegraph Group Ltd for extracts from the following: 'It's a dirty job, but if he didn't do it…' by Jonny Beardsall in *Telegraph Weekend*, 5 June 1999 (p75); 'Happy hero of the silent era' by Mark Monahan in *The Daily Telegraph*, 29 March 1999 (p76), © Telegraph Group Limited (1999); 'Are you a maven or a connector?' by Damian Thompson in *The Daily Telegraph Arts & Books*, 6 May 2000, © Telegraph Group Limited (2000) (p38); David Higham Associates on behalf of the author for an extract from 'C'mon man – get a grip' by Geoffrey Wall in *Telegraph Weekend*, 26 September 1998 (p38); Kogan Page for an extract from *Careers in Catering, Hotel Administration and Management* by Russell Joseph, © Russell Joseph, 1997, Kogan Page Limited (p43) and for an extract from *Careers in Retailing* by Loulou Brown, © Loulou Brown, 1997, Kogan Page Limited (p45); Abner Stein on behalf of the authors and The Random House Group for an extract from *Getting to Yes* by Roger Fisher and William Ury published by Hutchinson. Used by permission of The Random House Group Limited (pp72–3); Anna Fox and Roger Highfield for an extract from 'Seeing is believing – any moment now …' in *The Daily Telegraph*, 26 April 2000 (p76); Michael O'Mara Books Ltd on behalf of the author for extracts from *How Household Names Began* (1997) (pp77, 162); Atlantic Syndication for an extract from 'We lived without TV for a year – and loved it' by Miranda Ingram in *Daily Mail*, 17 August 2000 (p80); F&W Publications, Inc., excerpted from *Successful Scriptwriting* copyright © 1991 by Jurgan Wolff and Kerry Cox. Used with permission of Writer's Digest Books, and imprint of F&W Publications, Inc. All rights reserved (p81); Atlantic Syndication for extracts from 'Cheer up, life can only get worse!' by Quentin Letts in *Daily Mail*, 21 June 2000, 'What's cooking?' by Rosie Shepherd in *Night & Day*, 18 June 2000 (p119) and 'More than a game' by Stephen Ferns in *Evening Standard Supplement*, 25 February 2000 (p120); Dyson Appliances Ltd for an extract from 'Why we need a new patent law' by James Dyson, *James Dyson's History of Great Inventions*, Part 3, Introduction, 2000 in *Telegraph magazine* (p120); Paddy Burt for an extract from 'I wouldn't give Paddy Burt the mumps' in *Telegraph Travel*, 20 April 2000, from *Room Service*, Enigma (2000), © Paddy Burt (p122); Sheldon Press for an extract from *How to Improve your Confidence* by Dr Kenneth Hambly (1987) (p160); Telegraph Group Ltd for extracts from 'Caricature is packed with triple explosives' by Nicholas Garland in *The Daily Telegraph*, 8 June 2000 (p160), 'I think I have a way with pain' by Will Cohu in *The Daily Telegraph Arts & Books*, 6 May 2000 (p161), © Telegraph Group Limited (2000), and 'Rhythm 'n' roads' by Mick Brown in *Telegraph Travel*, 20 November 1999 (p161), © Telegraph Group Limited (1999).

Whilst every effort has been made to trace owners of copyright material in this book, there may have been some cases when the publishers have been unable to contact the owners. We should be grateful to hear from anyone who recognises copyright material and who is unacknowledged. We shall be pleased to make the necessary amendments in future editions of the book.

The authors and publishers would like to thank the following for permission to reproduce their photographic material:
Mary Evans Picture Library p176 (c); The Hulton Archive pp176 (a, b); Image Bank p173 (d); Pictor p172 (b); Superstock pp171 (c), 172 (a, c); Stone p171 (a), 174 (a), 175 (d, e); Telegraph Colour Library p171 (b, d), 173 (e), 174 (b, c).

Printed and bound in Spain
by Edelvives

2006 2005 2004 2003 2002
10 9 8 7 6 5 4 3 2 1

CONTENTS

THE NEW PROFICIENCY TESTBUILDER

The New Proficiency Testbuilder is much more than a book of Practice Tests. A completely new version for the Revised Proficiency exam in operation from December 2002, it is designed not only to enable students to do tests of exactly the kind they will encounter in the exam itself, but also to provide them with valuable further practice, guidance and explanation. This will enable them to prepare thoroughly for the exam and increase their ability to perform well in it.

The New Proficiency Testbuilder contains:

Four complete Practice Tests for the Cambridge Certificate of Proficiency in English

These tests reflect exactly the level and types of question to be found in the exam.

Further Practice and Guidance pages

These are included for each part of each paper and they come immediately after the part of the exam they relate to (see Contents). For each part of each paper, they include **What's Tested** sections, which provide detailed explanations of the precise focus of each part of the exam, and **Tips** sections, which provide advice on the best approaches to answering the questions. Throughout these pages, students are encouraged to draw their own conclusions as to what the correct answers to the questions in the test are, and the step-by-step approach taken enables students to develop and apply the right processes when answering the questions in the exam.

For PAPER 1 READING, the Further Practice and Guidance pages contain exercises and questions directly related to the questions in the test.

For PAPER 2 WRITING, the Further Practice and Guidance pages provide outlines enabling students to plan their answers. They also contain **samples** of each kind of writing that may be included in the exam (article, report, etc) for students to assess.

For PAPER 3 USE OF ENGLISH, the Further Practice and Guidance pages contain exercises and questions directly related to the questions in the test. They also contain exercises for planning the summary tasks and **samples** of summaries for students to assess.

For PAPER 4 LISTENING, the Further Practice and Guidance pages contain exercises directly related to the questions in the test.

For PAPER 5 SPEAKING, the Further Practice and Guidance pages provide exercises on vocabulary likely to be useful in general terms, exercises on vocabulary relating to the themes for discussion in the tests and practice in talking about pictures.

Key and Explanation

This contains full explanations of every answer to every question in the tests.

For PAPER 1 READING, this section contains detailed explanations not only of the correct choices, but also of why other options are incorrect. Within these explanations, key vocabulary in the texts is explained.

For PAPER 2 WRITING, this section contains task-specific mark schemes for each question and assessments of the sample answers.

For PAPER 3 USE OF ENGLISH, this section contains detailed explanations of the answers to each question, including grammatical and lexical information, mark schemes for the summaries and assessments of the sample summaries.

For PAPER 4 LISTENING, this section contains detailed explanations not only of the correct choices, but also of why the other options are incorrect. Within these explanations, key vocabulary in the pieces is explained.

For PAPER 5 SPEAKING, definitions are given of the vocabulary in the Further Practice and Guidance pages.

How to use the New Proficiency Testbuilder

Teachers and students who have the edition with key can use the book in a number of ways:

1 Simply follow the instructions page by page. Clear directions are given as to the order in which to do things. If you follow this order, you:

- complete one part of a paper, perhaps under exam conditions, and then

either

- do the Further Practice and Guidance pages relating to that part and check the answers to the questions in those pages. Then review the answers given to the questions in the test in the light of what has been learnt from doing the Further Practice and Guidance pages. Finally, check the answers to the questions in the test and go through the explanations of them.

Or

- check the answers to the questions in the test and go through the explanations of them if there are no Further Practice and Guidance pages and

then

- move on to the next part of the test.

2 Vary the order.

You may wish to do some of the Further Practice and Guidance pages before answering the questions in the test that they relate to. Alternatively, teachers may wish to do the Further Practice and Guidance pages as discussion or pairwork, or ask students to prepare them before class.

The Certificate of Proficiency in English

The following is a brief summary of what the exam consists of. Full details of what is tested in each Part of each Paper are given in the relevant Further Practice and Guidance pages.

PAPER 1 READING 1 hour 30 minutes

Part	Text	Question Type	Number of Questions	Number of Marks
1	3 short texts, each with 6 gaps	6 x 4-option multiple-choice questions per text, testing vocabulary, 1 mark per question	18	18
2	4 short texts with a linked theme	2 x 4-option multiple-choice questions per text, testing comprehension, 2 marks per question	8	16
3	1 long text with 7 gaps	choosing from 8 paragraphs to fill each gap, testing text structure and meaning, 2 marks per question	7	14
4	1 long text	7 x 4-option multiple-choice questions, testing comprehension, 2 marks per question	7	14
		Total	40	62

PAPER 2 WRITING 2 hours

Part	Question Types	Number of Words	Number of Marks
1	compulsory, may be an article, letter, essay or proposal	300–350	20
2	choice of one of three options (options are article, letter, proposal, report, review) or choice of one from three set book questions* *Candidates can choose from three set books, which are specified in the exam regulations each year. Since the set books change from year to year, these have not been included in this book.	300–350	20
	Total		40

PAPER 3 USE OF ENGLISH 1 hour 30 minutes

Part	Task	Question Type	Number of Questions	Number of Marks
1	1 short text with 15 gaps	filling each gap with one word, mostly testing grammar, 1 mark per question	15	15
2	1 short text with 10 gaps	filling each gap with one word formed from the word given, testing word formation, 1 mark per question	10	10
3	6 sets of three sentences, each with a gap	filling the gaps with one word that is appropriate in all three sentences, testing vocabulary, 2 marks per question	6	12

4	8 sentences to be rephrased	rephrasing the given sentence using a word supplied and the beginning and ending supplied, testing vocabulary and grammar, 2 marks per question	8	16
5	2 short texts, each with two questions Summary writing task	write answers to the two comprehension questions on each text, 2 marks per question, and write brief summary of both texts	4 1	8 14
		Total	44	75

PAPER 4 LISTENING approximately 40 minutes

Part	Piece	Question Type	Number of Questions	Number of Marks
1	4 short pieces	2 x 3-option multiple-choice questions per piece, testing comprehension, 1 mark per question	8	8
2	1 longer piece, usually a monologue	9 sentences to complete with information given in the piece, 1 mark per question	9	9
3	1 dialogue, often an interview	5 x 4-option multiple-choice questions, testing comprehension, 1 mark per question	5	5
4	1 discussion involving two speakers	6 x matching views to speaker expressing them (sometimes views are expressed by both speakers), 1 mark per question	6	6
		Total	28	28

PAPER 5 SPEAKING 19 minutes (usually two candidates and two examiners)

Part	Activity	Length
1	conversation between examiner and each candidate on general and social matters	3 minutes
2	talking about pictures, followed by conversation between candidates on topic arising from one or two of the pictures	4 minutes
3	each candidate talks for two minutes, based on prompts given to them on a card; candidates then discuss with each other and the examiner the topics related to the prompt cards for eight minutes	12 minutes
	Marks	20

Marks are worked out so that each paper is worth 40 marks. This gives a total of 200 marks, which can be divided by two to give a percentage. To pass, candidates need to score approximately 60%.

TEST ONE

PAPER 1 READING 1 hour 30 minutes

PART ONE

For questions 1–18, read the three texts below and decide which answer (A, B, C or D) best fits each gap. In the exam you will mark your answers on a separate answer sheet.

Living in Flats in Britain

The British have never **(1)** .... to flat dwelling in the way that other Europeans have. This is probably because of the English Channel. Continental European city dwellers had to build walls to keep out marauding invaders. Those who farmed the city hinterlands would **(2)** .... inside the walls and close the gates when danger approached. Space within the walls was at a **(3)** .... , so it made sense to pile one home above another in the form of flats. Flats were the **(4)** .... in cities like Paris from as early as the 15th century. Apart from the odd Viking, invaders were kept from British shores by the sea, allowing the British to live in houses **(5)** .... across the countryside in villages, hamlets and market towns, the only city of any size at that time being London. It was not until the industrial revolution started **(6)** .... people off the land into towns in the late 18th century that there was a demand for mass housing. Then, rooms in houses were rented by the poor and each family would share one room.

1	**A** fallen	**B** run	**C** taken	**D** given
2	**A** dash	**B** expedite	**C** gush	**D** inundate
3	**A** rarity	**B** shortcoming	**C** dearth	**D** premium
4	**A** average	**B** norm	**C** par	**D** yardstick
5	**A** messed	**B** scattered	**C** littered	**D** sprayed
6	**A** luring	**B** eliciting	**C** spurring	**D** inciting

Meeting Marvin Gaye

When I first met Marvin Gaye in his Sunset Strip studio, I had just completed a two-year project co-writing the autobiography of Ray Charles, an inspiring collaborator, but an authoritative and often **(7)** .... figure. Marvin came on like a brother. He was warm, witty and **(8)** .... to laugh. He spoke like he sang, in whisper-quiet melodies and soft falsettos. His conversation had a lyricism all of its **(9)** .... His affectations – a slight British accent when he was feeling aristocratic, for example – were more than **(10)** .... by his disarming sincerity. We became friends. I felt **(11)** .... to watch him work and play up-close. It soon became clear that, like his music, his personal life was filled with dramatic contradictions, a combination of charm and chaos. Because he was a hero of mine, and because his art was so dazzlingly beautiful – so self-contained, so accomplished, so **(12)** .... slick – it took me a while to realize my hero was drowning.

7	**A** distant	**B** faint	**C** secluded	**D** far-away
8	**A** prompt	**B** abrupt	**C** impulsive	**D** quick
9	**A** type	**B** self	**C** like	**D** own
10	**A** set against	**B** weighed up	**C** made up for	**D** settled up with
11	**A** advantageous	**B** privileged	**C** indulgent	**D** gainful
12	**A** appreciably	**B** fully	**C** utterly	**D** sorely

Sir John

Sir John did not seek to belittle and undermine for the sake of it. It was easy to mock – **(13)** .... , it was the instinctive reaction of any thinking being to the modern world – but great harm could be caused by thoughtless mockery. His intention was merely to instil a little humility. He was fighting a **(14)** .... battle, he knew. His colleagues – the psychiatric, the teaching and the social work professions – were all doing their **(15)** .... to raise people's self-esteem. It was their basic credo; everybody was **(16)** .... by low self-esteem. For Sir John, on the other hand, the self-esteem of most of the men and women he came across was far too high for their own **(17)** .... , or anybody else's, already. The job of the professors was not so much to promote the uncontrolled expansion of self-esteem **(18)** .... to forcibly ram it back into the Pandora's box from which it should never have been liberated, and then sit upon the lid.

13	**A** in that case	**B** indeed	**C** to that end	**D** still
14	**A** losing	**B** failing	**C** defeating	**D** wasting
15	**A** bounds	**B** excess	**C** lengths	**D** utmost
16	**A** afflicted	**B** sustained	**C** undergone	**D** grieved
17	**A** behalf	**B** avail	**C** good	**D** interest
18	**A** except	**B** so	**C** as	**D** just

Before you check your answers to Part One of the test, go on to pages 10–13.

WHAT'S TESTED

Part One of the Reading Paper focuses on vocabulary. Questions may test any of the following:

- **semantic precision** – choosing the word with the right meaning in the context. This does not involve completing a phrase or deciding according to grammatical structure; you must simply decide which option has the correct meaning in relation to the meaning of the sentence or the text as a whole.
- **collocation** – choosing which word goes together with another or others to form a phrase. It may be possible to fill the gap with another word that is not an option in the question, but only one of the words given as an option correctly completes the phrase.
- **complementation** – choosing the option that fits grammatically. More than one of the options may have the right meaning but only one will form a grammatically correct structure.
- **idioms** – phrases that have a special meaning as phrases, which may differ substantially from the meaning of the individual words in them. Questions testing idioms involve choosing which single word completes the idiom.
- **fixed phrases** – phrases in which the individual parts are always used together, and in which the meaning can be logically worked out from the meaning of the individual words in them. Questions testing fixed phrases involve knowing which single word completes them.
- **phrasal verbs** – phrases consisting of a verb followed by a preposition and/or an adverb which have a special meaning that cannot be worked out simply from the meaning of the verb. Questions may involve choosing which single word completes a phrasal verb or choosing from a set of complete phrasal verbs.
- **linkers** – words or phrases that connect sentences or parts of sentences. Questions testing linkers involve choosing from single-word linkers, deciding which word completes a linking phrase or choosing from complete linking phrases.

TIPS

- Read the text very carefully to make sure that the options you choose make sense in terms of the meaning of the text. If you only focus on a few words immediately before or after a gap, you may incorrectly choose an option that might seem to fit grammatically and in isolation, but does not fit in the context of the text.
- Make sure that the option you choose fits grammatically. It may be that more than one of the options fit the meaning of the text but that only one fits in grammatically.
- Don't choose an option simply because it looks like the 'hardest' word or because it is the only one that you don't know. The correct option may be a relatively simple word, though not used in a simple phrase or with its simplest meaning.

In each of the exercises below, choose which of the four options fits into each of the four sentences. Each exercise relates to the question with the same number in the test, and the options are the same as those given for that question in the test. This will help you to eliminate some of the incorrect options in the test or to confirm that you have selected the correct option.

Living in Flats in Britain

1 | *fallen* | *run* | *taken* | *given* |

A Tim has always been .... to dreams he has no hope of achieving.

B Louise has .... to life in her new country as if she'd been born there.

C Graham has .... into the habit of forgetting promises he has made.

D Julie has always .... to her friends whenever she has a problem.

2 | *dash* *expedite* *gush* *inundate* |

A The pipe broke and water started to .... out of it and onto the floor.
B To .... the bureaucratic process, I contacted the manager direct.
C I had to .... around to get everything ready for the trip in time.
D Fans started to .... the box office as soon as the tickets went on sale.

3 | *rarity* *shortcoming* *dearth* *premium* |

A Lack of patience is her main .... in her dealings with people.
B Ann got a job easily because people with her experience were at a ....
C Instances of that disease are a .... in this day and age.
D There is definitely a .... of young talent in sport these days.

4 | *average* *norm* *par* *yardstick* |

A His work became the .... by which everyone else's was measured.
B In this society, such behaviour is the ...., it's not an exception.
C My earnings at that time were well below the national ....
D Sudden changes are .... for the course in this company, as I've learnt.

5 | *messed* *scattered* *littered* *sprayed* |

A When he opened the bottle, everyone got .... with champagne.
B The room was .... with the remains of the previous night's party.
C All my plans got .... up because other people let me down.
D His office was untidy, with papers .... around all over the place.

6 | *luring* *eliciting* *spurring* *inciting* |

A Recent wins have been .... the team on to play better and better.
B I wrote them several letters, without .... a response.
C It was said that troublemakers were .... the protesters to riot.
D Clever advertising has been .... people into taking up this offer.

Meeting Marvin Gaye

7 | *distant* *faint* *secluded* *far-away* |

A It is hard to warm towards someone who is so .... with everyone else.
B They gave me only a .... outline of the project they had in mind.
C Fame caused her to lead a rather .... life, in her own private world.
D She had a .... look in her eyes, as if something was troubling her.

8 | *prompt* | *abrupt* | *impulsive* | *quick* |

A Frank is .... to blame other people when something goes wrong.
B He's .... and makes promises without thinking about the consequences.
C Hazel has a very .... manner, which many people find rude.
D I think it's important to be .... in replying to letters and messages.

9 | *type* | *self* | *like* | *own* |

A There was amazing scenery, the .... of which I had never seen before.
B People of his .... would lie to anyone if it was to their advantage.
C The island is unlike any other, as it has an atmosphere all its ....
D After a bad patch, Helen is back to her old .... again, I'm glad to say.

10 | *set against* | *weighed up* | *made up for* | *settled up with* |

A When I'd .... both sides of the argument, I made my decision.
B I hope this present has .... the fact that I forgot your birthday.
C When the cost was .... the benefits, the scheme looked good.
D She paid for both of us and I .... her when we got home.

11 | *advantageous* | *privileged* | *indulgent* | *gainful* |

A Doing this course might prove .... to me in my future career.
B She has rather .... parents, who give her everything she asks for.
C He said he felt .... when he was made captain of the national team.
D It took James some time to find .... employment when he left college.

12 | *appreciably* | *fully* | *utterly* | *sorely* |

A When Sally leaves this department, she will be .... missed.
B I think they're .... brilliant and they're my favourite group.
C I was .... expecting to have a bad day, but it turned out all right.
D Her health is .... better than it was a week or so ago.

Sir John

13 | *in that case* | *indeed* | *to that end* | *still* |

A You can't come on Friday? Well ...., we'll have to meet another day.
B I haven't got much money; .... , things could be a lot worse.
C I don't think you made a mistake; .... , I would have done the same.
D She wanted promotion and .... she set about impressing others.

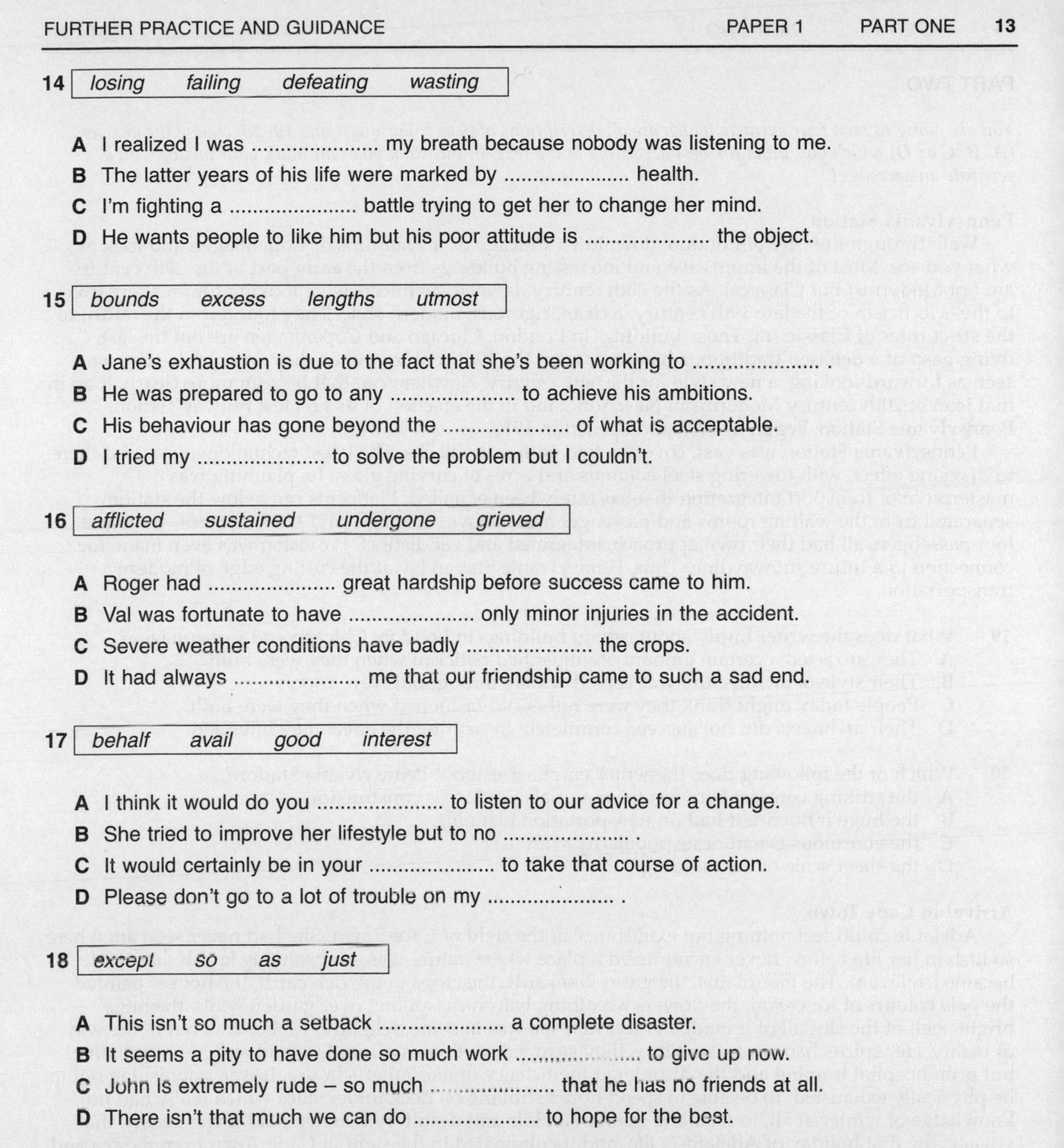

14 | *losing* | *failing* | *defeating* | *wasting* |

A I realized I was .... my breath because nobody was listening to me.

B The latter years of his life were marked by .... health.

C I'm fighting a .... battle trying to get her to change her mind.

D He wants people to like him but his poor attitude is .... the object.

15 | *bounds* | *excess* | *lengths* | *utmost* |

A Jane's exhaustion is due to the fact that she's been working to ....

B He was prepared to go to any .... to achieve his ambitions.

C His behaviour has gone beyond the .... of what is acceptable.

D I tried my .... to solve the problem but I couldn't.

16 | *afflicted* | *sustained* | *undergone* | *grieved* |

A Roger had .... great hardship before success came to him.

B Val was fortunate to have .... only minor injuries in the accident.

C Severe weather conditions have badly .... the crops.

D It had always .... me that our friendship came to such a sad end.

17 | *behalf* | *avail* | *good* | *interest* |

A I think it would do you .... to listen to our advice for a change.

B She tried to improve her lifestyle but to no ....

C It would certainly be in your .... to take that course of action.

D Please don't go to a lot of trouble on my ....

18 | *except* | *so* | *as* | *just* |

A This isn't so much a setback .... a complete disaster.

B It seems a pity to have done so much work .... to give up now.

C John is extremely rude – so much .... that he has no friends at all.

D There isn't that much we can do .... to hope for the best.

Now check your answers to these exercises. When you have done so, decide whether you wish to change any of your answers to Part One of the test. Then check your answers to Part One of the test.

PART TWO

*You are going to read four extracts which are all descriptions of places. For questions **19–26**, choose the answer (**A**, **B**, **C** or **D**) which you think fits best according to the text. In the exam you will mark your answers on a separate answer sheet.*

Pennsylvania Station

Walk through the City of London, downtown Chicago or the suburbs of Copenhagen and look at what you see. Most of the impressive and interesting buildings from the early part of the 20th century are not Modernist but Classical. As the 20th century dawned, architects were looking for an alternative to the eclecticism of the late 19th century; a clean, rigorous, modern style. They found it in the return to the strict rules of Classicism. Those buildings in London, Chicago and Copenhagen are not the last, dying gasp of a debased tradition, a hangover from the 19th century. When they were built, they were seen as forward-looking, a new style for the new century. Nowhere can that be seen more clearly than in that icon of 20th century Modernism, New York, and in the erection of its greatest railway station, Pennsylvania Station, begun in 1905 and opened in 1910.

Pennsylvania Station was vast, covering two entire city blocks. The latest technology was used there to dizzying effect, with towering steel columns and acres of curving glass. Its planning was a masterpiece of transport integration that has rarely been equalled. Platforms ran below the station, separated from the waiting rooms and passenger areas above. Carriage (and later car), bus, train and foot passengers all had their own approach, integrated and yet distinct. Provision was even made for connection to a future subway line. Thus, Pennsylvania Station lay at the cutting edge of modern transportation.

19 What does the writer imply about certain buildings in London, Chicago and Copenhagen?
A They attracted a certain amount of unjustified criticism when they were built.
B Their style of architecture was copied widely throughout New York.
C People today might think they were rather old-fashioned when they were built.
D Their architects did not succeed completely in creating the effect they intended.

20 Which of the following does the writer emphasize about Pennsylvania Station?
A the striking contrast between the materials used in its construction
B the huge influence it had on transportation planning
C the enormous extent of its popularity with users
D the sheer scale of the building

Arrival in Cape Town

Adelaide could feel nothing but exuberance at the sight of Cape Town. She had never seen anywhere so lush in her life before, never encountered a place where nature was so absolutely lavish that waste became irrelevant. The mountains, the green vineyards, the crops in the rich earth, the houses painted the pale colours of ice cream, the flowers wreathing balconies, spilling over garden walls, the huge bright shell of the sky, all of it made her feel that she was in some delightful limbo, well out of the way of reality. Her spirits had risen steadily as they steamed south away from England and her impressive but grim hospital training and the disordered inefficiency of her father's house. It was astonishing not to be physically exhausted, to be able to spend hours strolling on deck under skies which really had no knowledge of winter at all, to read and think in an idle and desultory manner. And it was reality, that voyage, the first holiday of Adelaide's life, and it culminated in the sight of Cape Town from the sea and the quayside where baskets of grapes and apples were dotted among military stores and pieces of artillery wrapped in sacking.

21 The writer says that, as she approached Cape Town, Adelaide was struck by
A how different it was from her expectations of it.
B the contrasts between the colours she saw.
C how pleasant life there seemed to be.
D the apparent neatness of the place.

22 We learn from the extract that it was unusual for Adelaide to
A spend time aimlessly.
B be objective about her life in England.
C feel a desire to relax.
D be observant in other places.

My London

We map cities by private benchmarks which are meaningful only to us. The Greater London Council is responsible for a sprawl shaped like a rugby ball about 25 miles long and 20 miles wide; my London is a concise kidney-shaped patch within that space, in which no point is more than about seven miles from any other. I hardly ever trespass beyond those limits, and when I do I feel I'm in a foreign territory, a landscape of hazard and rumour. The constrictedness of this private city-within-a-city has the character of a self-fulfilling prophecy. Its boundaries, originally arrived at by chance and usage, grow more not less real the longer I live in London. I have friends who live in Clapham, only three miles away, but to visit them is a definite journey, for it involves crossing the river. I can, though, drop in on friends in Islington, twice as far away as Clapham, since it is in what I feel to be my own territory. When I first came to London, I moved about the city much more freely than I do now, I took the liberties of a tourist and measured distances in miles rather than by the relationship with the unknown. In Manhattan, on my first afternoon in New York, I asked the man I'd lunched with for directions to a part of downtown Brooklyn where I had to make a call. He puzzled over my question and eventually needed to look at my map; he had lived in New York for 25 years, and had last been to Brooklyn, just over the bridge from his office, 12 years ago.

23 The writer describes himself as someone who
- **A** has a tendency to get confused about the geography of cities.
- **B** has become less adventurous since arriving in London.
- **C** is too lazy to explore London more than he has done.
- **D** wants to conquer an instinctive fear of unfamiliar places.

24 The writer uses Clapham and Brooklyn to illustrate his belief that
- **A** some areas of cities have undeservedly bad reputations.
- **B** if you live in a city, it begins to seem smaller after a while.
- **C** some areas of cities are more attractive to visitors than to people who live there.
- **D** if you live in a city, distance has little to do with whether you visit an area or not.

Oxford

Oxford's main tourist attractions are reasonably proximate to one another and there are guide books a-plenty, translated into many languages. Thus it is that the day visitor may climb back into his luxury coach after viewing the fine University buildings clustered between the High and the Radcliffe Camera with the gratifying feeling that it has all been a compact, interesting visit to yet another of England's most beautiful cities. It is all very splendid: it is all a bit tiring. And so it is fortunate that the neighbouring Cornmarket can offer to the visitor its string of snack bars, coffee bars and burger bars in which to rest his feet and browse through his recently purchased literature about those other colleges and ecclesiastical edifices, their *line 8* dates and their benefactors, which thus far have fallen outside his rather arbitrary wanderings.

But perhaps by noon he's had enough, and quits such culture for the Westgate shopping *line 10* complex, only a pedestrian precinct away, and built on the old site of St Ebbe's, where the city fathers found the answer to their inner-city obsolescence in the full-scale flattening of the *line 12* ancient streets and houses, and their replacement by the concrete giants of supermarket stores *line 13* and municipal offices.

25 The writer implies that some tourists who visit Oxford
- **A** fail to appreciate the real beauty of the place.
- **B** end up reading about places they do not actually visit.
- **C** feel that the interesting buildings are too close together.
- **D** are given a false impression of the place.

26 Which of these words does the writer use to indicate his approval of buildings in Oxford?
- **A** edifices (line 8)
- **B** culture (line 10)
- **C** obsolescence (line 12)
- **D** giants (line 13)

Now check your answers to Part Two of the test.

PART THREE

*You are going to read an extract from a novel. Seven paragraphs have been removed from the extract. Choose from the paragraphs **A–H** the one which fits each gap **(27–33)**. There is one extra paragraph which you do not need to use. In the exam you will mark your answers on a separate answer sheet.*

Husband and Wife

Detective Inspector Luke Thanet was a happy man. He had an interesting job, no pressing financial worries, two healthy, lively children and, perhaps best of all, a wife who was all that any man could wish for.

27 ______

Reaching for his pipe, he tapped it out, scraped it, inspected it, blew through it, then filled it with loving care. 'It's nine o'clock,' Joan said. 'D'you want the news?' 'I don't think so. Do you?' 'Not particularly.'

28 ______

Now she fidgeted, crossed and re-crossed her legs, fiddled with her hair, chewed the tip of her thumb. Eventually, 'Book no good?' Thanet enquired. She looked up at once. 'Mmm? Oh, it's all right. Very interesting, in fact.' 'What's the matter, then?' She hesitated, gave him a speculative look. He laid down his newspaper. 'Come on, love. Out with it.'

29 ______

'Oh?' he said, warily. She looked at him with something approaching desperation. 'It's just that ... oh dear ... Look, you know we've said all along that when Ben starts school I'll go back to work? Well, that's only six months away now. So I really ought to start thinking about what I want to do.' 'I see,' Thanet said slowly. 'There you are. I knew you wouldn't like it.' 'Darling, don't be silly. It's just that, well, the idea will take a bit of getting used to after all this time, that's all.' 'Don't pretend,' she said. 'You're dead against it really, aren't you? I can tell.'

30 ______

Now, in a flash, he saw all of that changing. Uncomfortable adjustments would have to be made, there would be inconvenience, irritation, arguments. Theory and practice, he now realized, were very different matters. All very well, in the past, to contemplate with equanimity the prospect of Joan returning to work one day, but to accept that that day was almost here ... No, he didn't like it at all.

31 ______

'No. Oh, I did consider it seriously, at one time. I'm very interested, as you know. But ... I don't know, I'd like to feel I was doing something, well, less self-indulgent, more useful. Oh, dear, does that sound horribly priggish?'

32 ______

'Not in the least. What sort of thing did you have in mind?' 'Well, that's the trouble. I'm just not qualified for anything. That's why I feel I ought to start thinking about it now, so that if I have to do a course, or any special training, I can get organized for September.' 'Yes, I can see that. You haven't gone into it yet, then?'

33 ______

Very much later, he told himself, as he drove to work next morning. And preferably not at all.

A Not very inspiring, he thought guiltily, assessing the situation in the light of Joan's projected foray into the world of work. 'I meant it, you know. You go ahead, make enquiries, find out the sort of thing you'd enjoy.' But the false heartiness in his tone did not deceive and she bit her lip, glanced away from him.

B 'Nonsense,' he said. 'We've always said you would, when the children were old enough.' 'Oh, I know you've always *said* you wouldn't mind. But that's very different from not minding when it actually happens,' she replied. 'Anyway, I thought you'd more or less made up your mind to do an art course.'

C She went back to her book. Thanet picked up the newspaper. He hadn't been reading for more than a few minutes, however, when he realized that Joan was unusually restless. Normally, when she was reading, she plunged at once into total absorption. On one occasion, Thanet had counted up to a hundred from the time he asked her a question to the moment when she looked up, eyes unfocused, and said, 'What did you say?'

D 'I wanted to speak to you about it first. Oh, darling,' and she came to kneel before him, took his hands, 'you're sure you don't mind?' 'No,' he lied valiantly, 'I knew, of course, that the time would come, sooner or later ...'

E He grinned. 'To be honest, yes. But I know what you mean.' 'Do you?' she said eagerly. 'You don't think I'm being stupid?'

F And so it was that on this blustery March evening, blissfully unaware of the nasty little shock that Fate was preparing for him, he stretched his toes out to the fire, settled back into his armchair and reflected that he wouldn't change places with any man in the world.

G And she was right, of course, he was. They had been married for eight years now and for all that time Joan had been the good little wife who stayed at home, ran the house efficiently and without fuss, coped with two children and made sure that everything was geared to Thanet's convenience. Unlike the wives of so many of his colleagues, Joan had never complained or nagged over the demands of his job, the irregular hours.

H To his surprise, she still did not respond. 'Joan?' He was beginning to feel the first faint stirrings of alarm. She shook her head slowly then, a fierce little shake. 'Oh, it's all right. There's nothing wrong, not really. It's just that I've a nasty feeling you aren't going to like what I'm trying to pluck up the courage to say.'

Now check your answers to Part Three of the test.

PART FOUR

*You are going to read an extract from a book about the history of the US. For questions **34–40**, choose the answer (**A**, **B**, **C** or **D**) which you think fits best according to the text. In the exam you will mark your answers on a separate answer sheet.*

Progressives in the US

The United States had reached a point, in the closing years of the 19th century, when radical improvements in its political, social and economic arrangements were so plainly necessary that they were actually attempted, and therefore may be called inevitable. Women and men, young and middle-aged, rich, poor and in-between, West, South and North, all acknowledged the necessity and had some hand in shaping the improvements. It was an epoch very much to the American taste, for it seemed a proof that faith in progress, and particularly in the potential for progress in America, was justified. The word 'progressive' had long been a favourite in common speech; now it became attached to a political party, a movement, an era. It remains a curiously empty word, but historians will never be able to do without it. And after all due reservations have been made, it would be churlish to deny that the United States did in many respects move forward during this period, did begin to tackle a good many serious problems intelligently. It is a moderately encouraging story.

Big business made itself felt at every stage in the progressive story, and not by any means as a purely reactionary force. All the same, it would be a mistake to suppose that business, however profoundly it had shaped and now coloured the day-to-day operations of American life, was the key to progressivism. Nor could the industrial working class, however active, muster the power necessary to dominate the epoch. That privilege belonged to the new middle class.

This class had emerged as, numerically, the chief beneficiary of the great transformation of American society. America's rapid development under the impact of industrialism and urbanization implied an equally rapidly developing need for professional services. The need for a new order was generally felt, and implied the recruitment and training of new men, and new women, to administer it. Society was now rich enough to pay for their services. Hence in the last decades of the 19th century there was a mushroom growth among the professions. Doctors and lawyers, of course; but also engineers, dentists, professors, journalists, social workers, architects. This was the age of the expert; he was given a free hand, such as he has seldom enjoyed since. Each new technical marvel – the telephone, the phonograph, the motor-car, the aeroplane – increased the faith that there was a sound technical answer to every problem, even to the problem of government. When a devastating hurricane and flood wrecked the port of Galveston, Texas, in 1901, the local businessmen proclaimed the regular authorities incompetent to handle the task of reconstruction and handed the city's government over to a commission of experts – a pattern that was to be widely followed in the next few years.

This may stand very well for what was happening generally. The new class, conscious of its power and numbers, was anxious to get hold of American society and remake it according to plan. All round were problems that needed solving – crime, disease, bad housing, political corruption – and the new class thought it knew what to do about them. Just as the experts themselves had taken advantage of a society open to the rise of the talented, so they wanted their disadvantaged fellow-citizens to rise also. And this democratic individualistic ideology made it seem perfectly legitimate to bid for political power, that is, for votes: to go down into that arena was simply to carry out one's civic duty. Motives did not need to be examined too closely, since they were self-evidently virtuous. What was new, and important at least to the experts, was the tool-kit they brought to their tasks: their improved spanners, so to speak. The new middle class set out to apply their spanners to such various contraptions as the state and city machines of the old political parties, and the new urban wastelands.

Behind the zeal of these technocrats lay an older tradition, betrayed in the word they used to describe the philanthropic centres they established in the slums, 'settlements': to them the cities were wildernesses, the inhabitants alien savages and the new settlers were bringers both of superior techniques and superior ideas, like the settlers of old. It is thus possible to see in the very approach of these progressives certain limitations, a certain inexperience, which were likely to impede their quest. They were mostly of old American stock, brought up on the old pieties, which their new expertise only veneered. The progressives were too conservative in their instincts, too parochial in their outlook, ever to propose, let alone carry out, fundamental changes in the American system.

Still, it cannot be denied that the progressives were an impressive generation, as intelligent, high-minded, energetic and good-hearted as any in American history. If their achievements were limited and flawed, they were real; they greatly assisted the adaptation of America to the requirements of modern government; and they laid the foundations, intellectual, personal, ideological – even organizational – of that liberalism which was to become one of the chief creative forces in American politics and society. This is not small praise.

34 What does the writer say about the word 'progressive' in the first paragraph?

A It should only be used with regard to this period in the US.
B No other word has been generally adopted to describe this period in the US.
C It was sometimes used inappropriately during this period in the US.
D No other word could have united diverse people during this period in the US.

35 What does the writer say about big business during this period?

A It ensured that the industrial working class was lacking in power.
B It paid too little attention to the importance of the new middle class.
C It was beginning to have too great an impact on everyday life in the US.
D It played a significant part in the development of progressivism.

36 The writer says that the 'mushroom growth' among the professions

A was expected to be only a short-term phenomenon.
B resulted from a desire among professionals for greater freedom.
C was a natural consequence of other changes at the time.
D resulted from fears among Americans about changes in their society.

37 The writer uses events in Galveston to illustrate

A the high regard in which specialists were held during that period.
B problems which had never been dealt with satisfactorily before.
C the speed at which solutions were found during that period.
D disagreements caused by the desire for technical solutions.

38 The writer says that when members of the new class tried to get political power,

A they sometimes underestimated the social problems of the time.
B people made assumptions about their reasons for doing so.
C they tended to overestimate the potential of their fellow citizens.
D people had realistic expectations of what they could achieve.

39 According to the writer, the use of the word 'settlements' reveals

A the insincerity of some of the progressives concerning social problems.
B the misunderstandings behind some of the progressives' beliefs.
C the confusion that surrounded the progressives' approach to problems.
D the similarities between the progressives and previous generations.

40 The writer's general view of the progressives is that

A they did not achieve as much as is widely supposed.
B their ideas were more radical than they believed.
C their impact was not enormous but it was lasting.
D they have not been given the credit they deserve.

Now check your answers to Part Four of the test.

PAPER 2 WRITING 2 hours

PART ONE

*You **must** answer this question. Write your answer in **300–350** words in an appropriate style. Write clearly in **pen**, not pencil. You may make alterations, but make sure your work is easy to read.*

1 You have seen the notice below at the end of an article in a magazine. The article was entitled *Too Much Too Young?* and consisted of a number of people who became rich and famous when they were very young describing the effects that this had on their lives. You decide to send in your **article** in response to the notice.

TOO MUCH TOO YOUNG?

As we regularly do, we're asking you, the readers, to add your contribution on the subject of one of our feature articles. So tell us what you think. Do young people get given too much too soon in their lives? We don't just mean famous youngsters, we mean youngsters in general. Are they spoilt? Do their parents indulge them too much? Is it better for them to go without certain things so that they learn the value of having to struggle to get what they want? Are they given the impression that life is easy because life is too easy for them? Or is it the opposite in a lot of cases? Is life too much of a struggle for too many youngsters? Maybe you have personal experience you'd like to share with the readers. We'll print some of your articles in future editions.

Write your **article**.

Before you write your article, go on to pages 21–23.

WHAT'S TESTED

In Part One of the Writing Paper you are required to present clear arguments and opinions, and to support them coherently with the appropriate register and tone. There are no choices and you will have to write one of the following:

- **an article** – a piece of writing on a given topic that could be published in the specified type of publication. The register and tone of the article should be appropriate in the circumstances indicated and some narrative or descriptive content may be required.
- **an essay** – a composition on a given topic, organized into an introduction, the expansion of points and a conclusion, so that it is a coherent whole. The reader should gain a clear understanding of the points made and the writer's purpose in writing it.
- **a letter** – probably a formal letter in which you present your opinions and make points in response to the material provided in the question. This may involve some narrative content in order to support and illustrate points made and opinions given.
- **a proposal** – a report concerning a future event or possibility, containing recommendations, reasons for making them, the advantages of accepting them and perhaps how their success could be judged. It should be presented in clear and appropriate sections, perhaps with relevant subject headings. The aim of a proposal is to persuade those reading it that the recommendations are justified and the register and tone should be appropriate for the readership mentioned in the question.

TIPS

When planning and writing your answer, there are a number of aspects to consider, as it will be judged according to the following criteria:

- **content** – you must cover all the points mentioned in the material in the question and expand on them. You may also add points of your own and expand on those. You may agree or disagree with any or all of the points presented in the material in the question.
- **range** – try to use as wide a range as possible of appropriate vocabulary and grammatical structures. If your answer consists only of simple vocabulary and basic structures, you will not get a very high mark, even if you make few or no mistakes.
- **accuracy** – be careful to ensure that the vocabulary you use is correct and that you do not make grammatical errors. It is advisable to check very carefully for accuracy when you have completed your answer.
- **appropriacy of register and format** – ensure that throughout your answer the register is appropriately formal, informal or neutral, taking into consideration the situation concerning the writing of the piece and the readership indicated in the question. You must also make sure that the format is suitable for the task you have been set, so that it is clear whether it is, for example, a letter or a proposal simply from the way it looks.
- **organization and cohesion** – make sure that your answer flows well and is divided clearly and logically into paragraphs or sections. Use appropriate linking words and phrases both between sentences and between paragraphs. There should be an appropriate beginning (for example, your purpose in writing a letter) and ending (for example, your conclusion concerning the given topic), and clear presentation and development of each of the points you make.
- **target reader** – your answer should have the desired effect on the reader, who would have no difficulty understanding your point of view, the points you make or exactly what you are proposing. The target reader would also feel that your answer is appropriately directed at them.

To plan your answer for Part One, complete the following notes.

1 Note down as briefly as possible the **topic** of your article.

....

2 List as briefly as possible the following:
- the **main points** raised in the notice which you will have to cover in your article
- the **views** you intend to express with regard to those points
- any **examples** you wish to give to support or illustrate your views

Main point	**View**	**Example**
Main point	**View**	**Example**
Main point	**View**	**Example**

3 List briefly any additional points you wish to make, including any personal experience you wish to include. You may not wish to include any additional points.

Additional point	**View**	**Example**
Additional point	**View**	**Example**

4 Now note briefly how your article will be organized by deciding what each part of it will contain. You may not wish to have as many paragraphs as are listed below.

Introduction
Paragraph 1
Paragraph 2
Paragraph 3
Paragraph 4
Paragraph 5
Conclusion

5 Now use these notes to write your article.

When you have written your answer, assess it in accordance with the task-specific mark scheme.

6 Now read through this sample answer for Part One and answer the questions that follow it.

I think it is very difficult to generalize the topic because it depends mainly on the environment the youngsters live in. The upbringing in a rich family is very different to growing up in a poor family. Children with rich parents have more opportunities to live an easier life.

I hold the view that many youngsters are spoilt because their parents try to calm their bad conscience (caused by too much work and less time, for example) by giving money or presents to them. They want to do as much as they can for their loved children and they want them to be happy and satisfied. And money and presents seem to be a good way to solve problems.

Parents want to support their children by giving money to them and make a good way of life possible (good education, ...). But this behaviour can cause difficulties for the spoilt youngsters. On the one hand they want to be independent as soon as possible, but on the other hand they can't manage their life on their own, because their caring parents 'did almost everything' for them so far. It is possible that young adults can't overcome financial problems or challenges which are common during their lifetime. It seems to be easier to live with money, but children can't live from their parents' support all the time. They have to learn that life is a hard struggle which includes big challenges they have to deal with.

I disagree that life is too much of a struggle for most of the youngsters, because they are not alone until they are 18–20 and leave their parents' home. But from then on it could be very difficult for spoilt children to cope with unusual situations.

All in all, I think that the upbringing is very important. A proper mixture of financial support, independence and struggle for life would be the best way to prepare youngsters for the 'hard life' outside their homes.

Content
Are all the main points raised in the notice covered? Where are these points covered? If any are not covered, which are missing? Are any additional points included? If so, what are they, and are they relevant?

Range
Is there a wide range of vocabulary and grammatical structures? If so, give examples. If there are occasions when the vocabulary or grammar is too simple, suggest alternatives.

Accuracy
Are there any mistakes in the use of vocabulary or grammar? Correct any that you find.

Appropriacy of register and format
Are the style and tone of the article appropriate? How would you describe them? Why are they appropriate or inappropriate? Is the format suitable for a magazine article? If so, why? If not, why not?

Organization and cohesion
Is the article well-organized in terms of the beginning, middle and end? Is it divided into paragraphs appropriately? Describe briefly the content of each paragraph. Does the article flow well in terms of the linking of points and ideas within paragraphs and between paragraphs? Give examples of places where the linking is good. If there are occasions when the linking is inadequate or inappropriate, suggest improvements.

Target reader
Do you feel that someone reading this article in a magazine would be clear what the writer's point of view is throughout it? If so, summarize the writer's point of view briefly. If not, say what you feel is unclear in the article.

Now check your assessment of this sample answer.

PART TWO

Write an answer to ***one*** *of the questions* ***2–5*** *in this part. Write your answer in* ***300–350*** *words in an appropriate style. Write clearly in* ***pen****, not pencil. You may make alterations, but make sure your work is easy to read.*

2 As part of a course assignment you have been asked to write a report analysing the organization where you work, or the institution where you study. Write your report, commenting on the organizational structure of the place, its strengths and weaknesses, and the performance and attitude of those who are in charge and those who work or study there.

Write your **report**.

3 A recent article in a travel magazine presented unflattering views of people of a variety of different nationalities. Write a letter to the magazine giving your views on some typical national stereotypes and describing what image you think people of your nationality have to outsiders, together with whether you think this image is accurate or not.

Write your **letter**. Do not write any postal addresses.

4 A local newspaper is running a competition for the most interesting review of an exhibition or museum. Write a review, describing the exhibition or museum you have chosen and commenting on why it is particularly worth visiting or why you would not recommend it to other people.

Write your **review**.

5 Set book questions – a choice from **(a)**, **(b)** and **(c)**.
In the exam you may choose to answer a question on one of the three set books.

When you have written your answer, assess it in accordance with the task-specific mark schemes.

PAPER 3 USE OF ENGLISH 1 hour 30 minutes

PART ONE

*For questions **1–15**, read the text below and think of the word which best fits each space. Use only **one** word in each space. There is an example at the beginning **(0)**. In the exam you will mark your answers on a separate answer sheet.*

Example:

0	*it*

Advertising in Britain

What does **(0)** ....*it*........ say about a nation that when a national newspaper recently set **(1)** .... to establish the best television adverts of all time, as **(2)** .... as 10,000 people responded? The answer lies **(3)** .... the fact that the British have developed an intense admiration for a genre that has developed into an art form in its **(4)** .... right. In 1955, when Gibbs SR toothpaste broadcast the first TV commercial, it was inconceivable that ads would ever end **(5)** .... being considered as sophisticated and innovative as the programmes surrounding **(6)** .... Yet by 1978, the author Jonathan Price was able to declare: 'Financially, commercials represent the pinnacle of our popular culture's artistic expression. More money and thought per second goes into **(7)** .... making and more cash flows from their impact than **(8)** .... the case for any movie, opera, stage play, painting or videotape.'

Today, **(9)** .... the explosion of channels and websites, there is more onus than ever **(10)** .... the advertiser to shock, amuse, enthral and entertain in its 30-second slot. But are ads really worthy **(11)** .... cultural appraisal, in the same way programmes **(12)** .... ? And what **(13)** .... an advertisement truly great? 'Aesthetically, it's something that is watchable for 1,000 viewings and still remains fresh,' says Robert Opie, founder of the Museum of Advertising and Packaging. 'Often, this is to **(14)** .... with perfect acting and with every single last detail **(15)** .... correct. There are so many layers that you can watch it many times, like listening to a piece of classical music.'

Before you check your answers to Part One of the test, go on to pages 26–27.

WHAT'S TESTED

Part One of the Use of English Paper is primarily a test of grammar, with many questions involving the completion of grammatical structures. Some questions may involve the completion of collocations, fixed phrases, idioms, phrasal verbs and complementation (for explanations of these terms, see the Further Practice and Guidance pages for Paper 1, Part One on page 10).

TIPS

- Read the whole text quickly before attempting to fill the gaps, as this will give you an idea of what it contains and help you to know what kind of answers will be required.
- Before deciding on an answer, read the whole sentence with the gap in it, and the sentences both before and after that – many answers may require you to see the flow and connections between ideas and information in the text. If you simply consider each gap in isolation, you may produce an answer that appears to make sense within the narrow context of the few words either side of the gap but in fact does not make sense within the context of the text.
- Remember that the majority of the answers will be what might be considered 'simple' words, although they will be placed within a relatively complex setting.

Look again at Part One of the test on page 25 and for each question, decide which of the four choices below best expresses the meaning of the part of the text in which the gap appears.

1 **a** succeeded in establishing
b started trying to establish
c proposed the establishment of
d devised a way of establishing

2 **a** approximately 10,000
b almost 10,000
c the high number of 10,000
d only 10,000

3 **a** contradicts the fact
b can be found by looking at the fact
c is concealed by the fact
d is the cause of the fact

4 **a** that can be regarded as distinct from others
b that is highly regarded
c as it should be
d despite opposition

5 **a** have the aim of being considered
b and not be considered
c no longer be considered
d be considered later

6 **a** that the adverts came in the middle of
b that the adverts tried to copy
c that were sophisticated and innovative
d that were popular at that time

7 **a** and creating commercials
b for example, creating commercials
c while creating commercials
d the creation of commercials

8 **a** than results from any movie, etc
b in contrast with what is said of movies, etc
c than anything else concerning movies, etc
d with the exception of the occasional movie, etc

9 **a** in spite of
b as a result of
c on the subject of
d in opposition to

10 **a** the advertiser has more opportunity to shock, etc
b the advertiser is keener to shock, etc
c the advertiser is expected to shock, etc
d advertisers are increasingly blamed for shocking, etc

11 **a** Are ads receiving the kind of cultural appraisal they deserve?
b Do ads deserve cultural appraisal?
c Why aren't ads the subject of cultural appraisal?
d Should ads receive a special kind of cultural appraisal?

12 **a** that compares them with programmes
b and is this true of programmes?
c although programmes are the subject of cultural appraisal
d just as programmes deserve cultural appraisal

13 **a** For what reasons can an advertisement be considered truly great?
b Why are some advertisements truly great while others are not?
c Is it possible for an advertisement to be truly great?
d What would be an example of a truly great advertisement?

14 **a** this results in
b this is connected with
c this makes sure of
d this takes into account

15 **a** the act of correcting all the details
b those details which are correct
c the fact that each detail is correct
d trying to make each detail correct

Now check your answers to this exercise. You may wish to change some of the answers you gave in the test after you have done this. Then check your answers to Part One of the test.

PART TWO

*For questions **16–25**, read the text below. Use the word given in **capitals** at the end of some of the lines to form a word that fits in the space in the same line. There is an example at the beginning **(0)**. In the exam you will mark your answers on a separate answer sheet.*

Example: | 0 | *necessity* |

Tube Inspired a Book

For many people, the London Underground is a grim **(0)** ......*necessity*...... that	**NECESSARY**
gets them from A to B. But for **(16)** .... author Preethi Nair, it is a	**BUD**
source of inspiration. She has just published her first novel, *Gypsy Masala* –	
a tale she dreamt up whilst commuting on the Metropolitan Line. 'Have	
you observed people on the tube?' she asks **(17)** .... 'Everyone	**ENTHUSE**
is in their own little world. I just used to sit there and imagine what	
kind of lives they led.'	
Gypsy Masala charts the adventures and **(18)** .... thoughts of	**INNER**
three members of an Indian family living in London, as they search for	
happiness. 'It is a story about following your dreams,' says Preethi,	
who gave up her high-pressure job as a management **(19)** .... in	**CONSULT**
order to go in **(20)** .... of her ambition of becoming a writer.	**PURSUE**
'It was a big risk but it was definitely the right decision in terms of peace	
of mind and **(21)** .... ,' she explains.	**CONTENT**
Preethi was born in a small village in the Indian state of Kerala and	
moved to London with her parents at the age of three. She says	
the striking contrast in cultures made a **(22)** .... impression	**LAST**
and is reflected in her story, which flits between the suburbs of London	
and **(23)** .... India. Many of the scenes in the book are based	**FAR**
on the place where she was born and spent long summer holidays.	
'It is a tiny village that is lost in time. There is still no **(24)** .... water	**RUN**
and it is quite difficult to get to. It is completely **(25)** .... , and so	**TOUCH**
beautiful,' she says.	

Now check your answers to Part Two of the test.

PART THREE

*For questions **26–31**, think of **one** word only which can be used appropriately in all three sentences. There is an example at the beginning **(0)**. In the exam you will write only the missing word on a separate answer sheet.*

Example:

0 You can stay with us if you like, we've got a .... room in our house.

It's very difficult to get .... parts for machines as old as this, so it's hard to get them repaired if they break down.

I like my job but the hours are long so it doesn't allow me much .... time.

0	*spare*

26 When I've had a .... day at work, all I want to do is go home and relax in front of the television.

You shouldn't have been so .... on Jackie – she only made a small mistake and there was no need to shout at her like that.

I'm a bit .... of hearing. Would you mind speaking up?

27 Ann is always gossiping about other people – I wish she'd .... her own business.

.... your head when you go through this doorway, it's rather low for someone tall.

Colin earns an absolute fortune in his job – .... you, he has to work extremely hard for it.

28 Elaine's self-confidence is just a .... because in fact she's a very shy person.

The arrangement is that we have to pay the builders half the money up .... and the other half once they've completed the work.

You must have got dressed in a hurry this morning – you've got your sweater on back to ....

29 Obviously, something had frightened the cat because it .... out of the house and up the road with an expression of panic on its face.

The critics .... her last film to shreds and one of them even called it 'comfortably the worst movie in living memory'.

Mike was obviously annoyed by the contents of the letter because as soon as he'd read it he .... it up and threw it in the bin.

30 I didn't want to arrive late so I left earlier than I needed to, just to be on the .... side.

Since they haven't phoned to tell us otherwise, I think it's .... to assume that they're still coming to see us next weekend.

Don't worry, I won't tell anyone what you've just told me – your secret is .... with me.

31 Katherine and her sister look so alike that I simply can't .... them apart.

I expect the boss is going to .... me off for not getting my work done on time again.

I bought my niece a toy clock because she's just learning to .... the time.

Now check your answers to Part Three of the test.

PART FOUR

*For questions **32–39**, complete the second sentence so that it has a similar meaning to the first sentence, using the word given. **Do not change the word given**. You must use between **three** and **eight** words, including the word given. There is an example at the beginning **(0)**.*

Example:

0 Robert was offended when he was left out of the team.
exception
Robert .... left out of the team.

The gap can be filled by the words 'took exception to being', so you write:

0	*took exception to being*

In the exam you will mark only the missing words on a separate answer sheet.

32 So that he would be able to leave the room quickly, Matthew stood by the door.
positioned
Matthew .... as to be able to leave the room quickly.

33 I haven't been told clearly what I'll have to do in my next project at work.
required
It hasn't been made .... me in my next project at work.

34 In my opinion, it was an absolute miracle that they survived the accident.
short
The fact that they survived the accident was .... , in my opinion.

35 What gave you the impression that Sue and Jack were going to split up?
led
What was .... that Sue and Jack were going to split up?

36 I tried as hard as I could to make sure that this problem would not arise.
power
I .... this problem from arising.

37 I don't think it was reasonable of you to complain so much about the service.
justified
I don't think you .... fuss about the service.

38 Laura was faced by a lot of problems during her childhood.
contend
Laura had a .... during her childhood.

39 The audience suddenly started to applaud loudly.
sudden
All .... from the audience.

Now check your answers to Part Four of the test.

PART FIVE

*For questions **40–44**, read the following texts on adolescence. For questions **40–43**, answer with a word or short phrase. You do not need to write complete sentences. For question **44**, write a summary according to the instructions given. In the exam you will mark your answers on a separate answer sheet.*

One of the more irritating conventional wisdoms of recent times is that adolescence is a horrendously traumatic and stressful phase of life characterized by rebellion and dissent. A somewhat unholy alliance of therapists, advertising moguls, pop pundits and preachers pontificates about the rupture that occurs with the entry into adolescent 5 status, the special and separate culture, the bewildering biological and psychological changes. The expectation is of trouble. This is not to suggest that adolescence is a golden age, a wondrous period of growth, self-exploration, self-discovery. It can be these things but it is also a time of pain, embarrassment, self-doubt and loss.

As a developmental phenomenon, adolescence is indeed unique to man. The 10 maturation of a human being takes many years. This delay in attainment of full growth and sexual maturity is seen by many experts to be essential to man's longer and richer development. Seen from such a perspective, adolescence acquires a positive evolutionary value. Easing the child into adulthood is the primary task of adolescence. Delay is its essence. The major conflict is between the urges prompted by biological maturity and 15 the slower, stuttering advances of psychological and social growth.

We adults worry about our teenagers getting into trouble, becoming distracted by sexuality, damaged by drugs, lured by ideological charlatanry, scarred by risk-taking, maimed by accidents. In truth we are scared, and understandably so, by the fact that they are growing up. In the course of that maturation we see, as in a mirror, our hopes 20 and fears and failures, achievements and inadequacies, as parents. The task of parents is to let go, of adolescents it is to cast off. For parents it is a time of loss, for the growing adult it is a time of challenge.

40 What point is the writer making by using the phrase 'a somewhat unholy alliance' (line 3)?

....

....

41 Explain in your own words the conflict mentioned in the second paragraph.

....

....

If you've got a teenager who is loud, moody, distant and rebellious, it won't make your life any more comfortable to know that this is normal, but it may at least put your mind at rest that you haven't gone badly wrong somewhere. The processes that teenagers go through, physical and emotional, are unavoidable if they are ever to reach maturity. There are no short cuts, no
5 cryogenic miracles that will suspend them in ice between the ages of 13 and 20. And in terms of their psychological development, it does appear that the more you try to hijack it, or delay it, or mould it in your very own image, the bigger the problems will be, especially for your child. If you don't allow them to grow up at the right time, they'll keep making dispirited efforts to do it for the rest of their lives. Or they'll give up, and knowing that they've been thwarted in a vital
10 piece of their development, they'll stay chronically angry with their parents, and chronically depressed with themselves. We all know people who'd be much healthier now if they hadn't been required to be so damn perfect 30 years ago.

At one and the same time a teenager is pulled back towards their childhood, with pangs of dependence, and onward to adulthood, with a longing for independence from their parents
15 and their history. So it's hardly surprising if their moods swing wildly from one extreme to another. The hallmarks of teenage moods are noisy exuberance or silence, with a face like thunder. When they're on an upward swing they burst with restless energy. They need to clatter and fidget around, they need their music to be on the loud side of loud, and they need to talk in a silly voice. Silly voices are a vital part of teenage culture. They may be caricatures of hapless
20 schoolteachers, or they may be original creations. Either way, they are a very effective way of separating those in the know from the uninitiated. Whole mealtimes may pass without a single intelligible word being said.

42 What, according to the writer, causes teenagers' mood swings?

....

....

43 What is said to be the role of silly voices in teenage culture?

....

....

44 In a paragraph of between **50 and 70** words, summarize **in your own words as far as possible**, what is said in the two texts concerning how parents should regard adolescence.

Before you check your answers to Part Five of the test, go on to pages 33–37.

WHAT'S TESTED

Questions 40–43

In Part Five of the Use of English Paper, questions 40–43 are comprehension questions about the texts. They focus on any of the following:

- **content** – points made or information included by the writer.
- **style** – the way in which the writer uses language in order to make points or convey views.
- **vocabulary** – the meaning of words and phrases in the context in which the writer uses them.
- **reference** – what a certain word or phrase in the text refers to elsewhere in the text.

TIPS

- You are not required to write complete sentences, so keep your answers as simple as possible. If you try to phrase your answer in a way that is too elaborate, you may make mistakes which spoil your answer and make it hard to understand. This will result in the unnecessary loss of marks for a question that in fact you do know the correct answer to.
- There are two marks for each question, but that does not necessarily mean that there are two separate elements for each answer. Make sure that you include both elements where there are two, but do not include something irrelevant simply because you think there should be a second element in your answer.
- In vocabulary questions, it is not assumed that you know the word or phrase tested. If you find you don't know it, try to work it out from the surrounding context.

The exercises below will help you to check whether the answers that you gave in the test are correct.

Question 40

1 What are 'conventional wisdoms' (line 1)?
 a outdated ideas
 b theories that have been proved
 c generally accepted views
 d beliefs copied from others

2 What are 'pundits' (line 3)?
 a people who express views which they think other people want to hear
 b people who give their opinions in public and are considered experts by some but not by others
 c people who say things in public which are intended to be controversial
 d people who are aware of the fact that the views they express have some influence on the thinking of other people

3 If someone 'pontificates' (line 4), they
 a say things which are inconsistent with things they previously said.
 b make statements which a number of other people do not take seriously.
 c speak in a way which is less impressive than they believe it to be.
 d give opinions confidently but without the expertise to support them.

4 What view of adolescence do the people referred to present?
 a a wholly inaccurate one
 b a contradictory one
 c a wholly negative one
 d a difficult one to prove

Question 41

1 In what sense is adolescence said to be 'unique to man' (line 9)?
 a because of its importance
 b because of how long it lasts
 c because it is not clearly understood
 d because it combines growth and sexual maturity

2 What is meant by 'Easing the child into adulthoood' (line 13)
- **a** taking the child gradually into adulthood
- **b** giving the child the impression that adulthood is easy
- **c** showing the child what adulthood really means
- **d** moving the child into adulthood with the right attitude

3 What does 'its essence' (line 14) refer to?
- **a** conflict
- **b** adulthood
- **c** adolescence
- **d** the child

4 What is meant by 'stuttering' (line 15) in this context?
- **a** confusing
- **b** unsuccessful
- **c** worrying
- **d** hesitant

Question 42

1 What does the phrase 'At one and the same time' (line 13) emphasize?
- **a** the similarity between actions
- **b** the speed of actions
- **c** the fact that actions happen together
- **d** the fact that actions happen suddenly

2 What are 'pangs' (line 13)?
- **a** painful feelings
- **b** feelings of relief
- **c** mixed feelings
- **d** vague feelings

3 If you have 'a longing' for something (line 14), you
- **a** regard it from a distance.
- **b** have a strong desire for it.
- **c** exaggerate it.
- **d** confidently expect it.

Question 43

1 'Silly voices' (line 19) are intended to
- **a** be amusing.
- **b** be offensive.
- **c** irritate others.
- **d** disguise feelings.

2 What is meant by 'those in the know' (line 21)?
- **a** people who behave in a way that is considered acceptable by the group they belong to
- **b** people belonging to a group who consider themselves better than others
- **c** people belonging to a group who are the only ones to be aware of something
- **d** people who understand something which others find it very difficult to understand

3 What is implied by the final sentence?
- **a** that mealtimes with adolescents are harder than other times
- **b** that parents do not understand what children are saying at mealtimes
- **c** that adolescents are often reluctant to talk at mealtimes
- **d** that parents only notice adolescents' behaviour at mealtimes

Now check your answers to these exercises and decide whether you wish to change any of the answers you gave in the test. Then check your answers to questions 40–43 in the test.

WHAT'S TESTED

Summary

For question 44 in Part Five of the Use of English Paper, you are asked to write a short summary of points made or information included in the two texts. The topic of the summary will be something that occurs in both texts. You are required to keep your summary within the word limit mentioned and include all relevant points in it. You should also write with accurate grammatical constructions and vocabulary and with appropriate linking so that it flows coherently, and you should rephrase rather than copy from the text.

TIPS

- You must only include points which are totally relevant to the topic of the summary, so it is essential to identify precisely what those points are before you start writing. Read the texts again, highlighting those parts of them which contain the relevant points that you must include.
- You will normally have to find four points to include, so make sure that you find everything in the texts that is relevant and should be included.
- The points that you need to include may be found in certain sections of each text or they may be scattered around in small parts of each text.
- This is not a composition, so keep the language that you use relatively simple. If you write long, elaborate sentences, you will not be able to cover all the main points in the required number of words and you may make unnecessary mistakes that result in the loss of marks.
- Don't copy whole sentences from the texts – you are supposed to cover the relevant points in your own words as far as possible; although of course it may be impossible not to use some words and phrases from the texts.
- Make sure that everything you write is grammatically accurate and that the points are linked in such a way that the summary flows well and makes sense as a whole.

Look at the highlighted parts of the texts and match them with the sentences which follow.

A One of the more irritating conventional wisdoms of recent times is that adolescence is a horrendously traumatic and stressful phase of life characterized by rebellion and dissent. A somewhat unholy alliance of therapists, advertising moguls, pop pundits and preachers pontificates about the rupture that occurs with the entry into adolescent status, the special and separate culture, the bewildering biological and psychological changes. **B** The expectation is of trouble. This is not to suggest that adolescence is a golden age, a wondrous period of growth, self-exploration, self-discovery. It can be these things but it is also a time of pain, embarrassment, self-doubt and loss.

As a developmental phenomenon, adolescence is indeed unique to man. The maturation of a human being takes many years. **C** This delay in attainment of full growth and sexual maturity is seen by many experts to be essential to man's longer and richer development. Seen from such a perspective, adolescence acquires a positive evolutionary value. Easing the child into adulthood is the primary task of adolescence. Delay is its essence. The major conflict is between the urges prompted by biological maturity and the slower, stuttering advances of psychological and social growth.

D We adults worry about our teenagers getting into trouble, becoming distracted by sexuality, damaged by drugs, lured by ideological charlatanry, scarred by risk-taking, maimed by accidents. **E** In truth we are scared, and understandably so, by the fact that they are growing up. In the course of that maturation we see, as in a mirror, our hopes and fears and failures, achievements and inadequacies, as parents. **F** The task of parents is to let go, of adolescents it is to cast off. For parents it is a time of loss, for the growing adult it is a time of challenge.

G If you've got a teenager who is loud, moody, distant and rebellious, it won't make your life any more comfortable to know that this is normal, but it may at least put your mind at rest that you haven't gone badly wrong somewhere. H The processes that teenagers go through, physical and emotional, are unavoidable if they are ever to reach maturity. There are no short cuts, no cryogenic miracles that will suspend them in ice between the ages of 13 and 20. I And in terms of their psychological development, it does appear that the more you try to hijack it, or delay it, or mould it in your very own image, the bigger the problems will be, especially for your child. If you don't allow them to grow up at the right time, they'll keep making dispirited efforts to do it for the rest of their lives. Or they'll give up, and knowing that they've been thwarted in a vital piece of their development, they'll stay chronically angry with their parents, and chronically depressed with themselves. J We all know people who'd be much healthier now if they hadn't been required to be so damn perfect 30 years ago.

At one and the same time a teenager is pulled back towards their childhood, with pangs of dependence, and onward to adulthood, with a longing for independence from their parents and their history. So it's hardly surprising if their moods swing wildly from one extreme to another. K The hallmarks of teenage moods are noisy exuberance or silence, with a face like thunder. L When they're on an upward swing they burst with restless energy. They need to clatter and fidget around, they need their music to be on the loud side of loud, and they need to talk in a silly voice. Silly voices are a vital part of teenage culture. They may be caricatures of hapless schoolteachers, or they may be original creations. Either way, they are a very effective way of separating those in the know from the uninitiated. Whole mealtimes may pass without a single intelligible word being said.

1 It is possible to see the effects of an unhappy adolescence in some adults. ☐

2 The process of adolescence can be seen as valuable in man's development. ☐

3 Parents analyse their own feelings and desires as parents during adolescence. ☐

4 Parents trying to affect the course of adolescence has bad results. ☐

5 Adolescents need to behave in a certain way when they are happy. ☐

6 Adolescence has both good and bad aspects. ☐

7 Changes during adolescence are inevitable. ☐

8 Parents worry about bad things happening to their children. ☐

9 Parents have to allow children to be independent of them. ☐

10 Parents of unpleasant adolescents should not blame themselves for this. ☐

11 Adolescence is seen as a terrible period. ☐

12 Teenagers experience extreme feelings. ☐

Now decide which of 1–12 above are relevant main points that should be included in the summary.

When you have done this, look again at your summary and decide whether you wish to change anything.

Sample Summary

Look at this sample summary and answer the questions that follow it.

> The most important thing that should be born in mind is that this period is a natural part of the growing up process with all its shocking and sometimes intolerable consequences. Both parties suffer many times, but it's mostly the adults task to try and be able to handle.
>
> But what to do? Instead of putting the problem off or exaggerating it, you should allow them (your children) to mature in their own way, giving them the most freedom possible, in spite of all your fears, and support them at the same time. Make this process as easy as possible for both of you.

1 Is anything irrelevant included or anything relevant not included? If so, what?
2 Are there any language mistakes? Correct any that you find.
3 Is the summary well-organized and does it make sense throughout?
4 Have any parts of the texts simply been copied in the summary? If so, where?
5 Is the summary within the specified word limit?

Now look again at your summary and decide whether you wish to change anything.

Then check your marks for your summary and read the assessment of this sample summary.

PAPER 4 LISTENING approximately 40 minutes

PART ONE

*You will hear four different extracts. For questions **1–8**, choose the answer (**A**, **B** or **C**) which fits best according to what you hear. There are two questions for each extract. In the exam you will hear each extract twice.*

Extract One

You hear a reviewer on a radio programme talking about a book.

1 The speaker says that the book's title refers to the point at which

A social epidemics are at their height.

B something becomes a social epidemic.

C people become concerned about social epidemics.

2 The speaker says that, in her opinion, the book

A presents some challenging conclusions.

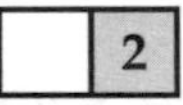

B is less complex than it may appear.

C uses terminology that may confuse readers.

Extract Two

You hear a reporter on a radio programme talking as he climbs a big rock.

3 One question the speaker asks himself is

A why he feels the way he does.

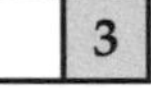

B where his climbing partner has gone.

C what has motivated him to climb the rock.

4 The speaker says that at this exact moment

A he doesn't care about the risk he is taking.

B he is relishing the experience.

C he feels that age is irrelevant.

Extract Three

You hear a scientist talking about a possible future technological development.

5 What does the speaker say about the basic needs of people?

A Technology cannot meet those needs completely.

B They make people resistant to changes in technology.

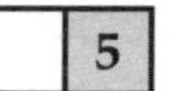

C They are not as great as is generally thought.

6 What does the speaker say about using prostheses for memory?

A It would work better with children than with adults.

B It would prove how important memory is.

C It would result in memories that are too efficient.

Extract Four

You hear part of a radio programme about literary festivals.

7 The interviewer says that when writers appear at events at literary festivals,

A they dislike being asked difficult questions.

B they find the experience easier if they read their own work.

C they seldom prepare as thoroughly as they should.

8 Why, according to William, do writers like meeting readers?

A Writers are made to feel they have succeeded in their aim.

B Writers want readers to know what they are really like.

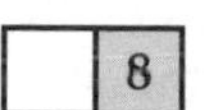

C Readers give writers ideas for future work.

Stop the recording when you hear 'That's the end of Part One'.

Before you check your answers to Part One of the test, go on to pages 40–42

WHAT'S TESTED

The questions in Part One of the Listening Paper test you on your ability to understand and interpret often complex points made, and information given by speakers, in four separate short pieces. Questions may focus on any of the following:

- **gist** – the general meaning of what a speaker says, based on more than one sentence or phrase.
- **detail** – a specific piece of information given or point made by a speaker, contained in a single phrase or sentence.
- **main idea** – the main point made by a speaker, rather than more minor points made or examples given.
- **function** – what a speaker is doing when speaking, for example, criticizing or apologizing.
- **purpose** – what a speaker is trying to achieve, what a speaker wants to happen as a result of speaking.
- **topic** – the subject matter of what a speaker says.
- **feeling** – the feeling expressed by a speaker.
- **attitude** – the way a speaker regards something or someone, as conveyed by what the speaker says.
- **opinion** – a view expressed or strongly implied by a speaker.

TIPS

- Don't rush into choosing the option that appears superficially to be the most plausible – what speakers say is often fairly complex and subtle.
- It is possible that more than one option in a question may be correct according to what the speaker says, but only one option will correctly answer the question that has been asked, so make sure that you read the question carefully.
- The two questions for each extract are likely to follow the sequence of what is said, with the first question about the first part of the piece and the second question about the second part. On occasions, however, questions may focus on the piece as a whole.
- If you find one of the extracts very difficult and are struggling with the questions on it, don't spend too much time on them so that you do not concentrate sufficiently on the next piece. If you do that, you may fail to answer questions on the next piece and lose marks unnecessarily.
- Use the pauses before and between the extracts to read the questions in advance, so that you are aware of the aspects of each piece that you will be tested on. Read the rubrics carefully too – they will give you the context for each of the pieces.
- Use the second listening to check your answers, even if you were confident of them on the first listening.
- Write your answers on the question paper as you listen. In the exam you will have five minutes at the end of the test to transfer your answers onto a separate answer sheet.

The exercises below will help you to eliminate the incorrect options in the questions in the test or to confirm that you have selected the right options.

Listen to each of the four extracts again and after each one, tick one or more boxes for the relevant questions.

Question 1 *Stop the recording when you hear 'take us by surprise'.*

Which of the following does the speaker say about the 'tipping point'?

a It is a phrase that is used for the book's title. ☐

b It refers to the sudden growth of a phenomenon. ☐

c After it, social epidemics cease to become more widespread. ☐

d It can be applied more to inventions than to ideas and diseases. ☐

e It is mostly associated with unwelcome social developments. ☐

f It refers to something becoming unexpectedly widespread. ☐

Question 2 *Stop the recording at the end of the first extract.*

Which of the following does the speaker say about the book?

- **a** It presents a detailed analysis of the causes of social epidemics. ☐
- **b** It does not make clear exactly what 'connectors' and 'mavens' are. ☐
- **c** It would be wrong to regard its analysis as a simplistic one. ☐
- **d** Not all the ideas in it are original. ☐
- **e** It suggests ways of dealing with social problems. ☐
- **f** It contains unorthodox ideas about what should be done about social problems. ☐

Question 3 *Stop the recording when you hear 'somewhere far above your head'.*

Which of the following does the speaker refer to?

- **a** being close to the top ☐
- **b** what the point of climbing the crag is for him ☐
- **c** the fact that he normally feels bad when he is high up ☐
- **d** the fact that there is nothing solid below him ☐
- **e** no longer being able to see his climbing partner ☐
- **f** the fact that his climbing partner is further up than him ☐

Question 4 *Stop the recording at the end of the second extract.*

Which of the following does the speaker mention?

- **a** the physical appearance of the object he is climbing ☐
- **b** the physical effects that climbing is having on him ☐
- **c** being glad that he is where he is ☐
- **d** regretting not having looked closely at his life insurance policy ☐
- **e** the appeal of danger to men of his age ☐
- **f** a belief that men of his age are good at dangerous activities ☐

Question 5 *Stop the recording when you hear 'existing biological substrata'.*

Which of the following does the speaker mention?

- **a** people's attitudes towards technology ☐
- **b** a belief that it will be possible to place technology inside the human body ☐
- **c** the idea that technology will replace functions of the human brain ☐
- **d** false assumptions about what the basic needs of people really are ☐
- **e** a belief that people's basic needs will remain the same ☐
- **f** the idea that technology could add to the way in which people function ☐

Question 6 *Stop the recording at the end of the third extract.*

Which of the following does the speaker say about memory?

a Prostheses would work better for memory than for other things. ☐

b Children's memories can be more easily manipulated than adults' memories. ☐

c Adults would benefit from remembering more about their childhoods. ☐

d People place greater emphasis on it than on other functions of the brain. ☐

e Different devices for recording memories would be needed for children and adults. ☐

f It is fortunate that people cannot remember everything. ☐

Question 7 *Stop the recording when you hear 'every couple of sentences'.*

Which of the following does the interviewer mention about literary festivals?

a something that writers seldom say about them ☐

b the amount of preparation required of writers before reading from their work ☐

c a misunderstanding writers have concerning what is expected of them ☐

d questions of a kind that writers are happy to be asked ☐

e questions which are not about the writer's own work ☐

f that writers are repeatedly asked the same questions ☐

Question 8 *Stop the recording at the end of the fourth extract.*

Which of the following does William say?

a Writers are not as miserable as people think they are. ☐

b Some writers never lose confidence in themselves. ☐

c Writers need to talk to people in order to get ideas. ☐

d Writers write with readers in mind. ☐

e Readers are sometimes surprised by what writers are really like. ☐

f Writers like to know that someone has read their work. ☐

Now check your answers to these exercises. When you have done so, listen again to Part One of the test and decide whether you wish to change any of the answers you gave. Then check your answers to Part One of the test.

PART TWO

*You will hear someone called Karen Williams talking about her career. For questions **9–17**, complete the sentences with a word or short phrase. In the exam you will hear the piece twice.*

At the end of her first work experience, Karen spent two days [9] and checking rooms with the floor housekeeper.

Her last work experience was spent in the hotel's [10].

The subject of Karen's next course was [11].

During her HND course, the subjects she had to study were business studies, hotel management, human resource management and [12].

The topic of her report was [13] in hotels.

In her report, she wrote reviews of various [14].

She joined an organization with the initials [15].

She got information from a magazine called [16].

In her present job, she has to deal with problems caused by the hotel being [17].

Stop the recording when you hear 'That's the end of Part Two'.

Now check your answers to Part Two of the test.

PART THREE

You will hear an interview with someone who consulted a 'life coach' to improve her life. For questions ***18-22****, choose the answer (****A, B, C*** *or* ***D****) which fits best according to what you hear. In the exam you will hear the piece twice.*

18 Brigid says that she consulted a life coach because

A she had read a great deal about them.

B both her work and home life were getting worse.

C other efforts to improve her life had failed.

D the changes she wanted to make were only small ones.

	18

19 What did Brigid's coach tell her about money?

A It would be very easy for Brigid to get a lot of it.

B Brigid's attitude towards it was uncharacteristic of her.

C Brigid placed too much emphasis on it in her life.

D Few people have the right attitude towards it.

	19

20 What does Brigid say about her reaction to her coach's advice on money?

A She felt silly repeating the words her coach gave her.

B She tried to hide the fact that she found it ridiculous.

C She felt a lot better as a result of following it.

D She found it difficult to understand at first.

	20

21 What does Brigid say happened during the other sessions?

A She was told that most people's problems had the same cause.

B Her powers of concentration improved.

C Some things she was told to do proved harder than others.

D She began to wonder why her problems had arisen in the first place.

	21

22 What has Brigid concluded?

A The benefits of coaching do not compensate for the effort required.

B She was too unselfish before she had coaching.

C She came to expect too much of her coach.

D It is best to limit the number of coaching sessions you have.

	22

Stop the recording when you hear 'That's the end of Part Three'.

Now check your answers to Part Three of the test.

PART FOUR

You will hear two shop managers, David and Katherine, talking about their jobs. For questions **23–28**, *decide whether the opinions are expressed by only one of the speakers, or whether the speakers agree.*

Write ***D*** *for David,*
K *for Katherine,*
or ***B*** *for Both, where they agree.*

In the exam you will hear the piece twice.

23 I put pressure on myself. [ ] 23

24 I don't like the idea that I've misjudged people. [ ] 24

25 I take certain action when there are not many customers. [ ] 25

26 The people working for me have certain expectations of me. [ ] 26

27 A certain doubt I had proved unjustified. [ ] 27

28 I take a certain approach to dealing with people's problems. [ ] 28

Stop the recording when you hear 'That's the end of Part Four'.

In the exam you will have five minutes at the end of the test to copy your answers onto a separate answer sheet.

Now check your answers to Part Four of the test.

PAPER 5 SPEAKING 19 minutes

PART ONE (3 MINUTES) GENERAL AND SOCIAL

Questions that may be addressed to either candidate.

- Whereabouts do you live?
- Could you describe the area / city you live in?
- What do you like / dislike about the area / city you live in?
- Can you describe the building you live in?
- Who do you live with and do you get on well with them?

- What's your favourite kind of music / performer / band?
- What's the best concert you've ever been to?
- What's the worst concert you've ever been to?
- What kind(s) of music / artist(s) is / are popular in your country at the moment?
- Do fashions in music change rapidly in your country?

PART TWO (4 MINUTES) CAREERS

For both candidates.

Choose two of the pictures on page 171 and describe what is happening in each of them.
(1 minute)

Now look at all of the pictures and answer one of these questions.
Which picture most closely corresponds with your own situation or how you see yourself in the future and which the least?
Which picture most closely corresponds with what you would most like to do and which the least?
Give your reasons in each case.
(3 minutes)

PART THREE (12 MINUTES) CHANGE AND STABILITY

In phase one of Part Three each candidate takes a long turn (2 minutes), followed by a brief response from the other candidate.

Prompt Card (a) *(Given to Candidate A, and a copy to Candidate B)*

Is change always a good thing?
- social change
- changes in personal life
- technological developments

One of the following questions for Candidate B (1 minute):

- What do you think?
- Is there anything you would like to add?
- Is there anything you don't agree with?
- How does this differ from your experience?

One of the following questions for both candidates (1 minute):

- Is there something which you believe will never change?
- What would you most like to change in your life?
- What changes in society would you most like to see?

Prompt Card (b) *(Given to Candidate B, and a copy to Candidate A)*

Is a certain amount of stability essential in life?
- childhood
- work
- society

One of the following questions for Candidate A (1 minute):

- What do you think?
- Is there anything you would like to add?
- Is there anything you don't agree with?
- How does this differ from your experience?

One of the following questions for both candidates (1 minute):

- Is there now less or more stability in people's working lives?
- Would you describe your childhood as a stable one?
- Is society now more or less stable than it used to be?

In phase two of Part Three there is a discussion on the general topic (4 minutes).
Possible general questions for both candidates on the topic of change and stability:

- Describe a change which you think has particularly benefited you personally.
- Describe a change which you think has been particularly bad for society.
- What changes have happened in the place where you live recently?
- Describe a situation which you think is particularly unstable.
- What are the causes of instability in society?
- Are there any disadvantages to growing up in a stable environment?

WHAT'S TESTED

In the Speaking Paper, you are required to do the following:

- have a conversation with the examiner about yourself and general social matters.
- talk about various pictures you are shown and discuss a topic arising from them, both with the examiner and the other candidate taking the test with you.
- talk on your own about another topic, based on a question and some brief ideas printed on a card that is given to you by the examiner.
- discuss the same topic further with the other candidate, prompted by questions from the examiner.

TIPS

Your performance in the Speaking Paper is judged according to the following criteria:

- **grammar** – your ability to use a wide range of grammatical structures appropriately and accurately.
- **vocabulary** – your ability to use a wide and appropriate range of vocabulary accurately in order to convey your precise meaning and to express attitudes, opinions and abstract ideas.
- **discourse management** – your ability to say things which form coherent speeches and make relevant and logical contributions to conversations. What you say should link together well, both with other things you say, and with what the other candidate and the examiner say.
- **pronunciation** – your ability not only to pronounce what you say so that it can easily be understood (although you do not have to try to sound exactly like a native speaker) but also to link words and phrases together smoothly. You should speak in such a way that appropriate words and phrases are emphasized, and the appropriate intonation is used to convey clearly the meaning of what you are saying.
- **interactive communication** – your ability to demonstrate conversation skills, such as knowing when you should speak and when it is someone else's turn to speak and keeping a conversation going by not hesitating too much. Coming up with something to say that enables the discussion to develop when it appears to be coming to an end before the subject has been fully covered is also important, as is making points of your own or responding to those made by others, so that you play a full part in the conversation.
- **global achievement scale** – your general performance in the Paper as a whole.

Part One: General and Social

Although this involves talking about yourself and general social matters, it is not simply a pleasant chat that doesn't really matter – you will be assessed on your performance in this part of the Paper in just the same way that you will be assessed in the other two parts.

You may feel that this is the only part of the Speaking Paper that you can really prepare for. However, beware! Do not prepare a fixed speech, learn it by heart and try to repeat it. Firstly, it will not sound natural and the examiners will know immediately that you are simply repeating something you have learnt – this will affect their assessment of your performance. Secondly, you cannot be sure what areas of discussion will come up – you may not be able to say anything that you prepared and therefore be unable to give natural or coherent answers to the questions that you are asked.

However, it is worth practising talking about a range of personal and general areas of conversation that *may* come up in the Paper.

With a partner, ask and answer questions about the following:

• where you live • your aims for the future • places you have travelled to	• your occupation • learning languages • spare time activities
• your own personality • your preferences in the arts • employment	• friends and family • the media • your social life

Part Two: Talking About Pictures

1 To talk coherently about a picture without having to point constantly to various parts of it, it is essential to know appropriate words and phrases for describing parts of a picture.

Look at the pictures on page 171 and describe them using the phrases below. With a partner, take it in turns to describe the content of each picture.

• in the foreground	• in the background
• in the top left-hand corner	• in the bottom left-hand corner
• in the top right-hand corner	• in the bottom right hand corner
• on the right-hand side	• on the left-hand side
• on/to the right of ...	• on/to the left of ...
• at the top	• at the bottom
• in front of ...	• behind ...
• next to/close to	• between ...
• facing ...	• opposite ...

2 When you are talking about a picture, you may need to guess or deduce what the situation is in the picture because you cannot be completely sure. Instead of constantly using very simple phrases for doing this, such as 'Maybe' or 'I think', try to vary the way in which you speculate on the content of the picture.

Look again at the pictures on page 171 and try to use as many as possible of the phrases below to introduce comments on them. With a partner, take it in turns to guess or deduce what is happening in each picture.

• I get the impression that ...	• The impression I get is that ...
• My impression is that ...	• It looks (to me) as if/as though ...
• I'd say ...	• I reckon ...
• I suppose ...	• I assume ...
• I expect ...	• I guess ...
• I imagine ...	• I suspect ...
• It would appear that ...	• I should think ...
• I've got a feeling that ...	• It's hard to say, but ...
• He/She/They seem(s) to ...	• He/She/They must/can't ...
• He/She/They seem(s) to have ...	• He/She/They must/can't have ...
• He/She/They seem(s) to be ...-ing	• He/She/They must/can't be ...-ing
• In my opinion/view ...	• He/She/They might/could ...
• The way I see it ...	• He/She/They might/could have ...
• If you ask me ...	• He/She/They might/could be ...-ing
• Judging by ...	• As far as I can tell/see ...
• It's (quite/fairly/highly) likely that ...	• ... is quite/fairly/highly likely to ...

TEST TWO

PAPER 1 READING 1 hour 30 minutes

PART ONE

*For questions **1–18**, read the three texts below and decide which answer (**A, B, C** or **D**) best fits each gap. In the exam you will mark your answers on a separate answer sheet.*

Spencer Tracy

Spencer Tracy was an enigma. He could be cruel and heartless toward some actors with whom he worked, but **(1)** .... kind to others. Director Robert Wise says, 'When we did a film called *Tribute to a Bad Man*, he couldn't have been more mean and nasty to his co-stars. He ignored and upstaged young Robert Francis to the **(2)** .... where the kid was hurt, bewildered and demoralized.' On the other hand, Robert Wagner says, 'After I worked with him in *The Mountain*, he became a sort of **(3)** .... father to me. We became good friends and he helped me in my development as an actor until the day he died.'

There was a similar dichotomy in Tracy's relations with directors. Generally he would **(4)** .... along with everything a director wanted, but as Stanley Kramer says, he could be difficult: 'There were times, when he disagreed with me, when he could wither me with a glance. If his forehead was shiny and I sent a make-up man over to powder-puff it, he'd push the man away.' These were comparatively **(5)** .... reactions, although with the highly respected Walter Lang, Tracy was **(6)** .... rude.

1	**A** acutely	**B** comprehensively	**C** overwhelmingly	**D** richly
2	**A** point	**B** amount	**C** degree	**D** end
3	**A** reserve	**B** substitute	**C** understudy	**D** proxy
4	**A** fall	**B** pull	**C** go	**D** bear
5	**A** low	**B** light	**C** small	**D** mild
6	**A** starkly	**B** straight	**C** fully	**D** downright

A Message for Lisa

It was nearly two weeks later that Lisa arrived at college to find there was a message for her. The voice teacher, Pete, said she'd have to go up to the head office to collect it. Lisa wanted to know what was in the message and who it was from, but the voice teacher insisted it was **(7)** .... 'Can't you just tell me?' Lisa pleaded, but Pete jutted his chin and said he was only obeying the rules. Lisa stretched her eyes at him. She had been brought up to be **(8)** .... of anyone who believed in rules.

The head office was on the third floor. Lisa's fantasies grew with each turn of the stairs. Each flap of swing door **(9)** .... sweeter and sweeter thoughts of her and Quentin's reconciliation. It **(10)** .... to her only a second before she slid through into the dusty light of the office that Quentin had no **(11)** .... of knowing that she was at college, and even if he did, it was unlikely he would know which college she was at.

'Lisa.' The head of department was talking to her. 'Someone has been looking for you.' Lisa's change of heart was so severe it **(12)** .... her breath away.

7	**A** confidential	**B** intimate	**C** clandestine	**D** undercover
8	**A** guarded	**B** uneasy	**C** wary	**D** edgy
9	**A** led	**B** arose	**C** brought	**D** put
10	**A** struck	**B** occurred	**C** dawned	**D** sprang
11	**A** access	**B** route	**C** scope	**D** way
12	**A** caught	**B** drew	**C** held	**D** took

The Vacuum Cleaner

When Hubert Cecil Booth visited the Empire Music Hall in London one afternoon in 1901, he wasn't **(13)** .... on saving the world. A fairground ride engineer, he went to a demonstration of a railway carriage cleaning machine. It was a bag that blew air into the carpet, raising the dust, which it hoped to catch in a box. Booth went backstage and suggested to the inventor that the machine should **(14)** .... , not blow. The inventor, he later recalled, **(15)** .... that this was impossible and then walked away.

(16) .... the problem over in a restaurant, Booth laid his handkerchief on a plush chair, put his lips against it, breathed in – and **(17)** .... on the dust. Then he went home and invented the vacuum cleaner. Not our push-along **(18)** .... , it was a roaring, red, horse-drawn machine. Booth sold several to royalty – a neat PR move – but preferred to hire them out for £13, the annual wages of a dirty-work servant. Guests at 'vacuum tea parties' watched the liveried male attendants feed hoses in through the windows and whisk away the dirt.

13	**A** envisaging	**B** aiming	**C** devising	**D** planning
14	**A** gasp	**B** puff	**C** suck	**D** gulp
15	**A** expressed	**B** remarked	**C** voiced	**D** uttered
16	**A** Mulling	**B** Reflecting	**C** Contemplating	**D** Dwelling
17	**A** strangled	**B** blocked	**C** choked	**D** clogged
18	**A** class	**B** variety	**C** category	**D** nature

Now check your answers to Part One of the test.

PART TWO

*You are going to read four extracts which are all concerned in some way with sport. For questions **19–26**, choose the answer (**A**, **B**, **C** or **D**) which you think fits best according to the text. In the exam you will mark your answers on a separate answer sheet.*

Manchester United

You get a whiff of it the moment you step off the tram at Old Trafford. Wafting down the Warwick Road, over the heads of the thousands making their way to Old Trafford Stadium to worship Manchester United, striking nostrils with even more force than that rich aromatic match-day odour of hot dogs is an unmistakable smell: money. The whiff is everywhere. Once a fortnight this quarter of a Manchester industrial estate hosts more than just a football match. It transmogrifies into a bazaar, as teeming, colourful and chaotic as anything in Istanbul. Every inch of pavement within half a mile of the ground is occupied by commerce. Stalls sell souvenir scarves, hats, badges and posters; a man trades in rare match programmes; boys with bin-liners jammed with T-shirts yell: 'Get yours, only a fiver'. *line 1* *line 6* *line 9*

But the most extraordinary sight comes once you have fought your way into the shadow of the ground itself. There, snaking round crush barriers cemented into the forecourt, is the queue for the Manchester United superstore. People already burdened by United apparel – shirts, sweaters, jackets, earrings – line up for at least an hour behind 2,000 others for the privilege of buying yet more stuff: 3-D posters, souvenir drinking mugs, duvet covers. A range of 1,500 items of United memorabilia is available to empty the pockets of the faithful. 'Sometimes on a match day,' says Edward Freedman, United's merchandising manager, whose office overlooks the superstore, 'the chairman comes here, and we both stand and look out over the queue. Then we smile at each other.'

19 Which word does the writer use to describe how busy the area around Old Trafford is?
A whiff (line 1)
B transmogrifies (line 6)
C teeming (line 6)
D jammed (line 9)

20 What does the writer suggest about the Manchester United superstore?
A People who buy goods there are surprised by how long they have to queue.
B The merchandising manager and chairman have made a major contribution to its success.
C Many of the goods sold there are of low quality.
D The number of goods individuals buy from it is remarkable.

Silly Sports

There is scarcely a human activity in the world that is not taken by some people with deadly seriousness. There is not a single sport that does not have its following of fanatics: people who will fall out over it, make lifelong friends through it, become better and wiser people through it, or perhaps become worse and more foolish. The urge to play, the urge for folly is something that goes very deep: deeper and older than the human species, as anyone who has seen a litter of kittens well knows. The Pouncing Game, the Tail-Chasing game, the Scragging Game: these are all sports with formal rules and accepted standards of behaviour. They are competitive, though in the main a kitten walks away from them unharmed.

In the end, it all comes down to Coleridge. Coleridge talked about the need for 'the willing suspension of disbelief'. He was talking about poetry, but it works just as well for sport. The obvious fact of the matter is that all sports are absurd: all are risible, all a complete waste of time. There is no other standpoint available to a person of logic. But of course, none of us is a person of logic, especially not where sport is concerned. However, we cannot suspend our disbelief at will. I confess I cannot watch golf without laughter.

21 The writer uses the games played by kittens as an example of
A how ridiculous sports may appear to others.
B the need for games to have properly worked-out rules.
C how instinctive the playing of sports is.
D the difference between animal and human behaviour.

22 The writer says that, in the context of sport, the 'suspension of disbelief' involves
A ignoring your awareness that every sport is ridiculous.
B acknowledging that some sports are more ridiculous than others.
C accepting that sport is important to a great many people.
D pretending that you are incapable of logical thought.

Football Clubs

What's going on? It's a football supporter's constant cry and lament. Beyond all things we crave reliable information, some sense of the inside workings of our clubs on which we can rely, and which acknowledges that our passionate and committed support of the team is met, in its own way, by the club's commitment to us. We are the children of neglectful parents; even repeated doses of callousness will never overcome our yearning for closeness and trust.

Football people keep themselves to themselves, because they are under siege from within and without. The supporters of a club are voracious for information, acknowledgement, and, above all, contact. They don't so much want to talk to the players as to touch them, to imbibe them. And the newspapers, radio and television have an unassuageable appetite for football news, trivia, gossip. Because the game, like all games, is fundamentally simple and intrinsically uninteresting, it is a constant challenge to the media to find something striking to say about it, to spice it up a little. Premiership football, particularly the behaviour both on and off the pitch of its players and management, is a subject of constant, and frequently unsympathetic, media attention. We may recall, for instance, the unconscionable treatment of former England manager Graham Taylor, a decent and competent man, pilloried by the tabloid press and made to look a fool by a slanted television documentary.

line 7 *line 8* *line 9* *line 14*

23 Which of the following words best reflects the writer's view of what football supporters are like?
A insensitive
B dependent
C assertive
D fickle

24 Which of these words does the writer use to make a criticism?
A voracious (line 7)
B imbibe (line 8)
C unassuageable (line 9)
D unconscionable (line 14)

The Professional Player

Rugby Union's transition from amateur to professional has affected the players more than anyone else. Suddenly there is no longer the luxury of margin of error. Suddenly the game ceases to be a hobby and becomes a job. Suddenly there is little scope for escape from rugby. Hobbies are vital avenues of release for us all. Sport starts life as a hobby for anyone who plays it at whatever level, but when it suddenly graduates to become a job, the necessary adjustment can be disconcerting, particularly when the sport in question has no lengthy culture of professionalism to inform it. Intense pressures start to close in. You are getting paid to be excellent and are devoting every last ounce of energy to that one end. Should imperfection ever blemish your excellence, it plagues your conscience, not only because you have always wanted to be the best but because you now have a duty to be the best. Pressures close in from the outside world too. The media may minutely scrutinize your performance (and your personal life) with the justification that you are now getting paid for it. The growing interest from the public and the love for their respective teams exact ever-higher expectations. While thousands enjoy the pre-match carnival outside, the echoes reverberate down to the quiet changing-rooms deep within the stadium.

25 The writer says that Rugby Union's change into being a professional sport
A is too recent for the players to have come to terms with it.
B has had an impact on the players that could not have been foreseen.
C has suggested that the sport itself is not suited to professionalism.
D is likely to have unforeseen consequences in the future.

26 The writer says that Rugby Union players now
A are required to put in more effort than is reasonable when playing.
B feel some resentment towards the fans who follow their teams.
C take criticism more seriously than they need to.
D feel guilty if they make mistakes when playing.

Before you check your answers to Part Two of the test, go on to pages 54–56.

WHAT'S TESTED

The questions in Part Two of the Reading Paper test you on your ability to understand and interpret the content and subtleties of a series of short texts related to a general topic. You are not required to make connections between the texts. Questions may focus on any of the following:

- **detail** – understanding of complex pieces of information and/or ideas that are clearly stated in the text.
- **opinion** – understanding of opinions expressed or referred to by the writer.
- **attitude** – understanding of feelings described in the text which either the writer or someone the writer refers to expresses.
- **tone** – identifying from the style of the text or a section of it the impression the writer wishes to create.
- **purpose** – identifying what the writer is trying to achieve in the text or a section of it.
- **main idea** – identifying the gist or the main topic of what is said in the text or a section of it, as opposed to minor points or details which exemplify general points.
- **implication** – interpreting what is not directly stated in the text but which instead is strongly suggested in such a way that it is clear that the writer intends the reader to make certain inferences.
- **exemplification** – understanding how a point made in the text is illustrated with examples.
- **imagery** – understanding why certain images are used, or how certain effects are achieved by the writer in order to indicate similarities and differences between things.
- **reference** – understanding of what words, phrases or sentences in the text refer to or relate to elsewhere in the text.

TIPS

- In multiple-choice questions such as those in this part of the Paper, it is essential to remember that more than one of the options given may be correct according to what is stated in the text but only one of the options will correctly answer the question that is asked. Don't choose the most appealing option superficially – it may be true, but it may not answer the question you have been asked.
- The questions follow the order of the text and often each question relates to each succeeding paragraph. Sometimes, though, questions may relate to the whole of the text.
- Before you attempt to answer any questions, skim through the whole text quickly. This will give you an idea of what it is about and enable you to approach the questions with some understanding of the text. If you start answering the questions too hastily, you may become confused by what you discover later in the text and have to start again, thus wasting valuable time.

The following exercises will help you to eliminate the incorrect options in the questions in the test or to confirm that you have selected the right options.

*Note: Questions marked * have more than one correct answer.*

Question 19

1 Is the place always busy?

....

2 What do the 'boys' referred to in the first paragraph have with them?

....

3 What two things do you get a 'whiff' of?

....

4* What is said of bazaars in Istanbul?

a They are constantly changing.
b They are full of people.
c They are interesting.
d They are full of contrasting smells.

Question 20

1* Which of the following are mentioned about the queue?

a the shape of it
b the writer's reaction to seeing it
c the feelings of the people in it
d the length of it

2 Which of the following does the writer mention concerning the merchandising manager and the chairman?
a their belief in their own abilities
b their reaction to seeing the queue
c their role in the superstore
d their attitude towards the way the superstore is run

3 Does the writer express a view on the quality of the goods sold in the superstore? If so, where?

....

4 What do the people in the queue have before they get into the superstore?

....

5 What do the people in the queue do when they get into the superstore?

....

Question 21

1* What does the writer say about sports people play?
a Some of them bear a resemblance to the games kittens play.
b All of them attract some people who do not find them ridiculous.
c They have both good and bad effects on people playing them.
d Some of them don't have rules that are consistently observed.

2* What does the writer say about the games played by kittens?
a They have more formal rules than some sports do.
b They reflect a natural need to play.
c They are different from the kind of games humans play.
d They may predate the games played by humans.

3 What is meant by 'folly'?
a seriousness
b silly behaviour
c competitiveness
d entertainment

4 If something 'goes very deep', it is something which
a you prefer to keep hidden.
b distinguishes you from others.
c is a basic part of your nature.
d you don't fully understand.

Question 22

1 If something is 'risible', it is
a criticized generally.
b given too much importance.
c appealing.
d ridiculous.

2 If you can do something 'at will', you can do it
a only when forced to.
b unconsciously.
c in order to fool others.
d any time you want to.

3 If you 'suspend your disbelief', you
a decide to accept something you know is not true.
b try to persuade others of something that isn't true.
c try to see more than one point of view.
d weigh something up before making a decision about it.

4 What does the writer's attitude to golf exemplify?
a the fact that he's more logical than some other people
b his belief that some sports really are ridiculous
c the fact that nobody is truly logical all the time
d his understanding of people who take sports seriously

Question 23

1 What does the writer say about the relationship between clubs and supporters?
a Supporters don't understand the problems faced by clubs.
b Supporters make unreasonable demands on clubs.
c Supporters want to feel that their relationship with clubs is mutual.

2 What is 'callousness'?
a cruelty
b kindness
c explanation

3 If you have a 'yearning' for something, you
a want it desperately.
b expect to receive it.
c treat it badly.

4 If you are assertive, you
a try forcefully to have your own requirements met.
b display great enthusiasm.
c behave with a considerable amount of tolerance.

5 If you are fickle, you
a attach great importance to something in particular.
b question what you are told by others.
c keep changing the object of your affections.

Question 24

1 What is 'imbibe' most likely to mean in the context?
a insult
b advise
c possess

2 What is 'unassuageable' most likely to mean in the context?
a strange
b unintelligent
c enormous

3 What is 'unconscionable' most likely to mean in the context?
a deserved
b unreasonable
c ambiguous

4 If you are 'voracious' for something, you
a are sceptical about it.
b want a great deal of it.
c do not receive as much of it as you should.

Question 25

1 If something is 'disconcerting', it
a constantly changes.
b disturbs you.
c causes disagreement.

2 If one thing 'informs' another, it
a influences the nature of it.
b makes it rigid.
c runs parallel to it.

3 What does the writer say about becoming a professional sportsman?
a People should be better prepared for it.
b It has different repercussions in different sports.
c It has certain implications in every sport.

4* What does the writer say about Rugby Union becoming a professional sport?
a It has required rapid changes in attitude.
b Further changes are likely to take place as a result of it.
c A decision may eventually be made to abandon the idea.
d Players have had difficulty in adapting to it.

Question 26

1 If you 'devote every last ounce of energy' to something, you
a feel you are required to exceed your limit.
b try as hard as you can.
c do more than is expected.

2 What is mentioned about the public?
a their increasing enthusiasm for Rugby Union
b their criticisms of the players
c the players' feelings about them

3* What is said about the media?
a They go into detail about players.
b They feel that Rugby Union being a professional sport justifies their treatment of players.
c Their coverage of the sport doesn't merit being taken seriously.

4 If something 'plagues your conscience', you
a feel bitter about it.
b worry about it.
c exaggerate it.

Now check your answers to these exercises. When you have done so, decide whether you wish to change any of your answers to Part Two of the test. Then check your answers to Part Two of the test.

PART THREE

*You are going to read an extract from an autobiography. Seven paragraphs have been removed from the extract. Choose from the paragraphs **A–H** the one which fits each gap (**27–33**). There is one extra paragraph which you do not need to use. In the exam you will mark your answers on a separate answer sheet.*

The Hammond Organ

It's September 1995 and I'm on my way home to Austin, Texas from Bangkok. Breaking the journey in Los Angeles, I spot an ad for an organ in the Classifieds. It's a 1954 Hammond B2. I can't resist this little gem, so I buy it – sight unseen – and arrange to have it collected, crated and trucked to Texas.

27	

Ever since I heard *Green Onions* by Booker T and the MG's on the radio, the sound of a Hammond organ has moved me. Although at the time I didn't know exactly what Booker T was playing, I knew I wanted to make that noise. I didn't even know how to play an organ, but the way it swirled and swam and bit your ears off, I knew somehow I had to have one. So I did my research in the music shops, and found out that the coolest-sounding organs were all Hammonds, but that the L100, while it still had that special sound, was lighter and cheaper than the other models. Not that any of them were cheap, which didn't much matter, because I had no money.

28	

But when I called them up, they were very helpful. There was no drawback. The only thing I could not do was move it, once they'd set it up. That wasn't going to be a problem. The problem would be explaining the arrival of this beautiful monster to Mum and Dad. But I wasn't thinking that far ahead. I wasn't really thinking at all, apart from wondering – when could it be delivered? 'Tomorrow.' 'Okay.' And that was it. The next morning at about 10am there was a knock at the door and two men in white coats were standing on the doorstep. After I'd signed papers and promised not to move it, we pushed the dining table and chairs back against the wall.

29	

It was all polished and shiny and made our dining room suite look quite tatty. They showed me how to start it up and we shook hands. It couldn't have been simpler. 'See you in two weeks then.' 'Yes, okay, bye.' Slam. 'Aarrgh!' I screamed and ran upstairs to get the record player from the bedroom, set it up on top of the bookcase, plonked *Green Onions* on the turntable and cranked it up! Yes, yes, yes, nothing could stop me now. I had lost my mind and I'd never find it again.

30	

The next thing to master was the Leslie cabinet. This was where the sound came out. The Leslie is a combined amplifier and speaker cabinet, but it has two speakers which point up and down. The sound travels through revolving rotors, which throws the music out in waves. It's what makes the sound of every Hammond bite and swim in your ears. You can regulate the speed it rotates and it's very powerful.

31	

When Dad came whistling his way up the path after work, I went to the door to head him off. 'Hello Dad.' 'What's up?' 'Nothing much. Well, I've got something to tell you.' 'Yes.' 'Er, Dad, you'll never guess what I've got.' 'What have you got?' 'A Hammond organ.'

32	

He was down the hall and peering round the door suspiciously before I could stop him. 'Blimey,' he said. 'Well, I'm blowed. Where's the dining room table gone?' He was in the doorway, trying to squeeze past the monster organ and the Leslie. 'It's great, isn't it?' 'Well, it's big ... how are we going to eat with this thing in here, and why didn't you ask me or your mum?' 'Sorry, but it'll only be here for a couple of weeks, listen to this.' I played the first part of *Green Onions* on it. 'Not bad, eh?' 'I dunno.' He was thinking. 'Here, don't say a word, let me break it to your mum.'

33	

I bought it on the 'never never'. Dad co-signed the hire purchase forms for me because I was under age.

A This meant that there was now enough room. Very carefully, they wheeled in a brand new Hammond organ and matching bench with the Playing Guide and connecting cables tucked inside the lid, and a brand new Leslie 147 speaker cabinet, which filled up the entire room. My face must have been a picture. This was the gear!

B I found all that out by fiddling around with it for hours that day until I got some results. Basically, I just taught myself. The wonderful thing about the Hammond is it sounds good without too much effort. It's not like the bagpipes or the violin, where even after a lot of work it can still sound bad!

C However, I never had any ambition as a kid to play the piano, let alone the organ. It was all my mum's fault. She'd had a dream of playing the piano since she was a kid, but growing up in the little town of Mountrath in the centre of Ireland, as one of 11 kids, there was hardly money for shoes let alone piano lessons. And as she hadn't been able to afford them when she was young, I was going to get them whether I wanted them or not.

D 'What's a Hammond organ?' 'It's free. I've got it for two weeks, then they'll come and take it away and no charge whatsoever.' 'Where is it then?' 'It's in the back room, it's fantastic and it's not costing a penny.'

E Then, thumbing through the back pages of the *Melody Maker*, I noticed an ad for Boosey and Hawkes, in Regent Street, who were offering to let me: 'Try a Hammond Organ in your own home on two weeks' free approval.' 'Yeah, right,' I thought, 'Pull the other one.' I tried to figure out what the catch could be, because I couldn't believe they'd let me get my sweaty hands on a genuine Hammond without money changing hands or at least making a promise to buy.

F Somehow I knew that meant it was going to be all right. The men in white coats came to take it away two weeks later and my new mahogany Hammond organ and matching Leslie cabinet arrived the following week.

G Sometimes, a smell can trigger a memory so strong and true it unravels years in an instant, like the smell of oil paint, which takes me straight back to my art school days. So, as they unbolt the container, even before I get to see how beautiful the instrument is, the combination of furniture polish and Hammond oil wafts up my nose and I get a flashback to 1964, when I caught that odd mixture for the first time.

H Now I had to figure out how to play the beast and get the same sound as that. Carefully listening to sustained notes on the record, I pushed and pulled the drawer bars in and out until I got the same sound. Then, if I played the part right, the sound would change – just like the record.

Now check your answers to Part Three of the test.

PART FOUR

*You are going to read an extract from a novel. For questions **34–40**, choose the answer (**A**, **B**, **C** or **D**) which you think fits best according to the text. In the exam you will mark your answers on a separate answer sheet.*

Piper and Buxxy

It was a great double act. Piper looking relaxed but dependable in a conservative, lightweight suit. Art Buxxy, the showman, doing what he did well. It was a big moment for both of them. They had to secure $200 million from their audience.

Piper warmed up the crowd. In a reasonable, persuasive voice he talked in abstract terms about the remarkable financial opportunity that the Tahiti represented. There was talk of numbers, strategy, competitive analysis. Enough to make us think that the Tahiti was in safe hands, not enough to bore us. ..

Despite the outward reserve, as he warmed up to his presentation, Piper did let some of the excitement he felt for the project show through. Standing there, tall, tanned, elegantly but conservatively dressed, speaking in a manner that was more suited to the Harvard Club than a casino, he gave his audience reassurance. Despite appearances, the Tahiti must be a respectable, conservative investment, or why would someone like Irwin Piper be involved with it?

Then it was Art Buxxy's turn. Buxxy was a small man with a nut-brown face, longish blow-dried grey hair and bundles of enthusiasm. He was hardly ever still, and when he was, it was for a melodramatic pause, to let the full consequence of what he had just said sink in. His abrasive, rough-edged manner jolted his audience after the smooth Piper, but within a minute his energetic charm had already bewitched us all. Selling was his calling, and the Tahiti was the love of his life. He used all his skills. We were captivated. And I think most of us were sold.

They took us on a tour of the complex. Seen through Buxxy's eyes, the tackiness and the loneliness of a big casino disappeared. We saw the glamour, the glitter, the amazing technological effects. He took us to see the private rooms where the high-rollers played, wallowing in sophistication, power and money. By the time we had returned to the conference room where he had started his pitch, I could feel the majority of the audience would write out a cheque there and then.

'Any questions?'

Silence. No difficult questions about Piper's background. No tedious questions about percentage drop of slots against tables, high-roller comps, or blue-collar busing costs. Even the most cynical investor was under the spell of the greatest casino on earth. At least temporarily.

I had thought through this moment carefully. I stood up. Piper's eyebrows pulled together slightly, in the barest trace of a frown. 'Yes?'

'I have two questions for Mr Piper.' The audience were looking at me with mild interest. My English accent jarred in the glitzy Las Vegas surroundings. Piper was staring at me hard. 'First – has the Nevada Gaming Commission scrutinized your previous investments?' The audience stirred a little, but not much. Piper stiffened. 'Second – can you comment on an investment you made in a clinic for executive stress in Britain?'

I sat down. The audience reaction was mixed. Some faces bore disapproval; I was a spoil-sport to try and take cheap shots at these great guys and their great casino. A few sat up and took notice.

Piper rose to his feet. He was as unruffled and urbane as ever. 'I would be happy to answer those questions. First, the Commission checks out all applicants for gambling licences very thoroughly. Second, I have a large portfolio of investments. I believe a few years ago these included some properties in England, but I don't have the details at my fingertips. Any other questions?' He looked around the audience quickly.

This was a dangerous moment for Piper. Until now he had had his listeners eating out of his hand. But he hadn't answered my questions properly. If anyone pursued him on this, then doubts might creep in. But I wasn't going to push it any further. I had achieved my objective. He knew I knew, and he knew I would tell.

Half an hour later, I was having a cup of coffee in the atrium, when a bellboy came over to me. 'Excuse me sir, Mr Piper would like you to join him in his suite.' That didn't take him long, I thought, as I put down my cup and followed the bellboy to the elevators.

Piper's suite was on the top floor of the hotel. Piper was alone in the room. He beckoned me to a seat. I perched on the flimsy-looking Georgian sofa, whilst he sat in one of the high-backed mahogany armchairs. Gone was all the civilized politeness. Piper was angry.

'What the hell do you think you were doing out there?' he said. 'I am not some two-bit bond salesman you can play games with. I am a powerful man in this town. I've got money, and I've got lawyers. And if you mention Bladenham Hall one more time, or even allude to it, I will sue. I will sue you for so much that your great-grandchildren will still be paying off your debts a hundred years from now.'

Piper, angry, was impressive. For a moment he had me on the defensive. If I had upset such a powerful man, I had surely made a mistake. The moment passed.

'I thought you would be interested in this,' I said, untucking the newspaper I had been carrying under my arm. It was a copy of the *Sun* of several years ago. On page two was the headline 'City Slickers' Saucy Retreat'. Under this was a photograph of Bladenham Hall and an article about how a Mr Irwin Piper was helping police with their enquiries.

Piper went purple. 'If you dare show that to anyone, I'll have my lawyers right on to you immediately. That is if I don't tear you apart myself.'

Paradoxically, Piper losing control helped me stay calm. He didn't seem quite so powerful.

34 When he addressed the audience, Irwin Piper gave the impression that

A it was not his primary purpose to get the audience to invest in the project.
B he was less comfortable talking about details than about general principles.
C he was not the sort of person who would normally associate himself with such a project.
D there were already plenty of people who were keen to invest in the project.

35 The narrator says that Art Buxxy's style of addressing the audience

A contained certain elements he may not have been aware of.
B came as something of a shock to them.
C involved making his most important points first.
D contrasted with his physical appearance.

36 When they went on a tour of the complex,

A it appeared that some members of the audience had never been inside a casino before.
B Buxxy diverted the audience's attention away from the less attractive aspects of casinos.
C it was clear the project was at a more advanced stage than the audience had realized.
D Buxxy encouraged the audience to picture themselves playing there.

37 When the narrator asked his questions,

A he feared that the audience would not take him seriously because of his accent.
B Piper reacted initially as if he had been expecting the questions to be asked.
C he did so because he was surprised by the audience's apparent trust in the project.
D it seemed that some of the audience considered he had no right to ask such questions.

38 When Piper stood up and answered the narrator's questions,

A he knew that the audience would not be convinced by his reply.
B he claimed that the questions concerned trivial matters.
C the narrator decided that he had conveyed a clear message to Piper.
D it was clear to the audience that he was ill at ease.

39 When the narrator went to see Piper in his suite,

A he had been expecting Piper to seek a confrontation with him.
B he briefly feared that he had been wrong to doubt Piper's honesty.
C what Piper first said to him was what he had expected him to say.
D Piper made it clear that other people had regretted underestimating him.

40 Piper's reaction to seeing the newspaper article indicated to the narrator that Piper

A had a tendency to make threats he could not actually carry out.
B was not able to dictate events as much as he thought he was.
C had proved capable of inflicting physical violence himself.
D did not realize what sort of article it was.

Now check your answers to Part Four of the test.

PAPER 2 WRITING 2 hours

PART ONE

*You **must** answer this question. Write your answer in **300–350** words in an appropriate style. Write clearly in **pen**, not pencil. You may make alterations, but make sure your work is easy to read.*

1 You have read a newspaper article about the relationships between different generations. The extract below is the conclusion of the article. Readers have been asked to respond to the article. You decide to write a **letter** responding to the points raised and expressing your own views.

> Years ago, you were always reading about the so-called 'generation gap' and all about the conflict between the rebellious young and their mystified parents.
>
> Well, you may not read so much about it any more, but it's still there. Perhaps it's just human nature that children, their parents and even their parents' parents are poles apart. Perhaps it's just the natural result of time passing that each generation sees the one that follows them as being in some way 'not like we were'. Perhaps people of every generation, as they get older, look back on a 'golden age' that may never really have existed.
>
> Perhaps the generations just aren't meant to get along.

Write your **letter**. Do not write any postal addresses.

When you have written your answer, assess it in accordance with the task-specific mark scheme.

PART TWO

*Write an answer to **one** of the questions **2–5** in this part. Write your answer in **300–350** words in an appropriate style. Write clearly in **pen**, not pencil. You may make alterations, but make sure your work is easy to read.*

2 The authorities at the place where you study or work have decided to look into the possibility of a student or staff representative group being set up. You have been asked to write a proposal for the setting up of such a representative group. Write your proposal, outlining reasons for setting it up, how it should be set up, what issues it could deal with and what the advantages of having such a group would be.

Write your **proposal**.

3 A magazine you read has asked readers to send in reviews of particular TV channels or radio stations. Write a review of a TV channel or radio station, commenting on the type and/or mixture of programmes it broadcasts, the standard of its broadcasts, which people it generally appeals to and how it compares to other TV channels or radio stations.

Write your **review**.

4 A series of articles is being published in a magazine you read under the title *Tell Me What It's All About*. The articles are all attempts to explain something that is currently popular to people who have never heard of it and know nothing whatsoever about it. Readers have been invited to send in their own articles under this title. Write your article, remembering that it must assume no knowledge of its subject on the part of the reader.

Write your **article**.

5 Set book questions – a choice from **(a)**, **(b)** and **(c)**.
In the exam you may choose to answer a question on one of the three set books.

Before you write your answer, go on to pages 63–65.

WHAT'S TESTED

Questions 2–4

In Part Two of the Writing Paper, you may choose one of three different types of writing. The choices you are given may include any of the following:

- **an article** – a piece of writing on a given topic that would be suitable for the specified type of publication.
- **a letter** – probably a formal or fairly formal letter, in which you may be required to give opinions, explain reasons for writing the letter, describe events or request actions.
- **a proposal** – a report concerning a future event or possibility, containing recommendations, with the aim of persuading the reader or readers that the recommendations are justified. It should be presented in clear and appropriate sections, perhaps with relevant subject headings.
- **a review** – this may be about anything that gets reviewed in publications, from films to hotels, and it should include both a description of the subject of the review and your views on it. You will obviously need to include a range of vocabulary associated with that particular subject, and the review should be written in a style that is appropriate for the specified type of publication.
- **a report** – this involves the presentation and analysis of information in clear and logical sections, perhaps with section headings. The report must be in a style suitable for the specified reader or readers of it, for example, a boss or colleagues. It will normally focus on a situation that exists or events that have happened (rather than on the future, which is the focus of a proposal in this Paper).

Question 5

In Part Two of the Writing Paper, you may prefer to write about one of the three set books. If so, you may choose one of three questions, which are each about one of the books. Questions on the set books may require you to write any of the following:

- **an essay** – a composition on a given topic connected with the book, organized into an introduction, the expansion of points and a conclusion, so that it is a coherent whole.
- **an article** (see notes above for questions 2–4)
- **a letter** (see notes above for questions 2–4)
- **a review** (see notes above for questions 2–4)
- **a report** (see notes above for questions 2–4)

TIPS

Answers to Part Two of the Writing Paper are judged according to the same criteria as those for Part One, as follows (for details on these criteria, see page 21):

- **content**
- **range**
- **accuracy**
- **appropriacy of register and format**
- **organization and cohesion**
- **target reader**

Remember also the following:

- marks will be reduced for answers that are significantly shorter than the specified number of words.
- spelling and punctuation are taken into consideration in the marking – a significant number of spelling mistakes will affect your marks, as will insufficient or inappropriate punctuation.
- handwriting should be as neat as possible – if the examiner has trouble reading your answers, your marks will be affected.

To plan your answer for question 3 in Part Two, complete the following notes.

1 Note down as briefly as possible the **topic** of your review.

....

2 List as briefly as possible the following:
- the **main points** in the question which you will have to cover in your review
- the **comments and opinions** you wish to give with regard to these points
- any **examples** you plan to give to support or illustrate these comments/opinions

Main point	Comments/Opinions	Example
Main point	**Comments/Opinions**	**Example**
Main point	**Comments/Opinions**	**Example**

3 List briefly any additional points you wish to make, which are not mentioned in the question but which you think are relevant to the topic. You may not wish to include any additional points.

Additional point	Comments/Opinions	Example
Additional point	**Comments/Opinions**	**Example**

4 Now note briefly how your review will be organized by deciding what each part of it will contain. You may not wish to have as many paragraphs as are listed below.

Introduction
Paragraph 1
Paragraph 2
Paragraph 3
Paragraph 4
Paragraph 5
Ending

5 Now use these notes to write your review.

When you have written your answer, assess it in accordance with the task-specific mark scheme.

6 Now read this sample answer for question 3 in Part Two and answer the questions that follow it.

As a keen reader of your magazine, I noticed the appeal in your last issue for writing a review of my favourite TV channel or radio station, which is here to follow.

The radio channel I've chosen to write about is called FIZZ FM. Many of your other readers may not have heard about this channel. The reason is that it's only on air between 11pm and 4am. It's a private channel only run by five people.

The main aim of FIZZ FM is to entertain people who have to work or get up either late at night or early in the morning. So it does not appeal to a certain social or age group, but to particular work groups such as nurses, bakers, etc. Nevertheless, it's very popular with people from 14 to 25 who, even if they don't have to, get up in the middle of the night just to listen to that programme.

Concerning their mixture of programmes, they don't have a fixed schedule. It's a 'colourful' mix of music (from the 60s, 70s, 80s, 90s, ...), news and discussions. Everything is very easy going, so it can happen that there is a whole night of music, followed by a night of discussions about anything. The coordinators of FIZZ FM want to make it easier for working people who have to face a long day full of work.

Though it's not a very busy or (sometimes) interesting station, it is able to compete against bigger stations, because a broad range of people enjoy listening to it. To my mind, this is because of its unique style and appearance. These people have successfully filled a gap in the market without having the problem of competing against others, just because other stations don't care about that time of day.

Perhaps now more people will tune in to FIZZ FM, who knows?

Content

Are all the main points mentioned in the question covered? Where are these points covered? If any are not covered, which are missing? Are any additional points included? If so, what are they, and are they relevant?

Range

Is there a wide range of vocabulary and grammatical structures? If so, give examples. If there are occasions when the vocabulary or grammar is too simple, suggest alternatives.

Accuracy

Are there any mistakes in the use of vocabulary or grammar? Correct any that you find.

Appropriacy of register and format

Are the style and tone of the review appropriate? How would you describe them? Why are they appropriate or inappropriate? Is the format suitable for a review? If so, why? If not, why not?

Organization and cohesion

Is the review well-organized in terms of the beginning, the middle and the end? Is it divided into paragraphs appropriately? Describe briefly the content of each paragraph. Does the review flow well in terms of the linking of points and ideas within paragraphs and between paragraphs? Give examples of places where the linking is good. If there are occasions when the linking is inadequate or inappropriate, suggest improvements.

Target reader

Do you feel that someone reading this review would be clear about what the writer is describing and the writer's views on it? If so, summarize the review briefly. If not, say what you feel is unclear in the it.

Now check your assessment of this sample answer.

PAPER 3 USE OF ENGLISH 1 hour 30 minutes

PART ONE

*For questions **1–15**, read the text below and think of the word which best fits each space. Use only **one** word in each space. There is an example at the beginning **(0)**. In the exam you will mark your answers on a separate answer sheet.*

Example: | **0** | *that* |

Laughing is Good for You – Seriously

It is a sad fact **(0)** .....*that*..... adults laugh far less than children, sometimes **(1)** .... as much as a couple of hundred times a day. Just take a **(2)** .... at people's faces on the way to work or in the office: you'll be lucky to see a smile, let **(3)** .... hear a laugh. This is a shame – especially in **(4)** .... of the fact that scientists have proved that laughing is good for you. 'When you laugh,' says psychologist David Cohen, 'it produces the feel-good hormones, endorphins. It counters the effects of stress **(5)** .... enhances the immune system.'

There are many **(6)** .... why we might laugh less in adult life: perhaps we are too work-obsessed, or too embarrassed to **(7)** .... our emotions show. Some psychologists simply believe that children have more naive responses, and as adults we naturally grow **(8)** .... of spontaneous reactions. Luckily, **(9)** .... , it is possible to relearn the art of laughter. In India, 'laughter clinics' have been growing **(10)** .... popularity over the last few years, **(11)** .... to the efforts of Dr Madan Kataria, **(12)** .... work has won him **(13)** .... devoted following. Dr Kataria believes that his laughing techniques can help to strengthen the immune system and lower stress levels, **(14)** .... other things. He teaches his patients different laughs or giggles to relax specific parts of the body. In 1998, when Dr Kataria organized a World Laughter Day at Bombay racetrack, 10,000 people **(15)** .... up.

Now check your answers to Part One of the test.

PART TWO

*For questions **16–25**, read the text below. Use the word given in **capitals** at the end of some of the lines to form a word that fits in the space in the same line. There is an example at the beginning **(0)**. In the exam you will mark your answers on a separate answer sheet.*

Example: | **0** | *considerable* |

King of the Watchmakers

For a period of its history, the city of Coventry had a **(0)** ....*considerable*.....	**CONSIDER**
reputation as the main centre of clock and watchmaking in Britain, and Coventry	
timepieces made then were **(16)** .... with both quality and	**SYNONYM**
(17) .... Few people in the city today will have heard of	**RELY**
Samuel Watson, but he almost **(18)** .... paved the way for Coventry's	**HAND**
involvement in the clock and watch business. He was at the **(19)**	**FRONT**
of the watchmaking revolution in the 1680s, and although it is not known how	
Watson became involved in the trade, he was a trailblazer for others.	
Watson made his name in 1682 when he sold a clock to King Charles II and was	
invited to be the King's **(20)** .... The following year he began	**MATHEMATICS**
work on an astronomical clock for the King, complete with planets and signs	
of the zodiac, which took seven years to build. It not only told the time of day	
but also the **(21)** .... changes of the planets. Queen Mary acquired	**POSITION**
it in 1691 and it is still in the **(22)** .... of the Royal Family.	**OWN**
He built several other clocks, and by 1690 the clamour for Watson's clocks was	
such that he left Coventry and took up **(23)** .... in London.	**RESIDE**
He became Master of the London Clockmakers' Company in 1692, which is	
testament to his **(24)** .... in the growing industry.	**STAND**
In 1712, Samuel Watson's name disappears from the records of the London	
Clockmakers' Company, and the **(25)** .... is that he died in that year.	**LIKELY**

Before you check your answers to Part Two of the test, go on to pages 68–69

WHAT'S TESTED

Part Two of the Use of English Paper is primarily a vocabulary test, in which you have to form words in different parts of speech from the words given. Questions may involve any of the following:

- changing or adding to the end of the word given, for example to form a noun from a given verb or an adjective from a given noun – the majority of the questions usually fall into this category.
- the use of prefixes, for example when a negative form of a word has to be formed.
- forming a compound word, either by adding another word to the word given, or by both adding a word to the word given and changing the form of the word given.

TIPS

- First of all, decide from the context what part of speech the word you have to form must be – do you have to form a noun, an adjective, an adverb, a verb?
- Then decide what the meaning of that word is most likely to be and whether it will require a prefix or be a compound word.
- If you are sure that your decisions about both the above are correct but do not know the actual word required, use your knowledge of the language to produce a word which you feel sounds correct. Your guess may be right, and if you put no answer at all, you certainly won't get a mark!

1 *Look again at Part Two of this test on page 67 and then for each question, decide which of the choices **a–d** best expresses the meaning of the word that should fill the gap.*
2 *Then decide which of the words listed could fill the gap for that question. Some of the words listed do not exist at all. Identify the words which **do** exist and try to match them to any of the meanings **a–d** given.*
3 *You may wish to change some of the answers you gave in the test after you have done these exercises.*

16 **a** incomparable objects
b always made to the same standard
c considered to mean
d in the same way

synonymatic
synonymists
synonymous
synonymally
synonymized

17 **a** in such a way that they could be relied upon
b being in a position of relying on
c dependence
d the fact of being something that can be relied upon

reliance
reliability
reliably
reliant
reliableness

18 **a** earlier
b in an authoritarian way
c conveniently
d alone

single-handedly
handfully
handily
high-handedly
beforehand

19 **a** most important position
b concerning the front
c outside
d being in the position of facing

frontage
frontal
forefront
fronting
facefront

20 **a** involving mathematics
b branch of mathematics
c expert in mathematics
d good at mathematics

mathematical
mathematician
mathematicist
mathematicalist
mathematicate

21 **a** having a certain position
b putting into positions
c relating to position
d forcing someone/something into a position

positionalized
positional
positionful
imposition
positionalizing

22 **a** the person owning
b the act of becoming owned by
c the fact of being owned by
d something owned

ownering
owning
ownerdom
ownership
ownerhood

23 **a** connected with the place where someone lives
b a person who lives in a particular place
c the situation of living in a particular place
d employment

resident
residential
residency
residence
residentity

24 **a** reputation
b extraordinary
c being able to endure
d attitude

standpoint
standing
withstanding
outstanding
standence

25 **a** evidence
b explanation
c guess
d probability

likelihood
likeliness
likelibility
likeliance
likeliment

Now check your answers to these exercises and to Part Two of the test.

PART THREE

*For questions **26–31**, think of **one** word only which can be used appropriately in all three sentences. There is an example at the beginning **(0)**. In the exam you will write only the missing word on a separate answer sheet.*

Example:

0 You can stay with us if you like, we've got a .... room in our house.

It's very difficult to get .... parts for machines as old as this, so it's hard to get them repaired if they break down.

I like my job but the hours are long so it doesn't allow me much .... time.

0	*spare*

26 Don't cheat – you've just put a card down and it's my .... now.

I'm exhausted because it's been very busy at work and I've been on the .... all day.

Daniel had a .... at fixing the washing machine but he couldn't make it work properly.

27 It's .... as well I remembered to take the map with me, or we'd never have found our way there.

There's no need to get upset .... because I've said I don't agree with you.

Do you think you could phone back in about ten minutes – I can't speak to you .... now.

28 They .... to lose a lot of money if they are forced to close down their business.

He has treated me very badly for a long time and I think that the time has now come for me to .... up to him.

Wendy is extremely selfish and she can't .... it when she doesn't get her own way.

29 I didn't have a view of the sea from my hotel room because there was a .... big block of flats in the way.

The town where I live is not very well-known and doesn't attract a .... many visitors.

I didn't want to go into .... detail at that point, so I said I would discuss the matter further the following day.

30 In a united .... of defiance, the protesters refused to disperse when ordered to do so by the police.

The burglars were in the .... of breaking in when he spotted them and called the police.

His .... was not well received by the audience and he left the stage to total silence.

31 If you wait outside the building at six o'clock, I'll .... you up in the car.

He obviously wanted to .... a fight with me but I refused to react to his aggressive behaviour.

Most fans regarded him as one of the best players in the country and were astonished when the selectors didn't .... him for the national team.

Now check your answers to Part Three of the test.

PART FOUR

For questions ***32–39****, complete the second sentence so that it has a similar meaning to the first sentence, using the word given.* ***Do not change the word given.*** *You must use between* ***three*** *and* ***eight*** *words, including the word given. There is an example at the beginning* ***(0)****.*

Example:

0 Robert was offended when he was left out of the team.
exception
Robert .... left out of the team.

The gap can be filled by the words 'took exception to being', so you write:

0	*took exception to being*

In the exam you will mark only the missing words on a separate answer sheet.

32 David played the main role when the proposal was drafted.
instrumental
David .... of the proposal.

33 If you hadn't changed our original agreement, everything would have been fine.
stuck
Had .... agreed, everything would have been fine.

34 I think you should have some consideration for those who don't have lives as privileged as yours.
spare
I think you should .... lives aren't as privileged as yours.

35 We decided to stay for longer because we were so thrilled by the place.
prolong
We decided to .... we by the place.

36 Competitors were amazed by how shrewdly he conducted his business affairs.
marvelled
Competitors .... which he conducted his business affairs.

37 I didn't want to give up while some hope of success remained.
defeat
I was loath .... some hope of success.

38 After a long hard journey, I cheered up when I saw my home.
sight
After a long hard journey, my spirits .... of my home.

39 Your attitude to life would be greatly improved by regular exercise.
wonders
Regular exercise would .... at life.

Now check your answers to Part Four of the test.

PART FIVE

*For questions **40–44**, read the following texts on popular culture. For questions **40–43**, answer with a word or short phrase. You do not need to write complete sentences. For question **44**, write a summary according to the instructions given. In the exam you will mark your answers on a separate answer sheet.*

Until recently, the study of popular culture has taken two main directions. The less productive has been that which has celebrated popular culture without situating it in the context of power and the dominant forces in a society. It has been a consensual model, which views popular culture as a form of the natural management of social differences out of which a final harmony is produced. It is a democratic version, which merely resituates the cultural life of a nation in the popular rather than the highbrow.

The other direction has been to situate popular culture firmly within the context of power, but to emphasize so strongly the forces of domination as to make it appear impossible for a genuine popular culture to exist at all. What replaces it is a mass culture imposed on people by a culture industry whose interests are in direct opposition to theirs. A mass culture produces a quiescent, passive mass of people, totally disempowered and helpless.

Recently, however, a third direction has begun to emerge. It sees popular culture as a site of struggle. While accepting the power of the forces of dominance, it focuses rather upon the popular tactics by which these forces are coped with, are evaded or are resisted. Instead of concentrating on the omnipresent, insidious practices of the dominant ideology, it attempts to understand the everyday resistances and evasions that make the ideology work so hard and insistently to maintain itself. This approach sees popular culture as potentially, and often actually, progressive and it is essentially optimistic, for it finds in the vigour and vitality of the people evidence both of the possibility of social change and of the motivation to drive it.

40 What, in the context, is meant by 'the highbrow' (line 6)?

....

....

41 What is said about 'the dominant ideology' in the third paragraph?

....

....

Popular culture in industrial societies is contradictory to its core. On the one hand it is industrialized – its commodities produced and distributed by a profit-motivated industry that follows only its own economic interests. But on the other hand, it is of the people, and the people's interests are not those of the industry – as is evidenced by the number of films,
5 records and other products that the people make into expensive failures. To be incorporated into popular culture, a commodity must also bear the interests of the people. Popular culture is not consumption, it is culture – the active process of generating and circulating meanings and pleasures within a social system: culture, however industrialized, can never be adequately described in terms of the buying and selling of commodities.

10 Culture is a living, active process: it can be developed only from within, it cannot be imposed from without or above. The fears of the mass culture theorists have not been borne out in practice because mass culture is such a contradiction in terms that it cannot exist. A homogeneous, externally produced culture cannot be sold ready-made to the masses: culture simply does not work like that. Nor do the people behave or live like the masses, an
15 aggregation of alienated, one–dimensional persons whose only relationship to the system that enslaves them is one of unwitting dupes. Popular culture is made by the people, not produced by the culture industry. All the culture industries can do is produce a repertoire of cultural resources for the various formations of the people to use or reject in the ongoing process of producing their popular culture.

42 What point does the writer use some films and records to illustrate?

....

....

43 What, in the context, is meant by the phrase 'unwitting dupes' (line 16)?

....

....

44 In a paragraph of between **50 and 70** words, summarize **in your own words as far as possible**, the theories as to what produces popular culture which are described in the two texts.

Before you check your answers to Part Five of the test, go on to page 74.

Sample Summary

Look at this sample summary and answer the questions that follow it.

> One theory is that popular culture develops democratically and not by people with power in society. Some people disagree and say that it is imposed on people by powerful forces and is really a mass culture. Another idea is that it results from people acting in opposition to powerful forces in society. It is also thought by some people that popular culture is created by people themselves and is not something they are forced to accept by businesses that want to make money.

1 Is anything irrelevant included or anything relevant not included?

2 Are there any language mistakes? Correct any that you find.

3 Is the summary well-organized and does it make sense throughout?

4 Have any parts of the texts simply been copied in the summary? If so, where?

5 Is the summary within the specified word limit?

Now look again at your summary and decide whether you wish to change anything.

Then check your marks for your summary and read the assessment of this sample summary.

PAPER 4 LISTENING approximately 40 minutes

PART ONE

*You will hear four different extracts. For questions **1–8**, choose the answer (**A**, **B** or **C**) which fits best according to what you hear. There are two questions for each extract. In the exam you will hear each extract twice.*

Extract One

You hear part of a talk about negotiating with others.

1 The speaker says that both soft and hard ways of negotiating

A are more suitable in some situations than in others.

B tend to result in outcomes that were not anticipated.

C indicate a lack of confidence on the part of those using them.

[ ] 1

2 The speaker says that principled negotiation involves

A accepting that life can be unfair.

B greater effort from both sides.

C the use of objective criteria.

[ ] 2

Extract Two

You hear part of a radio programme about a pottery.

3 What does the reporter emphasize about the pottery?

A how seldom anyone visits it these days

B how deceptive its appearance is

C how much it seems to belong to a previous era

[ ] 3

4 When describing the history of the pottery, Roly Curtis

A mentions a problem common to many potteries.

B refers to a mistake he believes was made.

C expresses support for what his father did.

[ ] 4

Extract Three

You hear part of a radio programme about the stars of silent films.

5 The speaker says that Harold Lloyd became very successful because he

A acted on a suggestion made by a colleague.

B changed the character he portrayed in films.

C became more ambitious than he had previously been.

6 The speaker says that Lloyd's career suffered because

A his character's attitude ceased to be appealing.

B he was reluctant to make films with sound.

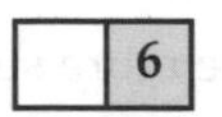

C he lost confidence in his abilities as a performer.

Extract Four

You hear the introduction to a radio science programme.

7 The speaker describes a process by which the brain

A changes previous perceptions about events.

B discards irrelevant information about events.

C waits before focusing on events.

8 What does the speaker say about the research he mentions?

A It has been influenced by the methods used for live TV broadcasts.

B It adds useful information to what is already known.

C It is likely to be disproved by other research.

Stop the recording when you hear 'That's the end of Part One'.

Now check your answers to Part One of the test.

PART TWO

*You will hear part of a radio programme, in which the history of Ty-Phoo Tipps – a brand of tea that is well-known in Britain – is described. For questions **9–17**, complete the sentences with a word or short phrase. In the exam you will hear the piece twice.*

In 1835, William Sumner appeared in a publication called the [9].

At the beginning of the 20th century, the Sumners' business sold [*and* 10] in addition to groceries.

Mary found that a certain type of tea was good for [11].

John was told that people would not wish to buy tea that resembled [12].

John thought that the name he chose for the tea sounded like a word that was [13].

The name of the tea has a double 'p' because of a [14].

To promote the tea, customers were offered a big [15].

John wanted people to know his tea came from the [16].

John was given an honour for his [17].

Stop the recording when you hear 'That's the end of Part Two'.

Before you check your answers to Part Two of the test, go on to pages 78–79.

WHAT'S TESTED

Part Two of the Listening Paper is the productive task, in which you have to write words and phrases to complete sentences with information that you hear in the piece.

TIPS

- You will normally be required to write only words and phrases that are actually said in the piece. If you attempt to rephrase what you hear, for example by using different vocabulary or changing the grammatical structure, you may make unnecessary mistakes and lose marks, even though you understood perfectly what was said in the piece.
- Don't spend too much time on a question you are having difficulty with – this may mean that you miss the information required for subsequent questions, which you may have been able to answer more easily.
- Use the pause of 45 seconds before the piece is heard to look carefully at the questions so that you are prepared for the kind of answer that will be required in each case. This will also give you a good idea of the kind of information the piece will contain.
- Pay close attention to any words that appear after the gap in a question, as these will affect the nature of the answer that is required.
- Use the second listening to check answers you were confident about on the first listening and to fill in answers to questions you were unable to answer then.

Listen to Part Two of the test again and do the exercises below. They will give you clues to the answers to each question in the test.

Question 9 *Stop the recording when you hear 'came from China'.*

The gap should be filled by a title referring to

a a particular region.

b a list of businesses.

c certain kinds of shop.

Question 10 *Stop the recording when you hear 'life was good'.*

The gap should be filled by words describing

a food and drink.

b types of drink.

c drinks and household goods.

Question 11 *Stop the recording when you hear 'why Sumner did not sell it'.*

The gap should be filled by a word or phrase describing

a an illness.

b a mood.

c a physical feature.

Question 12 *Stop the recording when you hear 'under a brand name'.*

The gap should be filled by a word or phrase describing

a a block of something.

b the colour of something.

c small particles of something.

Question 13 *Stop the recording when you hear 'Ty-Phoo could and was'.*

The gap should be filled by a word or phrase referring to

a a type of product.

b a region.

c the length of words.

Question 14 *Stop the recording when you hear 'stick with this spelling'.*

The gap should be filled by a word or phrase describing

a a sound.

b a decision.

c an action.

Question 15 *Stop the recording when you hear 'cream and biscuits'.*

The gap should be filled by a word or phrase describing

a an object.

b a sum of money.

c an event.

Question 16 *Stop the recording when you hear 'inserted them in the packets of tea'.*

The gap should be filled by a word or phrase describing

a a geographical area.

b part of a plant.

c a process.

Question 17 *Stop the recording at the end of the piece.*

The gap should be filled by a word or phrase connected with

a commercial success.

b helping others.

c employment.

Now check your answers to these exercises. When you have done so, listen again to Part Two of the test and decide whether you wish to change any of the answers you gave. Then check your answers to Part Two of the test.

PART THREE

You will hear an interview with someone whose family spent a year living without television. For questions ***18–22****, choose the answer (****A****,* ***B****,* ***C*** *or* ***D****) which fits best according to what you hear. In the exam you will hear the piece twice.*

18 One reason why the family decided not to have a television was that

A the reception from the communal aerial was often poor.

B they did not think the satellite technician would do the job properly.

C linking up with the communal aerial was complicated.

D they preferred to enjoy the beauty of their new surroundings.

[ ] 18

19 One thing that Miranda enjoyed about not having a television was

A telling other people about what they did instead.

B returning to hobbies they had previously given up.

C observing the reaction of others when they found out.

D feeling more energetic during the evening.

[ ] 19

20 Miranda says that one disadvantage of not having a television was

A the fact that they could not follow their favourite series.

B a constant desire to be more up to date with the news.

C being unable to discuss topics they had previously discussed.

D feeling out of touch with what other people talked about.

[ ] 20

21 What does Miranda say about getting connected again?

A She felt it would be of some benefit to the whole family.

B She agreed because her attitude towards television had changed.

C She initially disagreed with her husband about doing so.

D She felt that they were doing so because they were lazy people.

[ ] 21

22 Miranda says that since they got a television again, her children

A are more able to distinguish good programmes from rubbish.

B sometimes refuse to watch it when she suggests they do so.

C have decided not to return to the habit of watching it.

D never watch it simply because they are feeling lazy.

[ ] 22

Stop the recording when you hear 'That's the end of Part Three'.

Now check your answers to Part Three of the test.

PART FOUR

You will hear two people who work together writing scripts for television comedy series, Sara and Vic, talking about collaborating as writers. For questions **23–28**, *decide whether the opinions are expressed by only one of the speakers, or whether the speakers agree.*

Write **S** *for Sara,*
V *for Vic,*
or **B** *for Both, where they agree.*

In the exam you will hear the piece twice.

23 It can get harder for collaborators to agree when they've been collaborating for a while. [ ] 23

24 A partner can resolve your doubts about something you have written. [ ] 24

25 My personality leads me to a certain type of writing. [ ] 25

26 It's wrong to have too much personal involvement in your work. [ ] 26

27 Big arguments between partners do not necessarily destroy their relationship. [ ] 27

28 It is easy for one partner to cover for another if the need arises. [ ] 28

Stop the recording when you hear 'That's the end of Part Four'.

In the exam you will have five minutes at the end of the test to copy your answers onto a separate answer sheet.

Now check your answers to Part Four of the test.

PAPER 5 SPEAKING 19 minutes

PART ONE (3 MINUTES) GENERAL AND SOCIAL

Questions that may be addressed to either candidate.

- What is your purpose in taking this exam?
- What are your short-term and long-term aims?
- What will you have to do to achieve them?
- What are your friends' aims for the future?
- Do you think they will achieve them?

- Do you tend to get nervous, and if so, in what circumstances?
- What are the best ways of overcoming nervousness?
- What aspect(s) of your personality do you particularly like?
- What aspect(s) of your personality do you like the least?
- Do you think your personality has changed over the years?

PART TWO (4 MINUTES) GOOD AND BAD MOODS

For both candidates.

Choose two of the pictures on pages 172–173 and describe what is happening in each of them.
(1 minute)

Now look at all of the pictures and answer one of these questions.
Which of the feelings shown in the pictures are the most and the least typical of you?
Can you describe an event that has made you feel like the person/people in one of the pictures?
(3 minutes)

PART THREE (12 MINUTES) CONFLICT AND COOPERATION

In phase one of Part Three each candidate takes a long turn (2 minutes), followed by a brief response from the other candidate.

Prompt Card (a) *(Given to Candidate A, and a copy to Candidate B)*

What are the most common causes of conflict?
- greed/envy
- personality clashes
- desire for superiority

One of the following questions for Candidate B (1 minute):

- What do you think?
- Is there anything you would like to add?
- Is there anything you don't agree with?
- How does this differ from your experience?

One of the following questions for both candidates (1 minute):

- Is it simply human nature for conflicts to arise?
- Describe a conflict which you think could have been avoided.
- What sort of people are you most likely to come into conflict with?

Prompt Card (b) *(Given to Candidate B, and a copy to Candidate A)*

In what ways is cooperation essential?
- problem-solving
- between nations
- team games

One of the following questions for Candidate A (1 minute):

- What do you think?
- Is there anything you would like to add?
- Is there anything you don't agree with?
- How does this differ from your experience?

One of the following questions for both candidates (1 minute):

- Can people be taught to cooperate with others and if so, how?
- Is there something that you would be or have been unwilling to cooperate on?
- What typically makes people uncooperative?

In phase two of Part Three there is a discussion on the general topic (4 minutes).
Possible general questions for both candidates on the topic of conflict and cooperation:

- Describe an occasion when you were in conflict with someone else. What was the outcome?
- Describe an occasion when cooperation had a positive effect.
- Describe an experience you have had as a member of a team.
- Are you good at handling conflicts or do you try to avoid them?
- Describe a problem which you think could be solved by cooperation.
- Are there any situations in which cooperation is simply impossible?

Part Two: Describing Feelings

In the Speaking Paper, you may need to talk about your own or other people's feelings. To do this, you will need to know and use appropriately a wide range of words connected with feelings.

To check or add to your vocabulary on this subject, look at the adjectives below, decide whether each one is used for describing a feeling of sadness, anger, anxiety, shock or confusion and list them in the appropriate columns.

irate	flustered	infuriated
agitated	outraged	stunned
enraged	dismayed	downcast
bewildered	concerned	appalled
dispirited	distressed	wound up
taken aback	mad	despondent
tense	baffled	resentful
devastated	bothered	unnerved
apprehensive	edgy	petrified
flabbergasted	dejected	distraught
harassed	astounded	bemused
thrown	perplexed	cross
touchy	worked up	
staggered	speechless	

Sadness	Anger	Anxiety	Shock	Confusion

Now check your answers to this exercise.

Part Three: Topic Vocabulary

In Part Three of this test, you are required to talk about the topic of conflict and cooperation. To check or add to your vocabulary on this subject, look at the words and phrases below. List them in the appropriate column. Then decide whether they are verbs, adjectives or nouns and label them appropriately. Then note down the precise meaning of each one (you may need to consult a dictionary) and try to think of sentences in which you could use them.

reconcile	fall out	intervene
collaborate	antagonize	animosity
antipathy	squabble	mollify
appease	concede	camaraderie
conciliatory	bone of contention	unanimous
set-to	take issue with	see eye to eye
join forces	acrimonious	acquiesce
pacify	feud	defuse
enmity	harmony	grant
acknowledge	pool	hostility
strife	in accord	incompatible
showdown	band together	bicker
altercation	win over	bad blood
wrangle	mediate	accommodating
allow	concerted effort	give and take
rivalry	consensus	placate
in concert	friction	

Conflict	Cooperation	Agree	Try To Create Agreement

Now check your answers to this exercise.

TEST THREE

PAPER 1 READING 1 hour 30 minutes

PART ONE

*For questions **1–18**, read the three texts below and decide which answer (**A**, **B**, **C** or **D**) best fits each gap. In the exam you will mark your answers on a separate answer sheet.*

Seriousness

'Is it serious?' we ask the doctor. 'I'm not **(1)** .... ,' we tell the child. 'What's so funny?' says the voice of authority from classroom to army camp to editorial page of the newspaper. The threat of seriousness **(2)** .... our lives. Life is weighty, important, grave, critical, momentous. But though wise people spend their days trying to stay away from serious matters, there are other people who frankly **(3)** .... in them. They look serious, think about serious things, pick serious topics and speak about them seriously.

Why do they do it? My guess is self-loathing. 'Serious' people are dense and know it. But, they think, if they can be grave enough about some problem somewhere in the world, their gravity will **(4)** .... for the fact that – like most people – they don't know what's going on there, and – like all people – they don't know what to do about it.

Seriousness **(5)** .... weight to bad arguments. If a person is earnest enough about what he says, he must have *some* point. Seriousness is also the only practical tone to take when lying. The phrase 'to lie with a **(6)** .... face' is well-known. All lies are told in this way. It's truth that's said with a dismissive giggle.

1	**A** tricking	**B** cracking	**C** tickling	**D** kidding
2	**A** preys	**B** looms	**C** haunts	**D** hangs
3	**A** relish	**B** savour	**C** wallow	**D** cherish
4	**A** balance	**B** reconcile	**C** redeem	**D** compensate
5	**A** lends	**B** gains	**C** holds	**D** hands
6	**A** smooth	**B** straight	**C** plain	**D** clear

Horses

Of the more than 4,000 species of mammals that have inhabited our earth over the past 10,000 years, the horse is one of fewer than a dozen which have been successfully domesticated. Domestication is not simply a **(7)** .... of human intention. If it were, it is possible that we would now be sitting in our fireside chairs with a hyena curled at our feet.

Much of what we take for **(8)** .... as useful in the modern horse – speed, size and intelligence, for example – can be explained through the evolutionary changes it has **(9)** .... in response to a changing diet. As the Ice Age advanced and forests died away, to be replaced by windswept savannah, many herbivores were **(10)** .... to change their diets from leaves to grass. The little leaf-browsing predecessor of our modern horse – the ur-horse – began to change and adapt to a new ecological niche on the plains. The head **(11)** .... longer, with the eye positioned at some distance from the mouth, so that in exposed spaces it could keep a careful **(12)** .... for predators while it grazed. A larger brain began to develop, probably because, as a grazer, it needed greater tactile sensitivity in its lips to choose its food.

7	**A** concern	**B** business	**C** point	**D** matter
8	**A** assumed	**B** granted	**C** given	**D** read
9	**A** subjected	**B** undergone	**C** submitted	**D** committed
10	**A** coerced	**B** enforced	**C** compelled	**D** necessitated
11	**A** expanded	**B** increased	**C** grew	**D** enlarged
12	**A** lookout	**B** heed	**C** vigilance	**D** alert

Afternoon Tea

In far too many places in England today, the agreeable habit of taking afternoon tea has vanished. 'Such a shocking waste of time,' says one. 'Quite unnecessary, if one has had lunch or **(13)** .... to eat in the evening,' says another.

All very true, **(14)** .... , but what a lot of innocent pleasure these strong-minded people are missing! The very ritual of tea-making, warming the pot, making sure that the water is just boiling, inhaling the fragrant steam, arranging the tea-cosy to fit snugly around the container, all the preliminaries **(15)** .... up to the exquisite pleasure of **(16)** .... the brew from thin porcelain, and helping oneself to hot buttered scones and strawberry jam, a slice of feather-light sponge cake or home-made shortbread. Taking tea is a highly civilized pastime, and fortunately is still in favour in Thrush Green, where the inhabitants have got it down to a **(17)** .... art. It is common **(18)** .... in that pleasant village to invite friends to tea rather than lunch or dinner.

13	**A** designs	**B** proposes	**C** views	**D** minds
14	**A** no doubt	**B** no wonder	**C** no matter	**D** no way
15	**A** draw	**B** come	**C** lead	**D** run
16	**A** quenching	**B** nibbling	**C** munching	**D** sipping
17	**A** fine	**B** sheer	**C** rare	**D** pure
18	**A** custom	**B** practice	**C** habit	**D** procedure

Now check your answers to Part One of the test.

PART TWO

*You are going to read four extracts which are all descriptions of people. For questions **19–26**, choose the answer (**A**, **B**, **C** or **D**) which you think fits best according to the text. In the exam you will mark your answers on a separate answer sheet.*

FDR

The man who spoke to the American people on 4th March 1933, having overcome fearful blows in his own life, was well qualified to tell them that they were not and could not be defeated. But what inspired them was more than grit. It was more than his gallantry and charm, of which he made no use on 4th March. At bottom, Franklin Roosevelt was a man of power and vision. He was a master politician, who took command with absolute authority: he knew that he could save the country and that no one else could. His strength and ability went along with a profound, creative desire to shape America for a better future: his administration was to pursue reform as well as recovery. On Inauguration Day his hearers sensed above all his inner certainty and his deep sympathy with their plight.

Those closer to FDR (as he was soon known) discovered that he was better able to respond to people in numbers, at a distance, than to the needs of intimates. Like many a man who is totally committed to his career – in Roosevelt's case it might for once be truer to say wedded to his destiny – he was highly egoistic. At close quarters he could be evasive, cold, occasionally brutal, if others grew too demanding. If they kept their place he could be patient and generous; but who can always know his place? Many paid in the end a very high price for the privilege of working for FDR. Yet so intoxicating was his leadership that few seem to have regretted it. They felt it was enough to have served his great purposes.

19 According to the writer, one reason why FDR appealed to the American people was that
A he was not afraid to point out to them what their faults were.
B he seemed to have ideas that went beyond solving their immediate problems.
C he told them that determination alone would not transform the country.
D he was open about the unfortunate aspects of his personal life.

20 The writer says that people who came into close contact with FDR
A sometimes could not help doing something he found unacceptable.
B often found themselves defending his behaviour to outsiders.
C realized that he pretended to be more unpleasant than he really was.
D knew immediately that their relationship with him was likely to be short-lived.

Kenneth Williams

Kenneth Williams was not an international star. Cross the Atlantic and few will know the name. In his native Britain – a country he was never happy to leave – he was the antithesis of the showbiz personality. He was a combination of show-off and virtual recluse. In this age of the megastar who exists by virtue of the fact that to succeed at all, you have to be as easily recognized by people eating with chopsticks in Hong Kong, drinking Borscht in Moscow, enjoying a hamburger in New York and a plate of fish and chips in London, Williams again seems an aberration. At home he *was* a star – the kind who would bring taxi drivers shuddering to a halt as they saw him cross the road, who could send up the figures for a radio or TV show simply by saying his catchphrase, 'Stop messing about'.

Until now, the book on Kenneth Williams has remained closed. People who say they knew him well did so from their own necessarily limited perspective. His fellow radio personality and close friend, Derek Nimmo, put it perfectly in perspective when he said that he metaphorically kept all his friends in separate rooms – and none of them knew what was going on in the room next door. It was sometimes more than a metaphorical room. Being ensconced with him in a particular place was to have a wall built around you, even if you couldn't see it. This book, therefore, is an attempt to bring the walls down.

21 According to the writer, Kenneth Williams was an 'aberration' partly because
A he had no desire to be a star outside his native country.
B he did not realize how big a star he really was.
C he appealed to people who might not have been expected to like him.
D he was a very big star purely in his own country.

22 What are the 'walls' that the writer is going to try to bring down?
A Kenneth Williams' attempts to ensure that the truth about him was not made public
B the steps taken by Kenneth Williams' friends to keep information about him private
C the different aspects of Kenneth Williams' life which he kept separate
D Kenneth Williams' attempts to disguise his true feelings

My Brother Charles

My brother Charles left school with no talents discernible to his teachers. He works now in the electrical goods department of Temple's, Glebeland's magnificent department store built to outdo the great London stores and once boasting a small Arcadian bower on its roof, complete with green sward, rippling brooks and a herd of grazing cattle. That was a long time ago, of course, and Charles must content himself with a more mundane environment amongst an assorted miscellany of vacuum cleaners, hand whisks and radiograms. Charles seems neither particularly happy nor particularly unhappy with his life. I think that most of his time is taken up with daydreaming. He's the kind of boy – I can't imagine ever thinking of Charles as a man – who believes that *at any moment* something incredibly exciting might unexpectedly happen and change his life forever. Much like everyone else in fact. 'Don't you think that something,' his eyes nearly pop out of his head as he searches for the words to articulate the feeling, 'that something's about to happen?' 'No,' I lie, for there's no point in encouraging him. 'I'm just marking time at Temple's,' Charles says, in explanation of his remarkably dull outer life.

23 What do we learn about Charles' job?

A He regards it as satisfactory for the time being.
B It is with a company that is less successful than it used to be.
C He finds it more interesting than he appears to.
D It is with a company that makes little demand on its employees.

24 Which of the following best describes the writer's attitude towards her brother?

A She feels that what he says could be expressed better.
B She considers herself to have nothing in common with him.
C She regards him as an immature person.
D She feels that he is not fulfilling his potential.

John Lennon

John's cruelty was not confined to words; he would lash out instinctively at anyone who angered him. Extreme hostility coupled with extreme defensiveness characterizes the essential Lennon, early and late. These attitudes gripped John so powerfully that they bent him into a distinctive shape and gave him his characteristic gait. 'He used to walk,' recalled Pete Shotton, 'all hunched up, his eyes and head down, like a scared rabbit driven into a corner but ready to lash out.' Like most bullies, Lennon was frightened at heart. He sought to dominate through sheer aggression, especially by launching surprise attacks; but if he ran into someone bigger or braver, he would resort to psychological tactics, according to Shotton, 'undermining them by abuse or sarcasm.' If all else failed, Lennon would take to his heels. At school, John and Pete were often caned by the headmaster, the notorious Ernie Taylor, but no matter how much Lennon was beaten, he never mended his ways. Instead, he adopted the attitude that he was beyond the pale, so what did it matter what he did or how much he was punished?

25 The writer believes that John Lennon's behaviour illustrates the theory that

A cruel words are more hurtful than cruel actions.
B people who are nasty to others lack confidence in themselves.
C the way people walk is indicative of their personalities.
D fear is more powerful than other emotions.

26 According to the writer, why didn't Lennon change?

A He had no respect for his headmaster.
B He always got his own way in the end through bullying.
C He felt that others admired him for his refusal to conform.
D He decided that he was an outcast.

Now check your answers to Part Two of the test.

PART THREE

*You are going to read a newspaper article. Seven paragraphs have been removed from the article. Choose from the paragraphs **A–H** the one which fits each gap (**27–33**). There is one extra paragraph which you do not need to use. In the exam you will mark your answers on a separate answer sheet.*

The Perils of Pizza Making

It looks easy but it really isn't, says Chandos Elletson, whose efforts turned out far from perfect.

My first pizza was cremated. I hadn't even got to the toppings, let alone the tossing stage. I was stuck on the rolling-out bit. I fast discovered that specialist pizza chefs – pizzaioli – don't use rolling pins, they use their hands to shape the dough into perfect circles. Francesco Sarritzu, the pizzaiolo at The Park restaurant in Queen's Park, London, where I went to be trainee for the evening, took one look at my sorry effort and sighed.

27 ____

Real, or original, pizza is an art: the pizzaiolo is baker, fire stoker and cook. A wood-burning oven is an essential part of the proceedings. However, before the pizzas get to the fire, they have to be properly shaped and it was this procedure that was causing me all the grief.

28 ____

From here it was all hands. He pressed out the dough with his fingers, all the time working in flour and pressing the edges out until a small round circle had emerged. He then threw it into his hands, twirling it to shake off the excess flour. He did not toss it in the air. 'Tossing is for show,' he said disdainfully. 'It is not necessary.' Once the flour was shaken off, he put the dough onto the steel work surface with one half of it hanging over the edge. One hand pressed and stretched and the other pulled in the opposite direction. Before you could say 'pizza Margherita' there was a perfect circle ready to be topped.

29 ____

The object is to press out the edges, not the centre, using the flour to dry out the stickiness. However, the temptation to press everything in sight to make it stretch into a circular shape is too strong; before I knew it, I had thick edges and a thin centre.

30 ____

Then I noticed, to my horror, that some customers were watching me. 'Shall we watch the man make the pizza?' a man asked his young daughter, who he was holding in his arms.

31 ____

A hole appeared in the centre. 'Look, Daddy. There's a hole,' the little girl said. I looked up from my work, crestfallen. I was defeated. 'It's my first evening,' I admitted. Francesco stepped in with the paddle and my second pizza went where the first one had gone: on the fire. We all watched it go up in flames.

32 ____

Francesco noticed and applauded. I wanted to call back the little girl and tell her: 'I can do it! It's just like swimming!' My base was not perfectly round but it was not bad. It wasn't perfectly even but it was certainly an improvement. We decided to top it. We put on a thin smear of tomato sauce and some mozzarella.

33 ____

When I got there, Francesco showed me where to put it. There was a point in the deep oven away from the fire, where the pizzas go when they are first put into the oven. I put the long handle deep into the oven and, feeling the heat on my arms, brought it back sharply. The pizza slid onto the floor of the oven. My first pizza was in the oven and not being burnt alive.

A To put those things right, I did as Francesco had done and slapped it with the palm of my hand. This made me feel better and I slapped it again. Next, I did some twirling and the flour showered everywhere.

B Instead, Francesco quickly made one of his own to act as a comparison. When they were done and brought from the oven, we had a tasting. The result was astonishing. Mine was tough and crunchy in places, not bad in others. His was perfectly crispy and soft everywhere.

C Having done that, it was time to get it on to the paddle, which felt like a pole vault. With one determined shove, the pizza went on halfway. Another shove forward got it on completely but put an ugly buckle in it. I turned and headed for the oven.

D Francesco made it look easy. He showed me what to do again and I tried to take it in. The chilled dough balls, pre-weighed at 170g, were all ready in a special fridge below the work counter. The dough was sticky and Francesco worked fast. First it was dropped into a large pile of flour and then it was mixed with a small handful of polenta.

E Clearly, the stage was all mine. I had been told to concentrate on the edges using the flat edge of my hand under my little finger. I started to work the dough and tried to stretch it. It did begin to take shape, but as soon as I let it go it just went back again and didn't get any bigger. I felt more and more eyes on me. Then the worst thing happened.

F That was because it wasn't so much a circle as an early map of the world. Silently, Francesco reached for his pizza paddle, scooped it up and threw it disdainfully into the red-hot stone oven, where it burnt rapidly on top of a funeral pyre of burning wood. I made up my mind that my future efforts would be good enough to be spared the death sentence.

G I was baffled and embarrassed as it did so, but I thought I was onto something. On my next attempt, I quickly got to the shaping stage with half the pizza hanging over the edge. This was where I had gone wrong. Using only the bottom edge of my hands with my fingers working the edges, I started to do the breast stroke: fingers together, fingers apart, working and stretching. It began to work.

H I moved nervously into position to have a go at achieving the same result myself. I scooped up a piece of dough from its snug tray. It immediately stuck to my fingers and when I threw it at the flour, it just remained stuck. I had to pull it off. The first bit is easy, or so it seems, but unless you follow the right procedure you sow the seeds of later failure.

Before you check your answers to Part Three of the test, go on to pages 92–96 .

WHAT'S TESTED

In Part Three of the Reading Paper, you are required to work out how the various parts of a text fit together. This involves making sure that each paragraph you choose fits into the gap that you place it in for the following reasons:

- **cohesion** – each paragraph must fit in because there is a grammatical match with something in the paragraph before it and/or after it.
- **coherence** – each paragraph must fit in because it makes sense in terms of the meaning of the previous and/or next paragraph.
- **text structure** – each paragraph must fit in because it flows logically at that point in the text in terms of its line of development (for example, the argument being put forward, the series of events being described).
- **global meaning** – each paragraph must fit in because it can only be put in that place in terms of the meaning of the text as a whole.

TIPS

- There are two key issues for identifying the correct paragraph to fill a particular gap. The paragraph must fit grammatically in terms of pronouns, verb forms, linking words and phrases and it must fit in with the sense of what went before and what comes after the gap. Several options may superficially appear to fit a given gap because they meet one of these two requirements but only one will meet them both. For example, a paragraph may seem to fit in perfectly in terms of what is happening in the text, but be incorrect because it contains a pronoun that cannot refer to anything in the previous paragraph.
- Before you start trying to fill any of the gaps, read quickly through the whole of the text with gaps in it. This will give you a general idea of what the whole text is about and what might be missing from it. As a result, you may well have an idea of what you are looking for when you come to select from the missing paragraphs. If you simply plunge in and start trying to fill gaps immediately, you may well find that you have to keep changing your answers because what you discover further on in the text shows you that answers you have given are wrong. This, of course, wastes time.
- Remember that if you decide to change an answer, this may well have a knock-on effect on other answers you have given, which may also need changing.

The exercises below will help you to see whether you have given the correct answers for each of the questions in this part of the test.

For each of the questions in these exercises, two of the choices given are correct and two are not. Check your answers to each question in each exercise as soon as you have given them. When you have answered question 3 in each exercise, check that the answer that you gave in the test conforms with the answers that you gave to question 3.

Question 27

1 Read the first paragraph. Which of the following are mentioned?

a Francesco's reaction to a pizza that the writer had prepared ☐

b a task successfully completed by the writer ☐

c the writer's failure to do something well ☑

d a series of mistakes made by the writer ☐

2 Read the paragraph after gap 27. Which of the following are mentioned?

a the way in which a pizza should be prepared before it is cooked ☐

b a pizza made by the writer being eaten ☐

c the writer's difficulty in carrying out an operation ☐

d the writer preparing a pizza that was ready to go into the oven ☐

3 Which of the following would the missing paragraph most logically contain?

a something Francesco did with a pizza prepared by the writer ☐

b the writer feeling encouraged that he was improving ☐

c a description of a pizza prepared by the writer ☐

d a reference to correcting a number of errors ☐

Question 28

1 Read the paragraph before gap 28 again. Which of the following are mentioned?

a the writer managing to prepare a pizza properly ☐

b the writer doing something according to Francesco's instructions ☐

c the fact that there are certain rules to preparing a pizza ☐

d a particular skill that the writer could not master ☐

2 Read the paragraph after gap 28. Which of the following are mentioned?

a the writer beginning an attempt at something ☐

b Francesco showing the writer how something is done ☐

c various elements in the preparation of a pizza ☐

d the writer's reaction to doing something badly ☐

3 Which of the following would the missing paragraph most logically contain?

a the writer taking a completed pizza to the oven ☐

b a description of one stage of preparing a pizza ☐

c something that happened to a pizza the writer was preparing ☐

d the writer observing Francesco in action ☐

Question 29

1 Read the paragraph before gap 29 again. Which of the following are mentioned?

a the way to prepare a pizza of a certain shape ☐

b the writer's own efforts at preparing a pizza ☐

c the writer being observed by others ☐

d the successful completion of a process ☐

2 Read the paragraph after gap 29. Which of the following are mentioned?

a a mistake that it is easy to make ☐

b the writer correcting previous errors ☐

c the writer's feelings about a pizza he had prepared ☐

d how to achieve a certain result ☐

3 Which of the following would the missing paragraph most logically contain?

a the writer's reaction to a disaster ☐

b the writer attempting to copy something ☐

c the fact that it was now the writer's turn to do something ☐

d Francesco deciding on an alternative course of action ☐

Question 30

1 Read the paragraph before gap 30 again. Which of the following are mentioned?

a the writer correcting a previous error ☐

b a reason why it is hard to perform a particular operation ☐

c Francesco observing what the writer was doing ☐

d ways in which what the writer was doing went wrong ☐

2 Read the paragraph after gap 30. Which of the following are mentioned?

a the writer starting a process ☐

b the writer looking at the pizza he was preparing ☐

c the writer's reaction to becoming aware of something ☐

d the writer being observed by strangers ☐

3 Which of the following would the missing paragraph most logically contain?

a a reference to solving more than one problem ☐

b the writer doing something that might look foolish ☐

c the writer sampling a pizza he had made ☐

d the writer taking over from Francesco ☐

Question 31

1 Read the paragraph before gap 31 again. Which of the following are mentioned?

a the writer feeling some pressure ☐

b the writer feeling encouraged ☐

c the writer completing a pizza so that it could go into the oven ☐

d a sense of expectation on the part of someone else ☐

2 Read the paragraph after gap 31. Which of the following are mentioned?

a a reason for the writer to give up ☐

b a description of what happened to a pizza the writer had made ☐

c the writer's pizza being repaired ☐

d a movement made by the writer ☐

3 Which of the following would the missing paragraph most logically contain?

a a reference to a pizza being eaten ☐

b a reference to something disastrous ☐

c the writer's inability to do what he knew he should do ☐

d a reference to pizzas the writer would subsequently prepare ☐

Question 32

1 Read the paragraph before gap 32 again. Which of the following are mentioned?

a a repetition of events ☐

b Francesco making a pizza himself ☐

c Francesco attempting to rectify an error ☐

d the destruction of something the writer had done ☐

2 Read the paragraph after gap 32. Which of the following are mentioned?

a a decision to proceed with a pizza prepared by the writer ☐

b the fact that the writer had made too many mistakes ☐

c the writer feeling dispirited ☐

d a positive reaction from Francesco ☐

3 Which of the following would the missing paragraph most logically contain?

a an improvement made by the writer ☐

b the writer tasting a pizza he had made ☐

c something that suddenly went wrong with the writer's pizza ☐

d a reference to the writer's feelings about a failure of his ☐

Question 33

1 Read the paragraph before gap 33 again. Which of the following are mentioned?

a the end of part of a process ☐

b confusion on the part of the writer ☐

c the writer's sense of satisfaction ☐

d the beginning of a process again ☐

2 Read the final paragraph. Which of the following are mentioned?

a problems that always affect the cooking of pizzas ☐

b something the writer learnt about the cooking of pizzas ☐

c an improvement on a previous event ☐

d something Francesco did that was unlike common practice ☐

3 Which of the following would the missing paragraph most logically contain?

a the writer's failure to prepare a pizza correctly ☐

b a reference to the early stages of preparing a pizza ☐

c the next stage of a process ☐

d a movement in a certain direction ☐

Now check your answers to these exercises. When you have done so, decide whether you wish to change any of your answers to Part Three of the test. Then check your answers to Part Three of the test.

PART FOUR

*You are going to read an extract from a magazine article about a chess champion. For questions **34–40**, choose the answer (**A**, **B**, **C** or **D**) which you think fits best according to the text. In the exam you will mark your answers on a separate answer sheet.*

The Chess Player

In the corner of the room sits the pub champion. He looks like the classic chess bum. Untidy hair. Big beard. His possessions in a white polythene bag by his feet. The chess board is also made of polythene, and the pieces of plastic. The 'table' is an up-ended keg of beer. The pub champion is playing some kid genius from out of town who has just won a London grandmaster tournament. He is called David R. Norwood (I know. The boy wonder, all of 19, gave me his business card. It said 'David R. Norwood. International Chess Master'). Now David R. Norwood is, as he will be the first to admit, one of the hottest properties on the international chess circuit.

But something funny is happening in his games – played at the rate of about one every ten minutes – against the pub champion. David R. Norwood is not winning any. And he is not merely losing. He is being taken apart. In the argot of the chess player, he is being 'busted'. But David R. does not seem too worried about this denouement. Occasionally he will say, with a smile, 'Hey, you're not such a bad player.' His opponent, Jonathan Speelman, the pub champion, only laughs and sets up the pieces for the next act of slaughter. It is a joke, of course. He is not merely 'not a bad player'. He is possibly the best player in the Western world.

After Jon had finally exhausted David R. Norwood's enthusiasm, I asked whether he would mind playing me. Not at all, he said, and played game after game against me until I became more bored by losing than he did by winning. 'Why,' I asked, 'do you put up with playing chess jerks like me?' 'Because I like to play with the pieces,' was the instant and unanswerable reply. My impression while playing Jon was slightly different, namely that the pieces enjoyed playing with him. He gives them the time of their life. These plastic pieces, property of the pub, had probably never before experienced more than the intellectual equivalent of being cooped up in a shed. With Jon, they were roaming free across vast expanses.

His friends, incidentally, do not call him Jon. They do not call him Speelman either. They call him 'Spess'. This stems from a report in *The Times* about ten years ago of a tournament in which Speelman was taking part. But, *Times* sub-editors being *Times* sub-editors, his name inadvertently came out as 'Specimen'. In view of his rather weird appearance, fellow chess players decided that this was, if not his real name, at least descriptively accurate, and so Specimen, and then later Spess, he became.

On many personal matters, Jon Speelman is difficult to interview. He is very self-conscious, a keen practitioner of self-psychoanalysis. The result is that he is only too aware of the implications which might be drawn from anything he might say. Worse, he was so concerned about what I was writing down that he would stare at my pad when I noted anything, attempting to read my scribble upside-down. In an effort to counter this awkward turning of the tables, I began deliberately to write in messier and messier scrawl. Afterwards I was quite unable to read many of my own notes. Later I surmised that the chess player in Speelman had calculated that his scrutiny of my notepad would have this effect, and that it was a deliberate attempt to reduce the number of personal details I would be able to decipher. If that sounds convoluted, it is quite in character with Speelman's way of playing chess. Some great players reveal their greatness through the simplicity of their methods. Others, more unusually, have a genius to confuse, an ability to generate chaos, out of which only they can perceive a clear path to victory. This is Speelman's method.

But such a style is one which makes enormous demands on the exponent's nervous system. When he plays, Speelman is all nervous, twitchy movement. His hands play with his beard, his glasses, anything he can reach. He makes strange clicking noises. He will get up from the board and stand over it and his opponent, nodding his head as if checking through the variations. ('He goes there, I go there, he goes there ...') I asked him how many moves he can see ahead. 'It's a silly question,' he replied, 'but it's not too difficult to imagine a position in which one could calculate 25 moves ahead.' 25 moves on each side, he means. That is 50 moves in total. Try saying 'he goes there, I go there' 25 times. Now you get the picture. *line 40*

William Hartston, the former British chess champion, told me that playing Speelman was like playing 'an old fridge, one of those where the door shuts with a big clunk. You can't see inside, but the thing is whirring and shaking and something is certainly going on in an undirected sort of way.' The fridge is, of course, an innocent and harmless object of domestic pleasure, and Hartston chose that metaphor quite deliberately. The point is, as Jon Speelman explains, 'I do want to win at chess, but I don't want my opponent to lose.' How very different from Bobby Fischer, who declared on coast-to-coast US television, 'I like to crush the other guy's ego.'

34 In the first paragraph, the writer implies that

A he found David R. Norwood rather arrogant.
B it is strange for chess players to have business cards.
C the best chess players tend to be scruffy in appearance.
D he likes to see chess played in informal surroundings.

35 What does the writer say about the games between David R. Norwood and Jonathan Speelman?

A They might have different outcomes if they were being played in a real tournament.
B They indicate that Jonathan Speelman does not have a high regard for David R. Norwood.
C They involve David R. Norwood making jokes to cover his embarrassment.
D They indicate that there is a huge gulf between the standard of the two players.

36 When the writer played Jonathan Speelman, he felt that Speelman

A preferred just to play than to indulge in polite conversation as well.
B had an approach to the game that made other approaches seem limited in comparison.
C was doing his best not to let the games bore him.
D was adopting an approach he would not use if he was playing in a serious game.

37 What does the writer say about Speelman's nickname?

A It indicates that he is regarded as a rather distant figure.
B It is not very flattering.
C It is connected with his style of playing.
D It was first used as a joke.

38 The writer says that Speelman tried to read the notes he was making because

A he saw it as the kind of thing the writer would expect of him.
B he felt that he could get a clear picture of a person from the way they wrote.
C he was aware that this would put the writer off while he was making them.
D he wanted to make sure that certain complex points he made were correctly understood.

39 When the writer says 'Now you get the picture' (line 48), he is emphasizing

A how complex a serious game of chess can be.
B how extraordinary Speelman believes his style of play is.
C how incredible the mental feat Speelman performs is.
D how peculiar Speelman might appear to others to be.

40 The writer says that an old fridge is an apt metaphor for Speelman because

A Speelman's style of playing is deceptive.
B Speelman's appearance contrasts with his shrewdness.
C Speelman likes to create a false impression of himself.
D Speelman is generous in victory.

Now check your answers to Part Four of the test.

PAPER 2 WRITING 2 hours

PART ONE

*You **must** answer this question. Write your answer in **300–350** words in an appropriate style. Write clearly in **pen**, not pencil. You may make alterations, but make sure your work is easy to read.*

1 You are a member of a committee which is responsible for organizing local events. Following a recent meeting, you have received this note from the chairman of the committee concerning the organization of a week-long arts festival. Write your **proposal** for the arts festival, covering the points mentioned in the note.

> I hope you remember agreeing to put together the proposal for the arts festival! The whole committee will need to approve it at the next meeting, so obviously we need it to be as detailed as possible.
> As well as all the events you think it should include and an outline timetable, we'll need to know how you visualize them being organized (who will get involved in organizing them, etc), why you think they will be popular with people around here, where they'll take place and precisely what each event will consist of. And anything else you think relevant, of course.
> Thanks for volunteering.

Write your **proposal.**

Before you write your proposal, go on to pages 100–102.

PART ONE

For information on What's Tested and Tips see page 21.

To plan your answer for Part One, complete the following notes.

1 Note down as briefly as possible the **topic** of your proposal.

....

2 List as briefly as possible the following:
- the **main points** in the note which you will have to cover in your proposal
- the **details** that need to be included for each of those points
- any **reasons** you wish to give in support of the details

Main point	**Details**	**Reasons**
Main point	**Details**	**Reasons**
Main point	**Details**	**Reasons**

3 List briefly any additional points you wish to make, which are not mentioned in the question but which you think are relevant to the topic. You may not wish to include any additional points.

Additional point	**Details**	**Reasons**
Additional point	**Details**	**Reasons**

4 Now note briefly how your proposal will be organized by deciding what each part of it will contain. You may not wish to have as many sections as are listed below.

Opening
Section 1
Section 2
Section 3
Section 4

Section 5
Section 6
Ending

5 Now use these notes to write your proposal.

When you have written your answer, assess it in accordance with the task-specific mark scheme.

6 **Now read through this sample answer for Part One and answer the questions that follow it.**

PROPOSAL FOR THE ARTS FESTIVAL

As the arts festival will be held in the week of the half-term holidays, we have already agreed on the main cooperation and help from the side of the local arts academy students. Generally, the whole academy is willing to contribute a great deal. The teachers are ready to give two-day courses in sculpture, painting and pottery for amateurs or the ones that want to try. Students would contribute with their paintings and performances in the local theatre. There will also be three exhibitions in the Town Hall and a new play by Kaspar (our local dramatic group) in the local theatre.

Let me introduce the exact timetable:

THE TOWN HALL will be open from 9am to 5pm. We have ten local artists wanting to present their work, but capacity to show only three of them closely. We could also exhibit individual paintings from different artists. I am leaving this to the committee to decide. In case this is successful, I suggest to keep the exhibition open for the public for four more weeks.

THE LOCAL THEATRE will be open from 2pm to 4pm for performances by students of the arts academy. From 7pm, plays by Kaspar or a guest. We have three very different dramatic groups that want to perform. We can choose one guest that will alternate with Kaspar or they can take turns with a few groups. I suggest we keep every second day for Kaspar as people will be coming to see them and their new performance particularly.

THE ARTS ACADEMY can be open for the public from 10am to 4pm. If agreed, there is an option of two courses in arts. One would take place on Monday and Tuesday and one on Thursday and Friday. Fees need to be discussed. The exhibition held in the academy would consist of students' as well as teachers' works of art.

According to an agreement with other members of the committee on the exact structure of the exhibitions and performances, I will be pleased to provide you with the names of the artists as well as examples of their work. They are all very keen to contribute to the arts festival and willing to cooperate.

Content
Are all the main points mentioned in the question covered? Where are these points covered. If any are not covered, which are missing? Are any additional points included? If so, what are they, and are they relevant?

Range
Is there a wide range of vocabulary and grammatical structures? If so, give examples. If there are occasions when the vocabulary or grammar is too simple, suggest alternatives.

Accuracy
Are there any mistakes in the use of vocabulary or grammar? Correct any that you find.

Appropriacy of register and format
Are the style and tone of the proposal appropriate? How would you describe them? Why are they appropriate or inappropriate? Is the format suitable for a proposal? If so, why? If not, why not?

Organization and cohesion
Is the proposal well-organized in terms of being divided into sections appropriately? Describe briefly the content of each section. Does the proposal flow well in terms of the linking of points and ideas within sections and between sections? Give examples of places where the linking is good. If there are occasions when the linking is inadequate or inappropriate, suggest improvements.

Target reader
Do you feel that someone reading this proposal would be clear what the writer is proposing, and why? If so, summarize the proposal briefly. If not, say what you feel is unclear in it.

Now check your assessment of this sample answer.

PART TWO

*Write an answer to **one** of the questions **2–5** in this part. Write your answer in **300–350** words in an appropriate style. Write clearly in **pen**, not pencil. You may make alterations, but make sure your work is easy to read.*

2 A magazine is running a competition for the best article entitled *The Day That Changed My Life*. Write an article for this competition, explaining the background to what happened, the details of what happened and the effect it had on your life.

Write your **article**.

3 An arts magazine has started a section called *Answer The Critics*, in which readers are invited to respond to the reviews written by the magazine's critics with reviews of their own. Write a review of something you have seen (a film, show, play or TV programme) or read, giving your own opinions on it and comparing your views with those of the critics.

Write your **review**.

4 You recently stayed at one of a chain of large hotels and encountered a number of problems during your stay which you feel were the fault of the company. Write a letter to the company's head office, detailing the problems that you had, describing what happened when you complained to the hotel staff about them. Suggest ways in which the hotel group could improve its service to customers.

Write your **letter**. Do not write any postal addresses.

5 Set book questions – a choice from **(a)**, **(b)** and **(c)**.
In the exam you may choose to answer a question on one of the three set books.

Before you write your answer, go on to pages 104–106.

PART TWO

For information on What's Tested and Tips see page 63.
To plan your answer for question 4 in Part Two, complete the following notes.

1 Note down as briefly as possible the **topic** of your letter.

....

2 List as briefly as possible the following:
- the **problems** that you had at the hotel
- **what happened** when you complained at the time
- your **suggestions** as to how the hotel could improve

Problem	**What happened**	**Suggestion**
Problem	**What happened**	**Suggestion**
Problem	**What happened**	**Suggestion**

3 List briefly any additional points you wish to make about the hotel which you think are relevant. You may not wish to include any additional points.

Additional point	**What happened**	**Suggestion**
Additional point	**What happened**	**Suggestion**

4 Now note briefly how your letter will be organized by deciding what each part of it will contain. You may not wish to have as many paragraphs as are listed below.

Opening
Paragraph 1
Paragraph 2
Paragraph 3
Paragraph 4

Paragraph 5
Paragraph 6
Ending

5 Now use these notes to write your letter.

When you have written your answer, assess it in accordance with the task-specific mark scheme.

6 Now read through this sample answer for question 4 in Part Two and answer the questions that follow it.

Dear Sir or Madam,

I'm writing to complain about your Hotel Blue Star, where I was staying for two nights on 24th–25th of November during my business trip. Despite of recommendations of a friend of mine, I encountered three major problems that made my stay rather unpleasant and unnecessarily complicated. Although the hotel facilities were of high standard, certainly cannot say the same about your service.

For the first night I reserved a table for four people in your hotel restaurant. For some reason the reservation had not been made and my business partners and I had to wait in the lobby for more than half an hour to get a table. Considering that my guests were some of the most important business partners of mine, this was most unpleasant.

The next evening I arrived at the hotel very tired at 7pm, hoping that my dinner, which I ordered in the morning, will be delivered to my room at 7.30pm. At 8 o'clock, starving, I rang the restaurant. They knew nothing about my order. Therefore I had to wait for my dinner for another 45 minutes to be ready.

The same evening I rang the reception, asking them to prepare my bill for the following morning as I was about to leave at 6am for the airport and could not wait. This had not been done either, which meant another wait for me. It took more than 20 minutes to get my bill ready. Not mentioning that my taxi booking was omitted too.

I strongly advise you to inform your hotel staff in the reception as well as in the restaurant about the appalling service I had to endure and instruct them in the service they should provide, especially for business people, who usually lack the time for waiting. I don't require any financial compensation, although your apology and information about steps that have been taken to avoid such a situation in the future is awaited.

Yours faithfully,

Content
Are all the main points mentioned in the question covered? Where are these points covered? If any are not covered, which are missing? Are any additional points included? If so, what are they, and are they relevant?

Range
Is there a wide range of vocabulary and grammatical structures? If so, give examples. If there are occasions when the vocabulary or grammar is too simple, suggest alternatives.

Accuracy
Are there any mistakes in the use of vocabulary or grammar? Correct any that you find.

Appropriacy of register and format
Are the style and tone of the letter appropriate? How would you describe them? Why are they appropriate or inappropriate? Is the format suitable for a letter of this kind? If so, why? If not, why not?

Organization and cohesion
Is the letter well-organized in terms of the beginning, middle and end? Is it divided into paragraphs appropriately? Describe briefly the content of each paragraph. Does the letter flow well in terms of the linking of points and ideas within paragraphs and between paragraphs? Give examples of places where the linking is good. If there are occasions when the linking is inadequate or inappropriate, suggest improvements.

Target reader
Do you feel that someone reading this letter would be clear what the writer's point of view is throughout it? If so, summarize the writer's point of view briefly. If not, say what you feel is unclear in the letter.

Now check your assessment of this sample answer.

PAPER 3 USE OF ENGLISH 1 hour 30 minutes

PART ONE

*For questions **1–15**, read the text below and think of the word which best fits each space. Use only **one** word in each space. There is an example at the beginning **(0)**. In the exam you will mark your answers on a separate answer sheet.*

Example:

0	*and*

Celebrity Crossover

It is not surprising that actors want to be pop stars, **(0)** .....*and*..... vice versa. **(1)** .... that is deep in a part of our brain that most of us manage to keep **(2)** .... control, we all want to be pop stars and actors.

Sadly, there's nothing about the **(3)** .... profession that automatically qualifies you for the other, **(4)** .... , of course, for the fact that famous actors and singers are already surrounded by people who never **(5)** .... no to them. **(6)** .... the whole, pop stars tend to fare better on screen than their **(7)** .... numbers do on CD. Let's **(8)** .... it: not being able to act is no big drawback in Hollywood, whereas not being able to play or sing still tends to count **(9)** .... you in the recording studio.

Some stars do display a genuine proficiency in both disciplines, and a few even maintain successful careers in both fields, but this just **(10)** .... a bad example for all the others. **(11)** .... every success, there are two dozen failures. And most of them have no idea **(12)** .... terrible they are. **(13)** .... as power tends to corrupt, so celebrity tends to destroy the ability to gauge whether or not you're making a fool of **(14)** ....

But perhaps we shouldn't criticize celebrities for trying to expand their horizons in this way. **(15)** .... there is one good thing about actors trying to sing and singers trying to act, it is that it keeps them all too busy to write books.

Now check your answers to Part One of the test.

PART TWO

*For questions **16–25**, read the text below. Use the word given in **capitals** at the end of some of the lines to form a word that fits in the space in the same line. There is an example at the beginning **(0)**. In the exam you will mark your answers on a separate answer sheet.*

Example: | 0 | *refusal* |

Captain Webb

Captain Matthew Webb is fortunate in being remembered as the first man to	
swim the English Channel, rather than the one who later tried, and failed, to	
plunge through the Niagara Falls. If ever a man possessed	
self-confidence, it was Webb; but it was his stubborn **(0)** ....*refusal*........	**REFUSE**
to give up that eventually proved his **(16)**	**UNDO**
Unwilling to recognize the Channel crossing as the peak of his career,	
he went on and on, addicted to glory, literally swimming himself to death.	
Webb astonished the British nation on August 25th, 1875, with a Channel	
crossing that took a mammoth 21 hours and 45 minutes. He had entered	
the sea a merchant-ship captain living in **(17)** .... , but he emerged	**OBSCURE**
in France, stung by jellyfish and half-dead with **(18)** .... , a	**EXHAUST**
national hero. He was feted, mobbed and cheered wherever he went; his appearance	
in the City of London brought business to a **(19)** .... Alarmed by	**STAND**
the sudden attention, the normally **(20)** .... Webb fled	**FEAR**
to his native Shropshire.	
But all this **(21)** .... was too much for him, and he made the	**STAR**
fatal error of many a pop star in later years.	
Craving **(22)** .... , he very nearly dissolved himself in a series	**APPLAUD**
of marathon swims for money, including a six-day **(23)**	**ENDURE**
contest. Then he sailed for America, where he had a **(24)**	**PUNISH**
schedule of long swims. It was America that lured Webb to the final act in his	
tragedy; his crazed attempt to swim the Niagara River beneath the Falls in	
June 1883. **(25)** .... of all advice, he dived in from a boat and	**REGARD**
subsided forever into the boiling rapids.	

Now check your answers to Part Two of the test.

PART THREE

*For questions **26–31**, think of **one** word only which can be used appropriately in all three sentences. There is an example at the beginning **(0)**. In the exam you will write only the missing word on a separate answer sheet.*

Example:

0 You can stay with us if you like, we've got a .... room in our house.

It's very difficult to get .... parts for machines as old as this, so it's hard to get them repaired if they break down.

I like my job but the hours are long so it doesn't allow me much .... time.

0	*spare*

26 People say that Frank is a nasty individual but whenever I've met him, I've always .... him very pleasant.

You've .... fault with absolutely everything at the hotel – I've never known anyone complain so much!

Despite all the evidence against him, he was .... not guilty when the case came to court.

27 The team showed no improvement on their previous terrible performances and so it was inevitable that they would lose .... again.

A change in the law has been agreed but the government have .... to announce exactly when it will come into force.

I expect John will contact me with the details but as .... I haven't heard from him.

28 Suddenly becoming very famous went to his .... and he became extremely arrogant.

There had been a lot of discontent among the staff and matters came to a .... at the monthly meeting, when an argument broke out.

The groups' most loyal fans were at the .... of the queue, having waited overnight for the concert tickets to go on sale.

29 I was sitting at the next table to them so I couldn't .... overhearing their conversation.

My financial situation is pretty bad anyway, so this unexpected bill doesn't exactly ....

I wish you wouldn't .... yourself to my CDs without asking me first.

30 He used to be one of the top players in the world but he has now had a .... of 15 consecutive matches without a single victory.

Leaving college without completing the course may seem like a good idea now, but I think you may come to regret it in the long ....

The film is about someone who escapes from prison and goes on the ....

31 There was a very .... contrast between the scenes of wealth I saw in some parts of the country and the scenes of poverty I witnessed in others.

Trudy is a very .... businesswoman and that is what has enabled her to make all the right decisions for her company.

There was a very .... bend in the road and for a moment I nearly lost control of the car.

Before you check your answers to Part Three of the test, go on to pages 110–112.

WHAT'S TESTED

Part Three of the Use of English Paper is primarily testing you on vocabulary. You are required to think of a single word that could fit with the correct meaning into three different sentences. The words tested are words that can have different meanings in different contexts and which can be used to form phrases with different meanings. In some cases, therefore, the word fits because it is the correct word in the context; in other cases, it fits because it correctly completes a phrase such as a collocation, an idiom, a fixed phrase, or a phrasal verb (for explanations of these terms, see the Further Practice and Guidance pages for Paper 1, Part One on page 10).

TIPS

- Remember that the word you require will always be the same part of speech – it will not, for example, be a noun in one sentence and a verb in another, even if it is a word that is identical as a noun or a verb (for example, *change*).
- It is highly likely that more than one word could fit the gap in any one of the three sentences. Therefore, even if you are certain that a particular word fits into one of the sentences, it does not necessarily mean that it is the answer.

1 *Look at each of the three sentences for each question in the test again and decide which of the choices **a–c** is closest in meaning to the sentence or to the part of the sentence around the gap.*
2 *Then decide which of the words in the box could fit into the gap in that sentence. More than one of the words in the box may fit. One of the words you choose in each exercise should be the correct answer to the question in the test.*
3 *When you have done these exercises, you may wish to change some of your answers to the test.*

Question 26

First sentence

a Whenever I've met Frank, I've tried to encourage him to be pleasant.
b My personal experiences of Frank have all indicated to me that he is pleasant.
c When people ask me about Frank, I always describe him as a pleasant person.

thought	*told*	*considered*	*passed*	*discovered*

Second sentence

a There is nothing at this hotel which is satisfactory for you.
b You have been responsible for everything going wrong at this hotel.
c You have been justified in your behaviour at this hotel.

taken	*picked*	*seen*	*made*	*put*

Third sentence

a It became clear during the court case that he was not guilty.
b He declared at the beginning of the court case that he was innocent.
c It was decided at the end of the court case that he was innocent.

given	*pronounced*	*found*	*stated*	*agreed*

Question 27

First sentence

a It was certain that they would be unluckily defeated again.
b It was no surprise at all that another defeat was added to the previous ones.
c This defeat was worse than those that went before it.

even	*only*	*once*	*just*	*slightly*

Second sentence

a The government have decided against announcing it at this point in time.
b The government have set a date in the future for announcing it.
c The government have not announced it so far but are expected to do so.

quite	*still*	*against*	*over*	*so*

Third sentence

a Up until now, John has not contacted me.
b With regard to that, John has not contacted me.
c Despite that, John has not contacted me.

such	*far*	*yet*	*though*	*for*

Question 28

First sentence

a Becoming famous suddenly had a certain disadvantage for him.
b Achieving fame resulted in him having a very high opinion of himself.
c As a result of fame, his outward behaviour concealed what he was really like.

heart	*core*	*head*	*crown*	*pinnacle*

Second sentence

a The situation reached a point where something had to happen.
b There was a development which confused the situation.
c The situation arose unexpectedly.

climax	*peak*	*height*	*conclusion*	*summit*

Third sentence

a The queue consisted of the group's most loyal fans.
b The group's most loyal fans were the first people in the queue.
c The group's most loyal fans were tired by the time the tickets went on sale.

tip	*lead*	*front*	*top*	*limit*

Question 29

First sentence

a I was very surprised by what I heard of their conversation.
b I tried to listen to their conversation but I couldn't hear it clearly.
c It was impossible for me not to unintentionally hear what they said.

bear	*avoid*	*save*	*refrain*	*aid*

Second sentence

a This unexpected bill doesn't make much difference to my financial situation.
b This unexpected bill certainly doesn't improve my financial situation.
c This unexpected bill isn't an enormous surprise to me.

support	*stand*	*assist*	*mind*	*turn*

Third sentence

a You should get my permission before you take my CDs.
b You take my CDs even though I've told you not to.
c You weren't expecting me to notice that you had taken my CDs.

avail	*help*	*serve*	*hand*	*take*

Question 30

First sentence

a He is the first player to lose as many as 15 consecutive matches.
b He has lost all his matches and has no more matches to play.
c He has not won any of his last 15 matches.

course	*spell*	*string*	*trend*	*flow*

Second sentence

a You may spend a lot of time regretting it in the future.
b It is something you may regret at some point further in the future.
c It is possible that you will start to regret it in the near future.

term	*period*	*line*	*stream*	*patch*

Third sentence

a The film is about someone who is concerned more about the future than the present.
b The film is about someone who never has any luck.
c The film is about someone who tries to avoid being caught by the police.

flight	*rush*	*stretch*	*run*	*round*

Question 31

First sentence

a The difference between the scenes of wealth and the scenes of poverty was very noticeable.
b It is hard to describe the difference between the scenes of wealth and the scenes of poverty.
c People seldom comment on the difference between the scenes of wealth and the scenes of poverty.

striking	*marked*	*crisp*	*intricate*	*distinguished*

Second sentence

a Trudy is constantly changing her way of thinking according to changes in situations.
b Trudy is much more perceptive than she appears to be.
c Trudy is highly intelligent and quick to understand situations.

sharp	*severe*	*astute*	*perceptive*	*curt*

Third sentence

a The road changed direction suddenly and to a great extent.
b Part of the road had a very bad surface for driving.
c The road went suddenly from the top of a hill to the bottom of it.

harsh	*tight*	*stern*	*sheer*	*steep*

Now check your answers to these exercises and to Part Three of the test.

PART FOUR

For questions ***32–39****, complete the second sentence so that it has a similar meaning to the first sentence, using the word given.* ***Do not change the word given.*** *You must use between* ***three*** *and* ***eight*** *words, including the word given. There is an example at the beginning* ***(0)****.*

Example:

0 Robert was offended when he was left out of the team.
exception
Robert .... left out of the team.

The gap can be filled by the words 'took exception to being', so you write:

0	*took exception to being*

In the exam you will mark only the missing words on a separate answer sheet.

32 If Tony hadn't interfered, there would have been no problems yesterday, I'm sure.
smoothly
Without Tony's .... yesterday, I'm sure.

33 I said that I thought he was wrong about the best way for us to proceed.
issue
I .... best we should proceed.

34 He didn't want to get into a position where he might lose all his money.
possibility
He didn't want to expose .... all his money.

35 The company received an enormous number of calls responding to the advert.
deluged
The company .... response to the advert.

36 The manager said that he had paid attention to my complaints and would take the appropriate action.
note
The manager said that he had .... accordingly.

37 We'll have to make sure that costs are as low as possible or we'll have no money left.
minimum
We'll have to keep .... ourselves with no money left.

38 His behaviour at the conference gave him the bad reputation he now has.
conducted
The way .... in the bad reputation he now has.

39 Her work didn't meet the standards that were considered acceptable.
conform
Her work .... acceptable standards.

Now check your answers to Part Four of the test.

PART FIVE

*For questions **40–44**, read the following texts on the English class system. For questions **40–43**, answer with a word or short phrase. You do not need to write complete sentences. For question **44**, write a summary according to the instructions given. In the exam you will mark your answers on a separate answer sheet.*

It is a commonplace of English politicians and journalists that in recent years 'class distinctions' have been 'diminishing' or 'disappearing'. This does not prove that classes actually do exist. It does indicate, though, that people *believe* that classes exist, and are influenced in their behaviour by that belief. What people believe is true, so the truism
5 goes, is true. But truisms do not take us very far, since a more important question might be 'how true?' or, rather, 'how significant?' in relation to all the other social phenomena in which people believe or by which they are affected. One can go further and say that a pragmatic assessment of a range of evidence suggests that there is a strong presumption that classes do indeed exist, though again the question of how
10 *important* they are must remain for later exploration.

Why do I pussyfoot around the topic of the existence and significance of class when there are shelves groaning with books which demonstrate conclusively the existence of gross inequalities in the distribution of, let us say, political and economic power, of housing accommodation and of educational opportunity? The problem, and it is the
15 problem that lies at the heart of the dialectic between the image and the reality of class, is that while the existence of *inequality* can be clearly demonstrated, it is not so clear that the demonstrable inequalities are related to *class* in any fully acceptable sense of that term. Statistical studies have to depend on the manner in which official bodies serve up the raw statistics. The national censuses do, in presenting their findings, offer
20 a range of 'social classes', 'socio-economic groups' or 'occupational groupings', but none of these coincides with the notions of class actually found in everyday speech, in the newspapers or in historical studies of the period under review.

40 What point does the writer make about the truism mentioned in the first paragraph, with regard to classes?

....

....

41 What does the writer mean by the phrase 'there are shelves groaning with books' (line 12)?

....

....

About three years ago, when I rather tentatively suggested writing a book about the English class system, people drew away from me in horror. 'But that's all finished,' they said nervously, 'no-one gives a hoot any more. Look at the young.' It was plain that since the egalitarian shake-up of recent decades, class as a subject had become the ultimate obscenity.

5 Three years of research later, I can assure you that the class system is alive and well and living in people's minds in England. There may have been an enormous shift of wealth between rich and poor. Every day Jack may be getting nearer his master financially, but social stratification remains incredibly resistant to change. It takes more than jeans and a taste in pop music to make even the young all one class. In fact, a whole new generation has appeared who
10 wants the boundaries re-defined. Added to this is the colossal success of all those television serials and plays about the upper classes. The fact that they have all been set in the past – because nostalgia excuses everything, enabling people to click their tongues over the out-dated inequalities, yet guiltily enjoy the sense of hierarchy – must mean a hankering after some kind of social pecking order.

15 What struck me, however, as soon as I started the book, was the enormity of the task I had taken on. It was like trying to catalogue the sea. For the whole system, despite its stratification, is constantly forming and re-forming like coral. To me, the system seemed like a huge striped football shirt that had run in the wash, with each layer blurring into the next one, and snobbery being the fiercest at the place where one stripe merged with another.

42 What, according to the writer, has been the result of the 'enormous shift of wealth between rich and poor' mentioned in the second paragraph?

....

....

43 In your own words, explain the reasons given for the popularity of television serials and plays about the upper classes.

....

....

44 In a paragraph of between **50 and 70** words, summarize **in your own words as far as possible,** the problems associated with analysing the English class system that are mentioned in the two texts.

Before you check your answers to Part Five of the test, go on to pages 116–118.

Questions 40–43

For information on What's Tested and Tips see the Further Practice and Guidance pages for Paper 3, Part 5 on page 33.

The exercises below will help you to check whether the answers you gave in the test are correct.

Question 40

1 What is a 'commonplace' (line 1)?
a a comment that is frequently made and is neither new nor interesting
b a belief that is widely held but is contested by a number of people
c a remark that is made often in order to influence people's beliefs
d something that becomes less accurate with the passage of time

2 What is a 'truism' (line 4)?
a a belief that other people believe to be only partly true
b something that people want to believe is true
c a statement that is so obviously true that it does not really need making
d something that is not true at first but becomes true

3 What do 'how true?' and 'how significant?' (line 6) refer to?
a the idea that class distinctions are disappearing
b the existence of classes
c social phenomena other than class
d questions that people in general ask themselves

Question 41

1 What is meant by 'pussyfoot around' (line 11)?
a make statements about which might seem ambiguous
b talk about in a way that suggests it should not be taken seriously
c try to avoid talking about so as not to say anything that might offend
d address in a way that is bound to provoke disagreement

2 A person might 'groan' as a result of
a feeling comfortable.
b talking for a long time.
c pressure.
d feeling relieved.

Question 42

1 What is the writer emphasizing when she says that the class system is 'alive and well' (line 5)?
a that she is glad that the class system still exists
b that the class system certainly has not disappeared
c that the class system is more important than it used to be
d that there is much to admire in the class system

2 'Jack' is meant to represent
a people who do not approve of the class system.
b people who do not conform with ideas about the class system.
c people who suffer as a result of the class system.
d people who do not belong to the upper classes.

Question 43

1 What is 'nostalgia' (line 12)?
a a desire to learn from the past
b a romantic view of the past
c commonly held views of the past
d distance from the past

2 What is meant in the context by 'click their tongues' (line 12)?
a express disapproval
b act surprised
c sound pleased
d talk excitedly

3 What is a 'hankering' (line 13)?
a a belief based on experience
b a fixed view
c a sudden feeling
d a strong desire

4 What is a 'pecking order' (line 14)?
a a sense of duty
b an order of importance
c a logical order
d an order that is changing

Now check your answers to these exercises and decide whether you wish to change any of the answers you gave in the test.

Question 44 Summary

For information on What's Tested and Tips see the Further Practice and Guidance pages for Paper 3, Part Five on page 35.

Look at the highlighted parts of the texts and match them with the sentences which follow.

A It is a commonplace of English politicians and journalists that in recent years 'class distinctions' have been 'diminishing' or 'disappearing'. **B** This does not prove that classes actually do exist. It does indicate, though, that people believe that classes exist, and are influenced in their behaviour by that belief. What people believe is true, so the truism goes, is true. But truisms do not take us very far, since a more important question might be 'how true?' or, rather, 'how significant?' in relation to all the other social phenomena in which people believe or by which they are affected. **C** One can go further and say that a pragmatic assessment of a range of evidence suggests that there is a strong presumption that classes do indeed exist, though again the question of how *important* they are must remain for later exploration.

Why do I pussyfoot around the topic of the existence and significance of class when there are shelves groaning with books which demonstrate conclusively the existence of gross inequalities in the distribution of, let us say, political and economic power, of housing accommodation and of educational opportunity? **D** The problem, and it is the problem that lies at the heart of the dialectic between the image and the reality of class, is that while the existence of *inequality* can be clearly demonstrated, it is not so clear that the demonstrable inequalities are related to *class* in any fully acceptable sense of that term. **E** Statistical studies have to depend on the manner in which official bodies serve up the raw statistics. **F** The national censuses do, in presenting their findings, offer a range of 'social classes', 'socio-economic groups' or 'occupational groupings', but none of these coincides with the notions of class actually found in everyday speech, in the newspapers or in historical studies of the period under review.

G About three years ago, when I rather tentatively suggested writing a book about the English class system, people drew away from me in horror. 'But that's all finished,' they said nervously, 'no-one gives a hoot any more. Look at the young.' **H** It was plain that since the egalitarian shake-up of recent decades, class as a subject had become the ultimate obscenity.

Three years of research later, I can assure you that the class system is alive and well and living in people's minds in England. There may have been an enormous shift of wealth between rich and poor. Every day Jack may be getting nearer his master financially, but social stratification remains incredibly resistant to change. **I** It takes more than jeans and a taste in pop music to make even the young all one class. **J** In fact, a whole new generation has appeared who wants the boundaries redefined. Added to this is the colossal success of all those television serials and plays about the upper classes. The fact that they have all been set in the past – because nostalgia excuses everything, enabling people to click their tongues over the out-dated inequalities, yet guiltily enjoy the sense of hierarchy – must mean a hankering after some kind of social pecking order.

K What struck me, however, as soon as I started the book, was the enormity of the task I had taken on. It was like trying to catalogue the sea. For the whole system, despite its stratification, is constantly forming and re-forming like coral. **L** To me, the system seemed like a huge striped football shirt that had run in the wash, with each layer blurring into the next one, and snobbery being the fiercest at the place where one stripe merged with another.

1 Some people want there to be new definitions of classes. ☐

2 Many people believe in the existence of the class system. ☐

3 Information given on society does not match ideas about it found elsewhere. ☐

4 It is hard to define the characteristics of any particular class. ☐

5 Some people say that the class system is not as strong as it was. ☐

6 Distinctions between different classes are not clearly defined. ☐

7 It is possible to prove that not everyone is treated the same but not that this is connected with class. ☐

8 Class is no longer seen as a suitable topic for discussion. ☐

9 The class system is always changing. ☐

10 Information on society is influenced by the way it is presented. ☐

11 It is not certain that there is a class system. ☐

12 There is a belief that people are no longer interested in the topic of class. ☐

Now decide which of 1–12 above are relevant main points that should be included in the summary.

When you have done this, look again at your summary and decide whether you wish to change anything.

Sample Summary

Now look at this sample summary and answer the questions that follow it.

> People commonly believe that classes exist, although the question of how important they are has not been explored. Many books point to different social inequalities, but don't prove their relation to classes. 'Class' in such books has a different meaning. However, some people believe that among young generation classes don't exist.
>
> After a three-year research the writer found that classes do exist in people's minds. They want to know the class boundaries. But to do this is impossible. The classes keep changing, socially and financially merge and de-merge.

1 Is anything irrelevant included or anything relevant not included? If so, what?
2 Are there any language mistakes? Correct any that you find.
3 Is the summary well-organized and does it make sense throughout?
4 Have any parts of the texts simply been copied in the summary? If so, where?
5 Is the summary within the specified word limit?

Now look again at your summary and decide whether you wish to change anything.

Then check your marks for your summary and read the assessment of this sample summary.

PAPER 4 LISTENING approximately 40 minutes

PART ONE

*You will hear four different extracts. For questions **1–8**, choose the answer (**A**, **B** or **C**) which fits best according to what you hear. There are two questions for each extract. In the exam you will hear each extract twice.*

Extract One

You hear part of a radio programme about British attitudes.

1 The speaker says that one example of British people's pessimism is their

A calm response to problems that affect them personally.

B acceptance of what they are told by administrators.

C tendency to exaggerate potential problems.

[ ] 1

2 What does the speaker say about British children?

A They come to appreciate irony later in life.

B It comes naturally to them to be pessimistic.

C They are aware of having a peculiar sense of humour.

[ ] 2

Extract Two

You hear the introduction to a radio programme about food.

3 Brian J. Ford believes that in the future people's attitudes to food

A will be influenced by discoveries about old age.

B will reflect a growing interest in the whole subject of food.

C will focus more on what they can eat than on what they shouldn't.

[ ] 3

4 Ford believes that some of today's snack foods will be regarded as

A worse than today's junk food.

B unsuitable for consumption.

C more harmful than they really are.

[ ] 4

Extract Three

You hear part of a radio programme about children and sport.

5 What does the speaker say about certain fathers today?

A They ignore sensible advice that is given to them.

B They are primarily motivated by the desire for financial gain.

C They do not realize how hard it is to succeed in sport.

6 The speaker warns against

A taking the enjoyment out of sport for children.

B investing money in a child's sporting future.

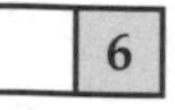

C taking children's sporting activities seriously.

Extract Four

You hear the introduction to a radio programme about inventors.

7 The speaker says that Edison's comment

A reflects the naivety of inventors.

B sums up the unpredictability of an inventor's life.

C is as true today as when he made it.

8 What does the speaker say about the rules concerning English patents?

A He can understand why they remain in force.

B They have always put inventors at a disadvantage.

C Some inventors do not abide by them.

Stop the recording when you hear 'That's the end of Part One'.

Now check your answers to Part One of the test.

PART TWO

You will hear a radio report about interactive science and technology centres in Britain. For questions ***9–17****, complete the sentences with a word or short phrase. In the exam you will hear the piece twice.*

The area on which the National Stone Centre stands has been used for a long time for the mining of

[*and*] **9**.

Visitors to the centre are surprised to discover how much stone people

[ ] **10**.

Examples of the use of stone in construction shown are [*and*] **11**.

The headmaster describes the centre as an excellent [ ] **12**.

The first interactive gallery in Britain was called [ ] **13**.

At Techniquest, there are structures which [ ] **14**.

At Techniquest, a special [ ] **15** is used for teaching people about centrifugal force.

People can learn about the effect that [ ] **16** can have on each other at Techniquest.

A dragon is used for teaching people about [ ] **17** at Techniquest.

Stop the recording when you hear 'That's the end of Part Two'.

Now check your answers to Part Two of the test.

PART THREE

*You will hear an interview with someone who reviews hotels. For questions **18–22**, choose the answer (**A**, **B**, **C** or **D**) which fits best according to what you hear. In the exam you will hear the piece twice.*

18 What does Paddy say about some readers of her column?

A They suspect that she enjoys criticizing hotels.

B Her attitude to hotels has changed because of their response.

C Her comments match their experiences of hotels.

D They prefer reading about hotels they would not want to visit.

[ ] **18**

19 What does Paddy say about some hotelkeepers?

A They sometimes have to force themselves to have a sense of humour.

B They would be more suited to a different profession.

C They expect to receive negative comments about their hotels.

D They are surprised that they become friends of hers.

[ ] **19**

20 Paddy says that some hotelkeepers she has contacted about the book have

A realized that she does not really have an assistant called Emily.

B corrected inaccuracies that were in her review of their hotels.

C responded favourably despite criticisms she had made.

D made her wonder whether her reviews of their hotels were unfair.

[ ] **20**

21 Paddy says that one hotelkeeper she spoke to told her that

A other people are unlikely to be treated in the same way in hotels as she is.

B he was unwilling to discuss some of the comments in her review.

C her reviews did not have as much influence as she believed.

D he no longer wanted his hotel to appear in the book.

[ ] **21**

22 The same owner also told her that

A he had passed information about her to other hotels.

B he resented her description of him in her review.

C he did not understand why she wanted to put his hotel in her book.

D there was nothing distinctive about her physical appearance.

[ ] **22**

Stop the recording when you hear 'That's the end of Part Three'.

Before you check your answers to Part Three of the test, go on to pages 123–125

WHAT'S TESTED

The questions in Part Three of the Listening Paper test you on your ability to understand and interpret often complex points made and information given by speakers in conversation, particularly in an interview situation. Questions may focus on any of the following:

- **opinion** – a view expressed by a speaker.
- **gist** – the general meaning of what a speaker says, or the main point a speaker makes.
- **detail** – specific information given or a particular point made by a speaker.
- **inference** – something which is not directly stated by a speaker but which is strongly implied.

TIPS

- Questions follow the order of what is said in the piece – for example, questions on an interview may cover each succeeding answer given by the person being interviewed.
- Don't rush into choosing the option that appears superficially to be the most plausible – what speakers say is often fairly complex and subtle.
- It is possible that more than one option in a question may be correct according to what the speaker says, but only one option will correctly answer the question that has been asked, so make sure that you read the question carefully.
- If you find a question particularly difficult, don't spend so much time on it that you do not concentrate sufficiently on what comes next in the piece. If you do that, you may fail to answer the next question, which may have presented you with considerably less difficulty.
- Use the pause of one minute before the piece to read the questions in advance, so that you are aware of the aspects of it that you will be tested on.
- Use the second listening to check your answers even if you were confident of them on the first listening, as well as to answer questions you were unable to do then.

Listen to Part Three of the test again and do the exercises below. They will help you to eliminate the incorrect options in the questions in the test or to confirm that you have selected the right options. In each exercise, tick one or more boxes.

Question 18 *Stop the recording when Paddy says 'some awful ones, too'.*

Which of the following does Paddy mention in her first speech?

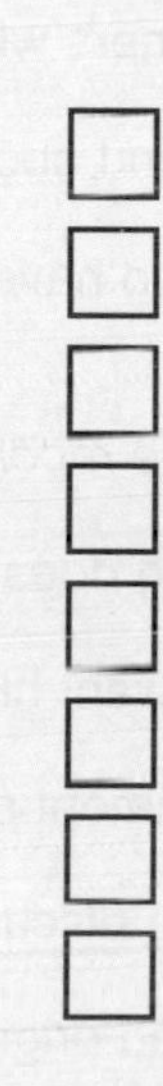

a a feeling of optimism whenever she goes to a hotel

b hotels whose appearances are deceptive

c a desire on her part to find things wrong with hotels

d the influence that readers' letters have had on her

e a reference to highly critical reviews of hotels she has written

f readers' own opinions of hotels she has reviewed

g a comment on how enjoyable her critical reviews of hotels are

h a comment about hotels she approves of in her reviews

Question 19 *Stop the recording when Paddy says 'have become friends'.*

Which of the following does Paddy refer to in her second speech?

- **a** hotelkeepers who are aware of reasons why their hotels deserve criticism ☐
- **b** circumstances in which she does not feel good about criticizing a hotel ☐
- **c** hotelkeepers who would prefer to be in a different line of work ☐
- **d** hotelkeepers she thinks would make excellent performers ☐
- **e** the kind of hotelkeepers most likely to have a sense of humour ☐
- **f** the reaction of hotelkeepers when she gives their hotels bad reviews ☐
- **g** hotelkeepers who she thinks disguise their true feelings about her reviews ☐
- **h** how strange it is that she has become friends with certain hotelkeepers ☐

Question 20 *Stop the recording when Paddy says 'behind-the-scenes stories'.*

Which of the following does Paddy mention in her third speech?

- **a** realizing that some details in her original reviews were inaccurate ☐
- **b** the fact that she has enjoyed getting into contact with hotel owners ☐
- **c** the reason why she sometimes pretends to be someone else ☐
- **d** occasions when she has regretted pretending to be someone else ☐
- **e** hotel owners protesting about the reviews she wrote about their hotels ☐
- **f** asking hotel owners whether their hotels have got better since her review ☐
- **g** changing her mind about whether some hotels were really as bad as she said ☐
- **h** hotel owners who have been pleased to give her further information ☐

Question 21 *Stop the recording when Paddy says 'the last thing I want'.*

Which of the following does Paddy mention concerning the hotel owner in her fourth speech?

- **a** why he did not want his hotel to be included in her book ☐
- **b** a particular comment she had made that he strongly disagreed with ☐
- **c** his reluctance to discuss her review of his hotel in detail ☐
- **d** why his hotel had originally been included in the book but then removed ☐
- **e** occasions when people have told him that Paddy's reviews were wrong ☐
- **f** a comment he made about the effect that her reviews have on people ☐
- **g** his belief that she only likes hotels where she is treated as important ☐
- **h** a belief he has about what she likes about hotels that is not true ☐

Question 22 *Stop the recording at the end of the interview.*

Which of the following does Paddy refer to concerning the hotel owner in her final speech?

a people wanting to know what Paddy looked like ☐

b details he gave that would enable hotels to know when she was visiting them ☐

c his opinion of the way she looked ☐

d people telling him that his description of Paddy was inaccurate ☐

e his realization that appearing in the book would be free ☐

f his confusion as to the purpose of her book ☐

g the possibility that he found her description of him flattering ☐

h a comment he made on her description of him ☐

Now check your answers to these exercises. When you have done so, listen again to Part Three of the test and decide whether you wish to change any of the answers you gave. Then check your answers to Part Three of the test.

PART FOUR

You will hear two friends, Helen and Tony, discussing various aspects of modern technology in everyday life. For questions **23–28**, *decide whether the opinions are expressed by only one of the speakers, or whether the speakers agree.*

Write **H** *for Helen,*
T *for Tony,*
or **B** *for Both, where they agree.*

In the exam you will hear the piece twice.

23 Being contactable all the time is not necessarily a good idea. [ ] 23

24 E-mails encourage laziness of thought. [ ] 24

25 Popular music isn't as good as it used to be because of technology. [ ] 25

26 Watching sport on TV has been made more interesting by modern technology. [ ] 26

27 There is no real demand for some aspects of modern technology. [ ] 27

28 Some innovations of modern technology will disappear in the future. [ ] 28

Stop the recording when you hear 'That's the end of Part Four'.

In the exam you will have five minutes at the end of the test to copy your answers onto a separate answer sheet.

Now check your answers to Part Four of the test.

PAPER 5 SPEAKING 19 minutes

PART ONE (3 MINUTES) GENERAL AND SOCIAL

Questions that may be addressed to either candidate.

- Describe your journey here today.
- What do you like/dislike about a journey you regularly take?
- Describe a typical day for you.
- What do you like most about the routines in your life?
- What do you like least about the routines in your life?

- What is the employment situation like where you live?
- Do you think it is likely to change in the future?
- Has it changed in comparison with the past?
- What would make/has made you move away from the place you come from?
- Is it common for people to leave the place you come from?

PART TWO (4 MINUTES) HEALTH AND EXERCISE

For both candidates.

Choose two of the pictures on pages 174–175 and describe what is happening in each of them. (1 minute)

Now look at all of the pictures and answer one of these questions.
Which of the scenes most closely corresponds with your lifestyle and which the least?
What are the most common attitudes in your society towards the activities shown in the pictures?
(3 minutes)

PART THREE (12 MINUTES) RULES AND REGULATIONS

In phase one of Part Three each candidate takes a long turn (2 minutes), followed by a brief response from the other candidate.

Prompt Card (a) *(Given to Candidate A, and a copy to Candidate B)*

In what ways is it important to have rules and regulations?
- order rather than chaos in society
- children / school
- crime and punishment

One of the following questions for Candidate B (1 minute):

- What do you think?
- Is there anything you would like to add?
- Is there anything you don't agree with?
- How does this differ from your experience?

One of the following questions for both candidates (1 minute):

- Are you someone who is happy to conform or are you rebellious?
- Which laws are the most commonly broken ones in your society?
- What is the common attitude towards the law and order authorities in your society?

Prompt Card (b) *(Given to Candidate B, and a copy to Candidate A)*

What are the most important rules of personal behaviour?
- politeness / rudeness
- honesty / dishonesty
- being reliable / unreliable

One of the following questions for Candidate A (1 minute):

- What do you think?
- Is there anything you would like to add?
- Is there anything you don't agree with?
- How does this differ from your experience?

One of the following questions for both candidates (1 minute):

- What rules of behaviour in your society do / would foreigners find it hard to conform to?
- Describe a ceremony that is common in your society.
- Do young people in general in your society behave in a conventional way?

In phase two of Part Three there is a discussion on the general topic (4 minutes).
Possible general questions for both candidates on the topic of rules and regulations:

- Is there a rule or law that you find particularly ridiculous?
- If you could introduce one rule or law, what would it be?
- Have you ever broken the rules when playing a game or sport? What happened as a result?
- Are ideas about personal behaviour changing in your society?
- Describe an occasion when you did not act according to your own rules of behaviour. What happened as a result?
- Describe someone whose general behaviour you particularly disapprove of.

Part Two: Describing Movement

In the Speaking Paper, you may need to describe movements, perhaps of people in the pictures. To check or add to your vocabulary on that subject, look at the list of verbs below and put them into the categories given. Then note down the precise meaning of each one (you may need to consult a dictionary) and try to think of sentences in which you could use them.

limp	stagger	quiver	chuck
nudge	rock	amble	thump
prod	hurl	tear	tremble
trot	hobble	fling	shiver
wander	toss	stroll	shove
sling	punch	dash	shuffle
poke	totter	hop	slap
sprint	shudder	dig	whack

Walk/Run	Shake	Hit	Throw

Now check your answers to this exercise.

Describing Vocal Sounds

You may need to describe the sounds that people make, perhaps the sounds you think people in the pictures are making. To check or add to your vocabulary on that subject, look at the list of verbs below and put them into the categories given. Then note down the precise meaning of each one (you may need to consult a dictionary) and try to think of sentences in which you could use them.

whoop	shriek	yell	holler
mutter	chuckle	mumble	whine
whisper	jabber	jeer	wail
bellow	snigger	gibber	drone
weep	groan	cackle	titter
murmur	chatter	howl	babble
giggle	natter	whimper	sob
roar	whinge	grumble	moan

Shout	Speak/Talk	Laugh	Sound Unhappy/ Complain

Now check your answers to this exercise.

Topic Vocabulary

In Part Three of this test, you are required to talk about the topic of rules and regulations. To check or add to your vocabulary on this subject, look at the words and phrases below. Group them together under the headings given. Then decide whether they are verbs, adjectives or nouns and label them appropriately. Then note down the precise meaning of each one (you may need to consult a dictionary) and try to think of sentences in which you could use them.

breach enforce comply infringe unruly defy	conservative conform observe protocol naughty stick-in-the-mud	binding middle-of-the-road idiosyncratic contravene unorthodox dissent	adhere to etiquette offbeat rebel sin cheeky	toe the line abide by insubordinate eccentric reactionary petty

Obeying Rules	Not Obeying Rules	Conventional	Unconventional

Now complete this table for forming words connected with this subject.

Verb	Adjective	Noun	Adverb	Opposites
1 behave	–		–	(verb) (noun)
2 conform	–	(noun) (person)	–	(person)
3	cheeky			
4 defy				
5 obey				(verb) (adj) (noun) (adv)
6 rebel		(noun) (person)		–

Now check your answers to these exercises.

TEST FOUR

PAPER 1 READING 1 hour 30 minutes

PART ONE

*For questions **1–18**, read the three texts below and decide which answer (**A**, **B**, **C** or **D**) best fits each gap. In the exam you will mark your answers on a separate answer sheet.*

Television Documentaries

Here's a new game for you. Watch a documentary with the sound turned down and make up your own commentary. It's great for parties. You **(1)** .... all your guests to stand outside and then they come in one at a time and have a **(2)** .... at guessing what it's about.

It's only when you turn down the sound that you realize just how **(3)** .... the pictures are to most documentaries. I expect you've noticed by now that television is primarily a visual medium. TV directors get into a terrible **(4)** .... if there's nothing to show you. They don't mind so much if there's nothing to tell you – 80% of television has nothing to say – but no director has ever turned to a cameraman and asked: 'What are you doing here?'

The most insuperable problem with a large **(5)** .... of documentaries is that they are working in the wrong medium. They ought to be newsprint articles. You can say more in print. You can say it better. And it's interactive. The readers can go at their own **(6)** .... Television is hampered by having to fill the screen and move at the approximate speed of the slowest member of the audience.

1	**A** have	**B** sort	**C** get	**D** settle
2	**A** bid	**B** stab	**C** venture	**D** speculation
3	**A** irrelevant	**B** incompatible	**C** inconsistent	**D** incongruous
4	**A** lather	**B** fuss	**C** ado	**D** stir
5	**A** fraction	**B** proportion	**C** ratio	**D** bulk
6	**A** time	**B** flow	**C** course	**D** pace

The Rejected Novel

'You've not had much luck with the book, I hear.'

That had to be the understatement of the year. My novel had been rejected four times **(7)** .... far. I've no doubt that behind my **(8)** .... the family were having a good snigger. Rhona of course had been the loyal exception, though I admit that her piteous expressions when the thing limped home battered by franking stamps were harder to **(9)** .... than her sister's outright sarcasm: 'Has your boomerang got back yet, Patton?' she'd enquire, while her husband Jack would give the knife an extra twist by asking if I'd managed to sell any of my daubs. Which meant that he presumed I'd **(10)** .... my job on the railways to pursue a painting career. Maybe I should have. The manuscript had begun to show bruises from its days, weeks and months buried in the 'slush pile' of various publishing firms. Actual criticism of the novel by its rejectors was very **(11)** .... on the ground, although the consensus of opinion seemed to indicate that its main weakness **(12)** .... in its apparent 'lack of plot'.

7	**A** yet	**B** thus	**C** hence	**D** by
8	**A** back	**B** head	**C** ears	**D** face
9	**A** bear	**B** defy	**C** cope	**D** resist
10	**A** broken off	**B** wound up	**C** pulled out	**D** packed in
11	**A** light	**B** shallow	**C** thin	**D** scant
12	**A** stood	**B** revolved	**C** lay	**D** centred

Loneliness in the City

For the really lonely individual in the city, life becomes a string of disconnected occasions. Eating by himself in a restaurant he feels conspicuous; he tries to **(13)** .... the eyes of other lone diners, **(14)** .... himself the subject of other people's conversations, sees a world divided into two groups – the majority; complacent couples, parties and families, and an envious minority of single people. He takes **(15)** .... at the imagined snubs or cursory service of the waiter. He calls for his bill with the coffee, knowing he has no further excuse to **(16)** .... put. In a phone booth, he makes a cliffhanger out of the ringing tone, and **(17)** .... with relief when it is answered. When his own phone stays silent for a day, he suspects a conspiracy to drop him, and **(18)** .... the operator to check his line. At a party, he stays too long, since there is nothing to follow it.

13	**A** set	**B** make	**C** take	**D** catch
14	**A** conceives	**B** infers	**C** imagines	**D** fantasizes
15	**A** offence	**B** indignation	**C** outrage	**D** insult
16	**A** stick	**B** hang	**C** stay	**D** hold
17	**A** blows	**B** sighs	**C** yawns	**D** snorts
18	**A** persists	**B** pesters	**C** perseveres	**D** pleads

Now check your answers to Part One of the test.

PART TWO

You are going to read four extracts which are all about the writers' school days. For questions **19–26**, *choose the answer (***A***,* **B***,* **C** *or* **D***) which you think fits best according to the text. In the exam you will mark your answers on a separate answer sheet.*

The Eleven Plus Exam

At school, particularly when I was ten or eleven, I was suffocated by the amount of normality I was subjected to. I knew how to count, and yet they, the teachers, pushed all these complex forms of mathematics down my throat. I could read, but I wasn't allowed to read what I wanted. I was force-fed the school syllabus, and all because it was deemed to be the standard. And someone had decided that children should be judged at the age of eleven so that they could be segregated for the rest of their lives. No consideration was given for talents outside the limited range required by the examining board. The misfits were destined to become factory fodder, farm workers or manual workers like my father, with no incentive to achieve or realize their potential.

I sat at my desk on the day of the Eleven Plus exam and looked at my paper. I felt it was more than my intelligence that was being tested, it was my whole being. I had to decide either to play the game their way, and succeed or fail according to their rules, or take my own route. I decided to settle my own fate. I signed my name at the top of the paper, and did nothing more for the rest of the exam. The room was silent, apart from the anxious scratching of pencils, and yet inside my head was a triumphant explosion, like the opening cannon shot of war. I had made my first statement to the world. But it was also like watching opportunity float away on a piece of paper down the river. It would damage me, but at the same time it was a victory. For the first time in my life I realized that it would be a battle between me and them.

19 The writer implies in the first paragraph that his school days were characterized by
A a system which benefited none of the pupils at his school.
B his belief that he would not end up in the same sort of job his father had.
C his belief that he had abilities that the school system did not cater for.
D a refusal on his part to do what teachers expected of him.

20 When the writer decided not to answer any of the questions in the exam, he
A was fully aware of the consequences of what he was doing.
B did so because he feared that the exam would suggest he was not very intelligent.
C told himself that doing so would not have long-term consequences.
D thought it was the logical thing to do in view of his behaviour at school.

A Good Education

I was part of a typical black family. My parents were strict with us. The traditional and most important essence of life was obtaining a good education, which to the black immigrants was the key to success, a way out of the ruck. Most parents dreamed of their offspring becoming lawyers, doctors, teachers – professions they thought that schooling could provide. It was a perfectly natural point of view. My parents, like thousands of other black people, had scrimped and scraped and saved for years to ensure that we had a better life. The jobs they had when they came to Britain were menial, jobs that nobody else would deign to do. They did all that so that we would have better opportunities, and they expected us to grab them when they came along. Dad always said that he wanted me to seize all the opportunities he had missed. I suppose that I shall say the same thing to my family when the time comes. Even over ten generations, the same story will be repeated. *line 1* *line 6* *line 7*

Sport didn't have any priority at all in this kind of philosophy; with Mum and Dad it was way down low on the list. One day I came home from training and Mum asked, 'How much do they pay you for all this running?'

I laughed. 'You go because you enjoy it,' I replied.

'You mean to say that you go out in all weathers – hail, rain, snow, sunshine – and run up and down for nothing?'

I said, 'That's how it goes, Mum.'

She was totally nonplussed. *line 19*

21 The writer implies that his parents' attitude to education
- **A** is a bit less common now than it was then.
- **B** was something that put pressure on him.
- **C** was unique to black people in Britain.
- **D** resulted from mistakes they felt they had made.

22 Which of these words suggests criticism on the part of the writer?
- **A** strict (line 1)
- **B** scrimped (line 6)
- **C** deign (line 7)
- **D** nonplussed (line 19)

A Child of My Time

I was just a typical child of my time, I suppose – open to everything. I was being a teenager: curious, rebellious, in quest of the forbidden. You heard about these hip clubs in London from a friend who had heard it from another friend who had actually been to one. The names alone took on a magical talismanic quality: the Marquee, Ronnie Scott's. I used to come up from school and go to clubs when I was about 16. I was dazzled by this scene, rudimentary as it was. I was just a girl from the provinces, going up to the big city to see what gives. I didn't know anybody, I was alone and unapproachable; I never spoke to anyone. I was putting together a persona out of a lot of diverse elements. The 1960s hadn't happened yet, there were only hazy intimations of what was coming. I thought maybe there was a bit more to it than shuffling around smoky clubs and I was hellbent on being there when it happened, whatever it was!

Somewhere in the back of my mind I had made a decision to leave home, to break away. My mother never suspected this. I've always laid my plans very secretively and never let anyone in on them, which more often than not has turned out to be a mistake. I didn't know that it was possible to talk things over with people and not lose everything in the process – I thought the minute you confided anything it would be gone or they would try to stop you. This was definitely true of my mother. I learned very young to conceal my innermost thoughts from her.

23 The writer says that when she went to clubs in London,
- **A** she found that they sometimes fell short of her expectations of them.
- **B** she felt that she was too young to fit in properly in them.
- **C** she unconsciously began to develop into a different kind of person.
- **D** she felt that the future would bring developments that would be more exciting.

24 What does the writer say about her mother?
- **A** Something she later learned in life did not apply to her mother.
- **B** She inherited a lack of openness with others from her mother.
- **C** She never revealed her private feelings to her mother.
- **D** Her tendency to be secretive stemmed from a desire not to upset her mother.

The Royal High School

Attendance at the Royal High School became more and more of a penance. The attitude of many teachers towards pupils was deplorable. They seemed to regard us as something of a nuisance and an interruption to their daily routine. There were exceptions. One devoted history teacher came up with a scheme by which any pupil who discovered a genuine error in any history text would be awarded an extra one per cent in the term examination. The enthusiasm with which his pupils combed their texts for mistakes was impressive, though there were rumours that their parents had been drawn into the research. Inevitably, a market economy developed around this precious information. Confident boys placed suspected errors on the market, charging rates according to the probability of acceptance. It was good practice for life, of a kind.

In the autumn of 1935, my father saw an advertisement for a Civil Service competition for a single appointment as a sorting clerk and telegraphist, and announced that I should apply. Sons in those days did exactly what their fathers told them to do, or at least I did, so at the age of 16 I sat the examination. I took first place in the city, to my own astonishment and my family's, and on the morning the brown envelope came my father told me that I could leave school that day. I went to the Rector's office and told him that I was going. The Rector, a very elevated person named Dr King Gillies, told me in omniscient tones that I was being very foolish, that I could expect only to become a butcher's delivery boy – the ultimate social disgrace. I spoiled his day by showing him the letter from the Civil Service Commission. And so my formal education ended.

25 What does the writer say about his school days in the first paragraph?

A They made him more competitive than he otherwise would have been.
B He feels that his attitude towards them was not totally justified.
C Something that happened then taught him about human nature.
D The action of one teacher caused problems for him in particular.

26 What does the writer imply about the Rector?

A He was not as highly respected as he thought he was.
B He did not like being proved wrong.
C He was sad that the writer was leaving school.
D He disagreed with what the writer's father had done.

Now check your answers to Part Two of the test.

PART THREE

*You are going to read a newspaper article. Seven paragraphs have been removed from the article. Choose from the paragraphs **A–H** the one which fits each gap (**27–33**). There is one extra paragraph which you do not need to use. In the exam you will mark your answers on a separate answer sheet.*

Rainmaker with his Head in the Clouds

Critics dismissed Graeme Mather's attempts to make clouds rain. But now recent experiments appear to have vindicated him. Anjana Ahuya reports.

Dr Graeme Mather lived his life with his head in the clouds, as a documentary film to be shown this week shows. Against the advice of almost everybody else in the meteorological community, the Canadian scientist devoted his professional life to trying to make clouds rain.

27 ____

Before Dr Mather became involved, the science of weather modification had already claimed many reputations. The idea that clouds could be manipulated first circulated in the 1940s, and efforts gathered pace soon after the Second World War.

28 ____

However, the entire discipline fell into disrepute when commercial companies hijacked the idea, took it around the world, and then failed to deliver on their promises. Cloud-seeding, as the process was known, became the preserve of crackpots and charlatans.

29 ____

Scientists theorised that if they could inject the cloud with similarly shaped crystals, these imposter crystals would also act as frames around which droplets would clump. The cloud would then be tricked into raining. Silver iodide, whose crystals resemble those of ice, seemed the best bet. Sadly, none of the experiments, including Dr Mather's, which had been going for more than five years, seemed to work. Dr Mather was about to admit defeat when serendipity intervened.

30 ____

Dr Mather was convinced that something that the place was spewing into the atmosphere was encouraging the downpour. Subsequent experiments confirmed that hygroscopic salts pouring into the sky from there were responsible. Hygroscopic salts attract water – once in the atmosphere, the particles act as magnets around which raindrops can form.

31 ____

He was wary; Dr Mather was known to be a smooth-talking salesman. 'He was charming and charismatic, and many scientists don't trust that,' he says. 'He was also not well-published because he had been working in the commercial sector. Overall, he was regarded as a maverick. On that occasion, he presented results that I was convinced were impossible. Yet the statistical evidence was overwhelming, which I couldn't understand.'

32 ____

'If those findings can be reproduced there, it will be the most exciting thing to have happened in the field for 20 years. It will be remarkable because some of the results are not scientifically explainable.' He adds, however, that scientists must exercise caution because cloud-seeding is still mired in controversy. He also points out that, with water being such a precious resource, success will push the research into the political arena.

33 ____

Dr Cooper says: 'With the paper mill, he saw something that other people wouldn't have seen. I am still uncomfortable with his idea because it throws up major puzzles in cloud physics. But if Dr Mather was right, it will demonstrate that humans can change clouds in ways that were once thought impossible.'

A Dr Mather refused to be daunted by this image. After all, the principle seemed perfectly plausible. Water droplets are swept up to the top of the clouds on updrafts, where they become supercooled (ie, although the temperature is below freezing, the water remains liquid). When a supercooled droplet collides with an ice crystal, it freezes on contact and sticks. Successive collisions cause each ice crystal to accumulate more water droplets; the crystals grow until they become too heavy to remain suspended in the atmosphere. As the crystals fall through the cloud, they become raindrops. The ice crystals therefore act as frames to 'grow' raindrops.

B Dr Mather unfortunately will not be involved in the debate about such matters. He died aged 63, shortly before the documentary was completed. It will ensure that this smooth-talking maverick is given the recognition he deserves.

C He and a colleague decided to collect a last batch of data when they flew into a tiny but ferocious storm. That storm, Dr Mather says in the film, changed his life. Huge droplets were spattering on the tiny plane's windscreen. No such storm had been forecast. Back on the ground, they discovered the storm was located directly above a paper mill.

D A trial in Mexico has been running for two years, and the signs are promising. 'We were sufficiently encouraged in the first year to continue the seeding research. But the results are preliminary, because we have only a very small sample of clouds at the moment. We need to work over two more summers to reach a proper conclusion.'

E He arranged to fly to South Africa 'with the full intention of explaining what was wrong with the experiment'. Instead, he came back convinced that Dr Mather was on to something. He is now running two experiments, one in Arizona and one in northern Mexico, to try to verify the South African results. The experiments use potassium chloride, which is similar to table salt (sodium chloride) and, it is claimed, non-polluting.

F The scientific community remained sniffy in the face of this apparent proof. Foremost among the sceptics was Dr William Cooper, of the United States National Center for Atmospheric Research (NCAR). Dr Cooper, regarded as one of the world's finest cloud scientists, saw Dr Mather present his astonishing claims at a cloud physics conference in Montreal.

G They involved weather experts firing rockets into clouds to stop them producing hail, which damages crops. The clouds, it was hoped, would dissolve into a harmless shower.

H The desire to do so led him to set up a project in South Africa, which was ultimately to convince him that it was possible. As the programme reveals, experiments around the world appear to prove his faith was justified.

Now check your answers to Part Three of the test.

PART FOUR

*You are going to read an extract from a book about comedy. For questions **34–40**, choose the answer (**A**, **B**, **C** or **D**) which you think fits best according to the text. In the exam you will mark your answers on a separate answer sheet.*

Comedians

What drives moderately intelligent persons to put themselves up for acceptance or disparagement? In short, what sort of individual wants to be a comedian? When we hear the very word, what does the label suggest? Other professions, callings and occupations attract separate and distinct types of practitioner. Some stereotypes are so familiar as to be cheaply laughable examples from the world of travesty, among them absent-minded professors, venal lawyers, gloomy detectives and cynical reporters. But what corny characteristics do we attribute to comedians? To a man or woman, are they generally parsimonious, vulgar, shallow, arrogant, introspective, hysterically insecure, smug, autocratic, amoral, and selfish? Read their superficial stories in the tabloids and so they would appear.

Rather than look at the complete image, perhaps we need to explore the initial motives behind a choice of career. Consider first those who prefer a sort of anonymity in life, the ones who'd rather wear a uniform. The psychological make-up of individuals who actively seek to resign their individuality is apparent among those who surrender to the discipline of a military life. The emotional and intellectual course taken by those who are drawn to anonymity is easily observed but not easily deflected. They want to be told what to do and then be required to do it over and over again in the safety of a routine, often behind the disguises of a number or livery. If their egos ache with the need for recognition and praise, it's a pain that must be contained, frustrated or satisfied within the rut they occupy. The mere idea of standing up in front of an audience and demanding attention is abhorrent.

Nor will we find our comics among the doormats and dormice, the meek. There's precious little comedy in the lives of quiet hobbyists, bashful scholars, hermits, anchorites and recluses, the discreet and the modest, ones who deliberately select a position of obscurity and seclusion. Abiding quietly in this stratum of society, somewhere well below public attention level, there is humour, yes, since humour can endure in the least favourable circumstances, persisting like lichen in Antarctica. And jokes. Many lesser-known comedy writers compose their material in the secret corners of an unassuming existence. I know of two, both content to be minor figures in the civil service, who send in topical jokes to radio and TV shows on condition that their real names are not revealed.

In both cases I've noticed that their comic invention, though clever, is based upon wordplay, puns and similar equivoques, never an aggressive comic observation of life. Just as there may be a certain sterility in the self-effacement of a humble life, so it seems feasible that the selection process of what's funny is emasculated before it even commences. If you have no ginger and snap in your daily round, with little familiarity with strong emotions, it seems likely that your sense of fun will be limited by timidity to a simple juggling with language.

If the comedian's genesis is unlikely to be founded in social submission, it's also improbable among the top echelons of our civilization. Once again, *humour* can be found among the majestic. Nobles and royals, statesmen and lawmakers, have their wits. Jokes and jokers circulate at the loftiest level of every advanced nation but being high-born seems to carry no compulsion to make the hoi polloi laugh. Some of our rulers do make us laugh but that's not what they're paid to do. And, so with the constricted comedy of those who live a constricted life, that which amuses them may lack the common touch.

Having eliminated the parts of society unlikely to breed funnymen, it's to the middle ranks of humanity, beneath the exalted and above the invisible, that we must look to see where comics come from and why. And are they, like nurses and nuns, called to their vocation? As the mountain calls to the mountaineer and the pentameter to the poet, does the need of the mirthless masses summon forth funsters, ready to administer relief as their sole raison d'être? We've often heard it said that someone's a 'born comedian' but will it do for all of them or even most of them? Perhaps we like to think of our greatest jesters as we do our greatest painters and composers, preferring to believe that their gifts are inescapably driven to expression. But in our exploration of the comedy mind, hopefully finding some such, we are sure to find some quite otherwise.

It's possible that two of the only three things that all successful comedians have in common have already been offered to the reader; they don't arise from the obedient and they don't descend from the mighty. And the third is that they make us laugh and that's it. There is no other commonable property. Otherwise, they are as diverse as fingerprints. When I first took to the stage to deliver my untested notions of levity, I was a bit of a novelty. There were almost no educated, middle-class comedians around. The great majority of funsters were working class. But I already sensed the truth. That, although the tradition of working-class origins was strong in comedy performers, poverty didn't teach timing. Having holes in your shoes as a kid wasn't what made you quick-witted and no one ever learned how to do a perfect double-take by starving. Comedians are singular and so was I.

34 What does the writer imply about comedians in the first paragraph?

A People in certain other professions generally have a better image than them.
B It is possible that they are seen as possessing only negative characteristics.
C It is harder to generalize about them than about people in other professions.
D They often cannot understand why people make negative judgements of them.

35 What does the writer say about people who wear uniforms?

A They criticize performers for craving attention.
B It is unusual for them to break their normal patterns of thought.
C They are more aware of their inadequacies than others may think.
D The desires they have are never met when they are at work.

36 The writer says in the third paragraph that shy people

A may be able to write humorous material but could not perform it.
B are capable of being more humorous than they realize.
C fear that what they find humorous would not amuse others.
D do not get the recognition they deserve even if they are good at comedy.

37 In the fourth paragraph, the writer criticizes the kind of comedy he describes for its lack of

A originality.
B coherence.
C sophistication.
D spirit.

38 The writer says that people at the top of society

A have contempt for the humour of those at lower levels of society.
B take themselves too seriously to wish to amuse anybody.
C are unaware of how ridiculous they appear to others.
D would not be capable of becoming comedians even if they wanted to.

39 What does the writer wonder in the sixth paragraph?

A whether people's expectations of comedians are too high
B whether comedians can be considered great in the way that other people in the arts can
C whether it is inevitable that some people will become comedians
D whether comedians realize how significant they are in the lives of ordinary people

40 The writer's own experience as a comedian showed him that

A his background was likely to put him at a disadvantage.
B common notions about what comic performance required were wrong.
C success as a comedian depended more on technique than on background.
D comedians themselves disagreed with common theories on comedy.

Before you check your answers to Part Four of the test, go on to pages 140–142.

WHAT'S TESTED

The questions in Part Four of the Reading Paper test you on the same abilities as the questions in Part Two, except that in this part you are required to study one longer text rather than a series of short texts. As in Part Two, questions may focus on any of the following:

- **detail** – understanding of complex pieces of information and/or ideas that are clearly stated in the text.
- **opinion** – understanding of opinions expressed or referred to by the writer.
- **attitude** – understanding of feelings described in the text which either the writer or someone the writer refers to expresses.
- **tone** – identifying from the style of the text or a section of it the impression the writer wishes to create.
- **purpose** – identifying what the writer is trying to achieve in the text or a section of it.
- **main idea** – identifying the gist or the main topic of what is said in the text or a section of it, as opposed to minor points or details which exemplify general points.
- **implication** – interpreting what is not directly stated in the text but instead is strongly suggested in such a way that it is clear that the writer intends the reader to make certain inferences.
- **exemplification** – understanding how a point made in the text is illustrated with examples.
- **imagery** – understanding why certain images are used, or how certain effects are achieved by the writer in order to indicate similarities and differences between things.
- **reference** – understanding of what words, phrases or sentences in the text refer to or relate to elsewhere in the text.

TIPS

- In multiple-choice questions such as those in this part of the Paper, it is essential to remember that more than one of the options given may be correct according to what is stated in the text but only one of the options will correctly answer the question that is asked. Don't choose the most appealing option superficially – it may be true but it may not answer the question you have been asked.
- The questions follow the order of the text and often each question relates to each succeeding paragraph. The exception to this is any question about the text as a whole, which is always the last question.
- Before you attempt to answer any questions, skim through the whole text quickly. This will give you an idea of what it is about and enable you to approach the questions with some understanding of the text. If you start answering the questions too hastily, you may become confused by what you discover later in the text and have to start again, thus wasting valuable time.

The following exercises will help you to eliminate the incorrect options in the questions in the test or to confirm that you have selected the correct options.

Question 34 *Look at the first paragraph.*

1 Does the writer say that generalizations are made about people in other professions? If so, where?

....

2 Does the writer mention the view comedians have of other people's opinions of them? If so, where?

....

3 Match these adjectives from the first paragraph with the definitions given on the next page.

Adjectives

absent-minded ....
venal ....
gloomy ....
cynical ....
parsimonious ....
vulgar ....
shallow ....
arrogant ....
introspective ....
insecure ....
smug ....
autocratic ....
amoral ....
selfish ....

Definitions

a lacking confidence
b incapable of serious thought
c too self-confident
d too self-satisfied
e expecting to be obeyed at all times
f corrupt
g forgetful
h miserable
i rude and likely to offend
j having no principles
k mean
l tending to see only negative aspects
m thinking only of your own wishes
n tending to analyse yourself

Question 35 *Look at the second paragraph.*

1 Does the writer mention the view that people who wear uniforms hold concerning performing in public? If so, where?

....

2 If you are 'not easily deflected' from something,
a it is hard to stop you from continuing with it.
b it is hard for you to make others understand it.
c it is hard for you to be satisfied with it.
d it is hard for you to see the point of it.

3 Does the writer refer to the way in which people in uniforms see themselves? If so, where?

....

4 Does the writer say that people who wear uniforms may be treated well at work? If so, where?

....

Question 36 *Look at the third paragraph.*

1 What is meant by the word 'comics' in the context of the third paragraph?
a people who write comedy
b people who appreciate comedy
c people who perform comedy

2 What two things does the writer imply should be distinguished from comedy?

....

3 Does the writer mention what the two 'lesser-known comedy writers' he refers to think of the material they write? If so, where?

....

4 Does the writer give a reason why those writers don't want their names to be revealed? If so, what is it?

....

5 Which six words in the paragraph mean 'shy' or 'not wishing to attract attention'?

....

6 Does the writer refer to the success or otherwise of the comedy material written by shy people? If so, where?

....

Question 37 *Look at the fourth paragraph.*

1 What do 'puns' involve?
a humour that focuses on nonsense
b witty manipulation of the meanings of words
c jokes that may be regarded as being in bad taste

2 Which two words in the fourth paragraph are used with the meaning 'vigour' or 'liveliness'?

....

3 What is meant in the context by 'emasculated'?
a complicated
b weakened
c pre-determined
d made less acceptable

4 Which of the following does 'self-effacement' involve?
a vulgarity
b repetition
c modesty
d determination

Question 38 *Look at the fifth paragraph.*

1 What is meant by the phrase 'the hoi polloi'?
a the elite
b the masses
c one's peers

2 Does the writer refer to the opinions those at the top of society have of the sense of humour of people at other levels of society? If so, where?

....

3 Does the writer refer to those at the top of society being amusing? If so, where?

....

4 Does the writer say that people at the top of society do not realize that others laugh at them? If so, where?

....

5 What is meant by 'constricted'?
a disrespectful
b limited
c unconscious
d solemn

6 What is meant by the phrase 'the common touch'?
a the sense of responsibility required of those at the top of society
b the ability to relate to people at lower levels of society
c the ability to make general points about life
d the attitudes shared by the majority of society

Question 39 *Look at the sixth paragraph.*

1 What four words are used in the sixth paragraph with the meaning 'comedians'?

....

2 Does the writer refer to what comedians do for people? If so, what?

....

3 The writer compares comedians with other figures in the arts with regard to
a their popularity.
b how much talent they require.
c what motivates them.

4 If someone has a 'vocation', they
a feel compelled to take up a particular kind of work because of the expectations of others.
b feel that there is one particular type of work that they are naturally suited to.
c feel strongly attracted to a particular kind of work because others regard it as important.

5 What does the writer say about the expression 'a born comedian'?
a It highlights the importance of comedy.
b It is often used inaccurately.
c It may not apply to the majority of comedians.
d It suggests that comedians are different from other people in the arts.

Question 40 *Look at the final paragraph.*

1 Does the writer refer to something that happened to him because he was middle class? If so, where?

....

2 What three requirements for someone to be a good comedian does the writer mention in the final paragraph?

....

3 Does the writer say that he developed unconventional ideas about comic performance? If so, where?

....

4 Does the writer refer to the views on comedy held by comedians who were performing at the time when he started? If so, where?

....

5 What does the writer say about the working-class origins of comedians at that time? More than one of the choices is correct.
a They didn't determine whether comedians were good or not.
b They meant that the comedians had suffered in their lives.
c Some comedians thought that these origins made them appealing.
d It crossed his mind that he should pretend to have such origins.

6 What two words in the final paragraph mean 'dissimilar to each other'?

....

Now check your answers to these exercises. When you have done so, decide whether you wish to change any of your answers to Part Four of the test. Then check your answers to Part Four of the test.

PAPER 2 WRITING 2 hours

PART ONE

*You **must** answer this question. Write your answer in **300–350** words in an appropriate style. Write clearly in **pen**, not pencil. You may make alterations, but make sure your work is easy to read.*

1 As part of a course, you have been asked to write an essay based on the following extract from the introduction to a book about the Arts. Write your **essay**, giving your opinions on the points raised.

> And so the crux of the matter is this: what relevance do the Arts have in the lives of ordinary people? Are some sections of the Arts just for a small elite or can they appeal to a much wider audience? Can all sections of society get something from the Arts? And what about participation in the Arts? Should it be more widely encouraged, and if so, how?
> And finally: what good, if any, do the Arts do? These are the issues to be addressed in this book.

Write your **essay.**

Before you write your essay, go on to pages 144–146

PART ONE

For information on What's Tested and Tips see page 21.

To plan your answer for Part One, complete the following notes.

1 Note down as briefly as possible the **topic** of your essay.

....

2 List as briefly as possible the following:
- the **main points** in the question which you will have to cover in your essay
- the **comments and opinions** you wish to give with regard to these points
- the **examples** you plan to give to support or illustrate these comments/opinions

Main point	**Comments/Opinions**	**Examples**
Main point	**Comments/Opinions**	**Examples**
Main point	**Comments/Opinions**	**Examples**

3 List briefly any additional points you wish to make, which are not mentioned in the question but which you think are relevant to the topic. You may not wish to include any additional points.

Additional point	**Comments/Opinions**	**Examples**
Additional point	**Comments/Opinions**	**Examples**

4 Now note briefly how your essay will be organized by deciding what each part of it will contain. You may not wish to have as many paragraphs as are listed below.

Introduction
Paragraph 1
Paragraph 2
Paragraph 3

Paragraph 4
Paragraph 5
Paragraph 6
Conclusion

5 Now use these notes to write your essay.

When you have written your answer, assess it in accordance with the task-specific mark scheme.

6 Now read through this sample answer for Part One and answer the questions that follow it.

Yes, why do we have such a thing as arts in our society?

We have beautiful pictures on the walls of our homes. Pictures of naked women, picturesque country studies, views of Mediterranean emerald waters, boats, abstract coloured cubes, and so on. There are two sides to this coin. One side is the artists and the other side is the public that enjoys the arts.

Doing arts is in a way a very selfish act. The artist feels a need to express themselves on a piece of canvas, a piece of rock or whatever material they work with. They want to put a mark in history and show people their visions and ideas – in short, the way they want things to be. Whether it's passion, obsession or a way to control their environment, it's surely individual. But what they do have in common is that they choose to show people what they stand for with colours and shapes, working with their hands (or in some cases their whole body).

The public that buy arts, on the other hand, have different reasons for doing so. Some people mean that buying arts is a very materialistic act, the highest form of luxury. They have a need to possess a piece of vision, only to be able to discuss it at the coming dinner party and show it off in front of friends. This is unfortunately the truth in some cases.

Though others say that the arts have a deeper meaning to us humans than just to show it off in front of friends. For one thing, it shows us a more accessible picture of our own history. Since artists in all times have been influenced by their surroundings and the issues of their time, the arts often give us a better idea of our past, and certainly a much more colourful one than dusty books filled with numbers.

Arts in our homes are relevant for many reasons. They tickle our thoughts, give our minds something to work with. Arts on our wall have a positive psychological effect. And since the spirit lifts our whole being, they're also vital for our physical condition. Colours often put a smile on our faces and what could be more relevant than that? To make art more commonly enjoyed and appreciated, we need to encourage people on an early stage, so they see it as a natural thing in everyday life, not something snobby or posh for the very rich or the very interested, but also for the common person to help them see the beauty in what's common.

Content
Are all the main points mentioned in the question covered? Where are these points covered? If any are not covered, which are missing? Are any additional points included? If so, what are they, and are they relevant?

Range
Is there a wide range of vocabulary and grammatical structures? If so, give examples. If there are occasions when the vocabulary or grammar is too simple, suggest alternatives.

Accuracy
Are there any mistakes in the use of vocabulary or grammar? Correct any that you find.

Appropriacy of register and format
Are the style and tone of the essay appropriate? How would you describe them? Why are they appropriate or inappropriate? Is the format suitable for an essay? If so, why? If not, why not?

Organization and cohesion
Is the essay well-organized in terms of the beginning, the middle and the end? Is it divided into paragraphs appropriately? Describe briefly the content of each paragraph. Does the essay flow well in terms of the linking of points and ideas within paragraphs and between paragraphs? Give examples of places where the linking is good. If there are occasions when the linking is inadequate or inappropriate, suggest improvements.

Target reader
Do you feel that someone reading this essay would be clear throughout it what the writer is describing and their views on it? If so, summarize the essay briefly. If not, say what you feel is unclear in it.

Now check your assessment of this sample answer.

PART TWO

*Write an answer to **one** of the questions **2–5** in this part. Write your answer in **300–350** words in an appropriate style. Write clearly in **pen**, not pencil. You may make alterations, but make sure your work is easy to read.*

2 You work for a local newspaper, which is considering launching a weekly magazine supplement that would be included in the newspaper. You have been asked to conduct a survey of local people to find out what the supplement should contain. Write a report detailing the findings of the survey and what conclusions can be drawn from it.

Write your **report**.

3 A letter from a reader has recently been published in a newspaper you read, complaining that the newspaper is always full of bad news and never highlights the positive aspects of life. The newspaper has invited readers to write an article entitled *Reasons To Be Cheerful*. Write an article under that title, listing what you believe to be the good things in life, both for you personally and for people in general and giving your reasons for choosing them.

Write your **article**.

4 You have recently visited a city or area as a tourist and found that there are a number of aspects of your visit which you wish to comment on. Write a letter to the head of the tourist office for that area, describing the positive and/or negative aspects of your visit and making any suggestions you feel appropriate.

Write your **letter**. Do not write any postal addresses.

5 Set book questions – a choice from **(a)**, **(b)** and **(c)**.
In the exam you may choose to answer a question on one of the three set books.

Before you write your answer, go on to pages 148–150.

PART TWO

For information on What's Tested and Tips see page 63.

To plan your answer for question 2 in Part Two, complete the following notes.

1 Note down as briefly as possible the **topic** of your report.

....

2 List as briefly as possible the following:
- the **main points** in the question which you will have to cover in your report
- the **comments and opinions** you intend to give with regard to those points
- any **examples** you wish to give in support of your comments/opinions

Main point	Comments/Opinions	Examples
Main point	**Comments/Opinions**	**Examples**
Main point	**Comments/Opinions**	**Examples**

3 List briefly any additional points you wish to make, which are not mentioned in the question but which you think are relevant to the topic. You may not wish to include any additional points.

Additional point	Comments/Opinions	Examples
Additional point	**Comments/Opinions**	**Examples**

4 Now note briefly how your report will be organized by deciding what each part of it will contain. You may not wish to have as many paragraphs as are listed below.

Opening
Section 1
Section 2
Section 3

Section 4
Section 5
Section 6
Ending

5 Now use these notes to write your report.

When you have written your answer, assess it in accordance with the task-specific mark scheme.

6 Now read through this sample answer for question 2 in Part Two and answer the questions that follow it.

REPORT – WEEKLY MAGAZINE SUPPLEMENT

Research

I prepared a short questionnaire, in which people were asked whether they would be interested in reading a weekly magazine supplement and, if so, what they thought it should include. I listed various categories for sections and articles, and included 'other' for suggestions people might have that I hadn't included. I then spent a week asking people in the streets in the city centre for their views and completing the questionnaires with them. I got the views of 220 people of all ages.

Findings

In general, the people I spoke to were keen on the idea of the supplement, although 15 people said they couldn't see the point and wouldn't have enough time to read one. The idea of a sports section was the most popular, and about 60% of the people I spoke to thought this should have articles about the local clubs and interviews with the players – at the moment, the newspaper only has short match reports. Another popular idea was to have a section for hobbies, with details of clubs that people can join to do them – about 50% liked that idea. Also, about 40% said they would like longer reviews of films, plays and books because the ones in the paper are usually very short. Six people suggested that it would be a good idea to have a restaurant review column, which was not included in my questionnaire. The idea of having a weekly recipe was also quite popular. The most unpopular idea was to include articles about local politics – 80% of the people I spoke to said they didn't want this – and about 70% said they didn't want articles on environmental issues or financial matters.

Conclusions

It would appear that there is enough enthusiasm for the supplement to make it worth doing. However, my survey indicates that people would prefer it to be entertaining and enjoyable rather than having anything serious in it. It should concentrate on people's interests rather than more serious issues and clearly sports, hobbies and reviews should be covered in it.

Content
Are all the main points mentioned in the question covered? Where are these points covered? If any are not covered, which are missing? Are any additional points included? If so, what are they, and are they relevant?

Range
Is there a wide range of vocabulary and grammatical structures? If so, give examples. If there are occasions when the vocabulary or grammar is too simple, suggest alternatives.

Accuracy
Are there any mistakes in the use of vocabulary or grammar? Correct any that you find.

Appropriacy of register and format
Are the style and tone of the report appropriate? How would you describe them? Why are they appropriate or inappropriate? Is the format suitable for a report of this kind? If so, why? If not, why not?

Organization and cohesion
Is the report well-organized in terms of being divided into sections appropriately? Describe briefly the content of each section. Does the report flow well in terms of the linking of points and ideas within sections and between sections? Give examples of places where the linking is good. If there are occasions when the linking is inadequate or inappropriate, suggest improvements.

Target reader
Do you feel that someone reading this report would be clear throughout it what the writer is describing and what their views are? If so, summarize the report briefly. If not, say what you feel is unclear in it.

Now check your assessment of this sample answer.

PAPER 3 USE OF ENGLISH 1 hour 30 minutes

PART ONE

*For questions **1–15**, read the text below and think of the word which best fits each space. Use only **one** word in each space. There is an example at the beginning **(0)**. In the exam you will mark your answers on a separate answer sheet.*

Example:

0	*of*

The Slow Arrival of the Wheel

It is nearly impossible in our post-industrial society to conceive **(0)** ....*of*..... a world without wheels. From clocks to huge machinery and from cars to computer disks, **(1)** .... employs cogs, wheels or other types of cylindrical components that spin on an axis. **(2)** .... the wheel took a relatively long time to be invented and several civilizations reached a relatively high level of technological sophistication **(3)** .... it. The most likely explanation is **(4)** .... neither terrain nor climate suited the wheel. Until 10,000 BC, much of the world was **(5)** .... the grip of the last vestiges of the Ice Age. **(6)** .... was not under ice sheet was covered by desert, jungle or bog – conditions obviously unsuited for something like the wheel.

Most experts agree that the wheel evolved **(7)** .... the fact that Neolithic man was familiar with moving heavy objects **(8)** .... putting a roller, such as a tree trunk, under the load. **(9)** .... techniques were used to move the huge stone blocks to build the pyramids around 2980 BC and probably Stonehenge, which dates **(10)** .... to around 2000 BC. **(11)** .... technique for moving large, heavy objects was to place them on sledges and to put the sledges on rollers. In time, it is likely that the sledge wore grooves into the rollers **(12)** .... the result that ancient man had a ratio – a small turn of the inner edge of the worn groove generated a larger turn of the outer edge of the roller. The next **(13)** .... final step in the invention of the wheel was to reduce the weight of the roller by cutting away the wood between the grooves, in **(14)** .... way creating an axle with a wheel at each end. At last man **(15)** .... better indulge his passions for travel, speed and movement.

Now check your answers to Part One of the test.

PART TWO

*For questions **16–25**, read the text below. Use the word given in **capitals** at the end of some of the lines to form a word that fits in the space in the same line. There is an example at the beginning **(0)**. In the exam you will mark your answers on a separate answer sheet.*

Example:

0	*headlines*

The Word 'Bogus'

For years 'bogus' was a word the British read in newspaper **(0)** .....*headlines*.........	**LINE**
but tended not to say. Its popularity among the teenagers of America changed that,	
although they didn't use it with its original meaning. It came from the Wild West.	
Its first appearance in print, in 1827, was in the *Telegraph* of Painesville, Ohio,	
where it meant a machine for making **(16)** .... of coins.	**FORGE**
Soon, those 'boguses' were turning out 'bogus money' and the word had	
(17) .... a change from noun to adjective. By the end of the	**GO**
19th century, it was well-established in Britain, applied to anything false,	
spurious or intentionally **(18)** .... But the computer scientists of 1960s	**LEAD**
America, to whom we owe so much **(19)** .... innovation, redefined	**LANGUAGE**
it to mean 'non-functional', 'useless', or 'unbelievable', especially in relation	
to calculations and engineering ideas. This was followed by its	
(20) .... among Princeton and Yale graduates in the East Coast	**EMERGE**
computer community. But it was the **(21)** .... of the word by American	**ADOPT**
teenagers generally, who used it to mean simply 'bad', that led to it being	
widely used by their counterparts in Britain.	
(22) .... , 'bogus' is one of only about 1,300 English words for which	**INTEREST**
no sensible origin has emerged. The 1827 'bogus' machine seems to have been	
named by an **(23)** .... present at the time of its capture by police.	**LOOK**
But why that word? The *Oxford English Dictionary* suggests a connection	
with a New England word, 'tantrobogus', meaning the devil. A rival US account	
sees it as a **(24)** .... of the name of a forger, called Borghese or	**CORRUPT**
Borges. **(25)** .... , it has been connected with the French word 'bagasse',	**ELSE**
meaning the refuse from sugar-cane production.	

Now check your answers to Part Two of the test.

PART THREE

*For questions **26–31**, think of **one** word only which can be used appropriately in all three sentences. There is an example at the beginning **(0)**. In the exam you will write only the missing word on a separate answer sheet.*

***Example*:**

0 You can stay with us if you like, we've got a .... room in our house.

It's very difficult to get .... parts for machines as old as this, so it's hard to get them repaired if they break down.

I like my job but the hours are long so it doesn't allow me much .... time.

0	*spare*

26 From her description of events, it was hard to get a clear mental .... of exactly what happened.

As regards the economic situation, the overall .... looks much the same as it did six months ago.

For some reason, we never get a very good .... on this channel on our TV.

27 I was feeling a bit .... because I'd had a late night and I was beginning to get the flu.

I know you can't give me the exact figure but could you give me a .... idea of what it might cost?

The sea was very .... and I began to feel ill half-way across.

28 I know you're very upset now but I'm sure the feeling will .... soon.

His comment was so rude that I couldn't let it .... without telling him that I thought he shouldn't have said it.

It was so hot in that room that I felt I might .... out at any moment.

29 When all the facts came to .... , there was such a scandal that he was forced to resign.

We built a huge bonfire in the garden out of all our rubbish and set .... to it.

It has been decided that, in the .... of all the criticism it has received, the scheme will be abandoned.

30 The situation was already bad but your interference has made it worse ....

I feel a bit guilty about what happened; .... , there's nothing I could have done to prevent it so I know I shouldn't feel bad.

I haven't officially signed any agreement so I can .... change my mind if I want to.

31 After the concert, all the equipment was .... away and transported in a convoy of lorries to the next venue.

George .... in his job and went travelling around the world for a year.

The club was absolutely .... and there was no room at all on the dance floor.

Now check your answers to Part Three of the test.

PART FOUR

*For questions **32–39**, complete the second sentence so that it has a similar meaning to the first sentence, using the word given. **Do not change the word given.** You must use between **three** and **eight** words, including the word given. There is an example at the beginning **(0)**.*

Example:

0 Robert was offended when he was left out of the team.
exception
Robert .... left out of the team.

The gap can be filled by the words 'took exception to being', so you write:

0	*took exception to being*

In the exam you will mark only the missing words on a separate answer sheet.

32 The film was so controversial that it was banned in several parts of the world.
caused
Such was .... the film that it was banned in several parts of the world.

33 He had no idea what was going to happen to him when he walked into that room.
store
Little .... him when he walked into that room.

34 You shouldn't let trivial matters worry you so much.
prey
You shouldn't let trivial matters .... extent.

35 He became famous but it cost him his privacy.
expense
His rise .... of his privacy.

36 I helped Ray, with the result that his business became successful.
favour
I .... which his business became successful.

37 I had to wait for the manager for almost an hour before he would see me.
best
The manager kept .... an hour before he would see me.

38 I'll have to consider working abroad if an opportunity doesn't arise here soon.
near
Unless an opportunity presents .... future, I'll have to consider working abroad.

39 I wanted to make sure that all my good work wasn't wasted in that way.
waste
I wanted to prevent .... in that way.

Before you check your answers to Part Four of the test, go on to pages 155–156.

WHAT'S TESTED

Part Four of the Use of English Paper focuses on a mixture of grammar and vocabulary. The answer you write is divided into two distinct parts, each of which is worth one mark. This means that there are really two 'pieces of language' to produce for each answer. In any question, either of the 'pieces' may involve:

- the transformation of one grammatical structure into another, or
- the production of a lexical phrase, such as a fixed phrase, an idiom, a collocation, a phrasal verb, a linking phrase or a phrase with the correct complementation (for explanations of these terms, see the Further Practice & Guidance pages for Paper 1, Part One on page 10), or
- changing a word from one part of speech to another, such as forming a noun from a given adjective.

TIPS

- Remember that you cannot change the form of the word given to you for inclusion in your answer.
- Remember not to exceed the limit of eight words in your answer, or to use fewer than three.
- Remember to copy correctly any words in the sentence you are given which do not change in the answer – carelessness of that kind can unnecessarily cost you a mark.
- Always attempt a complete answer to each question – even if you are unsure that your whole answer is correct, it is possible that one of the two parts will be.
- Always read the words on both sides of the gap carefully, as these provide you with vital information about the nature of the correct answer.

1 *Look at each of the questions in the test again and decide which of the choices **a–e** in each exercise can correctly fill the first part (1) and then the second part (2) of the gap. More than one of the choices may be correct in each case.*

2 *When you have done these exercises, you may wish to change some of your answers to the test.*

Question 32

1	2
a caused	**a** the controversy by
b there caused a	**b** controversy caused by
c the	**c** controversially of
d it caused to be	**d** controversial for
e a	**e** controversy by

Question 33

1	2
a he knew	**a** what lay in store for
b did he know	**b** what was the store for
c knew he	**c** what set store by
d idea he had	**d** what the store was for
e did he realize	**e** what was in store for

Question 34

1	2
a prey on your mind	**a** to such an
b be prey to you	**b** to great
c cause you prey	**c** by that
d fall prey to you	**d** at so great an
e prey on you	**e** to such a great

Question 35

1	2
a up in fame	**a** came at the expense
b up to getting fame	**b** cost an expense
c to the fame	**c** meant the expense
d to fame	**d** led to expense
e in fame	**e** was at the expense

Question 36

1	2
a did Ray a favour,	**a** the result of
b was in Ray's favour,	**b** the result being
c found favour with Ray,	**c** as a result of
d made a favour to Ray,	**d** resulting in
e did a favour for Ray,	**e** with the result

Question 37

1	2
a me that I wait	**a** to the best of
b the wait on	**b** for at best
c me waiting	**c** at the best of times of
d me on waiting	**d** with the best of
e up my waiting	**e** for the best part of

Question 38

1	2
a to me	**a** for any near
b itself	**b** to the near
c me with	**c** in the near
d for me	**d** as my near
e itself to me	**e** within the near

Question 39

1	2
a that all my good work	**a** was a waste
b getting all my good work	**b** going to waste
c all my good work	**c** to waste
d from all my good work	**d** from being waste
e it that all my good work	**e** laying waste

Now check your answers to these exercises and to Part Four of the test.

PART FIVE

*For questions **40–44**, read the following texts on designers. For questions **40–43**, answer with a word or short phrase. You do not need to write complete sentences. For question **44**, write a summary according to the instructions given. In the exam you will mark your answers on a separate answer sheet.*

Designers do not manufacture things. All good designers ask questions of their client and spend time helping the client to clarify what he or she really wants. If the product is to be made to the designer's specifications, then the designer must ensure that the factory has the tools and the intelligence and that each element specified is practicable.
5 On complex jobs several product engineers will be involved, today with computer-aided software packages, to help to realize a design precisely. The greatest difference between the designer and the single independent craftsperson is that the craftsperson does not have the problem of communicating his or her intentions to others for translation into objects. The designer, however, must make his or her intentions explicit –
10 communication is at the heart of design.

Since the early 1950s, the activity of designing has been the subject of systematic and scientific analysis, it has been codified into set procedures, and it has become institutionalized by manufacturing corporations as part of the overall identity of the company. Designing the way a company looks and presents itself, and giving a 'family'
15 look to the design of the company's products, is an intricate and serious business. Designers visualize a company's ideology and their visualizations communicate that ideology to the world.

But design has not been thoroughly institutionalized. Design has also been claimed as art. Or, as Ettore Sottsass, a designer of enormous influence, once said: 'To me
20 design is a way of building up a possible figurative utopia or metaphor about life. Certainly to me design is not restricted to the necessity of giving form to a more or less stupid product for a more or less sophisticated industry.'

40 Explain in your own words exactly how design has become 'institutionalized' (line 13) since the 1950s.

....

....

41 In your own words, explain what points are made about design in the quote from Ettore Sottsass.

....

....

What is the proper role of a designer? Some have suggested that designers differ from engineers in that an engineer, although he or she might proceed intuitively, prefers to test and test, whereas a designer is entirely happy with intuitive judgments. But, unlike an engineer, a designer is not responsible for the structural failure of the product. This is not to imply that only engineers have responsibility for malfunction. Designers have a share of responsibility, especially in the design of the 'human/machine interface' – can this machine be operated safely at all times, are the switches, dials, levers or handles in the right place for a human to use effortlessly? The disciplines of ergonomics and product semantics are the disciplines of the designer's responsibility to the user.

The design-to-manufacture-to-sales-to-user process is a continuum. Between 'a designer' and 'a production line' there are many interpreters. These individuals (and their computers), together with other specialists such as marketing experts, exist to get an idea into reality and also to filter out as many uncertainties as possible before a design goes into production. Each person contributes to a design and although a designer may provide an important stylistic signature it is important not to confuse the idea of 'the designer' with that of 'the fine artist'.

Many modern designs, especially if we consider domestic consumer goods, office equipment, power tools, automobiles and aircraft, are *not* the fruits of one individual's mind, even if it can be beneficial from a marketing point of view to play up a single designer's name as a signature that gives a product a provenance in the same way that a painter signs his or her canvas. In relatively simple, fabricated, non-mechanical objects, such as printed textiles or tableware, or furniture, a single designer can claim responsibility for the design of the whole product. However, even here it is possible that others will interpret the designer's design so that it can be manufactured more easily.

42 Explain two ways in which the role of a designer differs from that of an engineer.

....

....

43 Why might a designer's name be highlighted with regard to a particular product?

....

....

44 In a paragraph of between **50 and 70** words, summarize **in your own words as far as possible** what is said in the two texts to be the role played by designers in the creation of products.

Before you check your answers to Part Five of the test, go on to page 159.

Sample Summary

Look at this sample summary and answer the questions that follow it.

> A designer is responsible for giving a practicable and pleasant look to a product of everyday use with regard to the will of the client and the given possibilities for production. He differs from a fine artist in that his idea of a design can never be final, for function has to be considered and it has to be made to work. This is done by an engineer, the designer only has to prove that it could work.

1 Is anything irrelevant included or anything relevant not included?
2 Are there any language mistakes? Correct any that you find.
3 Is the summary well-organized and does it make sense throughout?
4 Have any parts of the texts simply been copied in the summary? If so, where?
5 Is the summary within the specified word limit?

Now look again at your summary and decide whether you wish to change anything.

Then check your marks for your summary and read the assessment of this sample summary.

PAPER 4 LISTENING approximately 40 minutes

PART ONE

*You will hear four different extracts. For questions **1–8**, choose the answer (**A**, **B** or **C**) which fits best according to what you hear. There are two questions for each extract. In the exam you will hear each extract twice.*

Extract One

You hear a psychologist talking about confidence.

1 What does the speaker say about the word 'confidence'?

A Most dictionary definitions of it are inaccurate.

B It means a great deal more than simply 'self-assurance'.

1

C It is a hard word to define precisely.

2 What does the speaker say about having confidence?

A There is no one who doesn't wish to have it.

B It frequently changes into feeling superior.

2

C Some people are incapable of it.

Extract Two

You hear a political cartoonist talking about his work.

3 The speaker says that political cartoons are not 'rapier thrusts' because

A it is understood that they are fundamentally jokes.

B their power derives from a range of different aspects.

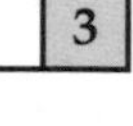

C they have a variety of different aims.

4 What does the speaker say about good caricatures?

A It is not possible for them to be subtle.

B They can make politicians change the way they behave.

4

C Politicians should be pleased when they are the subjects of them.

Extract Three

You hear a critic talking about a new book.

5 The speaker says that Goldman's latest book contains

A views even more negative than those in his previous book.

B confusing comments on actors and directors.

C criticism that may be unnecessarily harsh.

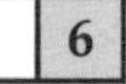

6 The speaker believes that Goldman

A exaggerates the difficulties of his occupation.

B has an unfavourable opinion of his own occupation.

C is unaware of how much his work is admired.

Extract Four

You hear a musician talking about American music.

7 What does the speaker say about the James Brown records he mentions?

A They conveyed a sense of joy.

B They were surprise hits.

C They were totally unlike Brown's other records.

8 The speaker says that people growing up in Britain in the 1960s

A had only a limited view of what America was like.

B had the same view of America as Americans did.

C felt that American music was more varied than British music.

Stop the recording when you hear 'That's the end of Part One'.

Now check your answers to Part One of the test.

PART TWO

*You will hear part of a radio programme about toys, in which the development of a famous toy called Meccano is described. For questions **9–17**, complete the sentences with a word or short phrase. In the exam you will hear the piece twice.*

Frank Hornby worked for a [9].

He was inspired by a book called [10].

The [11] that he invented did not work properly.

He started to consider the idea of [12] parts.

He decided that the parts would need to have a [13] in them.

The first parts he made were from a big [14].

The first object that was built with the new system was a [15].

The first name given to the new toy was [16].

Each Meccano set could be made bigger with the use of an [17].

Stop the recording when you hear 'That's the end of Part Two'.

Now check your answers to Part Two of the test.

PART THREE

*You will hear an interview with someone whose work is concerned with the design and marketing of products. For questions **18–22**, choose the answer (**A**, **B**, **C** or **D**) which fits best according to what you hear. In the exam you will hear the piece twice.*

18 David says that the session he has just conducted

A was longer than most sessions he conducts.

B illustrates his own beliefs about focus groups.

C is an example of a new approach to visual planning.

D concentrated as much on positive as on negative attitudes to cleaning.

[ ] 18

19 What did David know about cleaning products before the session?

A Some people could not make up their minds which ones to buy.

B Manufacturers were concerned about falling sales in them.

C Some of them looked too dull to appeal to shoppers.

D People felt that false claims were made about them.

[ ] 19

20 One of the comments made during the session referred to

A regarding the choice of a cleaning product as unimportant.

B cleaning products all looking the same.

C the deliberate misleading of shoppers.

D buying a cleaning product because it is familiar.

[ ] 20

21 David says that what the women produced when they were split into groups

A did not focus on what cleaning products actually do.

B presented contrasting images.

C was not what they had expected to produce.

D was similar to the presentation of other kinds of product.

[ ] 21

22 David says that he has concluded from the session that

A his firm's methods will need to change slightly.

B he was right to question a certain assumption.

C cleaning products do not fit into a general pattern.

D what he had previously thought was not entirely correct.

[ ] 22

Stop the recording when you hear 'That's the end of Part Three'.

Now check your answers to Part Three of the test.

PART FOUR

You will hear an artist, Karen, and a police officer, Graham, talking about attitudes towards authority. For questions **23–28**, *decide whether the opinions are expressed by only one of the speakers, or whether the speakers agree.*

Write **K** *for Karen,*
G *for Graham,*
or **B** *for Both, where they agree.*

In the exam you will hear the piece twice.

23 Being subjected to strict authority can make you feel better about yourself. [ ] **23**

24 Rebelling against authority is easier than being in authority. [ ] **24**

25 Some people are forced into a certain kind of behaviour. [ ] **25**

26 Extreme behaviour can cause problems for others. [ ] **26**

27 There is a limit to the extent to which people in authority should be influenced by others. [ ] **27**

28 People can be persuaded to accept things they are against. [ ] **28**

Stop the recording when you hear 'That's the end of Part Four'.

In the exam you will have five minutes at the end of the test to copy your answers onto a separate answer sheet.

Before you check your answers to Part Four of the test, go on to pages 165–166.

WHAT'S TESTED

Part Four of the Listening Paper requires you to identify who said what. Two speakers discuss a topic and give their opinions on it, and you have to decide whether only one of them expresses a particular view or both of them do.

TIPS

- The questions follow the order of what is said in the piece, with each one focusing on each succeeding point discussed by the speakers. However, be aware that questions do not necessarily focus on only one exchange of single speeches by each of the speakers – they may continue to talk about the relevant point after the first thing they say about it. For this reason, don't rush into answering the question as soon as they have both said something about that point – one or both of them may go on to say something else, with the result that the answer becomes 'Both' instead of just one of them.
- It may be that an answer is 'Both' and not only one of them as a result of one of the speakers saying only a short phrase or sentence that expresses a view, rather than a longer speech.
- A view may be strongly implied rather than directly stated.
- Where one of the speakers does not express the relevant view, that speaker may not directly disagree with it; they simply may not express actual agreement.
- Use the 30 second pause before the piece to look carefully at the questions so that you know what views you are listening for. Pay attention to the rubric, too – it will tell you exactly what the two people will be discussing.
- Use the second listening to confirm answers you gave on the first listening and to give any answers you were unable to do the first time.

Listen again to Part Four of the test and do the exercises below. They will help you to answer questions you were unable to in the test or to confirm answers that you gave. In each exercise, tick one or more boxes for what each of the speakers says. Tick the box in the first column for what Karen says and tick the box in the second column for what Graham says.

Question 23 *Stop the recording when Graham says 'I felt more capable of shining'.*

		K	G
a	I don't know how my attitude towards authority developed.		
b	Authority can be beneficial to you as an individual.		
c	I tend to have a negative view of authority.		
d	I have had positive experiences of authority.		
e	Authority can give you a sense of purpose.		
f	My attitude towards authority began in childhood.		

Question 24 *Stop the recording when Graham says 'a wholly good or wholly bad thing'.*

		K	G
a	It's wrong to see all authority figures as either good or bad.		
b	People who rebel are fundamentally selfish.		
c	There are practical reasons why authority figures exist.		
d	People in authority are subject to criticism.		
e	My personal circumstances have affected my attitude to authority.		
f	I have respect for those in authority.		

Question 25 *Stop the recording when Graham says 'is highly desirable'.* **K G**

a People should behave differently from normal in their free time.

b Some people react in totally opposite ways to authority.

c People's behaviour is dictated by the role they are playing.

d People think they are required to have a consistent attitude towards authority.

e People need to be responsible and rebellious at different times.

f My own attitude to authority is a healthy one.

Question 26 *Stop the recording when Graham says 'totally intransigent'.* **K G**

a Some people's desires either to conform or rebel are hidden.

b Some rebellious people behave in an unacceptable way.

c It's best to let contrasting aspects of your personality be revealed.

d Some people either always conform or always rebel.

e Some people's behaviour is too inflexible.

f Some people can both conform and rebel.

Question 27 *Stop the recording when Graham says 'whatever anyone says subsequently'.* **K G**

a Good authority figures consult others before taking action.

b People have to try hard to maintain a balance between obedience and disobedience.

c Good authority figures don't change their minds once they have made them up.

d People who have the right attitude towards authority as children make good authority figures later in life.

e Good authority figures tell others the reasons for actions they intend to take.

f Some people find it easier than others to combine obeying established rules and resisting authority.

Question 28 *Stop the recording at the end of the conversation.* **K G**

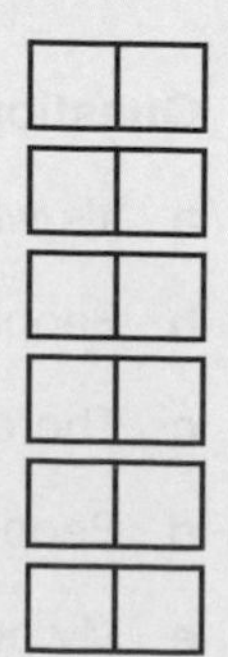

a Some authority figures behave as if they are more interested in the views of others than they really are.

b People like to feel that their views are taken into consideration by people in authority.

c Some authority figures are suspicious of people who disagree with them.

d I have personal experience of the right way for authority figures to behave.

e People can change their views on what people in authority have decided to do.

f Bad authority figures make illogical decisions.

Now check your answers to these exercises. When you have done so, listen again to Part Four of the test and decide whether you wish to change any of the answers you gave. Then check your answers to Part Four of the test.

PAPER 5 SPEAKING 19 minutes

PART ONE (3 MINUTES) GENERAL AND SOCIAL

Questions that may be addressed to either candidate.

- What kind of things do you do in your free time?
- How long have you been doing them?
- What is it about them that you enjoy particularly?
- Have you taken up any new activities in your free time recently? If so, why?
- Have you given up anything you used to do in your free time? If so, why?

- What countries or other parts of your country have you travelled to?
- What did you like most about these places?
- What did you like least about them?
- How did they compare with your expectations of them?
- Name one place you would not like to go to. What are your impressions of it?

PART TWO (4 MINUTES) HISTORY

For both candidates.

Choose two of the pictures on page 176 and describe what is happening in each of them.
(1 minute)

Now look at all of the pictures and answer one of these questions.
Which of these periods would you most and least like to have lived in? Give your reasons in each case.
If you had to choose another picture that showed a historical period that you would like to have lived in, what would it look like?
(3 minutes)

PART THREE (12 MINUTES) FASHION AND YOUTH

In phase one of Part Three each candidate takes a long turn (2 minutes), followed by a brief response from the other candidate.

Prompt Card (a) *(Given to Candidate A, and a copy to Candidate B)*

Why do so many people follow fashion?
- need to feel up to date
- commercial pressures
- how you look matters/has always mattered

One of the following questions for Candidate B (1 minute):

- What do you think?
- Is there anything you would like to add?
- Is there anything you don't agree with?
- How does this differ from your experience?

One of the following questions for both candidates (1 minute):
- Describe a fashion in clothes that you particularly like or liked.
- Describe a fashion in clothes that you particularly dislike or disliked.
- To what extent do you and your friends follow fashion?

Prompt Card (b) *(Given to Candidate B, and a copy to Candidate A)*

Is there too much emphasis on youth in modern life?
- the media/films/music
- what older people have to offer
- attitude in society to young and older people

One of the following questions for Candidate A (1 minute):

- What do you think?
- Is there anything you would like to add?
- Is there anything you don't agree with?
- How does this differ from your experience?

One of the following questions for both candidates (1 minute):
- Do people change as they get older and if so, in what ways?
- How much freedom do young people have in your society?
- What is the situation regarding the employment of older people in your society?

In phase two of Part Three there is a discussion on the general topic (4 minutes).

Possible general questions for both candidates on the topic of fashion and youth:

- How frequently do fashions in music change in your society?
- Is anything that was fashionable in the past now fashionable with a different generation in your society?
- Is it possible for older people to be fashionable?
- What, if any, restrictions do you think there should be on young people?
- Is there anything that is fashionable now that you think you will consider ridiculous when you look back on it when you're older?
- Describe an elderly person who you particularly admire.

Describing Personality

In the Speaking Paper, you may need to talk about your own or other people's personalities. To check or add to your vocabulary on this subject, look at the adjectives below and group them together under the headings given. Then note down the precise meaning of each one (you may need to consult a dictionary) and describe people you think they apply to, giving examples of their behaviour which justify your description of them.

considerate	tenacious	smug	calculating	condescending
mean	patronizing	big-headed	ignorant	affable
crafty	resolute	indulgent	lenient	tireless
ruthless	two-faced	persistent	pig-headed	surly
pompous	vindictive	snobbish	moody	assertive
compassionate	obstinate	aloof	tactful	mild-mannered
cunning	warm	pushy	devious	courteous
single-minded	spiteful	scheming	stuck-up	strong-willed
arrogant	intransigent	genial	supercilious	decent
hypocritical	conceited	petulant	narrow-minded	generous

Kind/Pleasant	Feeling Superior	Unkind/Unpleasant	Determined	Dishonest

Now check your answers to this exercise.

Part Three: Topic Vocabulary

1 In Part Three of this test, you are required to talk about the topic of fashion and youth. To check or add to your vocabulary on this subject, complete the words and phrases below.

Fashions/Fashionable	Unfashionable
_ _ fashion	_ _ _ _ _ fashion
a cr_ _ _	d _ _ _ _
a f _ _	outm _ _ _ _
all the r _ _ _	old h _ _
in v _ _ _ _	ob _ _ _ _ _
tr _ _ _ _	_ _ _ _ _ _ the times
cont _ _ _ _ _ _ _ _	anti _ _ _ _ _
_ _ _ _ _ setting	outd _ _ _ _

2 Now complete the words and phrases on the left so that they match the definitions on the right.

the y _ _ _ _	young people
a y _ _ _ _	a young person
a y _ _ _ _ _ _ _ _	a young person
y _ _ _ _ _ _ _	like young people
ch _ _ _ _ _ _	wrongly behaving like a child
imm _ _ _ _ _	more like a child than is acceptable
imm _ _ _ _ _ _ _ _	behaviour that is like a child's
j _ _ _ _ _ _ _	behaving like a foolish child
inf _ _ _ _ _ _	behaving like a small child
ad _ _ _ _ _ _ _ _	young person becoming an adult
ad _ _ _ _ _ _ _ _ _	period of becoming an adult
a k _ _	a child
a l _ _	a young boy
a y _ _	a badly behaved young man
a l _ _ _	a badly behaved young man
a h _ _ _ _ _ _ _	a violent young man

grow _ _	become an adult or start behaving like one
g _ _ _ _ _ _	like an adult
a g _ _ _ _ _ _	an adult
m _ _ _ _ _	like an adult
m _ _ _ _ _ _ _	behaviour like an adult's
getting _ _	becoming old
m _ _ _ _ _ a _ _ _	no longer young but not yet old
over the h _ _ _	too old to be at your best any longer
p _ _ _ it	too old to be at your best any longer
in your d _ _ _ _ _	very old and weak
an _ _ _ _ _	very old
s _ _ _ _ _	very old and suffering from mental weakness
s _ _ _ _ _ c _ _ _ _ _ _	an old or retired person
o _ _ a _ _	the later part of life
an o _ _ a _ _ p _ _ _ _ _ _ _ _	an old and retired person
e _ _ _ _ _ _	old (of people)
the e _ _ _ _ _ _	old people

Now check your answers to these exercises.

PAPER 5 SPEAKING

PART TWO (4 MINUTES)

Test 1: Careers

A

B

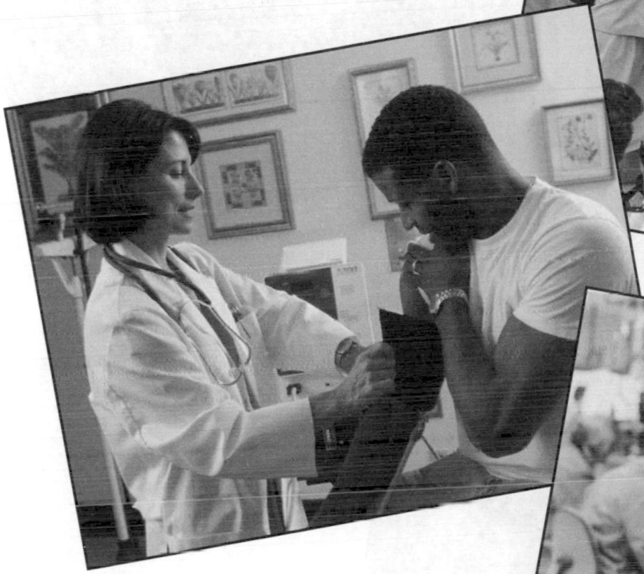

C

D

PAPER 5 SPEAKING

PART TWO (4 MINUTES)

Test 2: Good and Bad Moods

A

B

C

D

E

PAPER 5 SPEAKING

PART TWO (4 MINUTES)

Test 3: Health and Exercise

D

E

PAPER 5 SPEAKING

PART TWO (4 MINUTES)

Test 4: History

A

B

C

KEY AND EXPLANATION

TEST ONE

p8–13 PAPER 1 PART ONE

FURTHER PRACTICE AND GUIDANCE (p10–13)

For explanations, see the explanations to the questions in the test, which follow.

1 A given B taken
C fallen D run

2 A gush B expedite
C dash D inundate

3 A shortcoming B premium
C rarity D dearth

4 A yardstick B norm
C average D par

5 A sprayed B littered
C messed D scattered

6 A spurring B eliciting
C inciting D luring

7 A distant B faint
C secluded D far-away

8 A quick B impulsive
C abrupt D prompt

9 A like B type
C own D self

10 A weighed up B made up for
C set against D settled up with

11 A advantageous B indulgent
C privileged D gainful

12 A sorely B utterly
C fully D appreciably

13 A in that case B still
C indeed D to that end

14 A wasting B failing
C losing D defeating

15 A excess B lengths
C bounds D utmost

16 A undergone B sustained
C afflicted D grieved

17 A good B avail
C interest D behalf

18 A as B just
C so D except

p8–9 PAPER 1 PART ONE (TEST)

Note: all explanations in this part refer to the meaning or use of each option most closely related to the question, not necessarily to the only meaning or use of each option.

One mark per question (Total: 18)

Living in Flats in Britain

1 **C:** If you **take to something/doing something**, you start liking it or doing it habitually. The writer is saying that living in flats has never been as common or popular in Britain as in other European countries.
A: If you *fall to doing something* or *fall into the habit of doing something*, you begin doing something that is considered wrong or unpleasant for a period of time.
B: If you *run to someone*, you go to them in the hope that they will solve your problems without trying to solve them yourself. If *you can run to something*, you can afford to pay for it.
D: If *you are given to something/doing something*, you tend to do or experience something which is considered strange or unwise.
All the options complete phrasal verbs connected with the idea of habits, but only C fits the context as well as being grammatically correct (D might fit but would have to be passive).

2 **A:** If you **dash** somewhere, you go there very quickly because you are in a hurry. The writer is saying that people farming in areas away from cities in Continental Europe would hurry into the walls of the cities if an enemy was invading.
B: If you *expedite something*, particularly a process, you make it happen more quickly by taking certain action.
C: If liquids *gush*, they flow out of something in very large quantities.
D: If people *inundate* other people or places, they make contact with them in large numbers or send them large numbers of things, with the result that these people have difficulty in dealing with them all.
All the options relate to the speed or extent of movement or action, but only A fits the precise meaning in the context.

3 **D:** If something is **at a premium**, it is considered extremely valuable because it is in short supply and hard to obtain. The writer is saying that in Continental European cities, homes were built on top of each other because there wasn't much available space within the city walls.
A: If something is *a rarity*, it is very unusual because it rarely happens or exists.
B: *A shortcoming* is a fault in or negative aspect of someone's character, or a defect in something.
C: If there is *a dearth of* something, there is a lack or shortage of something and more of it is desirable.
All the options are related to a lack of something but only D completes the required fixed phrase.

4 **B:** If something is **the norm**, it is the normal situation or what normally happens. The writer is saying that most people lived in flats in cities such as Paris at that time.
A: If something is *average*, it is regarded as typical or normal statistically.
C: If something is *par for the course*, it is what normally happens and therefore it is what can be expected to happen.
D: *A yardstick* is a standard according to which things are measured or assessed in terms of success or quality.
All the options are connected with the idea of what is considered normal, but only B fits the precise meaning in the context.

5 **B:** If things are **scattered** somewhere, they are spread around various parts of an area. The writer is saying that, because Britain was seldom invaded, its people could live in places far apart from each other, rather than close together so that they could protect themselves from invaders.
A: If something gets *messed up*, it is caused to become disorganized or untidy or to go wrong.

C: If a place is *littered with* something, it is untidy because something has been left all over it.
D: If you get *sprayed with* something, you get hit by drops of a liquid that have burst out of something, often accidentally.
All the options relate to things being in different places or being untidy but only B fits the precise meaning in the context.

6 **A:** If something **lures you somewhere/into doing something**, it strongly tempts or attracts you to go somewhere or to do something. The writer is saying that people were attracted away from working on the land and went to work in factories in towns as a result of the industrial revolution.
B: If something *elicits* something such as a reply, it causes a reply to be given.
C: If something *spurs someone on/on to something*, it encourages or inspires them.
D: If something *incites something/someone to do something*, it causes something aggressive or causes them to do something aggressive.
All the options are related to the idea of encouraging or persuading people to do something, but only A fits the precise meaning in the context.

Meeting Marvin Gaye

7 **A:** If someone is **distant**, they are not friendly or communicative. The writer is saying that although he found it exciting to work with Ray Charles, he did not find him a very friendly person.
B: If something is *faint*, it is not clear or detailed.
C: If something is *secluded*, it is away from other people and very private.
D: A *far-away* place is physically a long distance away.
All the options are connected with the idea of distance or being apart from others, but only A can be used to describe a person's personality.

8 **D:** If you are **quick to do something**, you do it quickly, especially in response to something. The writer is saying that Marvin Gaye had a good sense of humour and laughed a lot.
A: If you are *prompt in doing something*, you do something that you are supposed to do without delay.
B: If you are *impulsive* or do something that is *impulsive*, you act or form a judgment suddenly or because of a sudden desire, rather than thinking carefully first.
C: If someone is *abrupt*, they say things quickly and then say nothing more, in a way that is considered rude.
All the options refer to speed, but only D is both appropriate in the context and fits grammatically (A might fit the meaning but it does not fit grammatically).

9 **D:** If something has **something all of its own**, it has a quality that is unique to it. The writer is saying that Marvin Gaye spoke in an almost poetic way that was unique to him.
A: Someone or something *of a certain type* belongs to a certain category and is typical of it.
B: A person's *self* is their normal personality and behaviour, what they are normally like.
C: *The like of something* is something similar to or comparable with it.
All the options refer to the nature of something, but only D completes the required fixed phrase.

10 **C:** If something **makes up for something**, it compensates for it so that something negative is balanced by something positive. The writer is saying that a positive aspect of Marvin Gaye's personality – his *disarming* (making people feel friendly towards him) *sincerity* – was much more important than an aspect of Marvin Gaye's personality he didn't like (his *affectations* – behaviour that is not natural and is intended to impress).
A: If you *set something against something else*, you judge something by comparing a positive aspect of it with a negative aspect or a negative aspect with a positive aspect.
B: If you *weigh something up*, you consider it carefully by looking at different aspects of it.
D: If you *settle up with someone*, you pay them the money that you owe them.
All the options are phrasal verbs connected with the idea of balancing things, but only C fits the meaning in the context.

11 **B:** If you feel **privileged**, you feel that something that has happened to you or been given to you is an honour and you are grateful for it and proud that you have been chosen for it. The writer is saying that he felt this way because he admired Marvin Gaye.
A: If something is *advantageous to you*, it benefits you or is useful to you.
C: If someone is *indulgent towards someone*, they have so much affection for them that they allow them to have or do anything they want.
D: If you find *gainful employment*, you do something which is profitable or earns you an acceptable amount of money.
All the options are connected with the idea of something benefiting someone, but only B can be used to describe a feeling.

12 **C: Utterly** means 'completely', 'totally' or 'absolutely' and can be used for emphasis with adjectives that convey both positive and negative ideas. The writer is saying that Marvin Gaye's work was done in a totally professional, highly efficient and highly organized way.
A: *Appreciably* means 'considerably' or 'much' and is used with comparative adjectives.
B: *Fully* means 'completely' or 'entirely', so that nothing could be added or so that the feeling described is as strong as it could be.
D: *Sorely* means 'very badly' or 'very much' and is used with this meaning in a few phrases such as *sorely missed, sorely tempted* and *sorely needed*.
All the options can be used with the meaning 'very' or 'very much', but only C can be used to form a correct collocation.

Sir John

13 **B: Indeed** means 'in fact', and is used for emphasizing the truth of something. The writer is saying that Sir John felt that it was not just easy to tell people he thought they were ridiculous, it seemed to him to be the natural thing for any logical person to do.
A: *In that case* means 'because that is the situation', and is used for introducing an alternative or suggested course of action as a result of that situation.
C: *To that end* means 'in order to achieve that'.
D: *Still* means 'even so', 'in spite of that', and is used for introducing a positive aspect after a negative one or a negative aspect after a positive one.
All the options are used for linking sentences or parts of sentences, but only B fits the context.

14 **A:** If you are **fighting a losing battle**, you are trying hard to achieve something which you are unlikely to achieve in the end. The writer is saying that Sir John was finding it impossible to get other people to have some *humility* (belief that you are no more important than anyone else).
B: If you have *failing health/eyesight*, your health or eyesight has become weak and is getting weaker.
C: If someone does something which *defeats the object*, it goes against what they are aiming to do themselves and makes it even harder for them to get what they want.
D: If you *waste your breath*, you tell people things which you think they should pay attention to but they take no notice of what you say.
All the options are related to the idea of failing to do something or losing in some way, but only A completes the required idiom.

15 D: If you **do your utmost to do something**, you try as hard as you can to do it. The writer is saying that Sir John's colleagues were all trying as hard as they could to make people have a higher opinion of themselves.
A: The *bounds of something* are the generally accepted limits of something, which should be kept to and not broken.
B: If you *do something to excess*, you do it more than you should or more than is considered acceptable.
C: If you *go to any/great lengths to do something*, you are willing to do anything / a great deal in order to achieve it.
All the options are connected with the idea of the limit or furthest extent of something, but only D completes the required fixed phrase.

16 A: If **someone/something is afflicted by something** or if **something afflicts someone/something**, they suffer as a result of it. The writer is saying that his colleagues all believed that everyone suffered from having a low opinion of themselves.
B: If *someone / something sustains something* bad, such as injury, defeat or damage, they suffer or experience it.
C: If *someone / something undergoes something*, they experience something unpleasant, such as an operation.
D: If something *grieves you*, it causes you to feel extreme unhappiness.
All the options are connected with the idea of suffering, but only A both fits the meaning in the context and is correct grammatically (B or C might fit but the verb would have to be active not passive).

17 C: If something is **for your own good**, it benefits you or is a good thing for you personally. The writer is saying that Sir John thought that the problem with people was that their opinion of themselves was too high, not too low.
A: If you do something *on someone's behalf* or *on behalf of someone*, you do it for them or instead of them because they are unable to do it themselves.
B: If you do something *to no avail*, you do it but it is not effective or successful and it does not have the desired result.
D: If something is *in your interest*, it benefits you or is of advantage to you.
All the options relate to something being to someone's advantage or not, but only C completes the required fixed phrase.

18 C: If something is **not so much** one thing **as** another, it is not really the first thing mentioned, it is really the second thing mentioned. The writer is saying that Sir John thought that professors shouldn't be trying to make people feel better about themselves, they should be trying to make sure they didn't have too high an opinion of themselves (in Greek mythology, Pandora's box was a box containing all the bad aspects of people, which Pandora opened).
A: If there is nothing you can do *except to do something*, the second thing is the only thing you can do.
B: *So much so that* ... means 'to such an extent that'.
D: *Just to do something* means 'simply or only to do it'.
All the options are used for linking phrases to express a particular meaning, but only C can be used to form a phrase with the correct meaning in the context.

p14–15 PAPER 1 PART TWO

Two marks per question (Total: 16)

Pennsylvania Station

19 C: The writer says that these buildings are *not the last, dying gasp* (literally, the final breath before dying) *of a debased* (having lost value or status) *tradition or a hangover* (something that is left after everything else connected with it has changed or disappeared) *from the 19th century*. By saying that they are not these things, he is implying that some people might think that they are. In fact, he says that the buildings did not follow the tradition of the 19th century because they were *an alternative to the eclecticism* (the use of a variety of styles rather than one single style) of that period. Instead, they were based on *a return to the strict rules of Classicism*. However, they were seen as *forward-looking* (modern and suitable for the future rather than belonging to the past). He is therefore saying that it would be wrong to think that the buildings were built in a style that was dying out when they were built, and implying that some people may think this was the case.
A: The writer does not say that they were criticized at all when they were built – they were seen as forward-looking and *a new style for the new century*. He does imply that criticizing them for being old-fashioned would have been unjustified, but he also implies that this didn't happen.
B: The writer says *Nowhere can that* (the new style) *be seen more clearly than in New York*, and in particular, he says, that style can be seen in the building of Pennsylvania Station. He describes New York as *an icon* (something or someone regarded as a symbol of a cultural phenomenon) *of 20th century Modernism*, which means that New York is full of Modernist buildings. However, in the second sentence, he says that some of the most impressive buildings of that period are not Modernist and he clearly includes Pennsylvania Station among these. He is therefore saying that Pennsylvania Station was different in style from other buildings in New York, many of which were Modernist, not implying that other buildings in New York were copied from and similar to it.
D: The writer says that the architects of these buildings wanted to find a style that differed from the style of their time – they wanted a *clean, rigorous* (in this context, simple and regular), *modern style* and that they found this style. Earlier, he says that such buildings are *impressive and interesting*, which shows that he likes them. He therefore implies that the architects succeeded in what they wanted to achieve in the design of these buildings.

20 D: The writer describes Pennsylvania Station as *vast* and his use of *entire* emphasizes that a building covering two blocks (in the US a 'block' is a section of a city consisting of a group of buildings with streets all around them) is very big. He also refers to the *dizzying* (causing you to feel that you cannot focus properly) *effect* created by the *towering* (very high) *steel columns* and the *acres* (an acre is a unit for measuring land; in this context it means 'large areas') *of curving glass*. All of this concerns the size and proportions of the building and of things in it.
A: The writer mentions steel and glass but this is not in order to emphasize the contrast between them, it is to refer to the extent to which they are used in the building.
B: The writer says that the building was *a masterpiece* (a brilliant piece of work) *of transport integration* (combining various different elements so that they work well together) and then describes how it was designed with regard to the various types of transport into and out of it. He also says that it was *at the cutting edge of modern transportation* (it was a very advanced form of it). He therefore emphasizes that it was an excellent building from the point of view of transport arrangements. However, although he says that it *has rarely been equalled* in terms of transport integration, which suggests that other places may have been influenced by it, his focus is on the station itself, not on its impact on transportation planning elsewhere.
C: The writer mentions people using the station and suggests that, since it was so well-planned, it was a good place from the point of view of passengers. However, he does not mention or emphasize their opinion of it.

Arrival in Cape Town

21 C: Adelaide felt *exuberance* (a lively, cheerful, excited feeling) when she saw Cape Town because it was *lush* (full of things growing healthily), nature there was *lavish* (widespread and rich in quality) to the extent that *waste became irrelevant* (there was so much that it didn't matter if some was wasted), and everything she saw that is listed in the third sentence made her feel that the place was *some delightful limbo* (in this context, a state that is so relaxed that no energy at all is spent) that was *well out of the way of reality* (apart from real life in a desirable way). For all these reasons, she clearly felt that it was a nice place to live in.
A: She had never seen or *encountered* (experienced) anywhere like Cape Town before but the writer does not say that she had had any ideas about it before she saw it.
B: Various colours are mentioned but she was struck by how attractive these colours were, not by any contrast between them.
D: Neatness was not one of the attractions of the place because flowers are described as *spilling over garden walls*, which suggests that they were allowed to grow over the edges of walls rather than being cut back so that everything would be neat and tidy.

22 A: One thing that was *astonishing* for Adelaide, because it differed from her normal life in England, was that she was able to *read and think in an idle* (lazy) and *desultory* (without any particular aim and without making much effort) *manner*. Usually, we are told, she was *physically exhausted* but now she was able to spend hours *strolling* (walking slowly and in a casual way, in no hurry to get anywhere in particular) on the deck of the ship.
B: She was clearly not happy with her life in England – leaving it had meant that her *spirits had risen* (she had become happier, more cheerful), her training there was *grim* (depressing) and she did not like her father's house. It is possible that being away from it enabled her to look at it objectively but we are not told that she did not already look at it objectively while she was there.
C: We learn that she was *physically exhausted* in England and that she was able to relax on the ship. However, it seems highly likely that she would have liked to be able to relax in England – being physically exhausted was clearly one of the aspects of her life in England that she was unhappy about.
D: She seems to have observed a very great deal as the ship approached Cape Town because a lot of things are described as being seen through her eyes. However, we are not told that being away from home has made her pay more attention to what can be seen or notice more – she may have been just as observant in England.

My London

23 B: The writer says that when he *first came to London*, he *moved about much more freely* than he does now. The reason for that is that he includes himself among people who *map cities by private benchmarks which are meaningful only to us* (think of the geography of cities in terms of reference points that are personal to them and which have no significance to anyone else). He explains that for him London is a smaller area within the *sprawl* (a.large area that has not been formally planned) that is officially Greater London and says *I hardly ever trespass beyond those limits* (I hardly ever go outside these personal boundaries; '*trespass*' literally means 'enter a place without authority or permission'). When he does so, he feels that he has gone into *a foreign territory, a landscape of hazard* (danger) *and rumour*. As a result, he prefers to drop in on (visit casually, especially without having previously arranged to do so) friends in Islington than to visit friends in Clapham, because, although Islington is further away from his home than Clapham, he considers Islington to be in his *own territory* and Clapham to be outside it. The point he is making, therefore, is that he doesn't travel as widely around London as when he first arrived there because he prefers to stay within the narrow area of it that he considers to be *my London*.
A: The writer says that Greater London is *shaped like a rugby ball*, whereas his London is a *concise* (small and neat) *kidney-shaped patch* (area) *within that space*. He therefore seems to have a clear picture of what these two areas look like on a map. In addition, he does not say that he tends to get lost in cities or that he fears he would get lost if he strayed outside the area he considers to be his territory – he simply prefers to stay within that territory and has a bad impression of anywhere that isn't in it.
C: He does not say that the reason for staying within what he regards as his territory is laziness. He says that the *constrictedness of this private city-within-a-city has the character of a self-fulfilling prophecy* (the restrictions imposed on you by feeling that only a certain part of a city is your territory are an inevitable result of this feeling). *Its boundaries, originally arrived at by chance and usage, grow more not less real* the longer he lives in London. (As he continues to live in London, the boundaries of what he considers his territory, which originally came into existence by chance and because of what he did habitually while living there, have begun to seem increasingly like genuine boundaries rather than the imaginary ones they really are.) He is therefore saying a reluctance to travel beyond what people who live in cities regard as their territory is a natural development, not the product of laziness.
D: The writer does say that he is someone who instinctively regards areas outside his *own territory* with suspicion and a certain amount of fear but he does not mention any desire to overcome this feeling. He presents it as a natural state of affairs for people who live in cities and describes it in a neutral way, making no reference to any desire to do anything to change it.

24 D: Clapham is a place that the writer implies he is reluctant to go to, even though it is closer to where he lives than Islington, which he is happy to go to. The man in New York had to look at the map in order to tell the writer how to get to Brooklyn – even though it was very close to his office, he had not been there for 12 years. Both of these examples illustrate the point the writer is making when he says that when he first came to London *he took the liberties of a tourist* (used the freedom to do things that tourists have) *and measured distances in miles rather than by the relationship with the unknown*. What he is saying is that people like him and the man in New York, people who live in cities, only go to places they know well and whether going to such places involves long or short journeys is irrelevant. They may not visit places like Clapham or Brooklyn, which are close to them, because they are not familiar with them, whereas they may visit places which are further away because they are familiar with them.
A: The writer does not say that Clapham and Brooklyn are places that are generally considered to be 'bad areas', he says that Clapham is outside what he considers to be his territory geographically and implies that the man in New York feels the same about Brooklyn.
B: The writer does not say that a city itself begins to seem smaller when you have lived there for some time; he says that you tend to regard only a certain area within it as 'your territory' and that you seldom go outside that area. Clapham and Brooklyn are examples of places outside his territory and the man in New York's territory.
C: The writer says that at first he *took the liberties of a tourist*, which involve looking at places in a city simply in terms of how far apart they are geographically and not in terms of whether they are familiar places or not. He is not saying that places like Clapham and Brooklyn appeal more or less to tourists than to people who live in London or New York. What he is implying is that, for tourists, the decision whether to visit such places would be based entirely on geographical distance, the distance that they would have to

travel to get to them. Tourists might visit a place because it is nearby, whereas people who live in a city might not visit nearby places because they do not regard them as being within their territory.

Oxford

25 B: The writer describes a visitor to Oxford sitting in one of its *string* (series) of snack bars, etc, in which he is able to *browse through* (look casually through) some literature he has just bought which includes details about buildings that have *thus far* (until now) *fallen outside* (not been included in) *his rather arbitrary wanderings* (random walks, not based on any planned or logical route). Since the writer says that visiting Oxford is *all a bit tiring*, the implication is that such a visitor may not go to these buildings he reads about while he is taking this opportunity to *rest his feet.*
A: The writer says that a day visitor to Oxford may get back onto the coach after their visit *with the gratifying* (pleasing, satisfying) feeling that they have had a *compact* (small and neat), *interesting visit* to one of *England's most beautiful cities.* He adds that the visitor will feel that it is *all very splendid* (wonderful and impressive). The implication here is that such a visitor will have appreciated the beauty of the place. The writer says that the visitor may have *had enough* (may not wish to continue visiting such buildings) by noon and go away from the old buildings and visit the shopping complex, but he doesn't imply the visitor didn't appreciate the beauty of Oxford before that or that the visitor goes to the shopping complex because of not appreciating the beauty of other parts.
C: The writer says that the main tourist attractions in Oxford are *reasonably proximate* (near) *to one another*, that there are *fine* (excellent) *University buildings clustered* (grouped closely together) *between* two places in Oxford and that a visit there is *compact.* He therefore says that interesting buildings there are close together but he does not imply that this is in any way a disadvantage – indeed, he says that this is a good thing.
D: The writer refers to the fact that there are *guide books a-plenty* (a great many of them) about Oxford and mentions literature about buildings in Oxford but he does not imply that information in these creates a false impression of Oxford. He also talks about visitors going to the Westgate shopping complex, which contrasts greatly with the old buildings elsewhere in Oxford, but he does not imply that either the old buildings or the shopping complex give visitors the wrong impression of the city – he merely says that the two things contrast.

26 B: The phrase *such culture*, which the visitor *quits* (leaves, abandons), refers back to both the main tourist attractions, such as the fine University buildings, and the literature about other buildings that the visitor has not visited. These are contrasted with the buildings to be found in the Westgate shopping complex, which are therefore not considered by the writer to be examples of *culture. Culture* in this context is used to mean 'the civilized, intellectual or artistic things produced by societies'. The writer therefore uses the word 'culture' to indicate that he believes the old buildings of Oxford such as those he mentions to be superior to those found in the Westgate shopping complex.
A: *Edifice* is a formal word meaning 'building'. The writer mentions *ecclesiastical* (connected with the Church) *edifices* and in the context this is a neutral term that implies neither disapproval nor approval. He does obviously prefer buildings such as these but the word 'edifices' does not convey this approval.
C: The writer says that the *inner-city obsolescence* (the fact of being out of date and therefore useless in the middle of a modern city) of the ancient streets and houses that used to be on the site of the old St Ebbe's was resolved by the *city fathers* (the authorities in charge of the city) by the *full-scale flattening* (the complete destruction) of them. He is therefore saying that they were knocked down because they were out of date in an inner city and he uses the word 'obsolescence' to describe the fact that they had become out of date, not to indicate either approval of them or of the buildings that replaced them.
D: The writer says that the ancient streets and houses were replaced by *concrete giants* (enormous things) such as supermarkets and *municipal* (local government) *offices*. The word 'giants' is used as a physical description of the size of these buildings, not as a term of approval of them – in fact, since they are not 'culture', he clearly disapproves of them.

p16–17 PAPER 1 PART THREE

Two marks per question (Total: 14)

Husband and Wife

27 F: In the opening paragraph we learn that Thanet is happy, and why.
In F, *And so* refers back to the fact that he was a happy man. Because of that, he relaxed in his armchair and *reflected* (thought about) how satisfied he was with his life. However, he was *blissfully unaware* (happy and unaware of a reason to be unhappy) that he was about to get a shock. In the paragraph after the gap he is still unaware of the shock to come, continues to relax, and he and his wife briefly talk about whether to watch the news on television or not.

28 C: In the paragraph before the gap they talk briefly about watching the news.
In C, they have stopped talking about that and Joan is reading her book again, while he reads a newspaper. He becomes aware that she is not concentrating on her book but is *restless* (unable to sit still because of feeling anxious) and this is very unusual because she usually concentrates fully when she is reading.
In the paragraph after the gap, she makes a number of nervous movements, which continue the description of her in C as *restless.* She *fidgeted* (moved around in her seat in a nervous manner), put one leg on top of the other and then reversed that, *fiddled with* (kept touching and rearranging) her hair and chewed the edge of her thumb.

29 H: In the paragraph before the gap he asks her if something is the matter and when she hesitates to reply he says *'Out with it'*, which means 'Tell me' or 'Say what you are thinking'.
In H, she still does not reply, he begins to feel the first *faint stirrings of alarm* (feelings of slight anxiety) and she eventually says that she thinks he isn't going to like the thing that she is *trying to pluck up* (gain or accumulate) *the courage* to tell him.
The paragraph after the gap begins with him replying to what she says at the end of H, *'Oh?'* in a way that is described as *warily* (suspiciously, cautiously). He replies in this way because in H he has begun to feel alarmed and she has told him that she needs courage to tell him what she is going to tell him. She then tells him that she has to start thinking about whether, as they have already agreed, she is going to return to work or not when *Ben* (their son) *starts school.*

30 G: In the paragraph before the gap, she says that she knew he wouldn't like the idea of her returning to work. He says that is not true but that it will take him some time to get used to the idea. She says that he is just pretending to approve and that in reality he is *dead against it* (completely opposed to it).
In G, we are told that *she was right* because *he was,* which refers back to the end of the preceding paragraph and

means that he was completely against the idea of her going back to work. We are then told that throughout the eight years they had been married, she had been *the good little wife* (this phrase is used to indicate a feeling that she had done what was expected of her without argument but implies that she would have had a right not to behave like this) who had not had a job and had brought up the children, looked after the home and made sure that everything *was geared to* (arranged in order to suit) *Thanet's convenience*. She was different from his colleagues' wives because she never *nagged* (continuously criticized or complained to someone, in this case her husband).
In the paragraph after the gap, we are told that now, *in a flash* (suddenly, very quickly), he *saw all of that changing*. The phrase *all of that* refers back to the whole situation concerning their arrangements that is described in G. He imagines that there will be problems if she returns to work.

31 B: In the paragraph before the gap, he has thought about how different theory and practice are – in the context, this means that when the idea of her returning to work was just an idea, it had been something he could *contemplate with equanimity* (think about in a calm manner), but now that it was a real possibility, he didn't like it at all.
In B, he begins by saying that it is not true that he is against the idea. The first thing he says, beginning *Nonsense*, refers back to what she says to him before the previous gap (gap 30) and he is denying the accusation she makes immediately before that gap. This reference back to something earlier in the text is logical because there is no conversation after the paragraph before gap 30 and this point in the text, so the next piece of dialogue continues the conversation from where it was left earlier. In B, she says that despite what he says, she thinks he is against the idea, and he then says that he thought she had decided to do an art course, not get a job.
In the paragraph after gap 31, *it* in her phrase *consider it seriously* refers to the art course he mentions at the end of B and she says that she was interested in doing such a course *at one time*.

32 E: In the paragraph before the gap, she says that she wants to do something less *self-indulgent* (only for her own enjoyment) and more useful and wonders whether saying this sounds *horribly priggish* (that indicates a belief that you are morally superior in a way that is very unappealing to others).
In E he replies *To be honest, yes*, which refers back to what she says at the end of the paragraph before the gap and means that he thinks what she has said does sound *horribly priggish*. He says that, however, he understands what she means, and she then asks him to confirm that he doesn't think she is being stupid in wanting to do something useful.
In the paragraph after the gap, he does confirm this – *Not in the least* refers back to what she asks at the end of E and means that he doesn't think she is being stupid at all. He then asks her what she is thinking of doing and she says that she doesn't know but feels she might need to do a course or some training.

33 D: In the paragraph before the gap, she says that she can arrange something for her to do by September and he asks whether she has *gone into* (investigated, made enquiries about) *it* (getting a job or doing a course or some training) *yet*.
In D her reply refers back to what he says at the end of the paragraph before the gap – when she says she wanted to speak to him about it *first*, she means she wanted to discuss it (the subject of her going back to work, doing a course or doing some training) before 'going into it'. She then asks if he is sure he doesn't mind and he says that he doesn't, lying *valiantly* (bravely) that he had been expecting this to happen *sooner or later* (at some point in the near or distant future, eventually).
In the final paragraph, the opening phrase refers back to the end of D, and means that he had been hoping that this would happen – that she would go back to work – *very much later* (a lot further in the future). *And preferably not at all* means that in fact he had hoped that it would never happen.

The paragraph which does not fit into any of the gaps is A.

p18–19 PAPER 1 PART FOUR

Two marks per question (Total: 14)

Progressives in the US

34 B: The writer says that the word 'progressive', which had previously been widely used in ordinary conversation, began to be used also at this time to describe a political party, a *movement* (a group of people with the same political beliefs and aims) and an *era* (a period in history). He says that it *remains a curiously empty word* (it is still a word which, strangely, has little or no meaning) but that *historians will never be able to do without it*. His point is that, although he doesn't think that the word adequately describes what it is meant to describe, historians have always used it to describe the period and continue to use it now.
A: The writer says that this was *an epoch* (a period) *very much to the American taste* (that appealed very much to Americans), in that it proved to them something they wanted to feel – that their belief in progress and in the idea that America was capable of it was *justified*. It is clear, therefore, that Americans at this time liked the idea that was signified by the word 'progressive', but the writer is not saying that it can be applied only to this period. He is simply saying that it was widely used and popular during this period.
C: The writer says that the word was widely used but he does not mention inappropriate use of it. In fact, he says that *after all due reservations have been made* (after all justified doubts have been expressed) *it would be churlish* (unfair and narrow-minded) *to deny* that the US did make progress during this period – his point here is therefore that the word is appropriate now and was appropriate then to some extent.
D: The writer does say that all kinds of different people were united during this period – he lists types of people all over America who *acknowledged* (accepted) *the necessity* (this refers to the necessity for *radical improvements* previously mentioned). He says that all these people *had a hand in* (played a part in) shaping these improvements. However, he does not say that the fact that the word 'progressive' came into use caused these people to unite – his point is that they became united in their common aims and that the word began to be applied to what they were doing.

35 D: The writer says that big business *made itself felt* (was a big factor that people were aware of) throughout this 'progressive' period but that this was *by no means as a purely reactionary force* (it was certainly not a force that was completely against change). His point here is that big business was to a certain extent, as might be expected, opposed to change but it was not entirely so, which means that its influence to a certain extent helped to bring about change. He then says that *All the same* (Despite this, in spite of the fact that big business to a certain extent encouraged change), it would be wrong to think that big business *was the key to* (the most important factor in) *progressivism*. His point, therefore, is that big business had a major influence on the way in which progressivism developed but that it was not the most significant contributor to it.

A: The writer says that the industrial working class, even though it was very active, could not *muster* (gather together, accumulate) *the power* that was necessary *to dominate the epoch* (to be the most powerful force of the period). However, he does not say that this was because big business prevented it from doing so.
B: The writer says that *That privilege* (the fortunate position of being the major force of the period) *belonged to the new middle class*. He is therefore saying that the new middle class became the dominant force, but he does not say that big business failed to pay enough attention to the rise of that class.
C: The writer says that big business *had shaped* (determined the nature of, greatly influenced) *and now coloured* (affected) everyday life in America. He is therefore saying that it had already had a great influence on daily life in America before this period.

36 C: The writer says that the new middle class had *emerged* (come out) *as the chief beneficiary of* (the people to benefit most from) the enormous change in American society because this change, which involved *industrialism and urbanization, implied* (in this context, this means 'had as its logical consequence') a need for professional services and that this in turn *implied* the need to recruit and train new people to supply these services. As a result, there was a *mushroom growth* (a sudden, rapid increase) *among the professions*. His point, therefore, is that the number of people working in the professions (he lists examples of these) grew suddenly and enormously because the great changes in American society had created a need for them.
A: The writer says that this was *the age* (historical period) *of the expert* and that these experts, the people working in the professions that he lists, were *given a free hand* (allowed to act without restrictions) of a kind that they have *seldom enjoyed since*. He is therefore saying that the way in which people in the professions worked was mostly only possible during that period, but he is not saying that people thought the rise in the numbers of them would not last for long.
B: The writer does say that the people in the professions enjoyed a freedom that they have hardly ever had since that period, but he does not say that the rise in their numbers was caused by a wish for fewer restrictions in the way they operated. Their numbers increased because of the demand for them, not because of their own desires.
D: The writer talks about the enormous changes in American society but he does not say that the American people were worried about these or that people in the professions helped the American people to come to terms with these changes. In fact, he says that the changes resulted in greater wealth in American society and that American society *was now rich enough* to pay for the professional services that the changes had created a need for.

37 A: The writer says that people had faith in experts and believed that *there was a sound* (sensible, functional) *technical answer to every problem, even to the problem of government*. In Galveston it was decided that politicians were not capable of solving the problems caused by the hurricane and flood and instead *a commission* (a group of people officially chosen to carry out a public task) *of experts* (people with specialist knowledge) was appointed to do that. This pattern – the appointment of experts rather than politicians to solve problems – was *widely followed* later. Therefore, the writer uses what happened in Galveston to illustrate the faith that people had in experts at the time.
B: It is clear that the people in Galveston did not think that politicians would be able to deal with the problems caused by the hurricane and flood as well as experts could, but the writer does not say or imply that problems caused by natural disasters were different from other problems, in the sense that authorities had always failed to solve problems of that particular kind.
C: The writer does not refer to how quickly the problems of Galveston were solved – his point is not that experts solved problems more quickly than *the regular authorities* (politicians), it is that experts and not politicians were given the responsibility for solving them.
D: The writer does not say that the fact that people wanted to be provided with technical solutions to problems resulted in disagreements, he is saying that it resulted in different people (experts, not politicians) being given the task of solving problems of the kind found in Galveston, with the expectation that they would be able to solve them.

38 B: The writer says that the new class wanted to change society and thought that it knew how to solve social problems. This new class, which consisted of experts, had themselves benefited from being in a society that was *open to the rise of the talented* (one in which talented people had the opportunity to do well) and they wanted people less fortunate than themselves to *rise* (improve their position) just as they had done. This *democratic individualistic ideology* (their political theory that society should be based on fair and equal treatment for everyone and the freedom of the individual) made people think that it was *legitimate* (reasonable) *to bid for* (to try to get) political power and that *to go down into that arena* (to enter the field of politics) *was simply to carry out one's civic duty* (to do what was expected of you as a citizen). When people did so (attempted to get elected to positions of political power), *Motives* (their reasons for doing so) *did not need to be examined too closely* because they were *self-evidently* (clearly, with no need for proof) *virtuous* (good, based on high moral standards). The writer's point here is therefore that people didn't wonder why members of the new class stood for election, because they believed they already knew why – it was assumed that they were doing so in order to improve the position of the disadvantaged people in society.
A: The writer says that there were social problems *All round* (in all places and parts of society) that had to be solved and he lists some of these problems. He says that the new class thought they knew how to solve these problems. However, he does not say that these problems were sometimes too great for them to solve or that some of them did not appreciate how great these problems were.
C: The writer says that their ideology was such that they believed that *their disadvantaged* (poor, lacking in the basic things considered essential to all members of society) *fellow citizens* should *rise* and that they tried to get political power in order to make this happen. However, he does not say that these disadvantaged people were not capable of doing what the new class thought they could do or that the new class had an unrealistic image of the disadvantaged people.
D: The writer says that these people brought a new *tool-kit* (set of tools in a bag – this is used here to refer to the expertise these people had) to the task of solving social problems and that in a way, they had *improved spanners* (a spanner is a tool for turning screws, etc; here it is used to mean that they had technical knowledge that was greater than people had previously had), which they tried to use when dealing with *contraptions* (this literally means 'strange or complicated machines') such as the existing political parties and the new *urban wastelands* (cities or parts of cities that were in poor condition and not serving any useful function). His point is that their methods for achieving their aims were new and practical and it is possible that as a result people thought that they could achieve their aims. However, he does not say that he believes that expectations of what they could achieve were realistic, he merely describes their attitudes, aims and methods.

39 D: The writer says that *Behind the zeal of these technocrats lay an older tradition* (an older tradition was the real but hidden basis for the enormous enthusiasm of these technical experts). The fact that they were in fact part of an older tradition was *betrayed* (in this context, this means 'unintentionally revealed') by their use of the word

settlements for the *philanthropic* (created by rich people to help poor people) centres they established in *the slums* (crowded districts of cities in which people live in terrible conditions). This word had previously been used by *the settlers of old* (people in the past who had been the first to go and live in various parts of America) to describe places they had established. Their use of the word *settlements* showed that they had the same attitudes as *the settlers of old* because the word had the same implications to them as it had to these settlers. This, he says, reveals *limitations* (abilities that are limited and do not go beyond a certain extent) in the new class that were likely to *impede their quest* (make it difficult or impossible for them to achieve what they were trying to achieve). They were mostly from *old American stock* (descended from American families that had been in existence for a long time), they had been brought up according to the *old pieties* (traditional religious and moral beliefs) and their new expertise only *veneered* these (only covered the surface of these so that they were still present just under the surface). Their use of the word 'settlements' therefore showed how much they had in common with previous generations, as a result of which they were too *conservative* (naturally reluctant to see major change) and too *parochial* (concerned with only local matters) to want or carry out major changes to American society.
A: The writer is not saying that the progressives were only pretending that they wanted to solve social problems because it would make them look good. He is saying that they had inherited an attitude towards cities which was part of a general attitude that prevented them from bringing about the enormous change they wanted to. He is not saying that they didn't genuinely care about disadvantaged people in cities, he is saying that their attitude towards them was the same as that of the old settlers towards the people in the places they settled in.
B: The writer is not saying that the word indicates that some of their beliefs were based on misunderstandings – he is not saying that their attitude towards cities indicated that they did not really understand them or that they had wrong ideas about the problems in them, he is saying that there was nothing new about their approach to solving the problems in them.
C: Their approach seems to have been clear and the writer does not say that they were not sure how to deal with the problems of cities – they believed they were bringing *superior* techniques and ideas to the problems. He says that their approach was *conservative* and *parochial* because of attitudes they inherited and that this prevented them from carrying out the changes they wanted, but he does not say that they were aware of this or that it meant that they were confused in their own minds.

40 C: The writer says that although their achievements were *limited and flawed* (imperfect, including negative aspects), they were *real* (the achievements genuinely did happen) in that they helped America to adapt to the needs of modern government and they *laid the foundations for the liberalism* (established the circumstances which made possible the tolerant attitude) that *was to become* (later became) a major factor in American politics and society. He is therefore saying that the progressives' influence on America was limited but that the influence they did have had important consequences beyond the period in which they were active.
A: The writer says that their achievements were limited but he does not say or imply that it is generally believed that they achieved more than they actually did.
B: The writer says that what they did resulted in major changes in America but he does not say that this was because they did not think their ideas were as radical as they really were, or that the changes that later took place would have surprised them because they were greater than what they had intended.
D: The writer describes them as *intelligent, high-minded* (having high moral principles), *energetic and good-hearted* (kind), which are all terms of praise, and talks about what they did achieve. He says that his comments on them are *not small praise*. He therefore gives them credit for their attitudes and their achievements, even though he says that their achievements were limited. However, he does not say or imply that they are not praised or regarded favourably by others to the extent that they should be.

PAPER 1:

PART ONE	18 marks
PART TWO	16 marks
PART THREE	14 marks
PART FOUR	14 marks
TOTAL	62 marks

To be converted into a score out of 40 marks.

p20–23 PAPER 2 PART ONE

Task-specific mark schemes

Each answer is given marks out of 20

Question 1

Content
Article should cover the points raised in the input article, for example, whether children and young people are given too much and think life is easy, and whether too many children and young people have a hard life. Candidates could include some personal experience.

Range
Language for expressing and supporting opinions. Candidates may support one of the two views as opposed to the other or present a balanced argument partially supporting both views.

Appropriacy of register and format
Register could be informal, formal or neutral as input article seems neutral. Article format – clearly divided, possibly short paragraphs. Article could have appropriate sub-headings.

Organization and cohesion
Clear development of argument, with each point expanded and probably exemplified. Clear and relatively brief introduction and conclusion. Appropriate paragraphing and linking.

Target reader
Would understand the writer's point of view fully and clearly.

FURTHER PRACTICE AND GUIDANCE (p21–23)

Assessment of sample answer

Content
The main points are fully covered and the article is directly relevant to them throughout. It focuses on the issue of whether young people are given too much by their parents and the consequences of this, and also addresses the issue of young people having a hard life. The candidate has not included personal experience but this is optional.

Range
There is some good use of vocabulary and structure, for example *depends mainly on* (first paragraph), *I hold the view* and *bad conscience* (second paragraph), the ending of a sentence with a preposition in *big challenges they have to deal with* (third

paragraph), *from then on* (fourth paragraph) and the use of *proper*, meaning 'appropriate' or 'correct' in the final paragraph. In general, the article is relatively simple in terms of vocabulary and structure, but not too much so.

Accuracy
There are a couple of relatively minor mistakes. In the first sentence, it should say *generalize on* or *about*; in the first sentence of the third paragraph, it should say *making* not *make*, to go with the previous structure *by giving*. These errors do not affect understanding of the points being made.

Appropriacy of register and format
The register of the article is suitably neutral, with a serious approach to the topic. Some of the piece involves short, sharp, sentences and this is entirely suited to an article, in terms of impact on the reader. The format is fine, with clearly divided paragraphs making and expanding separate points. There hasn't been an attempt to present the piece clearly as an article, with sub-headings, but this is not essential.

Organization and cohesion
The article is very well-organized. The first paragraph is an effective introduction in which the writer's main point is presented briefly; the second deals with the causes of the main point. The third paragraph deals with the results of it. The fourth paragraph disputes the opposite view and the final paragraph is an effective conclusion, which makes a suggestion rather than merely repeating any points made before. There is some excellent linking, for example *On the one hand ... but on the other hand* (third paragraph) and *All in all* (last paragraph).

Target reader
The writer's point of view is entirely clear and the reader would have no trouble in understanding that the writer is saying that parents spoil children, perhaps because they feel guilty about not giving them enough attention, that this can result in them being unable to deal with challenges later in life and that therefore their upbringing should involve preparation for adult life as well.

Assessment: A good, competent answer.

Mark: 14

p24 PAPER 2 PART TWO

Question 2

Content
Report should include:
- description of the organization's structure and comments on it
- evaluation of strengths and weakness of the organization
- description and evaluation of performance and attitude of those in charge
- description and evaluation of performance and attitude of those working/studying in the organization

Range
Language of analysis, evaluation and description, as well as language for expressing and supporting opinions.

Appropriacy of register and format
Register appropriate for report done as part of a course – formal or neutral. Report format: clear and brief introduction, followed by separate sections, probably with headings, dealing with each separate aspect required for the assignment, and perhaps a brief conclusion.

Organization and cohesion
The report should be well-structured, with description and comment appropriately linked.

Target reader
Would understand fully and clearly the structure of the organization and the writer's opinions on it.

Question 3

Content
Letter should describe one or more common national stereotypes and comment on them, and should describe stereotype of writer's nationality and comment on accuracy or otherwise of that.

Range
Language for describing and analysing and language for expressing and supporting opinions.

Appropriacy of register and format
Register appropriate for reader writing to magazine – could be formal, informal or neutral and perhaps even a mixture of these. Standard letter format.

Organization and cohesion
Clear introduction stating why reader has decided to write letter – to agree with the unflattering views expressed in the magazine article, disagree with them or both. Clear organization of points made: clear description of stereotypes and clear expression of views on them, with appropriate linking between stereotypes and comments on them. Clear paragraphing and appropriate linking between paragraphs. Clear, although probably brief, conclusion.

Target reader
Would understand what writer has described and writer's views on that.

Question 4

Content
Review should inform the writer as to content of exhibition or museum and what makes it special or particularly poor.

Range
Language of narration (to describe writer's visit), description (of exhibition or museum) and evaluation (writer's views).

Appropriacy of register and format
Register could be informal, formal or neutral – writer may wish to make review amusing or entertaining as the competition asks for 'the most interesting review'. Format should be appropriate to review: description followed by comment in each paragraph or in separate paragraphs.

Organization and cohesion
Clear development of points of view, with appropriate linking between description and comment and between different aspects of exhibition or museum.

Target reader
Would be informed as to content of exhibition or museum and any other relevant points concerning it. They would be able to decide whether they would be interested in visiting it or not. Reader would also find the review entertaining, as 'the most interesting review' is asked for.

PAPER 2:

PART ONE	20 marks
PART TWO	20 marks
TOTAL	40 marks

p25–27 PAPER 3 PART ONE

FURTHER PRACTICE AND GUIDANCE (p26–27)

Advertising in Britain

For explanations, see the explanations to the questions in the test, which follow.

1 b	2 c	3 b	4 a	5 d
6 a	7 d	8 a	9 b	10 c
11 b	12 d	13 a	14 b	15 c

p25 PAPER 3 PART ONE (TEST)

One mark per question (Total: 15)

1 **out:** If you *set out to do something,* you start taking action with the intention of achieving a particular aim. *Establish* here means 'discover and prove'. Clearly the newspaper in question asked readers to vote for their favourite adverts or to complete a survey or questionnaire.

2 **many:** The phrase *as many as* followed by a number is used for emphasizing that a number is considered high. In the next sentence, the writer says that British people admire television adverts and so it is clearly logical that a lot of them would have responded to the newspaper's attempt to find out what the best ones were.

3 **in:** If something abstract *lies in something* else, it exists or can be found there. The writer is saying that the reason why so many people responded is that British people admire television adverts.

4 **own:** If something exists *in its own right,* it exists separately from others with which it could be associated and has its own distinct identity. The writer is saying that television adverts have become a distinct art form, separate from other art forms.

5 **up:** If you *end up doing something,* you do it, or something happens, at the end of a series of events or a period of time. The writer is saying that it seemed impossible in 1955 that people would later think that TV commercials were as sophisticated and innovative as programmes.

6 **them:** This refers back to the *ads* (adverts/commercials) mentioned earlier in the sentence. The writer is saying that the programmes during which the ads appeared were considered sophisticated and innovative, but when adverts first appeared they were not.

7 **their:** This phrase means 'the making of them', 'them' being commercials. In this phrase 'making' is a noun, and it needs to be preceded by the plural possessive *their,* since it refers to 'commercials'. The writer is talking about how much money is spent and how much thought is given to produce each second of a TV commercial.

8 **is:** If something *is the case for something,* it is true of something. The writer is comparing television commercials and movies, opera, etc in terms both of what is involved in making them and the profits made from them and is saying that the amount is greater for commercials than for movies, etc. The verb *is* must be singular because the subject of it is *the case.*

9 **with:** *With* can be followed by a noun to link a sentence with the meaning 'Because of' or 'Following as a result of'. The writer is talking in this sentence about a result of the *explosion of* (sudden enormous increase in the number of) *channels and websites.*

10 **on:** If there is *onus on somebody to do something* or if *the onus is on somebody to do something,* they have a duty or responsibility to do it because it is expected of them. The writer is saying that advertisers are expected to make television commercials that shock, amuse, etc because those commercials have to grab people's attention, since they are faced by competition from commercials on other channels and on websites.

11 **of:** If something/somebody *is worthy of something,* they deserve to have or receive it. The writer is asking whether television adverts are important or serious enough for *cultural appraisal* (to have their quality or value assessed as if they are part of culture).

12 **are:** This refers back to *are* at the beginning of the sentence. The writer is saying that television programmes are *worthy of cultural appraisal* and wondering whether commercials are too.

13 **makes:** The writer is asking what causes an advertisement to be *truly great* (genuinely of excellent or outstanding quality), what qualities it has that make it possible for it to be considered wonderful.

14 **do:** If something *is to do with something,* it is connected with or related to it. In this sentence, *this* means 'whether an advertisement can still seem *fresh* (original and interesting) after you have watched it 1,000 times', which is Robert Opie's definition of a *truly great* advertisement. This, he says, involves the two aspects he mentions – acting and details.

15 **being:** The sentence means that for an advertisement to be truly great, the acting has to be perfect and *every single last detail* (absolutely every detail) has to be correct. The verb has to be in the *-ing* form because it is directly connected with the preposition *with.*

p28 PAPER 3 PART TWO

One mark per question (Total: 10)

Tube Inspired a Book

16 **budding:** If someone is described as *a budding something,* it means that they are beginning to become one and would like to be a good one. The writer is saying that Preethi Nair would like to be a successful author.

17 **enthusiastically:** If you are *enthusiastic about something,* you are very interested in or excited about it. The verb is *enthuse (about)* and the noun is *enthusiasm.* The writer is saying that Preethi Nair talks to her in an excited way.

18 **innermost:** Someone's *innermost thoughts/feelings* are their deepest and most private thoughts/feelings. The writer is saying that the book tells the reader the private thoughts of the characters in it.

19 **consultant:** A *consultant* is someone whose profession involves giving expert advice to companies. A *management consultant* is a consultant who advises companies on management methods and the training of managers. The writer says that people who do this job are under a lot of pressure.

20 **pursuit:** If you are *in pursuit of something,* you are trying to achieve or obtain it. We are told that Preethi Nair gave up her job so that she could try to achieve her ambition to be a writer.

21 contentment/contentedness: If you feel *contentment*, you are satisfied with the situation you are in or with life in general. The adjective is *content (with)* or *contented*. The verb phrase is *content yourself with something*, meaning 'be satisfied with something because it is the best you can have, even though it is not exactly what you want'. The word *contentedness*, which has the same meaning, is not often used. Preethi Nair is saying that giving up her job made her happier.

22 lasting: If something is *lasting* (adjective), it continues for a long time or has an effect that continues for a long time. The writer is saying that having two very different cultures in her background had a big effect on her.

23 far(-)away/far-off: *A far(-)away/far-off place* is one which is a long distance from where you are. The writer is saying that India is a long way from London.

24 running: *Running water* is a water supply that is provided through a system of pipes and taps rather than by means of getting water by hand from rivers or holes in the ground. Preethi is saying that the village in India where she was born does not have such a water supply.

25 untouched: If a place is described as *untouched*, it means that it has not been affected or changed by progress or the advances of the modern world, including tourism, and remains as it has been for a long time. Preethi is saying that the village in India where she was born has not changed or become modernized at all and remains beautiful.

p29 PAPER 3 PART THREE

Two marks per question (Total: 12)

26 hard: If you have a *hard day, week, time*, etc, you experience a period that is unpleasant and full of problems, as a result of which you are tired or unhappy. Many other adjectives would fit here to form correct collocations, such as *bad, terrible, tiring, tough, rough*, etc.
If you are *hard on someone*, you criticize them strongly or treat them severely, in a way that may be considered unfair. The adjectives *tough* and *rough* would both fit here to form correct collocations with the same meaning.
If you are *hard of hearing*, you cannot hear well, you are rather deaf.

27 mind: If you tell someone to *'mind your own business'*, you feel that they are interfering in or showing too much interest in something that concerns only you or someone else and does not concern them, and you are telling them to stop doing that.
If you tell someone to *mind something*, you are warning them to be careful about or pay attention to something, because they are in a situation of possible danger. The verb *watch* would also fit here, with the same meaning.
The phrase *mind you* is used to link two contrasting statements and to inform the person addressed that, although the first statement is true, the second statement is also true. 'Mind you' means 'but don't forget' or 'but you should realize or take into consideration that ...'.

28 front: A *front* is someone's outward behaviour or superficial appearance, when this is not genuine or sincere but has been deliberately created in order to give a certain impression. Several other nouns, such as *pretence, show, veneer*, etc would fit here with the same meaning.
If money is paid *up front*, it is paid in advance, before the person receiving it has done the work or supplied the goods that the payment is for.
If something, especially a piece of clothing, is *back to front*, it is wrongly arranged, so that the front is at the back and the back is at the front.

29 tore: If you *tear* somewhere or in a particular direction, you go there very quickly because you are in a hurry. Many other verbs meaning 'move quickly' would fit here, such as *ran, rushed, hurried*, etc.
If you *tear something to shreds*, you criticize it in the most severe way possible and have only very negative things to say about it. It is also possible to use the verb *ripped* to complete a phrase with the same meaning.
If you *tear something up*, you destroy pieces of paper by tearing them into pieces, because you are going to throw them away or because you are angry. The verb *ripped* could also fill this gap, with the same meaning.

30 safe: If you do something in order to *be on the safe side*, you do it because you want to be cautious and not take any risks.
If *it is safe to do something*, it is reasonable to do it because of the evidence available. Other adjectives could be used to complete this structure with the same meaning, such as *fair, reasonable*, etc.
If something such as a secret is *safe with someone*, they will not tell anyone else about it but will keep it secret.

31 tell: If you *can't tell things/people apart*, you are unable to distinguish between them and they seem to you to be the same.
If you *tell someone off*, you tell them in an angry way that you think they have done something bad or wrong. The verb 'slag' could also fill the gap here to form a phrase meaning 'criticize severely / say nasty things to or about' – this is a fairly common slang phrase.
If a child can *tell the time*, they have learnt to understand what the time is from looking at a clock or watch.

p30 PAPER 3 PART FOUR

Two marks per question (Total: 16)

32 positioned himself by the door (1 mark)
so (1 mark)
If you *position yourself somewhere*, you move to a particular place or put yourself in a particular physical position, usually because you have a reason for doing so. The linking structure *so as to do something* means 'in order to do something' or 'with the intention of doing something'.

33 clear to me (1 mark)
what will be required of (1 mark)
If you *make something clear to someone* or *something is made clear to someone*, they understand it fully because it is clearly expressed or explained to them. If *something is required of someone*, they are required or expected to do it, usually because it is what is demanded by someone in authority.

34 nothing short of (1 mark)
miraculous/a miracle (1 mark)
If something is described as *nothing short of + adjective/noun*, this means that it is absolutely equal to being that thing and not less than it. A *miracle* is something wonderful that happens and is completely unexpected because there is no reason to believe that it will happen. The adjective is *miraculous*.

35 it that/which (1 mark)
led you to believe (1 mark)
The structure *What + verb* can be transformed into the structure *What + to be + it + that/which + verb*. If something *leads you to believe that* something is the case, it causes you to believe or gives you the impression that it is the case.

36 did everything (with)in my power (1 mark)
to prevent/stop (1 mark)
If you *do everything (with)in your power to do something*, you try as hard as you possibly can in order to do it. If you make sure that something doesn't happen, you *prevent/stop something (from) happening*.

37 were justified in (1 mark)
making such a fuss (1 mark)
If you are *justified in doing something*, it is reasonable for you to do it and there are good reasons which mean that you are right to do it. If you *make a fuss (about something)*, you become more agitated than is necessary about something and this causes problems. The phrase *complain so much* has to be transformed into the phrase *make such a fuss* to convey the extent of the complaining.

38 a lot of problems to (1 mark)
contend with (1 mark)
The structure *was faced by + noun* can be transformed into the structure *had + noun + to face*. If you have to *contend with something*, you have to face it or deal with it and it is a difficult thing to overcome or solve.

39 of a sudden (1 mark)
there was loud applause (1 mark)
The phrase *all of a sudden* means 'suddenly' or 'quickly and unexpectedly'. The phrase *they started to applaud loudly* has to be transformed into the phrase *there was loud applause from them* – the verb *applaud* has to become the noun *applause* and the adverb *loudly* has to become the adjective *loud* to describe the applause. *There* has to be used as the subject, instead of *audience*.

p31–37 PAPER 3 PART FIVE

Questions 40–43

FURTHER PRACTICE AND GUIDANCE (p33–34)

For explanations, see the explanations to the questions in the test, which follow.

Question 40:	1 c	2 b	3 d	4 c
Question 41:	1 b	2 a	3 c	4 d
Question 42:	1 c	2 a	3 b	
Question 43:	1 a	2 c	3 b	

p31–32 PAPER 3 PART FIVE (TEST)

Questions 40–43

Two marks per question (Total: 8)

Answers that are similar to or cover the same points as those given here are acceptable, provided that they are clearly expressed.

40 that the people he refers to are a mixture of people he has a low opinion of and that therefore the entirely negative view they express about adolescence shouldn't be believed
Somewhat means 'rather' and an *unholy alliance* is a combination of people considered bad in some way, especially in the sense that they could be harmful to others. The people he lists include *pundits* (the word implies that they may not really be experts), and they are said to form a group which *pontificates* (the word implies that they don't know what they're talking about) concerning a number of negative aspects of adolescence, including *the rupture* (in this context meaning 'the end of friendly relations', presumably with parents) that occurs when adolescence begins. In the first sentence the writer has already made it clear that he finds it *irritating* (it annoys him) that one of the *conventional wisdoms* (commonly held or accepted opinions) these days is that adolescence is totally bad, for example in being *horrendously* (horribly, terribly) *traumatic* (causing extreme unhappiness or shock). He therefore doesn't agree with people who say it is totally bad and doesn't think that they are qualified to express an expert view.

41 the conflict during adolescence is caused by the fact that biological development is faster than psychological and social development
The writer says that the *advances of pyschological and social development* are *slower* and *stuttering* (in this context, hesitant and not progressing smoothly) in comparison with the *urges prompted by* (the strong desires caused by) *biological maturity*. This creates a conflict, because it means that full maturity is delayed. The writer's belief is that adolescence is *unique to man* because it is a long process involving this *delay in attainment of* (reaching) full maturity as an adult. He sees this as a positive aspect because it involves *easing the child into adulthood* (taking them into adulthood slowly and gently rather than suddenly) and therefore delay is the *essence* (the fundamental and most important characteristic) of adolescence.

42 the fact that adolescence involves a strong desire to remain a child and a strong desire to be an adult at the same time
The writer says that *at one and the same time* (at absolutely the same time), teenagers feel the *pangs of dependence* (strong and painful feelings that they want to remain dependent on their parents, as when they were younger children) and a *longing for* (a strong desire for) independence from their parents and their past that is associated with being an adult. For this reason, the writer says, *it's hardly surprising* (it is not surprising at all) that they have *mood swings* (constant changes in mood and state of mind).

43 they make teenagers feel that they are part of a distinct, separate group and that only members of that group understand each other
Silly voices are said to be *a vital* (extremely important) *part of teenage culture*. They may be *caricatures* (exaggerated imitations that make somebody look ridiculous in order to amuse others) of *hapless* (unfortunate, in this context in the sense that they may not know they are being made fun of) *schoolteachers* or they may be invented and not meant to represent real people. *Either way* (whether they are caricatures or original creations) their function is to separate *those in the know* (people belonging to a group who are the only ones to know or realize something) from *the uninitiated* (people who have no knowledge or experience of something that others do know about and have experienced). The writer is saying that silly voices are something that teenagers recognize when others in their group talk in them but that other people, in this case adults, especially their parents, don't see the point of or understand. If teenagers talk in silly voices when their parents are present, for example at mealtimes (the assumption here is that parents and children eat their meals together), parents don't understand anything they say and regard it all as impossible to understand.

Question 44 Summary

FURTHER PRACTICE AND GUIDANCE (p35–36)

For explanations, see the explanations to the summary in the test, which follow.

1 J	2 C	3 E	4 I	5 L	6 B
7 H	8 D	9 F	10 G	11 A	12 K

The relevant main points are **B, F, G, H, I.** The other points concern other aspects of adolescence but are not mainly about the attitude that parents should have towards it, which is the subject of the summary.

p32 PAPER 3 PART FIVE (TEST)

Question 44 Summary

One mark for each content point included from the following, maximum 4 marks

Note: the letters in brackets at the end of each explanation refer to the relevant sections of the texts highlighted in the Further Practice and Guidance pages.

(i) as both a good and a bad time/as something that has both positive and negative aspects
The writer says that although the *expectation is of trouble* (parents expect adolescence to be a period of difficulty because of what people say about it), it is not wholly that. It is not, he says, *a golden age* (a marvellous or *wondrous* – wonderful – period) but it can involve *growth* (in this context, psychological development as a person), *self-exploration* (trying new things in order to find out more about yourself) and *self-discovery* (finding out what your character is really like) as well as *pain, embarrassment, self-doubt* and *loss*. In other words, it has both positive and negative aspects. **(B)**

(ii) as a time when parents have to let their children become independent of them
The writer says that *the task of parents is to let go* – they have to 'release' their children, or allow them to be free, and the children have to *cast off* (release themselves, in the way that a boat is released by undoing the ropes that are attaching it to the shore). **(F)**

(iii) as a time when the bad behaviour of children is not the parents' fault
The writer says that if you are a parent with a teenage child who is *loud, moody, distant and rebellious,* you should realize that *this is normal*. Knowing this won't make it any easier to live with that child but it *may put your mind at rest* (it may make you stop worrying) as to whether you have *gone badly wrong somewhere* (made a terrible mistake, presumably in the way you have brought up that child or dealt with him or her). **(G)**

(iv) as something which has inevitable effects on children
The writer says that the physical and emotional changes that teenagers *go through* (experience) while becoming mature are *unavoidable* and that there are *no short cuts* (no ways of making things happen more quickly than they usually do or should do) and *no cryogenic miracles* (amazing acts, events or processes) that will enable teenagers to be frozen at the age of 13 and then emerge as adults at the age of 20, in this way avoiding the physical and emotional changes of adolescence. **(H)**

(v) as something which parents should not try to influence
The writer says if parents try to *hijack* (in this sense, take over and be in control of) or delay teenagers' psychological development, or try *to mould it in their own image* (influence it so that the child ends up being like the parents), the problems caused will be even greater. It may result in children *making dispirited efforts to do it* (trying to develop psychologically but in a discouraged way, with no expectation of succeeding) later in their lives or it may mean that they *give up* (stop trying to develop psychologically) and remain *chronically* (badly and for a long time) *angry* with their parents *and chronically depressed* with themselves because they know that they were *thwarted* (prevented from doing something they wanted and intended to do) by their parents with regard to *a vital piece of their development*. **(I)**

Marks out of 10 are then given for summary skills, based on the following criteria:

- *relevance*
- *accuracy*
- *organization*
- *rephrasing*
- *length*

FURTHER PRACTICE AND GUIDANCE (p37)

Assessment of sample summary

Content points:

1 Nothing irrelevant is included and most of the relevant points are included.

(i) This is not included, as there is no mention of adolescence having good as well as bad aspects.
(ii) This is included, in the penultimate sentence.
(iii) This is not included – there is reference to bad behaviour but not to parents realizing that it is not their fault.
(iv) This is included, in the first sentence.
(v) This is included, in the sentence beginning *Instead*.

Content: 3 marks

Summary skills:

2 There are a couple of minor errors – *born* should be *borne* in this sense of 'bear', there should be an apostrophe after *adults* (adults') and *handle* should be followed by 'it'. These errors do not affect understanding.
3 The summary is very well-organized and flows well, with good linking; for example the use of *with* in the first sentence and *Instead* and *in spite of* in the penultimate sentence.
4 The points made in the texts have been very skilfully reworded, with some very good language such as the passive of 'bear in mind', *intolerable consequences* and *mature in their own way*. Nothing has simply been copied from the texts.
5 The summary is about 20 words over the maximum length, because the final sentence of the first paragraph and the first sentence of the second paragraph repeat the subject of the question set, rather than answering it.

Summary skills: 6 marks

Sample summary total: 9 marks (out of 14)

PAPER 3:

PART ONE	15 marks
PART TWO	10 marks
PART THREE	12 marks
PART FOUR	16 marks
PART FIVE	
Questions 40–43	8 marks
Question 44	14 marks
TOTAL	75 marks

To be converted into a score out of 40 marks.

p38–42 PAPER 4 PART ONE

FURTHER PRACTICE AND GUIDANCE (p40–42)

For explanations, see the explanations to the questions in the test, which follow.

Question 1: a, b, f

Question 2: a, c, d, e, f

Question 3: a, b, c, d, e, f

Question 4: a, b, c, d, e

Question 5: b, e, f

Question 6: e, f

Question 7: a, b, d, e

Question 8: d, f

p38–39 PAPER 4 PART ONE (TEST)

Note: the letters in brackets refer to the relevant options in the questions in the Further Practice and Guidance pages.

One mark per question (Total: 8)

1 **B:** The speaker says that the title, which is *The Tipping Point*, is a *notion* around which the book is organized and that it describes *the moment when, to put it bluntly* (to phrase it in a direct, unsophisticated way), *a thing takes off* (suddenly becomes very popular or successful) *and becomes widespread in a particular society*. Since this is the central notion of the book, and the speaker has said that the book is a *wonderfully off-beat* (unconventional, unusual) *study of that little-understood social phenomenon, the social epidemic*, the speaker clearly means that the definition of a 'social epidemic' is 'something that becomes widespread in a particular society'. **(a, b)**
A: The speaker says that the title describes the point when something becomes widespread, but she does not say that this is the point at which it is at its most widespread, or imply that after that it becomes less widespread. **(c)**
C: The speaker gives examples of things that have *tipping points* – two of the examples are of inventions (fax machines and mobile phones) and the speaker says that *ideas and diseases* also have *tipping points*. She goes on to say that *the point is* (the important matter is) that social epidemics *usually take us by surprise*. Therefore, she is saying that whatever form the social epidemics take, they usually happen unexpectedly. This is not the same as saying that they worry people when they first happen. **(d, e, f)**

2 **A:** The speaker describes the book's writer as *coming out with ideas* (expressing ideas) – *not necessarily his own* (which may not be his own, original ideas) – *that make conventional solutions to social problems seem criminally naive* (so foolish and lacking in knowledge of the reality of something that they are disgraceful and totally unacceptable). The speaker is therefore saying that the writer, having studied social epidemics, comes to some unconventional conclusions about how to solve social problems, which disagree with and are far better than the ideas people normally have on that matter. **(d, e, f)**
B: The speaker says that Gladwell *makes sense of them* (social epidemics) by *anatomizing them* (examining them in enormous detail) and that he shows that they are heavily influenced by *connectors and mavens*. The speaker says that *Summarized like this* (If the book is summarized as simply an account of what 'connectors' and 'mavens' do), the writer's *dissection* (highly detailed examination) *sounds a bit crude* (seems rather simple and lacking in the required complexity). However, the speaker says, the book is *a very subtle piece of work* (it is clever, complex and not as straightforward as it may at first appear). **(a, c)**
C: The speaker refers to the writer's use of the terms 'connectors' and 'mavens'. She says that the writer defines connectors as people who *jump-start the epidemic* (cause it to start suddenly, as when a car engine starts as a result of the car being pushed) *by virtue of* (because of) *the people they know* – in other words, they know influential people and by telling them about something they can cause it to become a social epidemic. She says that there is a test in the book that lets readers find out whether *they qualify* (whether they can consider themselves 'connectors'). She says that 'mavens' are defined in the book as *specialists who possess the power of recommendation* (people who are experts in a particular field and whose recommendation of something to the public can make it become popular and widespread). She therefore explains what the terminology she mentions means but she does not say that readers will have difficulty understanding the terms. **(b)**

3 **C:** The speaker wonders *Why am I up here?* (Why am I high up *this crag*? – a steep, rough mass of rock) He wonders *What am I trying to prove?* (What do I want to show as a result of climbing the crag?) He wonders *why exactly* (the precise reason why) a man of his age (he implies that at the age of 46 he is old for such an activity) is *dangling over a void* (hanging or swinging over a large empty space below him). He says that there is no answer to *such fatuous* (stupid, foolish) *metaphysical questions* (philosophical questions concerning the meaning of life). He is therefore asking himself why he is doing it, what the point of it is. **(b, d)**
A: The speaker says that he is someone who feels *dizzy* (the uncomfortable feeling that everything is spinning round that some people have when ill or in high places) *near the edges of sea cliffs* (steep rocks on coasts) and *sweats* (produces liquid through the skin) *with fear at the top of towers* and implies that it is therefore strange for him to climb to the top of a rock. We know that he is high up and near the top because he says *Only 80 feet to the top*, indicating that he is only a short distance from the top. Feeling bad in high places is a common experience for him and so he doesn't wonder why he feels bad in the high place he is now. **(a, c)**
B: The speaker says that it is impossible to answer the questions he is asking himself when *your climbing partner has just disappeared from view* and is *somewhere far above your head* – clearly, his climbing partner has disappeared and he knows that he is a long way above him. He therefore doesn't wonder where his partner is, he has an idea where that person is. **(e, f)**

4 **B:** The speaker says that this is *the proverbial moment* (the moment that is well-known and talked about by a lot of people – he means that people who have done similar things talk afterwards about this moment during the

experience). He says that he is on a *great wrinkled slab of ancient geology* (a huge old rock that has lines in it rather than being smooth) and that, at this moment, he has a *palpitating* (with the heart beating very fast), *sweat-soaked* (very wet as a result of sweating), *miraculously* (very remarkably and unexpectedly) *heightened* (made very intense) *sense of existence* (feeling of being alive) and that he *wouldn't be anywhere else* (would not wish to be in any other place). He is therefore saying that he is experiencing a good feeling of great excitement and that he is very glad to be where he is. **(a, b, c)**
A: The speaker says that at this moment he realizes *with a keen pang of guilt* (with a strong and uncomfortable feeling of guilt) that he had forgotten to check *the small print* (the details in a legal document that are often printed in small type and which you might fail to notice or read but which may be very important) where it *states excluded risks* (where the document says which risks a person might take which the insurance policy will not cover). He is therefore saying that he did not look carefully at his life insurance policy to find out what the insurance company would refuse to pay money for if he had an accident as a result of taking a risk that is mentioned in the document. He does care about failing to do this; he says he feels guilty about it. **(d)**
C: The speaker says that the things mentioned in life insurance documents as activities that are not covered by the policy are the *awesomely* (enormously and very challengingly) *dangerous pursuits* (activities) *that men in their forties are so often drawn* (attracted) *to*. He is saying that men of his age (he is 46) are often attracted to dangerous sports of a kind excluded from insurance policies, but he is not saying that at this moment he feels that age does not matter when it comes to doing such activities. **(e, f)**

5 **A:** The speaker says that people's basic needs are *fixed by biology* (decided, determined by their physical structure and how they live) and that these needs have been the same for thousands of years and are unlikely to change for a long time. She lists some of these needs. She then says that the kind of *implants* she previously referred to (pieces of technology that would be small enough to put inside the body, that could perhaps be directly connected to the brain and which might *supplement* – add to – *the mind*) might be called *cognitive prostheses* (artificial parts which would aid the brain). However, she says that these would have to *build on top of the existing biological substrata* (add something to rather than replace the layers of biological need below them). In other words, she is saying that the implants produced by technology could not supply everything that human biology requires but they could help. **(b, c, e, f)**
B: The speaker says that while technology changes quickly, *people change slowly* and that their basic needs remain the same. However, she presents this merely as a statement of fact and does not say that this is because people do not want to change. On the contrary, she implies that they have no choice in the matter. **(a, e)**
C: The speaker lists people's needs but does not say that there are fewer of them than is generally thought or that those needs are less strong than is generally thought. **(d)**

6 **C:** The speaker talks about developing a toy teddy bear that could record a child's deepest thoughts and then replacing this when the child gets older with a device more suited to the age of the person which could do the same thing. After that, a device containing all the information so far gathered would be put into the brain and in this way a person would have in their brain a record of everything that had happened in their lives and everything they had thought in their lives. She says this is all possible, but then asks whether it is desirable for a person to be able to remember absolutely everything. She says this is not clear because our *fallible* (capable of making mistakes or, in this case, losing things) *memories* are *blessings* (very good things that you appreciate and are glad about) and that if we could remember everything, it would be difficult to distinguish important things from *trivia* (small, unimportant details or pieces of information). She is therefore saying that it would be a disadvantage to have a memory that worked so well that you could remember absolutely everything. **(c, e, f)**
A: The speaker talks about having different devices for children and older people to gather the information which would then be put into the brain by use of implants (prostheses). She doesn't say that such an idea would work better with children than with adults, she says that different devices would be suitable for each, and implies that both these devices would work equally well. **(b, e)**
B: The speaker says that prostheses would make memories work better but she does not say that it would show people that it is important to have a good memory. She says that prostheses would store both important and trivial memories, but this is not the same as saying that they would emphasize the importance of the power of memory itself. **(a, d)**

7 **B:** The interviewer says that writers who speak at literary festivals are *in quite a comfortable position* (do not have to worry and are not faced with difficulty) although they *rarely admit it* (they seldom say that this is the case, the implication being that perhaps they want people to feel that such appearances are hard work for them). She says that if they read from their own work, the only preparation they have to do is to give this work *a light dusting* (literally, to clean it a bit; in this context, to prepare something that has not been looked at or used for a while) when they are travelling to the event so that it is *in shape* (in good or suitable condition). Questions asked by the audience *on the back of* (in response to, as a result of) *such a sampling* (a small part of something bigger that is tried as an example) are gentle and *entirely on the author's own terms* (the questions are all questions that the author is willing and happy to answer). If writers *branch out* (move away from their normal area, in this case their own work), and into a different subject which they have a *proven* (known, established) involvement with, they may be asked *tougher* (more difficult) questions. She is therefore saying that the questions asked if writers read from their own work are easier than the ones asked if they talk about something else. **(a, b, d, e)**
A: The interviewer says that questions about subjects writers are involved with may be *tougher* but she adds that *writers are used to questions* because they *ask them of themselves every couple of sentences* – she is therefore saying that because they ask themselves questions all the time when they are writing, they are able to deal with being asked difficult questions by audiences and she does not imply that they dislike this, as it is something they are accustomed to. **(c, e, f)**
C: The interviewer talks about how little preparation may be required of writers before they appear at literary festivals but there is no implied criticism here, and she is not saying that they should prepare more thoroughly. In fact, she is saying that little preparation is required if they are going to read from their own work. When she says that writers rarely admit this, she is suggesting that they do not want people to know that little preparation is required, but she is not saying that this is because they know they should do more preparation. **(a, b)**

8 **A:** William says that it is *almost invariably* (nearly always) a pleasure to meet readers because *meeting those whose equally solitary experience* (this refers to readers, and William is saying that the experience of reading is as solitary – done alone – as the experience of writing) *completes the act begun in hope of contact* (makes writers feel that the act of writing, which they began with the hope that readers would read what they wrote and that in this way they would make contact with readers, has been successfully carried out). In other words, he is saying that when writers meet people who have read their books, they feel that they have made

contact with people through their writing, which was their aim when they started writing. He adds that the feeling that they have done this makes them feel relieved and encouraged, as well as pleased. **(d, f)**
B: William says that the existence of a writer is solitary and *mute* (silent, they don't speak to anyone when they are writing) and that this is like the life of someone suffering from the illness of depression. He says that all writers sometimes lose all confidence, as if a *trapdoor* (a door in a floor) has opened beneath them and they fall through it so that they are left *dangling* (hanging or swinging) above the empty space below it. He therefore talks about what writers really feel like when they are writing, but he does not say that they are keen for readers to realize that this is what it is like to be a writer. **(a, b, e)**
C: William says that writers often lose confidence and they gain *relief and encouragement* from meeting readers but he does not say that readers supply them with ideas they can use in the future. Instead, he is saying that readers make them feel good about what they have already written. **(c, f)**

p43 PAPER 4 PART TWO

One mark per question (Total: 9)

9 **planning rotas:** A *housekeeper* in a hotel is responsible for the good condition of the rooms, particularly with regard to the cleaning of them. The *floor housekeeper* is responsible for the rooms on one particular floor or storey of the hotel. A *rota* is a timetable or schedule saying when duties have to be carried out and who will do them at these times. In this case the rotas concerned the cleaning of rooms.

10 **front office:** The *front office* she refers to is clearly the reception area of the hotel, where staff deal with guests, rather than other offices in other parts of the hotel which guests do not go to.

11 **H(h)ospitality M(m)anagement:** In general terms, *hospitality* is the entertainment and treatment of guests. As a subject for study, it concerns hotels, restaurants, etc, and the management of them with regard to guests.

12 **operational techniques:** This means methods for carrying out activities and practices, in this case in a hotel. She also studied *human resource management*, which means the management of staff (also known as *personnel management*).

13 **green issues:** This means 'environmental matters' or 'matters which concern doing things which are good for or do not damage the environment'.

14 **give-aways:** A *give-away* is a free gift, something which is given to people that they do not have to pay for. She mentions soaps and shampoos as examples of things that hotels give to guests.

15 **HCIMA:** The full name of the organization she joined was the *Hotel and Catering International Management Association*.

16 **Caterer and Hotelkeeper:** This is clearly a *trade paper* or *trade journal* (a newspaper or magazine produced for and distributed among people working in a particular kind or area of business). A *caterer* is someone whose job involves providing food and drink for social events, companies, etc and a *hotelkeeper* is the manager or owner of a hotel.

17 **overbooked:** If a hotel is *overbooked*, an administrative mistake has been made and more people have booked rooms than there are rooms in the hotel, so it is impossible to accommodate all the people for whom bookings have been taken. The same verb is used with regard to an aircraft flight, when the number of passengers who have booked seats is greater than the number of seats on the aircraft.

p44 PAPER 4 PART THREE

One mark per question (Total: 5)

18 **D:** Brigid says that *all was not entirely well with* her life (not everything in her life was all right) but that there was *Nothing drastic* (nothing very seriously wrong). She simply felt *stuck* (as if she was not making progress) both in her working life and her personal life because she had too much to do and too little time in which to do it – when she says *ditto*, she means that that was her situation at home as well as at work. However, she *wasn't miserable enough* to get *therapy or counselling* (her situation wasn't bad enough for her to go to a psychiatrist or psychologist or to a counsellor – someone who gives professional advice about personal problems) and all she wanted to do was *get a little more from life* (enjoy life a bit more). She says that until recently, there would not have been many options for someone in her situation but now there are life coaches, who can help people in her situation.
A: She says that there are now *legions* (lots of) life coaches *out there* (in existence in a place) and that they help people who are frustrated and *down-at-heart* (unhappy), and she mentions what they do and how much they charge, but she does not say that she got this information from reading about them or that reading about them caused her to consult one.
B: She says that she had a small problem in her working life and her personal life and that the problem in both of them was the same (she felt *stuck and in need of change*), but she does not say that her situation was getting worse.
C: She says that she didn't feel that therapy or counselling were appropriate in her situation but she does not say that she had already tried them. She says that the options for someone in her situation were limited, but she does not say that she had tried any of these options.

19 **A:** Brigid's coach told her that she should consider herself a *magnet for* (someone or something which powerfully attracts) *money* and someone *to whom cash* (money that can be spent) *flows effortlessly* (without her having to make any effort).
B: She says that she agreed with her coach that her attitude to money was *rooted in childhood* (began and became established when she was a child) and she says that her coach told her that she had to *carve out* (create through effort) a completely new attitude, but she does not say that she was told that her attitude to money was untypical of her personality or that it differed from her attitude to other things.
C: She agreed with her coach that she had to do something about her *deeply ambivalent relationship with money*. This means that she had mixed feelings about money rather than a clear single attitude towards it, not that she gave it more importance than she should.
D: Her coach told her what her individual attitude to money should be but she does not say that her coach generalized about people's attitudes to money or said that most people have the wrong attitude to it.

20 **C:** Her coach advised her to repeat that she was ready to have the perfect life she deserved and she says that when she did this, it *cheered me up no end* (it made me feel much happier).
A: What she had to repeat was one of *a clutch of* (a small group of) *positive affirmations* (statements expressing a positive attitude) *with which to brainwash myself into* (force myself to accept the idea of) *readiness for riches* (being ready to be rich), and so the idea was that by repeating the words

she would convince herself that she was going to be rich. She says that she did repeat the words and it made her feel better but she does not say that she felt that repeating them was a silly thing to do while she was doing it, even though it is possible that this was the case.
B: When her coach told her that she would be rich, have a wonderful life and not feel guilty about it, she thought that this was a *preposterous* (totally ridiculous and unreasonable) idea and she *laughed out loud down the telephone*. She therefore did not conceal her feelings, she made them clear and expressed them openly.
D: She says that her coach was *undeterred* (not discouraged) by her *scepticism* (doubtful response to what someone claims) and told her to *suspend my disbelief* (decide to believe temporarily that something you know not be true is true). Her point is therefore not that her initial feeling was one of confusion but that she didn't believe what she was told and was then persuaded to accept it.

21 A: Brigid says that she was told that most people have the same aims with regard to their personal and working lives, their abilities and money and that the only thing that *stands in their way* (is an obstacle that prevents them from achieving their aims) *is childhood conditioning* (attitudes that were forced on them by other people and became their established attitudes when they were children). She was therefore told that most people's problems with regard to organizing their lives, *making the most of* (taking the greatest advantage possible of) their abilities and money resulted from their experiences during childhood.
B: She says that her work *came under close scrutiny* (was carefully analysed, presumably by both herself and her coach) and that she decided to concentrate on jobs that interested her. This means that she decided to direct her attention towards jobs that interested her rather than jobs that did not, but she does not say that she became able to *concentrate* (use her mind intensely) better.
C: She mentions several things that she was told to do. Firstly there was *the mandatory* (compulsory – presumably she means that people are always told to do this) *de-cluttering* (making things no longer in a state of disorder, tidying something which is untidy), which involved her throwing away useless things she had so that she would have room for all the *goodies* (desirable items) she would have when she was rich. Then she dealt with her financial situation and started saving money, and made changes in her working life. However, she does not say that she had more difficulty doing any one of these things than doing any of the others.
D: Her coach told her that her situation, like most people's, resulted from childhood, but she does not say that she herself began to wonder what had caused her to be in the situation she was in – she was told what the cause was.

22 B: Brigid says that she is still unsure about the *'me first' approach* but thinks that it is *a healthy counterbalance to* the *'me last'* attitude she used to have. What she means by this is that coaching has given her the attitude that she should be more selfish and see her interests and wishes as more important than those of others, and she is not completely comfortable with that idea. However, she thinks that it balances in a good way her previous attitude, which was to consider other people's interests and wishes more important than her own and to think of herself as the least important person. She therefore feels that her previous attitude was wrong and that it is right for her to be more selfish now.
A: She says that coaching *is hardly a soft option* (cannot be regarded as an easy choice requiring little effort) but that for her it provided *a great boost* (it had a very positive effect on her, gave her a great deal of help and encouragement). What she is saying is that coaching requires a lot of effort on the part of the person having it and that she put that effort in and got good results. She is not saying that it hasn't been worth it because there has been too much effort on her part and too few benefits for her in return.
C: She says that there have been *no instant miracles* (coaching has not had immediate wonderful results) but *things are looking up* (her situation is improving). However, she does not say that she began to expect that her coach would make miracles happen in her life; she simply says that miracles have not happened.
D: She says that if you have a coach, you have to deal with things that you have *put off* (delayed dealing with) because you have *the deadline* (point in time by which something must be done that has been fixed or imposed by someone else) *of the next session* (the next time you speak to your coach). If you haven't taken the appropriate action by that time, your coach will not wish to speak to you. What she is saying is that if you haven't done what you are supposed to do by a certain time, your coach may decide there is no point in having a session, and so this may limit the number of sessions you have. However, this is something the coach and not you would decide, so she is not saying that it's a good idea to have only a limited number of sessions.

p45 PAPER 4 PART FOUR

One mark per question (Total: 6)

23 D: David says *I am always competing with myself to beat last season's figures*, by which he means that he is always trying to improve on the sales made in the shop during the same period of the previous year. This is because *I get a kick out of making the best profit I can* (he gets a strong feeling of pleasure or excitement from it). He is therefore saying that his motivation for always trying to increase the profits made in the shop is a personal one – he likes to do better than he did before – and not that he is put under pressure by anyone else to do this.
Katherine talks about the demands of her job, saying *I have to be prepared to commit myself* (make firm decisions), *I thrive on* (thoroughly enjoy and am stimulated by) *the pressure*, that she is so busy *it's a kind of permanent 'high'* (a constant feeling of great pleasure or excitement) and that *you have to put your whole self into* (put all your energy and effort into) the job because *there are no half measures* (the job cannot be done with less than total effort and commitment). However, she does not say that any of the pressure she is under has been created by her, she simply says that it is part of the job.

24 K: Katherine says that she doesn't like losing staff, particularly if this involves her having to *terminate their employment* (sack them). If this happens, she believes that *among other things* (one of several reasons for it), it has happened because she *was wrong about them*. She is therefore saying that she doesn't like the feeling that she has to sack someone because she had got the wrong impression of them when she employed them and she should not have employed them in the first place.
David says that *it's all about people*, by which he means that the most important aspect of the job is dealing with people and he goes on to say that he enjoys dealing with people. He does not say that he feels the same as Katherine with regard to making wrong decisions when employing people.

25 K: Katherine says that one thing she does is to *conduct training on the sales floor when trade is slack*, which means that she trains the sales assistants in the part of the shop in which goods are sold when the shop is not busy because there are few customers.
David talks about various actions he takes, including *tight security*, and making checks and keeping records with regard to what comes into the shop and what goes out of it. He does this to *keep overheads* (the everyday expenses involved in running a business) *to a minimum*, presumably

to prevent goods from being stolen, but he does not say that he does any of these things only during quiet periods.

26 K: Katherine says that if you are in her position, *you mustn't let your staff see you falter* (appear to lack confidence at a particular point in time) *or hesitate* and that instead you must give them immediate answers. She says that things can be *hectic* (very busy) and that at such times you have to decide quickly on *deploying staff* (using members of staff in certain places and for certain purposes) and you *can't hang around* (delay or wait) wondering what to do. She is therefore saying that she has to act quickly because that is what her staff require of her. She doesn't want them to see her hesitate, which means that they do not expect her to do so.
David talks about enjoying solving problems and lists several of the kinds of problem he has to solve but he does not talk about his staff's attitude to this or say that they expect to see him solving these problems, even though this may well be the case.

27 D: David says that at first he thought that the staff might think he was *unapproachable* (unfriendly and cold, not someone that you can easily talk to) but that in fact this has not been the case because he has a *rapport* (a good relationship in which there is understanding between people) with all of them and they don't get *resentful* (annoyed because of feeling badly treated) or feel bad without saying anything.
Katherine says she likes *that side of things* (dealing with the staff's problems) and says that she could have made a career *behind the scenes* (in the background, not dealing directly with people) but prefers dealing with people. She does not, however, refer to having had any doubts, either about herself or her choice of career.

28 B: David says that his approach is to be *open with* (honest and willing to discuss matters with) the staff and that when they have problems (resulting from dissatisfaction at work presumably), he thinks of ways of changing what they do at work so that they *look beyond* what they consider to be *their immediate abilities* (think about what they might be capable of doing in the future, not only what they can do now).
Katherine says that her approach to customers who seem to have come to the shop only to complain is to *stand there and take what they say while they get it out of their systems* (not to speak but to allow them to get rid of their bad feelings by expressing them).

PAPER 4:

PART ONE	8 marks
PART TWO	9 marks
PART THREE	5 marks
PART FOUR	6 marks
TOTAL	28 marks

To be converted into a score out of 40 marks.

p44–49 PAPER 5

Marks out of 40 are given for performance in the speaking paper.

TEST TWO

p50–51 PAPER 1 PART ONE

Note: all explanations in this part refer to the meaning or use of each option most closely related to the question, not necessarily to the only meaning or use of each option.

One mark per question (Total: 18)

Spencer Tracy

1 **C:** If someone is **overwhelmingly kind, generous,** etc to someone else, they are so kind, generous, etc to them that the other person is amazed and moved emotionally by the treatment they receive. The writer is saying that Tracy was extremely unpleasant to some people and extremely nice to others.
A: If you are *acutely aware* of something or *acutely embarrassed* by something, you are extremely aware or embarrassed and experience the feeling very greatly. (*For me, it was an acutely embarrassing experience.*)
B: If someone is *comprehensively beaten, defeated,* etc, they lose badly and completely, for example in a sports match, a game or a battle. (*My team played very badly and were comprehensively defeated.*)
D: If something is *richly deserved* or if someone *richly deserves* something, it is fully deserved or they fully deserve it. (*His richly deserved success was long overdue./She richly deserves to be promoted.*)
All the options mean 'very' in some way, but only C can be used to form a collocation with 'kind'.

2 **A:** If something happens **to the point where** something else happens, it continues to happen until a time comes when it causes something else to happen. The writer is saying that Tracy treated Robert Francis so badly that Francis felt terrible.
B: *Amount* can be used in phrases like *a certain amount of* and *any/no amount of.* (*He felt a certain amount of guilt./No amount of money could compensate for their loss.*)
C: The same idea can also be expressed with the phrases *to such a degree/extent that* and *to the degree/extent that.* (*He annoyed people to such a degree/to the extent that he had absolutely no friends left.*)
D: The phrase *in the end* means 'finally' or 'eventually' and can be used to describe the result of something after a period of time. (*She was consistently rude to me and in the end I lost my temper with her.*)
All the options are connected with the idea of the extent of something or a time being reached when something happens, but only A can complete the linking phrase required and be followed by 'where'.

3 **B:** A **substitute** something, is someone or something that replaces the original or usual thing or person because the original or usual one is not available. The writer is saying that Tracy became like a father to Wagner, whose real father was presumably either not present or dead.
A: A *reserve* is a player who is named as someone who could play in a team if a member of that team was unable to play. (*The reserve goalkeeper was one of the members of the squad.*) Something that is a *reserve* is also something extra that can be used if required, especially if the main one can no longer be used (*a reserve petrol tank*).
C: An *understudy* is an actor who learns the part played by another actor so that they can replace that actor if they are unable to perform. (*The leading actress fell ill and her understudy had to play her part that night.*)
D: A *proxy* is someone who has the legal authority to act on behalf of someone else, especially when voting. (*As I was abroad at the time, I voted in the election by proxy.*)
All the options refer to someone who can replace someone, but only B fits the precise meaning in the context.

4 **C:** If you **go along with something,** you agree with, accept or co-operate with it. The writer is saying that Tracy usually did what directors asked him to do.
A: If you *fall in with something* or *fall into line with something,* you conform with it or agree to act in accordance with it. (*I'll fall in with whatever you choose./Despite his objections, he fell into line with the wishes of the majority.*)
B: If people *pull together,* they act together with a common aim and without letting any disagreements between them affect them. (*If the whole workforce pulls together, the company can be saved.*)
D: If you *bear with someone,* you are patient and tolerant towards them, rather than becoming annoyed with them because they are unable to do something that you want. (*If you'll just bear with me for a moment, I'll get you the information you want.*)
All the options are connected with the idea of people co-operating with each other, but only C correctly completes the required phrasal verb.

5 **D:** A **mild reaction, comment, criticism,** etc is one that is fairly gentle and not severe. The writer is saying that the reactions described were not particularly aggressive ones, in comparison with the way Tracy sometimes reacted.
A: A sound can be *low,* meaning 'not loud' (*She speaks in a low voice.*); lights can be *low,* meaning 'not bright' (*Turn the lights down low.*); heat in an oven, etc can be *low,* meaning 'warm but not hot'. (*Cook for 20 minutes on a low heat.*)
B: Weather conditions can be *light,* meaning 'not severe' (*a light shower*); a *light conversation* is one that is not serious; *light reading* is the reading of something purely for entertainment rather than for serious thought; a *light sentence* is a jail punishment given by a court that is not severe and does not involve going to jail for long.
C: *Small* can be used with the meaning 'not important, minor'. (*The differences between our attitudes are very small.*)
All the options can be used to mean 'not severe' 'not strong' or 'not great', but only D can form a collocation with 'reaction'.

6 **D:** If someone is **downright rude, lazy,** etc, they are completely rude, lazy, etc and their behaviour cannot be regarded in any other way. The word *downright* is used to express strong disapproval of such behaviour. The writer is saying that Tracy was extremely rude when he worked with Lang.
A: If something *contrasts starkly with* something else, the contrast between the two things is very obvious, very great and very noticeable. (*The building contrasts starkly with those surrounding it.*)
B: If you *tell someone something straight,* you say it directly and honestly, even though this might upset them. (*I told him straight that I couldn't stand him.*) If you *come/get straight to the point,* you say what you mean directly, without hesitation and without talking about other things first. (*Let's come/get straight to the point – this situation cannot continue any longer.*)
C: If you are *fully aware* of something or *fully expecting* something, you are completely aware of it or completely expecting it so that it is no surprise at all. (*I am fully aware of your opinion on this matter./She was fully expecting something like that to happen.*)
All the options can be used with the meaning 'clearly' or 'completely', but only D can form a collocation with 'rude'.

A Message for Lisa

7 **A:** If information is **confidential,** it is secret in the sense that it cannot be made known to anyone other than the specified people who are allowed to have it. The writer is saying that the teacher told Lisa he was not allowed to tell her what was in the message for her, which seemed ridiculous to her.
B: *Intimate details* are those which are private and personal to someone. (*I didn't want to tell a complete stranger all the intimate details of my life.*) If two people are *intimate,* their relationship is a very close one and they know each other's

private and personal details. (*I know her quite well but I'm not an intimate friend of hers.*)
C: *Clandestine* behaviour is done secretly, so that other people, who would disapprove, will not know about it. (*She had clandestine meetings with her lover.*)
D: Something that is *undercover* is done secretly because it may be regarded as breaking rules. (*The company was accused of making undercover payments to people in exchange for information on their rivals.*) *Undercover* work is work done by a spy or police officer to get information about people who do not know who they really are. (*Two officers went undercover to find out about the drug dealers in the area.*)
All the options mean 'secret' in some way, but only A fits the precise meaning in the context.

8 **C:** If you are **wary of somebody/something**, you are suspicious of them or cautious with regard to them, because you fear that they could cause you problems or do you harm. The writer is saying that Lisa had been taught as a child not to trust people who believed in rules.
A: If you speak or react in a *guarded* way, you do so cautiously. (*My comments were guarded because I didn't want to offend anyone.*)
B: If you are or feel *uneasy* (*about something*), you are anxious or worried about it. (*Joe is a rather aggressive person and he makes me feel uneasy.*)
D: If someone is *edgy*, they are nervous or agitated and likely to get upset or angry at any moment. (*George has got a lot on his mind and this has made him rather edgy.*)
All the options mean 'cautious' or 'nervous', but only C can be followed by 'of'.

9 **C:** If something **brings** something, it causes it to exist, results in it or is followed by it. The writer is saying that as Lisa walked towards the office to collect the message, she became more and more optimistic that it would result in her and Quentin being together again.
A: If something *leads to* something, it results in it or causes it. (*What was it that led to this problem?*) If you *lead someone to* a place, they follow you there. (*The hotel owner led me to my room.*)
B: If something *arises*, it occurs or appears. (*Whenever a serious problem arises, Helen panics.*) If something *arises from/out of something*, it happens or follows as a result of it. (*My interest in the theatre arose from/out of a visit to a play when I was very young.*)
D: If something *puts someone in mind of something*, it causes them to think about or remember it. (*This situation puts me in mind of something that happened to me many years ago.*)
All the options are connected with the idea of causing something, but only C fits grammatically.

10 **B:** If something **occurs to someone**, it comes into their mind or they realize it. The writer is saying that Lisa realized just before she reached the office that Quentin didn't know she was at college.
A: If something *strikes someone*, it comes into their mind suddenly or they suddenly become aware of it. (*It strikes me that there is a very simple solution to this.*)
C: If something *dawns on someone*, it becomes clear or obvious to them after a period of time. (*Gradually it dawned on me that he had been telling me lies.*)
D: If something *springs to mind*, it comes into someone's mind quickly or they suddenly think of it. (*I've been trying to come up with some new ideas but unfortunately nothing springs to mind at the moment.*)
All the options are connected with the idea of a thought coming into someone's mind, but only B fits grammatically.

11 **D:** If you *have no way of doing something*, it is impossible for you to do it. The writer is saying that Quentin couldn't have known that Lisa was at college.
A: If you *have no access to something*, you do not have the chance to have or use it as it is not available to you (*people with no access to a good education*).
B: *The route to something* is the way in which it is achieved or the process through which it is reached. (*It's a book which claims to teach you the route to success in business.*)
C: *Scope for something* is the opportunity for something to exist. (*In this job, there is scope for innovation.*)
All the options are connected with the idea of the ability to do or have something, but only D fits both in terms of the precise meaning in the context and grammatically.

12 **D:** If something **takes your breath away**, it surprises, pleases or excites you very much. The writer is saying that Lisa's mood changed so much and so quickly when the head of the department spoke to her that she was extremely surprised by this change.
A: If you *catch your breath*, you stop breathing for a moment because of a sudden feeling of fear or shock. (*When the figure suddenly appeared out of the darkness, I caught my breath.*)
B: If you *draw breath*, you breathe in after a period of not doing so. (*He spoke at great length, hardly drawing breath the whole time.*)
C: If you *hold your breath*, you deliberately stop breathing for a short time, perhaps because of fear or excitement. (*You have to hold your breath underwater./The competitors held their breath as the name of the winner was announced.*)
All the options can be used in phrases with 'breath', but only D completes the required idiom.

The Vacuum Cleaner

13 **D:** If you **plan on doing** something, you intend to do it, you consciously wish to do it. The writer is saying that Booth wasn't intending to do anything of enormous significance when he went to the event.
A: If you *envisage something/doing something*, you imagine it as a possibility in the future or you form a picture of it in your mind. (*I didn't envisage that there would be such complications./Do you envisage staying in this job for years?*)
B: If you *aim for/at/towards something*, you try to achieve it. (*In everything she does, she's always aiming at/for/towards success.*)
C: If you *devise something*, you create or produce it by planning it and thinking about it carefully. (*The local government have devised a new traffic scheme.*)
All the options are connected with the idea of planning or intending, but only D can be followed by 'on'.

14 **C:** If something such as a machine **sucks**, it draws in air, liquid, etc from outside. If a person **sucks something**, they draw liquid into the mouth using the lip muscles (*suck orange juice through a straw*) or they squeeze and roll it with the tongue while it is in the mouth (*suck a sweet/a child sucking his thumb*). The writer is saying that Booth told the inventor that his machine should take air in, not blow it out.
A: If you *gasp*, you take in air suddenly and quickly through the mouth, perhaps because you are very surprised or because you are having difficulty in breathing. (*The audience gasped at the sight of such extraordinary fireworks./The room filled with smoke and the people were gasping for breath.*)
B: If you *puff*, you breathe quickly and loudly as a result of using a lot of energy. (*He was puffing when he arrived at the top of the stairs.*) If you *puff on a cigarette*, you smoke it.
D: If you *gulp something*, you swallow it quickly and in large quantities. (*Don't gulp your drink or you'll choke.*) If you *gulp for/in air*, you breathe in air quickly and deeply because you are having difficulty in breathing normally. (*When I reached the surface, I was gulping for air.*)
All the options are connected with taking in air, but only C fits the precise meaning in the context.

15 B: If you **remark** that something is the case, you say that it is the case. The writer is talking about a comment the inventor made to Booth.
A: If you *express something* such as a feeling or opinion, you make it known (*express views in an article/express emotions/ express interest*).
C: If you *voice something* such as an opinion or feeling, you make it known through what you say (*voice objections/a meeting in which everyone voiced their opinions*).
D: If you *utter something*, you say it. (*She sat there all afternoon without uttering a word.*)
All the options mean 'say something' or 'make something known by speaking', but only B can be followed by that + clause – the other options are followed by an object.

16 A: If you **mull over something** or **mull something over**, you think about or consider it carefully for a long period. The writer is saying that Booth gave serious thought to the problem of how to get a machine to take in air while he was in the restaurant.
B: If you *reflect on something*, you think deeply and seriously about it (*reflect on past mistakes*).
C: If you *contemplate something/doing something*, you think carefully and deeply about it or you consider the possibility of it carefully. (*He sat there, contemplating what the best course of action was./I'm contemplating working abroad for a few years.*)
D: If you *dwell on something*, you continue to think or talk about it for a long time, perhaps longer than is necessary or desirable. (*Don't dwell on the things that have gone wrong – be positive.*)
All the options mean 'think about', but only A completes the required phrasal verb.

17 C: If you **choke** or **choke on something**, you become unable to breathe because something is preventing air from reaching your lungs or because something has become stuck in your throat. Usually this causes you to cough. The writer is saying that Booth had a problem because he breathed in the dust.
A: If someone *strangles someone*, they kill them or make it impossible for them to breathe by holding them round the throat and squeezing tightly. (*The victim was strangled with a rope.*)
B: If your nose is *blocked*, it is hard or impossible for you to breathe through it. (*I was suffering from a heavy cold and had a blocked nose.*)
D: If something is *clogged (up) with something*, it is blocked by it (*streets clogged (up) with traffic*).
All the options are connected in some way with difficulty in breathing and something being prevented from flowing, but only C fits the precise meaning in the context.

18 B: A **variety** of something can mean one type or example of something that differs from others that come into the same general category. The writer is saying that Booth's machine was not the same as vacuum cleaners as we know them today but it *was* a vacuum cleaner.
A: If something is in a *class*, it can be considered to belong to the same group as other, similar things (*For tax purposes, all such vehicles belong to the same class.*) or it is of a high quality. (*This computer is not in the same class as more modern models.*)
C: A *category* is a group of people or things that can be considered together because of what they have in common (*prisoners divided into categories/various categories of illness*).
D: The *nature* of something refers to its qualities or characteristics (*conduct research into the nature of the problem*). If something is *of a* certain *nature*, it is of that type or belongs to that category. (*He's not very good at jobs of a practical nature.*)
All the options can mean 'type', but only B fits the precise meaning in the context.

p52–56 PAPER 1 PART TWO

FURTHER PRACTICE AND GUIDANCE (54–56)

For explanations, see the explanations to the questions in the test, which follow.

Question 19
1 no, it gets busy on days when there is a match
2 bin-liners (plastic bags that are placed inside rubbish containers or bins for rubbish to be put into, so that it can be thrown away) containing T-shirts
3 hot dogs (snacks consisting of a roll of bread with a cooked sausage inside) and money
4 b and c

Question 20
1 a, b and d
2 b
3 no
4 a lot of merchandise they have already bought there
5 buy even more merchandise

Question 21: 1 a, b and c 2 b and d 3 b 4 c

Question 22: 1 d 2 d 3 a 4 b

Question 23: 1 c 2 a 3 a 4 a 5 c

Question 24: 1 c 2 c 3 b 4 b

Question 25: 1 b 2 a 3 c 4 a and d

Question 26: 1 b 2 a 3 a and b 4 b

p52–53 PAPER 1 PART TWO (TEST)

Note: the numbers in brackets after each explanation refer to the relevant question in the Further Practice and Guidance pages.

Two marks per question (Total: 16)

Manchester United

19 C: If a place is *teeming with people or things*, it is completely full of them and there is a great deal of activity there. The writer says that the area is like a bazaar in that it is *teeming, colourful* (not only in the sense of containing many colours but also meaning interesting and full of remarkable things) *and chaotic* (without order or organization). The idea that it is very busy is then reinforced by the reference to every bit of pavement being *occupied by commerce* (people selling things). **(4b, 4c)**
A: A *whiff* of something is a smell of something, especially one experienced only briefly, or a trace or hint of something. In this case the writer uses it with regard to food and money – he says you can smell the food, but even more powerfully you can detect that money is being made all around you. He does not use the word to refer to how busy the place is. **(3, 4d)**
B: If something *transmogrifies into* something else, it changes completely and becomes something totally different. *Transmogrifies* therefore refers to the industrial estate changing into a place like a bazaar in Istanbul on match days but the word itself does not refer to a place being busy. **(1, 4a)**
D: If something is *jammed with* something, a large quantity of something has been forced into it so that it is completely full and there is no room for anything else. In this case, the boys' bin-liners have been filled completely with T-shirts which they are trying to sell. The word is therefore used to describe the bags, not how busy the area is. **(2)**

20 **D:** The writer says that people *already burdened by United apparel* (already carrying or wearing clothes and other goods connected with Manchester United) *line up for the privilege of buying yet more stuff* (stand in a queue in order to buy even more goods connected with Manchester United). The word *privilege* (meaning a right or honour not given to most people) is used ironically here and the phrase *yet more stuff* emphasizes just how many goods these people buy from the superstore. The writer is therefore implying that he finds it strange that people are willing to queue for so long to buy goods from the shop and that he is surprised by the number of goods they buy individually. **(1b, 4, 5)**
A: The writer describes the queue as *the most extraordinary sight* but that is his opinion of it, not the feeling of those in it. He also describes it as *snaking round crush barriers* (twisting or winding round barriers erected to control crowds so that people in them do not press against each other too much) but this describes the shape and length of the queue, not the feelings of those in it. **(1a, 1c, 1d)**
B: The merchandising manager says that he and the chairman look at the queue and smile at each other – presumably because they are pleased to see how popular the superstore is and therefore how much money it makes for the club – but there is no mention of their role in its success and there is no implication on the part of the writer concerning that. **(2)**
C: The writer lists numerous items that are available at the superstore and mentions that over 1,500 items are available to *empty the pockets of the faithful* (for loyal supporters of the club to spend all their money on) but he does not refer to the quality of those goods. He is surprised by how many goods people buy, but he does not imply that those goods are of low quality. **(3)**

Silly Sports

21 **C:** The writer says that the *urge to play, the urge for folly is something that goes very deep* and that this urge can be seen if you watch kittens playing. He is therefore saying that the desire to play and do foolish things is a basic part of human nature (and that it is *older than the human species*) and that you can see this urge in action if you watch kittens playing. The kittens' games are therefore examples of the natural desire to play. **(2b, 2d, 3, 4)**
A: The writer says that all sports are regarded by some people with *deadly* (extreme) *seriousness* and that all sports are followed by *fanatics* (people who are extremely or too enthusiastic about them). He says that such sports may have a bad effect on people – for example, people may *fall out over it* (stop being friends with other people because of disagreements about the sport) – or they may prove beneficial to such people. He therefore implies that some people may regard certain sports as ridiculous but the games played by kittens are not examples of such sports – they are examples of the need to play, even if this need may result in sports that appear ridiculous to some. **(1b, 1c)**
B: The writer says that the games kittens play all have *formal rules and accepted standards of behaviour* and so it could be said that they have properly worked-out rules. However, these games are not used as examples of the need for games to have such rules. Instead, they exemplify the need to play. **(1d, 2a)**
D: The writer indicates that the games played by kittens that he mentions could be considered 'proper games' in the way that a human would understand that – they have rules and they are *competitive* although they usually do not result in physical injury. He is therefore suggesting that these games are similar to those played by humans, not different from them, and is using them to illustrate a similarity between humans and animals, not the differences between them. **(1a, 2c)**

22 **A:** The writer says that on the subject of sport *it all comes down to* (the whole issue centres on) a phrase used by the poet Coleridge with regard to poetry that can equally be applied to sport. The writer says that all sports are *absurd* and *risible* (ridiculous) and that if you are a logical person there is *no other standpoint* (no other way of looking at them). He then says that nobody is logical, particularly with regard to sport, which indicates that we do not regard sports as ridiculous. He then adds that we *cannot suspend our disbelief at will* (we cannot do so whenever we want to), which indicates that there are times when we do regard sports as ridiculous. Therefore the phrase '*suspension of disbelief*' must refer to deciding to forget about logical thought and consciously taking seriously something which you know isn't actually serious. In the wider sense, the phrase means choosing to believe that fictional characters and events are real in order to enjoy a piece of writing, a play, a film, etc. **(1, 2, 3)**
B: The writer says that he finds golf ridiculous – he cannot watch it *without laughter* – and that he cannot suspend his disbelief when it comes to golf. He therefore thinks that golf is more ridiculous than other sports but the phrase 'suspension of disbelief' does not refer to accepting that one thing can be taken more seriously than another or to comparing anything with something else. **(4b)**
C: The writer clearly accepts that sport is important to a great many people and that this involves them not applying logic to it. However, the phrase 'suspension of disbelief' does not refer to accepting that other people take something seriously when you do not. **(4d)**
D: The writer says that the 'suspension of disbelief' involves putting out of our minds what we know to be logically the case – that all sports are ridiculous. This is also said, in Coleridge's full phrase, to be *willing* – we want to do it and we know that we are doing it. The phrase therefore refers to adopting a particular attitude towards a particular subject at a particular time, not to pretending to have a general characteristic – the inability to think logically – at all times. **(4a, 4c)**

Football Clubs

23 **B:** The writer compares football supporters with *the children of neglectful parents* (children whose parents do not pay enough attention to or care enough for them) and says that their *yearning for closeness and trust* (their strong desire to have a close relationship with clubs and be able to trust what clubs tell them) remains despite repeated *doses of callousness* (occasions when they are treated extremely unkindly). He is therefore saying that they are dependent on (in the sense of needing) the clubs even though they feel that the clubs often do not treat them well. **(1c, 2, 3)**
A: The writer says that people in football *keep themselves to themselves* (avoid contact with other people) because they are *under siege from within and without* (they are under pressure or attack from people both inside and outside the club). However, his main point about supporters is not that they should be more sympathetic to the difficulties faced by those in football clubs, it is that supporters feel an intense personal involvement with clubs and want things from them. **(1a, 1b)**
C: Supporters are said to *crave* (have a very strong desire for) *reliable information* and to feel a sense that the supporters are as important to the club as the club is to the supporters (*that our passionate and committed support for the team is met, in its own way, by the club's commitment to us*). The writer is therefore saying that the supporters want certain things from the club but he makes no mention of how they try to get what they want, and no suggestion that they are forceful in their pursuit of it. **(4)**
D: The writer does not suggest that supporters keep changing their loyalties (supporting first one club and then another) or that they are sometimes enthusiastic in their support for a club and sometimes have no interest in it. On the contrary, his main point is that they always want to know what is happening at their club (*What's going on?* is

their *constant lament* – unhappy cry), despite feeling that the club cares less about them than they do about it. **(5)**

24 D: The writer describes Graham Taylor as a *decent and competent man* – he thinks he was a good person and good at his job – who was *pilloried* (publicly attacked and made to look ridiculous) by the *tabloid press* (the smaller, popular newspapers in Britain that have little in the way of serious news and frequently have a disrespectful tone with regard to people in the public eye), and made to look stupid by a television documentary that was *slanted* (not balanced, presenting a particular view without including other, contrary views). He therefore feels that Graham Taylor was treated extremely unfairly in a way that cannot be justified, and deserved better treatment. **(3)**
A: The writer says that supporters are *voracious for* (want a very great deal of, are very enthusiastic in their wish for) information from football clubs, but this is not a criticism – his overall tone suggests that he sympathizes with supporters on this matter and indeed states that he is one of them (the use of *We* in the first paragraph). **(4)**
B: The writer says that supporters *don't so much want to talk to the players* (even talking to them is not enough for the supporters) *as to touch them, to imbibe them* (they want to have physical contact with them, in some sense to absorb or possess them). He is therefore saying that supporters want extremely close personal contact with the players, but this is a description of how important the players are to the supporters, not a criticism of either group. **(1)**
C: The media, according to the writer, have an *unassuageable appetite for football news, trivia, gossip* (their desire for news, minor details and rumours is so great that it can never be satisfied). The writer is here simply stating that the media want a lot of information about football but he is not criticizing them for this. **(2)**

The Professional Player

25 A: The writer begins three sentences with *Suddenly* to emphasize how rapid the changes in Rugby Union have been since it became a professional sport. These sentences all refer back to his opening statement that the changes have *affected the players more than anyone else*. For the players, there is no longer *the luxury of margin of error* (they can no longer feel relaxed in the knowledge that they can make some mistakes without it mattering too much), their hobby has become their job and they have *no escape from rugby*. He says that *making the necessary adjustment* to a hobby becoming a job can be *disconcerting*, which suggests that players find the change confusing and disturbing and says that this is particularly true when the *sport in question* (the sport concerned) *has no lengthy culture of professionalism to inform it* (has not been a professional sport for long enough for it to have learnt from experience and for the nature of it to have developed as a result of experience). He is therefore saying that the changes in the sport have been rapid and enormous and that players have not had time to adjust to them because the sport has not been a professional one for long enough. **(1, 2, 4a, 4d)**
B: The writer makes a general point about when sport changes from being a hobby to being a job. Hobbies, he says, *are vital avenues of release for us all* (are extremely important as ways of escaping from pressure) and when a hobby *graduates* (in this sense moves on or progresses) to become a job, this can be *disconcerting*. He says therefore that this is always a possibility since it is true for all sports, and he therefore implies that the impact on the players of becoming professionals is not a surprise. **(3, 4a, 4d)**
C: The writer's point throughout the text is that there is a massive impact on players when a sport becomes professional. The impact on Rubgy Union players, he says, is even greater when they become professionals because the sport itself has not been professional for long. However, his topic is the effect of the change and he does not imply that Rugby Union should not have become a professional sport or that there is anything about it which makes it a mistake for it to have become professional. **(4c)**
D: The whole text focuses on the present situation with regard to the feelings and situation of players who have become professionals. The writer does not refer to the future or to any unexpected developments there may be then. **(4b, 4c)**

26 D: The writer says that, if you are a player, *Should imperfection ever blemish your excellence* (If any fault or mistake on your part ever spoils your performance, which is otherwise excellent), *it plagues your conscience* (you feel guilty about it for a long time afterwards and cannot forget about it), not only because you want to be the best but because you feel you *have a duty* to be the best, presumably because you are being paid. **(4)**
A: The writer says that as a player you are *devoting every last ounce of energy* (trying so hard that you couldn't try any harder) *to that end* (with the aim of being excellent). He is therefore saying that players have to put in an enormous amount of effort and describes why they feel they should do this, but he does not suggest that it is unreasonable that they should have to do this. **(1)**
B: The writer says that the public's growing interest and their love for the teams they support *exact ever-higher expectations* (produce expectations of the players on the part of the fans that get higher and higher). He says that while the fans are enjoying the entertainment before a match, the players can hear the sounds of the entertainment as it echoes inside the changing rooms where they are sitting quietly. He therefore implies that they are tense or concentrating before a match, rather than relaxing or enjoying themselves, and that this may be a result of the pressure they feel because of the expectations of fans. However, he does not refer to how the players feel about the fans, or to any feeling of annoyance at being badly or unfairly treated by fans that the players may have. **(2)**
C: The writer says that the media *minutely scrutinize* (analyse or examine in great detail) both how players play and their private lives and feel that this is justified because players are getting paid. He implies therefore that players do get criticized by the media, but he does not refer to any reaction to criticism on the part of the players or express any personal view as to how they should react to it. **(3)**

p57–58 PAPER 1 PART THREE

Two marks per question (Total: 14)

The Hammond Organ

27 G: In the opening paragraph, the writer has bought a Hammond organ *sight unseen* (without seeing it first) and arranged to have it delivered to his home in Texas.
In G, he talks about how a smell can *trigger a memory* (cause a memory to return suddenly) which *unravels the years in an instant* (takes you back in time immediately), and gives an example of such a smell. Then he talks about when *they* (the people delivering the organ) *unbolt the container* (the one in which the organ has been transported to him), and *before he sees the instrument* (the organ he has bought) – these are all references back to what he mentions in the opening paragraph. At this point, a smell *wafts* (floats) up his nose and gives him a *flashback* (a sudden image of a previous time) to 1964, when he first smelt it.
In the paragraph after the gap, he goes on to talk further about his first acquaintance with Hammond organs.

28 E: In the paragraph after gap 27, the writer talks about his desire when he was younger to own a Hammond organ. He says that he did some research into them but that, although

he discovered that some models were better than others, he couldn't buy any of them because he didn't have any money.
In E, the writer says that not having any money didn't matter because he then discovered that he could have one without having to pay for it. While he was *thumbing through* (looking casually through) a magazine, he saw an advert offering a Hammond organ *on two weeks' free approval* (an arrangement by which customers can try out goods free of charge for a given period, after which they either buy it or return it). He wondered if this offer was genuine – *Pull the other one* (an informal expression meaning 'I don't believe it'), he thought, and he wondered what *the catch* (the hidden disadvantage of an apparently attractive offer) was.
In the paragraph after gap 28, he says that he responded to this advert and phoned the company who had placed it. He discovered that the offer was genuine (the *drawback* in the second sentence refers back to *the catch* mentioned in E), as long as the organ wasn't removed once it had been delivered and *set up* (installed).

29 A: In the paragraph after gap 28, the writer talks about arranging for the organ to be delivered and the organ arriving the next morning. When it arrived, he and the men who brought it moved furniture in the house in order to create space for the organ.
In the first sentence of A, *This* refers to the action of moving tables and chairs back against the wall and the sentence means that as a result of doing that, enough space had been created for what the men had brought. The writer then lists what this consisted of and describes his excited reaction on seeing it all – when he says *My face must have been a picture,* he means 'I must have had an extraordinary expression on my face' and *This was the gear!* means 'This was exactly the equipment I wanted, this was the very best equipment'.
In the paragraph after gap 29, the first word *It* refers to *the gear* mentioned at the end of A, and he says that because it looked *polished and shiny*, it made the *dining room suite* (set of table and chairs) in his house look quite *tatty* (in poor condition as a result of being used for a long time).

30 H: In the paragraph after gap 29, the writer says that he was shown how to get the organ working. After that, he went to get the record that had first made him want to have a Hammond organ, *plonked* (an informal word meaning 'put') the record on the record player and *cranked it up* (an informal expression, here meaning 'played it at loud volume'). Then he describes the intense feeling he experienced now that he had the organ and could try to copy the record.
At the beginning of H, he says that at this point he had to work out how to play *the beast* (this literally means 'big animal' and here refers to the organ, which we already know is big) and how to get *the same sound as that* (*that* refers back to the record *Green Onions*, which he is playing and wants to copy at the end of the paragraph before gap 30). He then describes how he successfully attempted to make the same sounds with his organ as were on the record.
In the paragraph after gap 30, he goes on to talk about the next stage, the next thing he had to do after he had succeeded in working out how to get the right sound out of the organ. This was to *master* (become fully skilled in using) the piece of equipment that the sound came out of.

31 B: In the paragraph before gap 31, the writer describes how the Leslie cabinet works.
At the beginning of B, he says that he *found all that out* (*that* refers to 'how the Leslie cabinet worked', which he has just described in the preceding paragraph) by *fiddling around with it* (trying various different things, moving, turning, pressing, etc different parts; *it* refers back to the Leslie cabinet previously mentioned). He goes on to say that, unlike some other instruments, a Hammond organ can be made to produce a good sound without much effort.
In the paragraph after gap 31, he moves on to talk about what happened next, after he had found out how to get the equipment to work well – his father came home.

32 D: In the paragraph before gap 32, he describes his conversation with his father when he arrived home. He went to the door to *head him off* (to stand in his way so that he could not go in a certain direction, in this case into the room that now contained the organ) and told him about the organ. The first question in D is asked by his father, in response to the writer telling him that he has got a Hammond organ, which he tells him at the end of the preceding paragraph. The writer doesn't answer this question, but tells his father that the organ is free for two weeks. His father asks him where it is, and he tells him, adding that it is *fantastic* (marvellous, great) and repeating that it does not have to be paid for.
In the paragraph after gap 32, his father's reaction to learning all this is to go down the hall to the room where the writer has told him the organ is (which he does at the end of D). He describes his father as *peering* (looking closely and carefully) *round the door* to look at the organ.

33 F: In the paragraph before gap 33, the writer describes his father's reaction to seeing the organ. He is astonished – *Blimey* and *I'm blowed* are slang expressions expressing surprise. His father comments on how big the organ is and asks the writer why he didn't ask him and his mother before getting the organ. The writer apologizes and plays the organ to demonstrate how good it is. His father then says *Let me break it to your mum* (if you 'break something to someone', you tell them something that you think will upset them in a gentle way to try to minimize the effect the news has on them).
At the beginning of F, the writer says he believed *that meant it was going to be all right* (*that* here refers back to what his father said at the end of the preceding paragraph and *it* means the situation regarding the organ – clearly, he thinks that his father will persuade his mother to let him keep it and that he will also persuade her not to be angry with him). The writer then says that the organ was removed two weeks later and a new one brought for him the following week.
In the final paragraph, the writer explains how this – the fact that he got a new organ, as mentioned in F – was possible. It was possible because he bought it *on the 'never never'* (this and *hire purchase* are old-fashioned terms describing a system of credit by which you buy goods by making regular payments over a period of time). He was able to do this because, although he was too young to get credit, his father also signed the form, guaranteeing that he would make the payments if the writer did not.

The paragraph which does not fit into any of the gaps is C.

p59–60 PAPER 1 PART FOUR

Two marks per question (Total: 14)

Piper and Buxxy

34 C: Piper is said to have looked *relaxed and dependable* and there are two references to his *conservative* (respectable, traditional) style of dress. When he spoke, his *outward reserve* (the fact that he seemed like someone who tended not to express feelings or opinions) is mentioned and the fact that he *let some of his excitement for the project show through* indicates that he was so excited about the project that he could not conceal this excitement even though he was generally reserved when making his speech. The

narrator says that he provided the audience with *reassurance* (the confident feeling that there is nothing to worry or have doubts about) and made them feel that *Despite appearances* (Although it did not appear to be the case), *the Tahiti must be a respectable, conservative* (without involving much risk) *investment* – if it was not, *why would someone like Irwin Piper be involved with it?* In other words, the Tahiti did not look like a good thing for them to invest in and Piper seemed like a calm, quiet and respectable person who would not normally get involved with a casino. The fact that such a person was involved with it made them feel that it might be a suitable thing for them to get involved with too.
A: We learn that this was a *big moment* (a very important one) for both of them because they had to get their audience to invest $200 million. Piper tells them in a *reasonable, persuasive voice* that the Tahiti is a *remarkable financial opportunity for them*. He talked about *numbers, strategy, competitive analysis* (presumably, how the Tahiti could compete for customers). There is no mention of him talking about anything other than the business aspects of the Tahiti and so it must have been clear to the audience that his main purpose in his speech was to get them to invest money in the Tahiti.
B: He talked about the financial opportunity *in abstract terms* (in a general way, without going into detail) and he only talked about numbers, strategy and competitive analysis to the extent that the audience would be made to feel that the Tahiti was *in safe hands* (being efficiently run by trustworthy people), but he did not keep talking about these matters to the extent that the audience would get bored. We are therefore told that the audience felt that he spoke more in general terms and did not give much detail because he did not want to bore them, not because he was less comfortable when giving details.
D: He gave the audience the impression that they would be wise to invest in the project but he is not said to have mentioned whether anyone had already expressed an interest in investing in it. The phrase *competitive analysis* does not indicate that there was competition among people to invest; it is a term relating to the financial details of the project.

35 B: The narrator says that Buxxy's *abrasive* (direct, rather aggressive), *rough-edged* (unsophisticated) *manner jolted* (caused a sudden reaction in, resulting from shock) *his audience after the smooth* (sophisticated, charming but perhaps not sincere) *Piper*. In other words, Buxxy's manner was so different from and so much more energetic than Piper's, that the audience were initially shocked when he started to speak.
A: The narrator says that on the rare occasions when Buxxy was still during his speech, the fact that he stopped moving around was *for a melodramatic* (dramatic in an exaggerated way) *pause, to let the full consequence* (significance, importance) *of what he had just said sink in* (be absorbed or fully understood by the audience). It is therefore clear that the narrator believes that Buxxy put in these pauses deliberately, with a particular intention.
C: Although the audience were *bewitched* and *captivated* (both these words mean 'greatly attracted') by Buxxy and he paused to allow people to absorb the significance of things he had said, we are not told that the audience's reaction to him resulted from the first points he made or that he started off with his most important points.
D: His face and hair are described but the descriptions are factual rather than intended to convey any opinion of him, and the narrator does not say or imply that his manner came as a surprise because he looked like someone who would have a different manner of speaking.

36 B: The narrator says that *Seen through Buxxy's eyes* (As described by Buxxy), *the tackiness* (poor taste and poor quality) *and loneliness of a big casino disappeared* (they didn't notice it, it did not seem to them to exist) and they saw instead *the glamour, the glitter* (the excitement associated with the world of entertainment), *the amazing technological effects*. In other words, although the casino could have looked like a tacky and lonely place, they saw it as a glamorous, exciting place as a result of the way that Buxxy described it to them.
A: Most of the audience were obviously impressed by the tour because by the end of it they were ready to invest money in the casino immediately, but the narrator does not say that they were so impressed because it was the first time they had ever been inside a casino.
C: They were shown the private rooms where the *high-rollers* (people who gamble large sums of money) played and they saw the amazing technological effects, but the narrator does not say that the fact these things existed was unexpected or that they indicated that the project was nearer to completion than the audience had thought.
D: They were shown the rooms where the high-rollers played and the high-rollers are described as *wallowing in* (taking enormous, selfish pleasure in) *sophistication, power and money*. The audience are not described as doing so, and although it is likely that they were so impressed by this that they were willing to invest immediately because they imagined themselves playing in those rooms, the narrator does not say that Buxxy encouraged them to imagine themselves in those rooms.

37 D: The narrator says that when he sat down after asking his questions, some faces in the audience *bore* (had expressions of) *disapproval* and he thinks this was because they regarded him as *a spoil-sport* (someone who ruins the pleasure of others) who had taken *cheap shots at* (made unpleasant, unintelligent and unjustified comments about) the *great guys* (the wonderful men – Buxxy and Piper) and their casino. In other words, he felt that they looked as if they were angry with him and thought that he was not justified in asking the questions he asked.
A: He says that his English accent *jarred in the glitzy* (glamorous) *Las Vegas surroundings*, which means that it sounded strange and out of place there but he does not say or imply that he thought this meant people would not take him seriously.
B: When the narrator stood up, Piper's face showed the *barest trace of* (a very faint sign of) *a frown* (an expression of annoyance, worry or confusion), which shows that he was slightly concerned as to what the narrator would say. After the narrator's first question, Piper *stiffened* (his body became tense), which again indicates that he was concerned. If he had been expecting the narrator's questions, he would not have had either of these reactions.
C: The narrator says that nobody asked any difficult questions about Piper's background, or any *tedious* (dull, boring) questions about technical matters connected with the casino and that even *the most cynical* (negative in attitude, seeing only bad aspects) *investor was under the spell of* (had been completely charmed by, as if by magic) what they obviously thought was *the greatest casino on earth* – clearly the audience seemed to have faith in the project. However, this was not why he asked his questions. He had obviously been planning to ask them anyway because he says that he *had thought this moment through carefully*. He had therefore gone to the casino with the intention of asking these questions and the audience's attitude did not influence or cause that.

38 C: The narrator says that, although Piper had not answered his questions properly and that *if anyone pursued him on this* (if anyone asked him further questions about these matters), *doubts might start to creep in* (people might start to have doubts about him), *he wasn't going to push it* (it wasn't his intention to proceed with the matter or put pressure on him) *any further*. This was because he had achieved his *objective* (aim) which was that Piper would realize he knew something (presumably something bad about Piper) and that Piper would realize that he would tell others about it.
A: When Piper had answered the questions, he *looked*

around the audience quickly, presumably to see what their reaction was. It was *a dangerous moment* for him because until then the audience had been *eating out of his hand* (under his control, believing everything he said), but now *doubts might start to creep in* because he hadn't answered the questions properly. He was therefore worried that they might not find his answers convincing and he knew he had not answered the questions properly, but the narrator does not say or imply that the audience realized this.
B: Piper said that he was happy to answer the questions. To the first question he replies that all applications for gambling licences are checked out (this means the same as *scrutinized* in the narrator's question – checked or inspected thoroughly). To the second, he says that he has a lot of investments and doesn't have details of all of them *at my fingertips* (in a place close enough for him to get them immediately). In neither of these replies does he dismiss the questions as concerning only very minor matters and he seems to take them seriously.
D: The narrator says that when Piper *rose to his feet*, he was *as unruffled* (calm) *and urbane* (sophisticated) *as ever*. He therefore did not appear to the audience to be feeling uncomfortable, even though he probably was.

39 A: When the *bellboy* (a young man in a uniform who works in a hotel carrying bags, giving messages, etc, especially in the US) told the narrator that Piper would like to see him and he then made his way to Piper's suite, he thought *That didn't take him long*, which means that he was expecting Piper to ask for him at some point, although he had not expected it to happen so quickly.
B: After Piper had expressed his anger with the narrator and threatened to *sue* him (take him to court in a legal case in order to get money from him), the narrator felt that Piper had put him *on the defensive* (in a position in which he was under attack and could be defeated) for a moment. This was because he wondered whether he had made a mistake in upsetting such a powerful man – presumably because someone so powerful could do damage to him, particularly financially. He was therefore briefly concerned that he might regret upsetting Piper because of what Piper could do to him, not because he had begun to feel that he might have been mistaken in thinking that Piper was dishonest.
C: In Piper's first speech to him, he said that he wasn't a *two-bit* (unimportant, minor) *bond salesman* (a kind of financial trader) who the narrator *could play games with* (not take seriously, treat dishonestly) and that if he were to even *allude to* (refer indirectly to) a certain place again, he would sue him for so much money that he would not be able to pay off the debts in his lifetime. The fact that all this put the narrator *on the defensive* indicates that he had not been expecting him to say these things; if he had been expecting it, he would have been able to respond immediately.
D: Piper suggests that the narrator is treating him like a *two-bit bond salesman* and tells him that he is in fact rich and powerful and has lawyers he could use to hurt the narrator. He therefore does accuse the narrator of underestimating him. However, he does not refer to other people who have done this or to what he did to them as a result.

40 B: When the narrator showed Piper the newspaper article, he *went purple* (became so angry that his face became a purple colour), threatened to *have my lawyers right on you* (get my lawyers to deal with you directly) and threatened to *tear you apart myself* (destroy you physically through violence). This indicated to the narrator that Piper had lost control and he says that *Paradoxically* (Although the opposite would be logical or expected), the fact that he had lost control made him feel calm because Piper no longer seemed so powerful. The implication is that if Piper had remained calm, the narrator would have thought that he was powerful enough to harm him, but the fact that he lost control made it seem that he would not be able to do what he wanted and control the situation.
A: Piper threatens the narrator both with his lawyers and with physical violence. The narrator feels that because he has lost control when he makes these threats, it seems less likely that he will be able to carry them out than if he had said these things calmly, but he does not mention threats made by Piper to other people or imply that he often made threats he could not carry out.
C: Piper threatens the narrator with physical violence when he says that he will tear him apart himself but the narrator does not say or imply that Piper had ever actually been physically violent towards anyone before.
D: The article was clearly one about a scandal involving Piper. In the headline, 'City Slickers' is a slang phrase meaning 'people who live in a city and have well-paid jobs', 'Saucy' means 'naughty, especially in a sexual way', 'Retreat' means 'a private place where people can relax' and the phrase 'helping the police with their enquiries' usually implies that the person concerned is suspected of being involved in the crime being investigated. When Piper saw it, he went purple, lost control and started threatening the narrator, which indicates that he knew perfectly well what the article was about.

PAPER 1:

PART ONE	18 marks
PART TWO	16 marks
PART THREE	14 marks
PART FOUR	14 marks
TOTAL	62 marks

To be converted into a score out of 40 marks.

p61 PAPER 2 PART ONE

Task-specific mark schemes

Each answer is given marks out of 20

Question 1

Content
Letter should cover the points raised in the conclusion to the newspaper article – that the 'generation gap' still exists, that it may be inevitable, that people always believe their generation is in some way better than the next generation and that people have a romantic view of the past.

Range
Language for expressing and supporting opinions and language for analysing. Candidates may support or oppose any or all of the views expressed in the input, or they may support some and oppose others.

Appropriacy of register and format
Register should probably be formal or neutral, since the topic is a fairly serious one, although an amusing, informal letter is possible. Register should be consistent throughout.

Organization and cohesion
Standard letter format, with introduction mentioning reason for writing, clear organization of points in separate paragraphs dealing with each aspect of the topic and appropriate linking within and between paragraphs.

Target reader
Would understand fully and clearly the writer's point of view.

p62–65 PAPER 2 PART TWO

Question 2

Content
Proposal should include:
- reasons for setting up the group
- how the group should be set up, including personnel
- issues the group could deal with
- advantages of having the group

Range
Language of describing, hypothesizing and recommending, including expressing and supporting opinions.

Appropriacy of register and format
Register should be appropriate for relationship between student/employee writing the proposal and authority/employer who has requested it and will read it – formal or neutral. Proposal format of clearly separate sections, probably with section headings.

Organization and cohesion
Proposal should be organized into sections, each of which deals with each aspect mentioned in the input. Clear and brief introduction and conclusion. Appropriate linking within sections and perhaps also between sections.

Target reader
Would understand precisely what the writer is proposing and why.

Question 3

Content
Review should inform the reader about the TV channel or radio station, evaluate it in terms of what it broadcasts, describe the nature of its viewers or listeners and compare it with others.

Range
Language of description, evaluation, analysis and comparison.

Appropriacy of register and format
Register could be informal, formal or neutral but should be consistent throughout. Format should be appropriate for review – description followed by comment within paragraphs or in separate paragraphs.

Organization and cohesion
Clear development from description to comment and then to comparison, with paragraphing and linking – both within and between paragraphs – appropriate to this.

Target reader
Would be informed about the TV channel or radio station and be able to decide whether it would appeal to them, or whether their views on it match those of the writer.

FURTHER PRACTICE AND GUIDANCE (p63–65)

Assessment of sample answer

Content
The review covers all the aspects mentioned in the question. The writer describes and comments on what the radio station broadcasts, explains who its listeners are and why, and compares it with bigger radio stations in general terms.

Range
There is some very good use of vocabulary and structure, for example *on air* and *run by* (second paragraph), *even if they don't have to* and *the middle of the night* (third paragraph), *colourful* and *easy going* (fourth paragraph), *compete against*, *broad range* and *filled a gap in the market* (fifth paragraph) and *tune in to* (last sentence). The final sentence provides a lively and effective way of ending the review.

Accuracy
There are no actual mistakes in this review.

Appropriacy of register and format
The register is neutral throughout, with an informal final sentence, which is appropriate in the context. The format is appropriate, with each paragraph on different aspects of the radio station. The opening paragraph is not really part of the review, it is more of a note to the magazine itself, and perhaps this should not have been included.

Organization and cohesion
The review is very well-organized, with description of the various aspects of the radio station combined with comment on these in each paragraph. The second paragraph describes the radio station in general terms, the third paragraph talks about its listeners, the fourth paragraph talks about what it broadcasts and the fifth paragraph compares it in terms of bigger stations. There is some good linking throughout, for example the use of *but* after the negative verb in the second sentence of the third paragraph, *Nevertheless* (third paragraph), *Concerning* (fourth paragraph), *Though* (fifth paragraph) and *To my mind* (fifth paragraph).

Target reader
The reader would learn a great deal about a radio station that it is assumed they had not previously heard of, and would be in a position to decide whether it would appeal to them or not.

Assessment: A very good review, with few errors.

Mark: 14

Question 4

Content
Article should inform the reader about something which is popular but which it is assumed the reader doesn't know anything about, although they may be aware of its existence (this could be a fashion, a type of music, a social phenomenon, a commercial development, etc). It should explain what it is and why it is popular, and perhaps its background.

Range
Language of description, narration (if giving background), analysis and perhaps hypothesizing.

Appropriacy of register and format
Register could be formal, informal or neutral but should be consistent throughout. The format should be appropriate for an article – clearly divided paragraphs dealing with different aspects of the topic, perhaps with sub-headings.

Organization and cohesion
Clear introduction stating chosen topic and intention to explain to someone with no knowledge of it. Clear division into paragraphs dealing with background of the chosen topic, description of the nature of it, analysis of reasons for its popularity and perhaps the writer's own comments on it (the writer's views could also be expressed in a conclusion). Appropriate linking within and between paragraphs.

Target reader
Would understand fully and clearly what the writer has chosen as the subject of the article, having previously had no knowledge of it at all. Would also understand clearly and fully why it is popular and any views expressed on it by the writer.

PAPER 2:

PART ONE	20 marks
PART TWO	20 marks
TOTAL	40 marks

p66 PAPER 3 PART ONE

One mark per question (Total: 15)

Laughter is Good for You – Seriously

1 **by:** *By* is used to describe the amount by which something is greater or less than something else. The writer is comparing the number of times children laugh with the number of times adults laugh, and saying that adults laugh a couple of hundred times a day less than children do. Obviously, this is an enormous difference, and the figure is introduced by the phrase *as much as* to emphasize how great the difference is.

2 **look:** If you *take a look at someone/something*, you look at them. The writer is talking here about what you see if you look at people's faces. *Look* is the only noun that fits the meaning here and correctly forms a collocation with *take*.

3 **alone:** *Let alone* is a linking phrase meaning 'and therefore certainly / probably not', when the result of the first thing not being the case is that the second thing certainly or probably isn't the case. The writer is saying that, since you might not see someone smiling, you're very unlikely to see anyone laughing.

4 **view:** The phrase *in view of the fact that* means 'considering','taking into consideration' or 'because of'. The writer is saying that it's a pity people don't laugh more because it has been proved that doing so is good for you.

5 **and:** The writer is giving two ways in which laughing is good for you – it *counters* (acts against) stress and *enhances* (improves, makes more effective) the immune system, which is the body's natural defence against disease.

6 **reasons:** *Reason* is followed by *why*, not *because* in the structure *There is a/The reason + why + subject, verb,* etc. The writer is introducing an explanation of the causes of adults laughing much less than children.

7 **let:** If you *let something show*, you reveal it, rather than trying to keep it hidden. The word *let* is the only word that can complete this phrase so that it both has the right meaning in the context and is correct grammatically – *let* is followed by the infinitive without 'to' and there is no 'to' before 'show'.

8 **out:** If you *grow out of something*, you become too old, mature or big for it. The writer is saying that when people become adults they stop reacting in the *spontaneous* (natural, without first thinking or planning carefully) way that children do. No other word can complete the phrasal verb with this meaning.

9 **however:** The writer is contrasting two opposing ideas – that adults have lost the ability to laugh a lot and that they can learn how to laugh a lot again. The word *however* can be used within a sentence, usually with a comma on either side of it, to convey the meaning 'Although the first idea is true, the second idea is also true'.

10 **in:** If something *grows in something*, it gets or acquires more of it. The writer is saying that laughter clinics have become more popular. The preposition *in* is the only word that supplies the correct complementation for *grow* in the context of the meaning of the phrase.

11 **thanks/owing/due:** The writer is saying that laughter clinics have become more popular because of Dr Kataria's work. The linking phrases *thanks to, owing to* and *due to* all mean 'because of'.

12 **whose:** The relative *whose* means 'of whom'. In the context, this part of the sentence means 'and Dr Kataria's work has won him ...'.

13 **a:** In this sentence, *following* is a singular noun meaning 'group of supporters'. Since this group of supporters has not been previously mentioned, it must be preceded by the indefinite article, rather than the definite article or *this/that*.

14 **among:** The phrase *among other things* means that the things already mentioned are not the only things that could be mentioned, since other things could be included too. The writer is saying that Dr Kataria believes there are several benefits of his laughing techniques and those mentioned are only two of these – there are also others.

15 **turned/showed**: If someone *shows/turns up* somewhere, they arrive or appear there. The writer is saying that 10,000 people attended Dr Kataria's World Laughter Day. No other verbs complete a phrasal verb with this meaning.

p67–69 PAPER 3 PART TWO

FURTHER PRACTICE AND GUIDANCE (p68–69)

King of the Watchmakers

For explanations, see the explanations to the questions in the test, which follow.

16	c	**17**	d	**18**	d	**19**	a	**20**	c
21	c	**22**	c	**23**	c	**24**	a	**25**	d

p67 PAPER 3 PART TWO (TEST)

Note: the letters in brackets refer to the relevant options in the Further Practice and Guidance pages.

One mark per question (Total: 10)

16 **synonymous:** If a word is *synonymous with* another, it has the same meaning as it. More figuratively, if something is said to be *synonymous with* something else, it automatically involves it. In this context, the writer is saying that clocks and watches made in Coventry at that time were assumed to be excellent because they had a high reputation. **(c)**
The other words in the list do not exist.

17 **reliability:** If something such as a machine or piece of equipment possesses *reliability*, it always performs well without breaking down. The writer is saying that clocks and watches made in Coventry at that time were known to be both of high quality and reliable. **(d)**
Reliance on something is the situation of relying or depending on something in order to function, exist, succeed, etc (*the team's total reliance on one or two good players*). **(c)**
Reliably means 'in a way that can be relied on' (*a car that performs reliably over many years*). **(a)**
If you are *reliant on somebody/something*, you depend on them (*children who are totally reliant on their parents*). **(b)**
The word *reliableness* does not exist.

18 **single-handedly:** If someone does something *single-handedly*, they do it on their own and not with the help of

others. The writer is saying that Samuel Watson was almost alone in getting Coventry involved in the clock and watch business, he was almost the only person who *paved the way* for the city's involvement in it (created the situation which allowed the city to become involved in it). **(d)**
If something is *handily placed, situated, etc*, its place or position is convenient. (*The hotel is handily placed for all the city's main attractions.*) **(c)**
If someone is *high-handed*, they are in a position of power and authority and act towards others in a rude manner, without considering their wishes or consulting them (*a boss with a high-handed manner*). **(b)**
If something happens *beforehand*, it happens earlier, in advance of or before another event. (*I knew what I was doing because I'd checked beforehand.*) **(a)**
The word *handfully* does not exist.

19 forefront: If someone is *at the forefront of something*, they are a leader in it and have one of the most important positions in it. The writer is saying that Samuel Watson was a leading figure in the *watchmaking revolution* (the time of great change in watchmaking) in the 1680s and *a trailblazer for others* (a pioneer, someone doing something new after which others could follow). **(a)**
The *frontage* of a building is the front of it, especially if this is remarkable or interesting in some way (*a palace with an ornate frontage*). **(c)**
Frontal means relating to or from the front of something (*an army making a frontal attack*). **(b)**If something *fronts onto something*, the front of it faces something (*a house fronting onto the river*). **(d)**
The word *facefront* does not exist.

20 mathematician: A *mathematician* is an expert in mathematics or someone whose occupation is concerned with mathematics, for example, an academic. In those days, the King appointed various people as experts to work for him and one such was an expert in mathematics who would be called 'the King's mathematician'. **(c)**
Mathematical means connected with or consisting of mathematics (*a mathematical calculation*). **(a)**
The other words do not exist.

21 positional: This means 'connected with position'. The phrase *positional changes* means 'changes in position'. **(c)**
An *imposition* is either an occasion when something is forced on others by authority (*the imposition of new regulations by the government*) or an action that causes inconvenience. (*I hope it's not an imposition but could you give me a lift?*) **(d)**
The other words do not exist.

22 ownership: If something is *in the ownership of someone*, they own it. The writer is saying that the Royal Family still owns the astronomical clock made by Watson. **(c)**
Owning can be used in a noun phrase, with the meaning 'the fact or situation of owning'. (*The owning of vast numbers of houses and cars did not bring him happiness.*) It can therefore have the same meaning as *ownership*, but it cannot be used in the phrase *in the ... of.* **(c)**
The other words do not exist.

23 residence: If you *take up residence* somewhere, you go to live there. Someone's *residence* is a formal word for the place where they live or their address. We are told that Watson moved from Coventry and began to live in London. **(c)**
A *resident* of a place is someone who lives there, as opposed to a visitor. (*Local residents objected to plans for a music festival.*) In a hotel, a *resident* is a guest who is staying there. **(b)**
Residential means 'involving people living there rather than working there or living elsewhere' (*a residential area/a residential course*). **(a)**
Residency is a formal, legal word, meaning 'permission to live in a country that is not your own' (*be granted permanent residency*). **(c)**
A residency is a situation in which a performer is employed to work at a particular place over a period of time. (*The band got a residency at a local club, appearing every Tuesday night.*) **(d)**
The word *residentity* does not exist.

24 standing: A person's *standing* is their reputation or status in a profession or among a group of people. The writer is saying that the fact that Watson became *Master of the London Clockmakers' Company* (presumably a very important position for which only someone highly respected is chosen) *is testament to* (is proof of) how high his reputation was in that industry. **(a)**
A person's *standpoint* is their point of view, the position they are in from which they regard a certain matter or issue. (*From the standpoint of the employees, the management's decision is a bad one.*) **(d)**
If someone/something *withstands something*, they endure it and continue despite it (*materials which can withstand heavy impacts; a politician who could withstand great criticism*). **(c)**
If someone/something is *outstanding*, they are remarkable in a positive way, or conspicuously better than others (*an outstanding performer/an award for outstanding achievement*). **(b)**
The word *standence* does not exist.

25 likelihood: The *likelihood of something happening* is the chance of it happening. If *the likelihood is that* something is the case, it is probably the case. The writer is saying that because there are no records of Watson's name after 1712, it is reasonable to think that he probably died that year. **(d)**
The other words do not exist.

p70 PAPER 3 PART THREE

Two marks per question (Total: 12)

26 go: If it is *someone's go*, it is their turn to do something in a game. In this context, a game is being played which involves people putting cards down so that one person puts a card down, then another person puts a card down and so on. The noun *turn* would also fit with exactly the same meaning. (The verb *move* could not fit here, because it is used for games in which pieces are moved, such as chess, not for card games.)
If you *are on the go*, you are continually very busy and active over a period of time. The noun *move* could also fit here to form a phrase meaning 'constantly moving from place to place'.
If you *have a go at doing something*, you try to do it, although you are not confident that you will succeed. The nouns *stab*, *crack* and *shot* would also complete idioms with the same meaning.

27 just: The phrase *it's just as well* means 'it's fortunate/lucky that ...' or 'it's a good thing that ...'.
The adverb *just* can mean *simply* or *merely* and both of those words could fill the gap here. The sentence means 'The fact that I've said I don't agree with you is not a good enough reason for you to get upset.'
The phrase *just now* means 'at this exact moment' or 'during this particular period'. The adverb *right* could also fill the gap to form a phrase with exactly the same meaning.

28 stand: If you *stand to do something*, you are in a situation in which it is possible that you will do it or it will happen to you. With a slightly different meaning, *expect* could fill the gap here.
If you *stand up to someone*, you defend yourself against them and refuse to allow them to treat you badly.
If you *can't stand something* or *can't stand it when something happens*, you cannot endure it and it annoys or upsets you

because it is too much for you. The verbs *bear, tolerate* and *take* would all also fit here with exactly the same meaning.

29 **great:** *Great* can be used before *big* to emphasize that the thing being described is very, very big.
The phrase *a great many + plural noun* means 'a lot of'. The adjective *good* could also be used to form a phrase with this meaning.
Great detail means 'a lot of detail'. Other adjectives such as *enormous* could form collocations with 'detail' to express the same meaning.

30 **act:** An *act of + noun* is an action or something done that can be described in a particular way, shows something or represents a particular kind of action. An *act of defiance* is something that is done which is contrary to and shows a refusal to obey something which someone in authority has demanded. In the context, nouns such as *show* and *demonstration* could also fit with the same meaning.
If you are *in the act of doing something*, you are in the middle of doing it. The noun *process* could also fill the gap to form a phrase with exactly the same meaning.
A performer's *act* is what they do on stage when theirs is just one performance in a show in which various people perform separately. Usually comedians, singers, dancers or performers in a circus do an act. The noun *performance* would also fit here.

31 **pick:** If you *pick someone up* in your car, you collect them from a place, usually having previously arranged to do so, and then take them to another place in your car.
If you *pick a fight with someone*, you are responsible for starting a fight or argument between you and that person because you are the one who is aggressive first. The verb *start* could fill the gap to form a phrase with the same meaning.
If someone *is picked for something*, they are selected from a number of candidates by the people who are in charge of deciding who will be given the position in question. The verbs *choose* and *select* would also fill the gap here with the same meaning.

p71 PAPER 3 PART FOUR

Two marks per question (Total: 16)

32 **was instrumental in** (1 mark)
the drafting (1 mark)
If someone / something *is instrumental in something/doing something*, they are the cause of it or the most important reason why it happens. The verb *drafted* has to be transformed into the noun phrase *the drafting of*, meaning 'the process of drafting'.

33 **you stuck to/by** (1 mark)
what we originally (1 mark)
The third conditional structure *If + subject + had + past participle* can be transformed into the structure *Had + subject + past participle*. If you *stick to/by something*, you do not change it after you have agreed to it or decided on it. The verb *agreed* has to be given the subject *What* and the phrase *our original agreement* changed to *what we originally agreed* – 'original' has to become an adverb to describe the verb 'agreed' rather than an adjective describing the noun 'agreement'.

34 **spare a thought for** (1 mark)
those/(the) people whose (1 mark)
If you *spare a thought for someone*, you give them some consideration because they are in an unfortunate situation. The relative *who* comes before a verb or subject and has to be replaced by the structure *whose + noun* because *lives* is a noun.

35 **prolong our stay** (1 mark)
so thrilled were (1 mark)
If you *prolong something*, you make it last longer than had been arranged or than is necessary. The verb 'stay' has to become the noun 'stay' to provide the object that follows 'prolong'. The structure *subject + verb + so + adjective* has to be transformed into the emphatic structure, with the verb and subject inverted, *so + adjective + verb + subject*.

36 **marvelled at** (1 mark)
the shrewdness with (1 mark)
If you *marvel at something*, you are amazed by it and usually you also admire it very much. The structure *how + adverb* has to be transformed into the structure *the + noun + with + which* to describe how something is done. The noun from *shrewd* is *shrewdness*.

37 **to admit defeat** (1 mark)
while there was still/while there remained (1 mark)
If you are *loath to do something*, you are reluctant or unwilling to do it. If you *admit defeat*, you accept that you are not going to succeed and stop trying. The phrase *noun + to remain* has to be transformed into the structure *there + to be + still + noun* or, more formally, *there + to remain + noun*.

38 **rose/(were) lifted** (1 mark)
when I caught sight (1 mark)
If *your spirits rise/lift/are lifted*, you become happier or more cheerful after being unhappy, usually because of something that happens to cause this. If you *catch sight of something*, you see it suddenly or for a moment.

39 **do wonders for** (1mark)
the way you look (1 mark)
If something *does wonders for something/someone*, it is extremely beneficial for them because it changes them in a very positive way. The phrase *the way someone looks at something* has the same meaning as the phrase *someone's attitude to something*.

p72–74 PAPER 3 PART FIVE

Questions 40–43

Two marks per question (Total: 8)

Answers that are similar to or cover the same points as those given here are acceptable, provided that they are clearly expressed.

40 **intellectual, done by and appealing only to a small part of society who are highly educated and interested only in serious artistic or cultural matters, rather than ones which interest people in general**
The writer contrasts *the highbrow* with *the popular* with regard to culture – both words are adjectives used as nouns in this context, meaning 'highbrow things' and 'popular things'. In the context of anything connected with culture or the Arts, something which is *popular* is entertaining rather than serious and appeals to people who are not necessarily highly educated and who do not necessarily know much about the subject – it therefore has wide appeal. Something that is *highbrow* is serious and is aimed at and appeals to people who consider that they have good taste when it comes to that kind of cultural area – it therefore has narrow appeal, mostly to those with a keen interest in serious cultural matters.

41 **that it exists everywhere in society, that its influence may not be noticed but may be harmful, and that it has to make a big effort to continue to have an influence or exist**
Most of the third paragraph is about popular culture rather than the dominant ideology. What is said about the

dominant ideology is that it is *omnipresent* and *insidious* and that it has to *work hard and insistently to maintain itself.*

42 that popular culture is not simply a business, it also belongs to the people, and if people don't like something that has been produced in order to be popular, it will not become popular
The writer says that popular culture is *contradictory to its core* (the most fundamental point about it is that it has two opposing main aspects). It is a commercial industry whose main aim is profit but it is also *of the people*, and their interests may not be the same as those of the industry. This is shown by *the number of* (the implication here is that there are a large number of) films and records that *the people make into expensive failures* (they cost a lot of money to make but they are not successful because people do not buy them).

43 people who are being deceived by the system in their society but do not realize this
The writer is arguing that people who believe in *mass culture* rather than *popular culture* are wrong because *mass culture* does not exist. This is because people are not like *the masses* that theorists who believe in mass culture talk about. People are not, the writer says, *an aggregation* (collection) *of alienated* (not feeling that they are part of society), *one-dimensional persons* (people whose personalities have only one aspect) *whose only relationship to the system that enslaves them* (keeps them under strict control without any power or rights) *is one of unwitting* (unintentional, not being aware of what they are doing or what is happening) *dupes* (people who are tricked, victims of deception).

Question 44 Summary

One mark for each content point included from the following, maximum 4 marks

(i) It is democratic and has nothing to do with power.
In the first paragraph of the first text, the writer says that the *less productive* (less useful) view of popular culture has been one that is made *without situating it in the context of power and the dominant forces of society* (that has not considered it in relation to power and the most powerful forces in society). This view has been that popular culture is *consensual* (resulting from general agreement being reached) and *democratic* (resulting from the will of the people rather than being imposed by powerful forces), suggesting that popular culture results from society reaching a general agreement in a natural way about what constitutes culture, and that popular culture has been the result of this process of general agreement producing a culture that is popular rather than highbrow.

(ii) It is imposed in the form of a mass culture.
In the second paragraph of the first text, the writer says that another view of popular culture is that it results totally from power and the *forces of domination* in society and that therefore it isn't *a genuine popular culture*. Instead, it is a *mass culture*, which has been imposed on people by *a culture industry whose interests are in direct opposition to* the interests of the people. As a result, the people become a *quiescent* (quiet and obedient), *passive* (not taking control of what happens to them) *mass of people, totally disempowered* (having had all power taken away from them) *and helpless* (unable to do anything about their unfortunate situation).

(iii) It results from resistance to the powerful forces of the dominant ideology.
In the third paragraph of the first text, the writer says that another, more recent view, is that popular culture is *a site of struggle* (a place in which conflict is happening). This view concentrates on the *tactics* (planned methods for achieving something that involves defeating opposition) that are used so that the dominant forces in society can be *coped with, evaded* (dealt with by avoiding direct contact with) or *resisted*. Because of these *resistances and evasions*, the dominant ideology has difficulty in continuing to have a powerful influence. As a result, popular culture is seen as something that comes from the *vigour and vitality* (energy and liveliness) of the people and their desire to change society so that society is not dictated by the powerful forces of the dominant ideology.

(iv) It develops naturally as a result of the interests of people in general rather than simply being a commercial business.
In the first paragraph of the second text, the writer says that if something is to *be incorporated into* (become part of) popular culture, it has to match the interests of the people, rather than simply being a commercial *commodity* (something bought and sold). Popular culture is therefore not *consumption* (in this context, the purchase, ownership and use of goods for pleasure), it is something that gives *meanings and pleasures within a social system* (it has more social significance than consumption does).

(v) It is created by the people themselves.
In the second paragraph of the second text, the writer says that culture *can be developed only from within* (by people themselves in a society rather than by any outside force). It is therefore impossible for a *homogenous* (uniform, standard for all people in society), *externally produced culture* to be *sold ready-made* (complete and fully-formed before being sold) *to the masses*. People don't behave like that – they do not allow cultures to be imposed upon them. Instead, they produce their own cultures. As a result, the *culture industries* cannot force cultures on people, they can only *produce a repertoire of cultural resources* (a variety of available cultural resources from which some may be chosen or not chosen at any time) that people *use or reject* during the *ongoing* (continuing) *process* of producing their own popular culture. In other words, people use some of the things produced by the culture industries if they wish to and reject others, while they are producing their own popular culture.

Marks out of 10 are then given for summary skills, based on the following criteria:

- *relevance*
- *accuracy*
- *organization*
- *rephrasing*
- *length*

FURTHER PRACTICE AND GUIDANCE (p74)

Assessment of sample summary

Content points:

1 All the relevant points are made and nothing irrelevant is included.

(i) This is included in the first sentence.
(ii) This is included in the second sentence.
(iii) This is included in the third sentence.
(iv) This is included in the final sentence.
(v) This is also included in the final sentence.

Content: 4 marks

Summary skills:

2 There are no errors in the summary.
3 The summary is very well-organized, with each point made in separate sentences and appropriate linking.
4 Although some of the more specialized terms cannot really be rephrased, the summary accurately simplifies and rephrases the points made in the two texts.
5 The summary is within the word limit.

Summary skills: 10 marks

Sample summary total: 14 marks (out of 14)

PAPER 3:

PART ONE	15 marks
PART TWO	10 marks
PART THREE	12 marks
PART FOUR	16 marks
PART FIVE	
Questions 40–43	8 marks
Question 44	14 marks
TOTAL	75 marks

To be converted into a score out of 40 marks.

p75–76 PAPER 4 PART ONE

One mark per question (Total: 8)

1 **B:** The speaker says that soft negotiators want *an amicable* (friendly) *resolution* and *make concessions* (agree to let the other side have some things they are asking for), but that they *often end up exploited and feeling bitter* (the outcome is often that they feel someone has taken advantage of them and they feel annoyed that something has been unfair to them). Hard negotiators think that negotiation is *a contest of wills* (a struggle between people who are each determined to get what they want) and that the side that *holds out longer* (refuses to surrender or give in for the longest time) will be the side that *fares better* (gets the best result). However, they discover that their attitude has produced *an equally hard* (in this context, determined, tough) *response* from those they are negotiating with and this experience *exhausts them* (makes them very tired, uses all their energy) and damages their relationship with the other side. The speaker is therefore saying that both types of negotiator have certain expectations regarding what the results of their method of negotiating will be, but that both types find that the results are different from and worse than the results they had expected.
A: The speaker is not saying that it is better in some circumstances to be a soft negotiator and in others to be a hard negotiator, he is saying that both methods have disadvantages.
C: Although the speaker is saying that both methods can result in the negotiator feeling bad, he is not saying that they are not sure they will succeed during the time when they are negotiating. In fact, he suggests that they are confident then, because they expect their method to succeed.

2 **C:** The speaker says that through principled negotiation people *decide issues on their merits* (individually and objectively, rather than as part of a general theory or being influenced by personal feelings) and that the results of this method are *based on some fair standards independent of the will of either side* (they are reached according to generally accepted ideas of what is fair, which are not influenced by the personal wishes of the people involved in the negotiations).
A: The speaker says that people should *look for mutual gains* (try to gain things which are to the advantage of both of them) but that when their interests conflict they should reach an agreement that is objectively fair and that enables them both to *obtain what you are entitled to and still be decent* (honourable, behaving in a morally acceptable way). He is therefore saying that through principled negotiation people can get what is rightfully theirs, and so they will not feel that the outcome has been unfair to them.
B: The speaker says that principled negotiating does not involve *haggling* (bargaining, arguing involving both sides trying to get what they want) and that it also does not involve *tricks* or *posturing* (insincere or unnatural behaviour in order to create a certain impression or achieve a certain effect). Instead, it involves reaching an agreement that both sides can consider fair. The speaker does not say that this requires greater or less effort on the part of the negotiators than other methods of negotiating.

3 **C:** The reporter says that if you go to the shed, it is as if you *rewind* (this is what you do to make a tape go back to an earlier part or to the beginning, here it means 'go back') *to the Industrial Revolution* in the 19th century. She also says that Roly gets clay from the pit in a way that is *Like his father and grandfather before him* (the same as previous generations of his family did). The speaker therefore mentions twice the relationship between the pottery now and periods a long time in the past.
A: The speaker says that an old railway track is near to the pottery and that it leads to a *meadow* (a field) thick with bushes, plants and flowers and so it sounds as if the pottery is in an isolated place that few people go to apart from Roly, but the speaker does not say this or emphasize that it is a lonely place that people rarely visit.
B: The speaker talks about the *gloom* (darkness) of the place and mentions the door to the building and the colour of the building. However, she does not say that if you go inside the pottery, you are surprised to find that it contrasts with its external appearance.

4 **A:** Roly says that the pottery began to *decline* (do badly) as a result of *the advent* (arrival) *of the plastic bowl* (which was manufactured in factories rather than made individually in potteries) and that in the 1950s this was *a death blow to potteries countrywide* (something which caused potteries throughout the country to go out of business because they could not survive it).
B: He says that the pottery used to make *horticultural* (connected with gardening) *containers* and *domestic ware* (goods for use in the house), but that developments in the 1950s had a bad effect on it. He does not say that it was a mistake to make the kind of things it used to make or that any mistake was made with regard to developments in the 1950s, which he seems to see as having an inevitable result.
C: He says that his father was able to continue in business but that doing so involved *laying off* (making unemployed because there was no work to for them to do) the last four people still working there and producing pots that were more unusual. He probably does support what his father did but he does not say so or defend or justify his father's actions.

5 **B:** The first character mentioned is Lonesome Luke, who was *aggressive* and *a moderate hit* (quite but not very popular). Lloyd then decided to reject stylization *in favour of normality* (to portray a character that seemed like a real person rather than one that was clearly unrealistic and created just for film). The character he then created was someone that audiences could *readily* (easily) identify with (someone they felt was like them). This character was very successful and for ten years, while he was playing that character in films, Lloyd *could do no wrong* (everything he

did was very successful and popular) and audiences *flocked* (went in very large numbers) *to* his films.
A: It is not clear whether the idea for the new character came from Lloyd or his friend Roach. The speaker says that *history is divided* on this matter (some people who have done research, written books, etc on the subject say it was Lloyd and others say it was Roach). The speaker is therefore saying that it is not clear who *hit on* (thought of) the idea of the new character, and so she is not saying that it was definitely Roach's suggestion.
C: The speaker says that Lloyd felt that he was *not really good* when playing the character of Lonesome Luke and that he then played a character that was much more popular. However, she does not say that this was a result of his ambition increasing, and he may well have been extremely ambitious from the very start of his career.

6 **A:** The speaker says that there were two reasons why Lloyd's career suffered – the *double onslaught* (two things attacking) that *proved fatal to Lloyd's career* (that were disastrous for his career and caused it to end) were the invention of films with sound and the Depression of the 1930s in the US (this was a period of high unemployment during which a great many people were very poor). As a result of the latter, *his indomitable optimism was now incongruous* (his character's constant belief that everything would be all right despite the problems he was faced with didn't seem appropriate). The speaker is therefore saying that the attitude of Lloyd's character did not fit in with the general unhappy mood of the period and this was one of the two reasons why his career suffered.
B: Lloyd made one *talkie* (a film with sound rather than a silent film) and it was a *hit* (popular, a success) but he didn't make any more. The speaker says that this was because he was *instinctively a visual performer* (he was suited to doing things that were entertaining to watch rather than to dialogue). The speaker does not say or imply that Lloyd didn't want to make any more films with sound or that he was not keen to make the one that he did make. He may well have wanted to make other films with sound in order to continue his career but his style wasn't suited to films with sound and that is the other reason why his career came to an end.
C: The speaker says that Lloyd's highly successful character combined *lateral thinking* (a way of solving problems by means of ideas that may not seem logical) and *preternatural physical prowess* (physical strength that seemed to go beyond what is natural or normal) in order to *save the day* (prevent disaster when it seems certain to happen). She also says that the character's optimism didn't suit the times during the 1930s. However, nothing that the speaker says suggests that Lloyd himself began to lose confidence or that that was why his career suffered. His career suffered because of the arrival of films with sound and because of the Depression, not because he lost confidence in himself as a performer.

7 **C:** The speaker says that the brain waits before focusing on the present and collects *information from the future of an event* first. In other words, before thinking about what is happening now, we wait until the next thing has happened and then think about it. This is similar to what happens with live TV broadcasts; they are not genuinely live – what viewers see actually happened a few seconds earlier. The speaker says that the brain has a similar process of delay – it does not focus on what happens until a short time after it has happened, by which time something else has happened. He says that the brain develops *conscious awareness in an 'after-the-fact fashion'*, which means that it focuses on what happens after an event before *committing to a decision about what happened* (before making a firm decision about what happened in the actual event).
A: The speaker is not saying that people change their minds about something that happens. They don't have one perception and then later change it, they have no perception at all until after it has happened.
B: The speaker is not saying that the brain decides on what is important and what is not important when something happens, he is saying that it delays focusing on it until a short time after it has happened.

8 **B:** The speaker says that scientists have now measured the extent to which the brain delays before processing visual information and that in doing this they have provided *new insights into how we use vision to make sense of the world*. By saying that these are *new insights*, he is saying that their research has produced new information which helps us to understand something, and clearly this information adds to what is already known.
A: The speaker says that the brain's delay before focusing on an event is similar to the *slightly delayed broadcast of live TV shows*. The brain delays for *a minimum of 80 thousandths of a second* and he compares this with the delay in live TV broadcasts, which is *about three seconds*. He therefore compares the two delays but he does not say that the methods used in order to measure the length of the brain's delay were in any way based on the techniques used for live TV broadcasts. The scientists used a technique called *the flash-lag phenomenon* but he does not say that this was based in any way on the techniques used in TV.
C: The speaker says that the research has provided *new insights* and he refers to the scientists' report, but he does not say or imply that what they have discovered is probably going to be shown not to be correct or true. In fact, he seems to believe that the information is reliable, because it adds to what we know about the brain.

p77–79 PAPER 4 PART TWO

FURTHER PRACTICE AND GUIDANCE (p78–79)

For explanations, see the explanations to the questions in the test, which follow.

Question 9: b

Question 10: a

Question 11: a

Question 12: c

Question 13: b

Question 14: c

Question 15: a

Question 16: b

Question 17: b

p77 PAPER 4 PART TWO (TEST)

One mark per question (Total: 9)

9 **National Commercial Directory:** A *directory* is a reference book listing information such as names, addresses, telephone numbers, etc, usually in alphabetical order. In this case, clearly, the names and addresses of businesses throughout the country were listed under various categories. William Sumner was listed under the category Grocers and Tea Dealers.

10 **wines; spirits:** We are told that *at the turn of the 20th century* (at the beginning of it), William and his son John's business included *wines* and *spirits* (strong alcoholic drinks served in small quantities, such as whisky, vodka and gin) as well as groceries.

11 **indigestion:** Mary *suffered from indigestion* (a painful stomach complaint that usually lasts for a short time, resulting from problems when food passes into the stomach). She found that tea consisting of large leaves *aggravated her problem* (made it worse, more severe) but when she was sent some tea that consisted of small particles, she found that this *gave her great relief* (made the problem much better) and so she offered it to other people who had the same problem as a *'remedy'* (something that cures a medical problem).

12 **dust:** When John Sumner told his friend that he was going to buy *30 chests* (large, strong boxes in which tea was transported) of the tea Mary had discovered, the friend, who was a *wholesale tea merchant* (someone who traded in tea, in this case, selling it in large quantities to shopkeepers for sale to the public), told him that people would not want to buy it because it *looked little better than* (not much better than) *dust* (small particles of powder or dirt).

13 **oriental:** John wanted a name which *tripped off the tongue* (was easy and pleasant to say) and the name he *came up with* (produced, thought of) was *alliterative with* tea (both words in the name began with the same letter as tea) and had an *oriental sound* (sounded like a word from a language of the East, for example, Chinese or Japanese).

14 **printer's error:** The word 'Tipps' with two p's does not exist in English and presumably it was intended that the word would be 'Tips' (as in 'the ends or edges of something', in this context, the leaves of the tea plants). The double 'p', we are told, first happened *as a printer's error* – was the result of a mistake made by a printer, presumably when printing labels or something similar for the tea. Clearly, John Sumner decided not to change the spelling once that mistake had been made.

15 **jar of cream:** To encourage people to buy the tea, John offered anyone buying a certain quantity of it *a generous* (in the context of the size of something, this means 'large') *jar* (glass container in which certain kinds of food are sold or kept) *of cream.*

16 **edge of the leaf:** John brought back a kind of tea called *fannings*, and he *drew attention to* (tried to make people notice and realize, presumably in his advertising) the fact that this type of tea was taken from the edge of the leaf of a tea plant, and not from the *fibrous stalk* (the stem at the base of the plant, consisting of fibres), which contained the chemical tannin (which presumably people did not want in their tea).

17 **charitable work:** John received a *knighthood* (a high honour given by the British Queen or King for services to the country – the person awarded this is given the title 'Sir') *in recognition of* (as a sign of official praise for and approval of) *his charitable work* (his acts of charity, for example, giving money or other help to the less fortunate people in society, or helping or setting up organizations to provide such things). It was after his death that he helped his employees, all of whom *benefited under his will* (were left money by him in the legal document in which people say what will happen to their possessions and money after they die).

p80 PAPER 4 PART THREE

One mark per question (Total: 5)

18 **A:** Miranda says that the communal aerial (rod or tower that transmits TV signals) *sent fuzzy* (unclear, blurred) *pictures* every time it rained and that in Wales rain is *not a rare occurrence* (it happens regularly). In other words, the reception from the communal aerial was poor whenever it rained, and so this happened often.
B: When the satellite technician came to see them, he *saw not breathtaking natural beauty but obstacles* (he wasn't interested in how beautiful the place was, he only noticed the problems he would face if he tried to install satellite TV there). The point is not that they doubted his ability to install satellite TV, it is that he thought it would be very difficult or impossible to do so.
C: She doesn't say that it would be hard to link up with the communal aerial. She says that it would have been expensive to do so – they *could have spent a fortune laying cables to the nearest village* – and that the results would not have been good, because the reception was poor from the communal aerial and the entire system *went down* (stopped working completely) if *strong winds or stray animals* (animals that had wandered from the place where they should be) *knocked it out of kilter* (hit it so that it moved from its correct position).
D: She says that she *would love to be able to say* that they lived without TV by choice – that she threw the TV away or sold it – but that in fact *circumstances deprived us* (the situation they found themselves in meant that they couldn't have TV). She does say that they were living in a place of *breathtaking natural beauty* but that was not why they had no TV.

19 **C:** Miranda says that they started to *revel in our moral superiority* (to enjoy enormously the feeling that they were morally superior to people who had TV). When people started to ask them if they had watched a particular programme, Miranda *would watch their jaws drop* (their mouths open wide as an expression of astonishment) when they realized she had no TV, and they would wonder *what on earth* (an emphatic expression of surprise, indicating that it is extremely hard to know what the answer could be) the family did instead of watching TV. Clearly, therefore, she enjoyed seeing how surprised people were when they realized she and her family had no TV.
A: She says *At the risk of sounding unbearably smug,* which means 'I know that this might sound as if I am very pleased with myself in a way that others won't like', they did read more books, listen to more music and play more games. However, this is what she says to the interviewer, not what she said to people who found out that she didn't have a TV. She does not say that she told other people that they did these things instead, that she enjoyed doing so, or that she might have sounded self-satisfied when talking to them.
B: She says that they read more books, listened to more music and played more board games than before but this is not the same as saying that these were hobbies they had had and then stopped before moving to the cottage. It seems that in fact they did these things before, but when they moved to Wales they did them more.
D: She says that one enjoyable outcome was that they discovered the *untold* (very many), *long, pleasant and potentially fulfilling hours there are in an evening* – that evenings seemed a great deal longer and that it seemed that there was much more time in which to do things that make you feel happy and satisfied. She does not, however, say that these were energetic things or that they felt more energetic, and in fact implies that they felt more relaxed. In addition, she says that sometimes they *merely had an early night* (simply went to bed earlier than usual), which suggests they were more relaxed or tired rather than energetic.

20 D: Miranda says that they felt like *cultural oddities* (people who were not normal in terms of being part of the culture) because they did not understand when other people referred to well-known characters on TV or used a *catchphrase* (a phrase used often by a performer or in a programme that is associated with that person or programme by the public) from a popular TV programme. She therefore felt that it was a disadvantage that they were no longer informed about some of the things people talked about, because this made them feel they were in some way strange.
A: She talks about programmes that were popular but that they didn't know about because they did not have a TV, and these may have been series, but she does not say that they had previously liked particular series and were unhappy about not being able to follow them any more. She does say that they wished they could watch *big news events* on TV but these are not series.
B: She says that she and her husband were *confirmed news junkies* (people who were addicted to watching the news – *junkie* usually means 'person addicted to drugs') and that therefore they really missed watching the news on TV. However, she says that their addiction was only *mild* (not strong), and that after an *initial withdrawal* (an initial period of suffering because of the absence of something you are addicted to), *you hardly give it a second thought* (you hardly think about it at all). Their desire to watch the news was therefore not constant, it went away after a short period of time.
C: She says that they were in the habit of watching the news on TV and that a major disadvantage of not having a TV was that they couldn't do that, but she does not say that they normally discussed what was in the news and now couldn't. She says that other people talked about popular TV programmes and that they didn't know what these people were talking about because they hadn't watched them, but she does not say that previously they had discussed programmes they watched on TV.

21 A: Miranda says that she *went along with* (agreed to, accepted) having a TV installed because she is *certainly not one of those anti-TV types that believes the box* (an informal word for 'television set') *to be the source of all modern evil* (the cause of everything that is bad in the modern world). She says that she thinks there are lots of programmes on TV that are *interesting and rewarding* (worthwhile) *for both adults and children* and that television can be part of a *well-rounded* (appropriately balanced and varied) *life*. She is therefore saying that people of all ages – which in this context must include her, her husband and their children – benefit from having TV, and that was one of the reasons why she agreed to have a TV again.
B: She does not say that her attitude changed; it seems to have always been the same. She agreed because she thinks that TV is worth having and also because her husband wanted to have one, although she thinks this was because he wanted to play with the remote control device, not because he wanted to watch certain programmes. She doesn't say that she agreed because she had previously disapproved of TV and then approved of it.
C: She says that her husband *persevered with the satellite option* (continued to investigate the possibility of them having satellite TV installed) and says why she thinks he was so keen to have a TV again, but she does not refer to any disagreement between them about having a TV again.
D: Although she is in favour of TV, she says that *its insidiousness* (its ability to become powerful in a harmful way without people noticing that this has happened) *lies in its being an easy option* (results from the fact that it is an easy thing for people to do) because, like a *ready meal* (a meal you don't have to prepare yourself because it has already been prepared when you buy it), it *seduces you into forgetting the rewards that come from putting a bit more into life* (it persuades you by being attractive to forget that you can gain a great deal more satisfaction out of life if you put more effort into living your life). The point she is making is that TV can make people lazy or that watching it can be a result of their laziness, but she does not say that this was why her own family got a TV again. She was *apprehensive* (anxious) that it would dominate their lives and so she felt that it might make them lazy but she doesn't say that they got it because they were lazy – they got it because her husband wanted it and she thought that it was a good idea, despite the disadvantages that she talks about.

22 B: She says that she sometimes finds herself *proposing half an hour's viewing as an activity* to her children, but that they tend to refuse to do it if they think she is suggesting it because she wants to *sneak off* (go somewhere else quietly and secretly) and *do something without them* while they are watching TV.
A: She says that they *even watch rubbish from time to time* but not that the children now have a clearer idea of which programmes are rubbish and which programmes are worth watching. She also says that often, after ten minutes of watching TV, they decide that it's boring and switch it off, but she does not say that this is because they decide that some programmes are rubbish and others are not.
C: She says that they never had the habit of watching it, not that they have decided not to return to that habit. She says that their *year's abstinence must have coincided with their habit-forming years, so it's a habit they don't have* (the year they spent without a TV happened by chance during the same period in which their habits were beginning to form, so that in fact they formed the habit of not watching TV and never got into the habit of watching it).
D: She says that the children occasionally *slump* (sit in a tired or lazy way) and watch TV and that sometimes the whole family decide to *vegetate* (do nothing at all, be totally inactive) in front of the TV, which means that sometimes they do watch it because they are feeling lazy. She adds that to do this now is a deliberate choice rather than a habit.

p81 PAPER 4 PART FOUR

One mark per question (Total 6)

23 B: Sara says that their collaboration was *fun at first* and that *things started to get more and more serious* because after a while people tend to *believe strongly in your own ideas*, as a result of which *the art of compromise* can be a bit more difficult. She is saying that when people have been collaborating for some time, they become more determined for their own ideas to be accepted by the other person and so it is more difficult for them to reach agreements involving each person agreeing not to have everything they want.
Vic continues this point, saying that at first you lack confidence and need the other person to give their opinion but that as time passes, you become *more at ease* (relaxed and confident) and *more likely to rely on your own judgement* – he is saying that after a time, each collaborator has more confidence that they are right and so he strongly implies that it is harder for them to reach agreement when they disagree.

24 V: Sara says that collaborators *bounce ideas off each other* (try out ideas by getting a reaction from the other person) and that this is important in comedy writing, because you might think that something you have written is funny when in fact it's not funny at all, and it is important that your collaborator tells you that it isn't funny. She is not talking about situations in which you are not sure whether something is a good idea or not, she is talking about occasions when one person is sure that something is a good idea and the other makes them realize that it isn't. She

emphasizes *You really need to hear that* to indicate how important it is that your collaborator stops you from including something that isn't at all funny when you believe that it is funny.
Vic talks about when one person wants to try something risky in what they are writing, something that they think may be a bit *far out* (extreme), and says that their collaborator may give them *a bit more confidence* so that they *go ahead with the idea* (decide to carry it out or proceed with it, when previously it was in doubt). He is therefore saying that if you are doubtful about something you would like to try, your collaborator's opinion may make you feel that it is right to try it. He also says that this opinion may make you decide against trying it because it won't work.

25 S: Sara says that she loves dialogue and loves to talk. What she is saying is that because she is a person who likes talking, she also likes writing dialogue. She also says that she is *a very good story person*, which means that she is good at thinking of stories, whereas Vic is a *logical* person who gives her stories a structure so that they make sense.
Vic agrees with Sara about this, saying that Sara is *great at dialogue*, whereas his strength is in *story and structure*. However, he does not say anything about his own personality, he only talks about what each of them is best at in their work.

26 B: Sara says that you *can't be married to your work* (so involved with it that it takes over your personal life and is more than just a job) because *you'll never get anything done* if that is the situation.
Vic says that that is true not only for scriptwriters but for any kind of writer. He says that when he has written a play, he values the *feedback* (reaction, comments and criticism) he gets from other people about his work, but that some playwrights get personally upset if they are criticized because they feel that their work is *their baby* (something they have personally created and is of enormous personal importance to them). He thinks this is the wrong attitude and that *you have to accept criticism* if you are a writer.

27 V: Sara says that she has seen *teams involved in pitched battles* (violent or very aggressive arguments) but she does not say what the outcome of these was.
Vic interrupts Sara and says that they've *seen teams at each other's throats* (arguing aggressively with each other) *and they are still the best of friends* (their arguments have not prevented them from remaining close friends).

28 B: In answer to the question about one partner *slowing things down* or *not pitching in enough* (not making a big enough contribution), Sara says that *it all evens out* (it balances over a period of time) because when one of them is having a bad time and can't do enough of the work, the other one *pitches in a little more* (does more of the work).
Vic continues this point, implying agreement, and gives examples of why one of them might not be able to do their share of the work, adding that this is *no big deal* (not a big problem or important matter). He says that it is *just part of being a team*, and so he strongly implies that when one can't do enough of the work, the other does more to compensate for that.

PAPER 4:

PART ONE	8 marks
PART TWO	9 marks
PART THREE	5 marks
PART FOUR	6 marks
TOTAL	28 marks

To be converted into a score out of 40 marks.

p82–85 PAPER 5

FURTHER PRACTICE AND GUIDANCE (p84–85)

DESCRIBING FEELINGS

SADNESS

dispirited: discouraged or depressed because something bad has happened and as a result, something you hope for seems unlikely to happen
devastated: extremely unhappy and upset because of something terrible that has happened that affects you personally
dismayed: fairly unhappy because of something unexpected that has happened
distressed: very unhappy and suffering a great deal emotionally as a reaction to something
dejected: sad and depressed, and not feeling hopeful about the future
downcast: sad and depressed, especially in comparison with previously feeling happy or not feeling unhappy
despondent: without hope and therefore extremely unhappy
distraught: extremely unhappy and upset because of something terrible that has happened, especially when showing this by crying, etc

ANGER

irate: very angry (this word is used especially to describe other people, rather than yourself)
enraged: caused to feel or show that you feel very angry
touchy: easily offended or upset; sensitive and likely to get angry suddenly
mad: angry, in phrases such as *go mad* or be *mad at/with someone*
infuriated: extremely annoyed
resentful: annoyed for a long period after something that you consider unfair has happened
cross: fairly angry (this word is often used by adults talking to children)

ANXIETY

agitated: nervous and worried, especially when having previously been calm
tense: anxious and worried, especially when also silent
apprehensive: afraid that something bad or unpleasant may happen
harassed: feeling stressed and anxious because of pressure, having too many things to do, etc
concerned: worried
bothered: worried
edgy: nervous and therefore easily annoyed or upset
worked up: having got into a very worried or nervous state because of something that has happened
wound up: having got into a very anxious or stressed state because of something that has happened
unnerved: nervous after previously having been confident or relaxed, because something has happened to make you lose confidence or courage
petrified: extremely frightened

SHOCK

taken aback: greatly surprised by something that is said or happens and therefore unable to respond immediately
flabbergasted: completely amazed or astonished
staggered: extremely surprised or shocked
outraged: very shocked, and possibly also upset or angry, because of something that you consider morally wrong
astounded: extremely surprised or shocked
speechless: so surprised and shocked, and possibly also angry, that you are unable to speak
stunned: amazed; so surprised or shocked that you are unable to think clearly
appalled: very shocked because of something you consider totally unacceptable or disgusting

CONFUSION
bewildered: very or totally confused
thrown: confused or disturbed by something that has happened, so that you are unable to respond to it quickly or to continue what you were doing
flustered: confused and nervous because of trying to do too many things at the same time or because of not knowing what to do next
baffled: very confused and totally unable to understand, solve or answer something
perplexed: confused and worried, especially because you cannot understand why something has happened
bemused: confused and unable to think clearly

TOPIC VOCABULARY

CONFLICT
antipathy: (noun) If someone feels *antipathy towards* someone or there is *antipathy between* people, they strongly dislike that person or each other.
set-to: (noun) If someone has a *set-to with* someone, they have a big argument or a fight with them.
enmity: (noun) *Enmity towards someone/between people* is when people feel that someone is their enemy and therefore have aggressive and very unfriendly feelings towards them.
strife: (noun) Often used with an adjective to form phrases such as *political strife*, this means angry and violent disagreement or conflict.
showdown: (noun) A *showdown* is an occasion when people who disagree meet together in order to settle their dispute by arguing angrily.
altercation: (noun) An *altercation* is an argument or disagreement involving people shouting at or fighting with each other.
wrangle: (noun) In phrases such as *legal wrangle*, this means long and complicated argument.
rivalry: (noun) If there is *rivalry between* people, each is competing with the other in order to get something that both want or in order to be better than the other in some way.
fall out: (phrasal verb) If people *fall out with* each other, they have an argument or disagreement, as a result of which they are no longer friendly with each other.
antagonize: (verb) If someone *antagonizes someone*, they make them respond in an aggressive way by doing or saying something that makes them angry.
squabble: (verb/noun) If people *squabble with* each other or have a *squabble*, they argue with each other noisily, often about unimportant matters.
bone of contention: (idiom) If something is *a bone of contention between* people, it is a matter that they disagree about very strongly.
take issue with: (idiom) If you *take issue with someone*, you say that you disagree with them or you argue with them, rather than saying nothing.
acrimonious: (adjective) If something is *acrimonious*, it involves angry and bitter feelings and people being unpleasant to each other.
feud: (noun) If there is a *feud between* people, they have a disagreement that lasts for a long time and that involves them saying and doing nasty things to each other.
friction: (noun) If there is *friction between* people, they disagree with and dislike each other.
animosity: (noun) If you feel *animosity towards* someone, you strongly dislike them or have feelings of aggression towards them.
hostility: (noun) If you feel *hostility towards* someone, you feel aggressive towards them, as if you would like them to be harmed in some way.
incompatible: (adjective) If people are *incompatible with* each other, they can't live or work together in a reasonable way because they are so different from each other that they cannot have a friendly relationship.
bicker: (verb) If people *bicker with* each other, they argue about unimportant things, often in a way that is considered childish.
bad blood: (idiom) If there is *bad blood between* people, they dislike each other intensely, often as a result of particular things that have happened in the past.

COOPERATION
collaborate: (verb) If people *collaborate with* each other, they work together in order to produce or create something.
join forces: (idiom) If people *join forces*, they work together in order to achieve a common aim.
in concert: (idiom) If people do something *in concert*, they do it by working together.
harmony: (noun) If people are *in harmony*, they agree with each other, share the same opinions and attitudes, etc and therefore have a good relationship with each other.
pool: (verb) If people *pool something*, such as ideas, resources, etc, they put together what they each have so that together they can use the total of all the amounts.
in accord: (idiom) If people are *in accord* (*with* each other), they agree with each other on a particular matter.
band together: (idiom) If people *band together*, they join together to do something as a group.
concerted effort: (idiom) If people *make a concerted effort to do something*, they join with others and try to do it together.
camaraderie: (noun) If there is *camaraderie* among a group of people who spend a lot of time together, they like each other and are very friendly with each other as a group.
accommodating: (adjective) If someone is *accommodating*, they try to help someone get what they want rather than preventing them from having it.
give and take: (idiom) If something involves *give and take*, it involves people making compromises with each other so that they can avoid having a bad relationship.

AGREE
acknowledge: (verb) If you *acknowledge that* something is the case, you say that you accept that it is the case.
allow: (verb) If you *allow that* something is true, you agree or accept that it is true.
concede: (verb) If you *concede that* something is the case, you admit that it is the case, even though you wish that it was not.
consensus: (noun) If there is *(a) consensus*, there is general agreement among people about a particular matter.
unanimous: (adjective) If something is *unanimous*, it has the agreement of everyone involved in it. If people are *unanimous*, they all agree about something.
see eye to eye: (idiom) If you *see eye to eye with someone*, you are in complete agreement with them or have exactly the same opinions and attitudes.
acquiesce: (verb) If you *acquiesce in something*, you accept it or agree to it without protest or expressing opposition.
grant: (verb) If you say to someone *I grant you that* something is the case, you are telling them that you accept or admit that it is the case, even though there are other things which you do not accept or believe.

TRY TO CREATE AGREEMENT
reconcile: (verb) If people are *reconciled* (*with* each other), they re-establish a friendly relationship with each other after a period of disliking each other or having no contact with each other as the result of a disagreement.
appease: (verb) If you *appease someone*, you give them or allow them to have something that they want so that they stop being angry.
conciliatory: (adjective) If you do something *conciliatory*, you do something that is intended to stop someone from being angry, because it indicates that they can have something they want.
pacify: (verb) If you *pacify someone*, you cause them to stop being angry.
win over: (phrasal verb) If you *win someone over*, you convince them to agree with your point of view.
mediate: (verb) If you *mediate between* people, you try to persuade people who are in disagreement with each other to reach an agreement.
intervene: (verb) If you *intervene in* a situation or *intervene*

between people, you take action to resolve a disagreement or to prevent a dispute between people from getting worse or becoming violent.

mollify: (verb) If you *mollify someone,* you make them less angry about something.

defuse: (verb) If you *defuse something,* you make a situation in which people strongly oppose each other less serious, less severe or less likely to get worse or to result in violence.

placate: (verb) If you *placate someone,* you make them less angry about something.

p82–83 PAPER 5

Marks out of 40 are given for performance in the speaking paper.

TEST THREE

p86–87 PAPER 1 PART ONE

Note: all explanations in this part refer to the meaning or use of each option most closely related to the question, not necessarily to the only meaning or use of each option.

One mark per question (Total: 18)

Seriousness

1 **D:** If you say that you are **kidding**, or **kidding someone**, you say that you are not being serious and that you are joking, when the person you are talking to has not realized this and thinks that you are being serious. If you tell someone that you are **not kidding**, you are saying that you are being serious when they appear to think that you are joking. The writer is quoting something that parents tell their children when they want them to know they are being serious.
A: If you *trick someone*, you deceive them, so that they believe or do something as a result of something untrue that you said. (*I was tricked into buying some stolen goods.*)
B: If you *crack a joke*, you tell a joke. (*He spent the evening cracking jokes with his mates.*)
C: If you *tickle someone*, you touch them in such a way that they automatically laugh. (*She was tickling the baby's tummy.*) If something *tickles you*, it amuses you and makes you laugh. (*Something had obviously tickled him because he couldn't stop laughing.*)
All the options are connected with the idea of joking or not being serious or truthful, but A is the only one which both fits the meaning and does not have to be followed by an object.

2 **C:** If something **haunts you**, it is something unpleasant which is constantly present and which you cannot forget or put out of your mind. The writer is saying that people are always thinking about serious matters.
A: If something *preys on you* or *preys on your mind*, it troubles or worries you over a long period. (*His terrible treatment of her preyed on him/his mind for many years.*)
B: If something is *looming*, it seems likely to happen soon and it is unpleasant and frightening. (*The exams were looming and she was feeling more and more under pressure.*)
D: If something *hangs over you*, it is a threat or unpleasant possibility which is constantly present over a period of time. (*With the possibility of a court case hanging over him, he was unable to relax.*)
All the options mean 'worry someone', but C is the only one that fits grammatically because it is followed by an object.

3 **C:** If you **wallow in something**, you enjoy it enormously but this is regarded with disapproval. The writer is talking about people who get a lot of pleasure from being serious.
A: If you *relish something/doing something*, you enjoy or take pleasure from it. (*I don't relish the prospect of such a long, tiring journey.*)
B: If you *savour something*, you make sure that you enjoy a particular experience as fully as possible. (*He savoured the moment of victory.*)
D: If you *cherish something*, you think of it with great pleasure and it is very important to you. (*These are memories I will cherish in later life.*)
All the options are connected with the idea of getting great pleasure from something, but only C can be followed by 'in'.

4 **D:** If one thing **compensates for** another, it is something good or positive which balances something bad or negative. The writer is saying that some people think that if they are serious about a problem, this compensates for the fact that they don't understand it or know how to solve it.
A: If one thing *balances* another, it is equal to it and the result is a satisfactory situation. (*The problems involved in her job are balanced by the high salary she receives.*)
B: If you *reconcile something with something else*, you make the two things agree or work together in a satisfactory way, despite the fact that they are in opposition to each other. (*He had to reconcile his moral beliefs with his need to make money.*)
C: If something *redeems* something else, it is a good aspect of something but the other aspects of it are bad. (*The only redeeming feature of our awful holiday was the weather.*)
All the options are connected with the idea of something being good when other things are bad, but only D can be followed by 'for'.

5 **A:** If something **lends/gives weight to** something that someone has said or believes, it gives it power, importance or force and makes it more likely to be true or influential. The writer is saying that being serious makes a wrong opinion seem more acceptable.
B: If something *gains weight*, it becomes more powerful, important or forceful and therefore becomes more likely to be true or influential. (*My point of view has gained weight as a result of recent events.*)
C: If a theory or idea *holds water*, it appears likely to be true or believable when it is examined or considered. (*If you look at the evidence, you'll see that your theory doesn't hold water.*)
D: If you say that you *have to hand it to someone*, you are saying that they deserve the praise you are giving them. (*I have to hand it to Kevin – he always seems to know how to be in the right place at the right time.*)
All the options could form phrases connected with the idea of something becoming more powerful or justified, but only A completes the required fixed phrase.

6 **B:** If you have **a straight face**, you have a serious or sincere expression on your face, even though you are lying or joking or feeling amused. The writer is saying that the idea that people who are lying look serious when they are doing so is a common one.
A: If you describe someone as *smooth*, you are saying that they are charming and appear honest but that in fact they may be insincere and not to be trusted. (*Hugh is a smooth talker but don't believe everything he says.*)
C: If you describe something that is said as *plain*, you are saying that it is said in a direct and honest way. (*Helen has a reputation for plain speaking.*)
D: If you have *a clear conscience*, you do not feel guilty because you have not done anything wrong. (*I have a clear conscience about what happened because I was always honest.*)
All the options are connected with the idea of being honest or sincere, but only B completes the required idiom.

Horses

7 **D:** If something **is a matter of** something else, it results from it or depends on it. The writer is saying that the human desire to tame animals is not the only factor in whether or not they can be tamed, there are other factors too.
A: If something *is concerned with* something else, it is on the subject of it or connected with it. (*Her work is concerned with the investigation of serious diseases.*)
B: A *business* is a situation or something that is happening or has happened. (*I found the whole business very depressing so I tried not to get involved.*)
C: A *point* is a particular item or detail among others. (*Let's decide on the main points that we need to discuss.*)
All the options can mean 'thing related to a particular subject or situation', but only D correctly completes the required fixed phrase.

8 **B:** If you **take something/someone for granted**, their presence or value to you has been continuing for so long that you no longer appreciate them or show that you

appreciate them. If you *take it for granted that* something is the case, you believe that it is the case and that there is no need to check to make sure that it really is the case. The writer is describing the various characteristics of horses that people assume them to have.
A: If you *assume something*, you automatically believe it to be true or expect it to happen, even though there is no proof of this. (*I assume that you've already heard the news about George.*)
C: *Given something* means 'Taking into consideration something which is known to be true'. (*Given her lack of ambition, it's amazing that she became so successful.*) *Given that* ... means 'Since it is known to be true that ...'. (*Given that you've never done this kind of work before, I think you're doing quite well.*)
D: If you *take it as read* that something is the case, you believe or assume that something is the case and therefore feel that there is no need to check it. (*I'm taking it as read that you know the background to this situation.*)
All the options are connected with the idea of believing that something is the case, but only B correctly completes the required idiom.

9 **B:** If someone / something **undergoes something**, they experience something unpleasant or go through a process which results in change. The writer is saying that horses have changed as a result of changes in their diet.
A: If someone / something *is subjected to* something, they are made to experience something undesirable or forced to suffer it. (*We were subjected to a long speech from the boss about what we were doing wrong.*)
C: If someone *submits to something* or *submits themselves to something*, they accept the control or authority of something more powerful than them, rather than fighting against it. (*We had to submit (ourselves) to the wishes of the people in charge.*)
D: If someone *commits something*, they do something illegal or morally wrong (*commit a crime/a sin*). If someone *commits suicide*, they kill themselves.
All the options are connected with the idea of experiencing something or taking action, but only B both fits the meaning in the context and fits grammatically. A could fit the meaning but the verb would have to be in the passive form.

10 **C:** If someone is **compelled to do something**, they are forced to do it because of circumstances beyond their control or because someone makes them do it. The writer is saying that environmental changes forced animals to change their diets.
A: If you are *coerced into doing something*, you are forced to do it by someone who puts you under pressure or threatens you. (*He was coerced into signing the agreement because he was told he would lose his job if he didn't do so.*)
B: If someone *enforces something*, they make sure that it is obeyed because they are in authority. (*It is the responsibility of the police to enforce the law.*)
D: If something *necessitates something*, it makes it necessary. (*His plans for restructuring the company will necessitate a certain number of job losses.*)
All the options are connected with the idea of things happening because of force or because they cannot be avoided, but only C both fits the meaning in the context and fits grammatically. D fits the meaning, but the sentence would have to be changed so that the verb was active and followed by an object.

11 **C:** If something **grows + comparative adjective (longer, older, etc)**, it becomes longer, older, etc. The writer is talking about physical changes to the horse.
A: If something *expands*, it becomes bigger or wider. (*Metals expand when hot./The company has expanded and now has offices in several countries.*)
B: If something *increases*, it becomes bigger in number or size. (*The population of this city is increasing rapidly./I increased the speed at which I was working.*)
D: If something *enlarges* or someone *enlarges something*, it becomes larger or someone makes it larger. (*I enlarged the photograph of the children for my mother.*)
All the options mean 'get bigger in some way', but only C can be followed by a comparative adjective.

12 **A:** If you **keep a lookout for something** or if you **are on the lookout for something**, you look for it and make sure that you will notice it if it appears, either because it is dangerous and you want to avoid it or because it is something that you want. The writer is saying that the horse's eyes were positioned so that they could see whether they were in danger from other animals that might attack them.
B: If you *take heed of something* or *pay heed to something*, you take notice of it or pay attention to it, so that it has some influence on what you do or think. (*She took no heed of/paid no heed to my advice.*)
C: *Vigilance* is concentration or awareness involving looking out for possible danger, problems, etc. (*The police informed the residents that constant vigilance was required because a gang of burglars was operating in the area.*)
D: If you are *on the alert for something*, you are aware of possible danger and ready to react if it happens. (*Be on the alert for thieves if you go to that part of the city.*)
All the options are connected with the idea of being aware of the possibility of something or paying attention, but only A correctly completes the required idiom.

Afternoon Tea

13 **B:** If you **propose to do something**, you plan or intend to do it. The writer is saying that some people say that there is no point in having afternoon tea if you intend to have an evening meal.
A: If you *have designs on something*, you intend or wish to have it. (*Tim has designs on that sports car.*)
C: If you do something *with a view to doing* something else, you do it because you have a particular intention. (*She moved to another company with a view to rising to the top quickly.*)
D: If you *are minded to do something*, you intend or wish to do it. (*I am minded to write them a very strong letter of complaint.*)
All the options can be used to complete phrases which mean 'intend' or 'plan', but only B fits grammatically.

14 **A: No doubt** means 'very probably' or 'certainly' and is often used to say that one thing is the case but that something which contrasts with it or is opposite to it is also true. The writer is saying that people who think afternoon tea is unnecessary are probably right, but that they are missing something that is very enjoyable.
B: *No wonder* means 'It is not surprising that ...' and is used to say that something is logical in view of something else already known. (*'I've just been on holiday.'– 'No wonder you look so relaxed.'*)
C: *No matter* can be used to mean 'It isn't important' or 'It doesn't matter'. (*I can't meet you tonight.' – 'No matter, we'll fix up a different day.'*)
D: *No way* is an exclamation meaning 'Certainly not' or 'Under no circumstances'. (*'Will you do the washing up?' – 'No way, it's your turn.'*)
All the options are phrases that can be used to link within or between sentences, but only A fits the meaning in the context.

15 **C:** If something **leads up to something**, it forms a process or series of developments which results in a final outcome. The writer is talking about all the preparations for afternoon tea, which end with the pleasure of consuming it.
A: If something *draws to an end/a close*, it reaches its end. (*As the evening drew to a close, everyone got ready to go home.*)
B: If something *comes to an end/a close*, it reaches its end. (*She's hoping to get a job when her course comes to an end.*)
D: If something *runs to* a particular extent or amount, that is

the total extent or amount of it. (*The report runs to 20,000 words.*)
All the options can be used in phrases or phrasal verbs connected with the idea of something reaching an end, but only C correctly completes the required phrasal verb.

16 D: If you **sip something**, you drink a liquid by taking only very small quantities into your mouth at a time and without opening your mouth very wide. The writer is describing the act of consuming afternoon tea.
A: If a liquid *quenches your thirst*, the act of drinking it makes you no longer thirsty. (*I was very hot and needed a cold drink to quench my thirst.*)
B: If you *nibble something*, you eat it by taking small bites out of it at a time (*nibble a biscuit*).
C: If you *munch something*, you eat it by chewing it fairly loudly and energetically. (*He was munching an apple loudly.*)
All the options are connected with drinking or eating, but only D fits the meaning in the context.

17 A: If you **get something down to a fine art**, you learn to do it perfectly or become extremely skilled at it. The writer is saying that the people who live in Thrush Green are particularly good at preparing and enjoying afternoon tea.
B: *Sheer* means 'complete' or 'nothing but'. (*This is a work of sheer genius.*)
C: *Rare* can mean 'exceptionally good' as well as 'unusual' and 'happening only rarely'. (*He showed from an early age that he had a rare talent as a musician.*)
D: *Pure* can mean 'containing only the original or necessary elements and therefore as originally intended'. (*The necklace was made of pure gold.*)
All the options are connected with the meaning 'perfect', or 'complete', but only A correctly completes the required idiom.

18 B: If it is **common/standard practice to do something**, doing it is normal or common among a particular group of people in a particular place. The writer is saying that it is a custom in Thrush Green for people to invite others for afternoon tea rather than for a conventional meal.
A: If it is *someone's custom to do something*, they do it habitually. (*It is not my custom to lend money to people I hardly know.*)
C: If you *have a habit of/are in the habit of doing something*, it is something that you often do. (*Oliver has a habit of/is in the habit of offending people accidentally.*)
D: If something is *standard procedure*, it is the way that something is usually or officially done. (*I had to follow standard procedure, which meant filling in a lot of forms.*)
All the options are connected with habitual actions, but only B correctly completes the required collocation.

p88–89 PAPER 1 PART TWO

Two marks per question (Total: 16)

FDR

19 B: The writer says that what *inspired* the American people about Roosevelt was not just *grit* and his *gallantry and charm* but the fact that *At bottom* (basically), *he was a man of power and vision* (clear and wise ideas and plans for the future in general). The *power* was seen in the fact that *he took command with absolute authority*. The *vision* lay in his *profound* (deep), *creative desire to shape America for a better future*. It is implied that he made it clear that his *administration* (period of being President in the US) would *pursue* (make a great effort to achieve) *reform* (changes and improvements to a system) *as well as recovery* (returning something to its normal healthy state). Clearly, the country was experiencing problems because the people felt that he had *deep sympathy* with their *plight* (unhappy situation). The writer is therefore saying that the American people believed that Roosevelt would not only cause the recovery of the country but that he would have more than a short-term effect, in that he would introduce reform that would make the country better in the long term.
A: The writer does indicate that the country was going through a difficult period and that some people were suffering as a result, but he does not say that this was in any way the fault of the people themselves or that Roosevelt told them that it was. In addition, the writer is saying that Roosevelt was a courageous politician, but he does not say that this involved him having the courage to be critical of the American people.
C: The writer says that *what inspired them* (filled the American people with enthusiasm, hope, etc) *was more than grit* (determination to endure and succeed in difficult circumstances) and more than the *gallantry* (courage) *and charm* he possessed but did not use in that speech. He is therefore saying that Roosevelt possessed determination and courage but that these were not the only aspects of him that appealed to the American people. However, he is not saying that Roosevelt told them they needed to be determined in order for the country to change.
D: The writer says that Roosevelt had *overcome fearful* (terrible) *blows* (disasters, shocks that affect people very badly) *in his own life* and that this made him *well qualified to* (in a position where he had the experience that enabled him to) tell the American people that they *were not and could not be defeated*. He is therefore saying that because Roosevelt had experienced unfortunate events in his personal life and overcome the effects of them, he could tell the American people that they too could and would overcome the unfortunate situation they were in. However, he does not say that Roosevelt gave the American people details about what had happened to him personally or talked about his private life.

20 A: The writer says that FDR was not able to respond well to *the needs of intimates* (people in close contact with him) and that *At close quarters* (when in close contact with someone), he could be *evasive* (not completely direct or honest), *cold* (unfriendly, lacking in emotion) *and occasionally brutal* (very cruel), *if others grew too demanding*. However, if the people he was in close contact with *kept their place* (behaved correctly according to their rank or position, which presumably involved them doing what he told them and not being demanding), he could be *patient and generous*. However, the writer asks, *who can always know his place?* By this he means that some people could not always behave according to their rank or position because it is very hard for anyone to do so. He is therefore saying that some people close to FDR found it impossible to behave in the way he considered acceptable all the time.
B: We are told that FDR could be very unkind to people if they did something he disliked and that many people who were close to him *paid a very high price for* (suffered greatly in return for) *the privilege* (honour) *of working with him*. However, according to the writer, his leadership was so *intoxicating* (enormously exciting) that not many people regretted the experience because they felt pleased to have *served his great purposes*. The writer is therefore saying that even though some people who worked for him were treated very badly by him, they did not mind this, and he neither says nor implies that they felt they had to justify FDR's unkind behaviour to anyone.
C: The writer says that FDR was capable of being very kind as well as very unkind, but he does not say or imply that when he was being unkind he was only pretending or that those close to him felt that this was the case. On the contrary, being cruel to people was a genuine part of his character, we are told.
D: It is possible that some people who worked closely with him were only in that situation for a short time, because we are told that he was not patient with people who *grew too*

demanding, and the writer implies that it is very difficult for anyone to *know his place* all the time, so some people may have upset him very soon after coming into close contact with him. However, we are not told and the writer does not imply that some people only expected to be closely involved with him for a short time.

Kenneth Williams

21 D: The writer says that Williams *again seems an aberration* (a peculiar exception to what is normal) because he was not known by people all over the world and in *this age of the megastar*, megastars only exist *by virtue of* (because of) *the fact* nobody can be successful and a star unless they are recognized all over the world. Instead, Williams was a star only *At home* (in *his native Britain*). The writer is therefore saying that Williams was an exception to the norm because he was only a star in Britain and these days nobody is considered a star unless they are famous all over the world. The word *again* in the phrase *again seems an aberration* means that this is a further reason why he was an aberration. The first reason given is that he was *the antithesis* (opposite) *of the showbiz personality* (the kind of people typically associated with show business – the entertainment industry) in that he was *a combination of show-off* (someone who always wants to impress people by behaving in a very extrovert way) *and recluse* (someone who lives alone and very privately and avoids contact with others) – presumably the writer means that the normal showbiz personality is entirely 'show-off'.
A: The writer says that Williams *was never happy to leave Britain* but although that might well indicate that he was not interested in being a star in any other country as well, it is not what makes him an exception to the norm. We are not told that other people who were stars in Britain also wanted to be stars in other countries.
B: It seems likely that he did realize that he was a very big star in Britain because taxi drivers would come *shuddering to a halt* (they would stop so suddenly that their vehicles would shake) when they saw him. Moreover, the writer does not say that Williams' attitude to his fame in Britain was what made him an exception.
C: We are told that he appealed to taxi drivers and that he appealed to so many people that if he appeared on a show and simply said his *catchphrase* (a phrase always used by and associated with a particular entertainer) he could *send up figures* (cause the figures for the number of people watching or listening to a show to rise). However, we are not told that it was surprising that he appealed to certain people or that he was an exception because of the kind of people he appealed to.

22 C: The writer says that *the book on Kenneth Williams has remained closed* (nothing has been known about him) until now because people who say they knew him well only knew him *from their own necessarily limited perspective* (from their own point of view, which was inevitably a narrow one). This was because he *metaphorically* (not really, but in a way that can be imagined) *kept all his friends in separate rooms* and none of them knew what was happening in the next room. By this, the writer means that Williams kept all his relationships with his friends separate, so that each friend knew nothing about any of the others. If you were *ensconced* (settled in a place) *with him* somewhere, you felt that you were contained within a place with him and that you did not know what was going on in any other part of his life. The *walls* to which the writer refers are therefore the barriers that Williams seemed to build in order to keep each of his relationships separate. The writer says he is now going to try to bring those walls down and by this he therefore means that he is going to reveal the different parts of his life that Williams kept separate from all those involved in them.
A: The writer says that Williams liked to keep all his friendships separate but he does not mention any desire on Williams' part to keep things from the public, nor does he suggest that there were things which Williams was anxious to keep secret about himself. He merely says that he wanted to keep his friends separate from each other.
B: The writer says that Williams' friends didn't know anything about each other and that their friendships with him were therefore all entirely private. However, he does not say or imply that these friends took action to make sure that what they knew about him was known only by them – it was Williams who seems to have taken action to make sure they didn't know about each other.
D: We are not told that Williams hid his true feelings from people – he may have revealed them to each of his friends. What we are told is that he kept different parts of his life in separate compartments, with the result that none of his friends could have discussed him with each other.

My Brother Charles

23 A: Charles is said to be *neither particularly happy nor particularly unhappy with his life* and thinks that something extremely exciting that would change his life forever might happen *at any moment*. The writer puts this phrase in italics to emphasize that he really does always think that such a thing could happen at any time. Furthermore, Charles says that he is *just marking time* (doing something to pass the time until something more interesting presents itself) at the shop. He is therefore reasonably content to do the job he is doing at the moment, but only because he believes that everything will change for him at some point.
B: The writer says that when the shop was built, it was *magnificent*, it was meant to *outdo* (be better than) the *great London stores* and it used to have a countryside scene on its roof. These days it is a more *mundane* (dull, unremarkable) place. This does not mean that it is no longer as successful or profitable as when it was built, merely that it is different.
C: The writer says that because the shop is not as magnificent as it used to be, Charles has to *content himself* (be satisfied with) a duller environment in which he deals with a variety of different kinds of electrical equipment. She is therefore saying that he does not have interesting surroundings to amuse him but she does not say or imply that he finds the electrical equipment particularly interesting or that he likes his job more than he seems to.
D: Charles is said to spend most of his time *daydreaming* (thinking pleasant thoughts about other things rather than what you are supposed to be doing). He therefore doesn't seem to get on with his work but we are not told that he is able to do this because he is not given much work, or that his employers expect little from their staff. He may get into trouble for daydreaming, and he may be the only member of staff who spends most of their time doing it.

24 C: The writer says that she *can't imagine ever thinking of Charles as a man* after referring to him as a *boy*. What she means is that, regardless of his age, he seems to her to be a boy and she cannot imagine that he will ever seem like a fully-developed adult. She therefore feels that he still has the attitudes of a boy, rather than thinking like a man.
A: She says that when he talks about his belief that something exciting is going to happen, *his eyes nearly pop out of his head* (the mental effort makes his eyes open very widely) as he tries to find the right words *to articulate* (express clearly) *the feeling*. She is therefore saying that he finds it hard to express his feeling clearly but she does not say that he fails to do so or that there is a better way of expressing the feeling that he has.
B: She says that Charles believes that something exciting might happen at any time and in this belief he is *Much like everyone else*, which presumably includes her. Furthermore, when he asks her whether she too believes that something is about to happen and she replies 'No', she is lying, which means that she does believe it too.

D: She says that when he left school, he had *no talents discernible to* (that could be seen or noticed by) *his teachers*. Now, she says, he has a *remarkably dull outer life* (if you look at his life from the outside, it seems very dull). However, she does not say that he is capable of something better than the job he has, only that he thinks that something more exciting will come up for him.

John Lennon

25 B: The writer makes the generalization *Like most bullies* (people who get pleasure from hurting or frightening people who are weaker than them), *Lennon was frightened at heart* (in his real character rather than the way he appeared). He is therefore saying that Lennon's behaviour illustrates the belief that bullies are actually frightened people.
A: Lennon's cruelty is said to have been *not confined* (limited) *to words* because he would *lash out* (physically attack) *instinctively* (because it came naturally to him to do so) at anyone who made him angry. If he was faced by someone *bigger and braver*, he would *resort to* (use because another course of action did not work) *psychological* (involving the mind rather than physical action) *tactics* (methods for achieving an aim), which involved *undermining them* (making them lose confidence or power) *with abuse* (insults, nasty remarks) *or sarcasm* (remarks that involve saying the opposite of what you mean in order to make somebody look foolish). He was therefore cruel both with words and with physical actions but the writer does not say that one was more effective than the other or that this aspect of his behaviour exemplifies a particular theory.
C: It is said that Lennon's *characteristic gait* (typical way of walking), which involved him being *hunched up* (bent forward, with the neck and shoulders pulled together), resulted from his attitudes towards people, which were a mixture of *hostility* (aggression) and *defensiveness* (the anxious feeling resulting from the idea that you are being attacked). However, the writer does not say that this is something that is true of people in general, he only says that it was the case with Lennon.
D: The writer says that Lennon was basically a frightened person and he also seems to say that he frightened other people because he *sought to dominate* (tried to have complete control over) them *through sheer* (by means of nothing other than) *aggression*, for example by *launching* (putting into action) *surprise attacks*. However, he does not say or imply that fear is a stronger emotion than others in general terms – it may have been in Lennon's case and in the case of those he came into contact with, but the writer is not suggesting that fear affects people in general more than any other emotion.

26 D: The writer says that Lennon and his friend were *often caned* (hit with a stick used for punishment in schools) by the headmaster but that despite this, Lennon *never mended his ways* (improved his behaviour so that it was acceptable). Instead of doing that, he took the attitude that he was *beyond the pale* (considered generally unacceptable by people) and that, because of this, it didn't matter how he behaved or how much he was punished. In other words, the writer says that Lennon decided there was no point in him changing the way he behaved because it would make no difference to how he was treated or what people thought of him – he would remain unacceptable to them anyway.
A: The headmaster is described as *notorious* (well known for a bad reason), and the fact that he beat Lennon had no effect on him, so it is possible that he had no respect for him. However, this is not why he didn't change – that happened because he decided that he was not socially acceptable in general.
B: The writer says that *If all else failed* (if everything else that he had done had not worked), he would *take to his heels* (run away), which indicates that he was not always able to get what he wanted from bullying people.
C: The writer does not say that anyone admired Lennon for being a rebel. He certainly did refuse to conform but that was not because he was encouraged to do so by anyone else – it was because of his own image of himself.

p90–96 PAPER 1 PART THREE

The Perils of Pizza Making

FURTHER PRACTICE AND GUIDANCE (p92–96)

For explanations, see the explanations to the questions in the test, which follow.

Question 27
1 a and c 2 a and c 3 a and c

Question 28
1 c and d 2 b and c 3 b and d

Question 29
1 a and d 2 a and d 3 b and c

Question 30
1 b and d 2 c and d 3 a and b

Question 31
1 a and d 2 a and b 3 b and c

Question 32
1 a and d 2 a and d 3 a and d

Question 33
1 a and c 2 b and c 3 c and d

p90–91 PAPER 1 PART THREE (TEST)

Note: the numbers in brackets refer to the relevant question in the Further Practice and Guidance pages.

Two marks per question (Total: 14)

27 F: In the opening paragraph, the writer says that his first pizza was *cremated* (burnt to ashes, as is done with dead bodies in a ceremony at funerals) and that he hadn't even got to the stage of putting toppings on it. We therefore know that is was thrown away because it was useless. He then tells us that pizza dough should be made into perfect circles. Obviously he had failed to do that with his pizza **(1c)** and Francesco had looked at his *sorry effort* (poor attempt) and *sighed*, presumably with disappointment or disapproval **(1a)**.
In the first sentence of F, *it* refers to the pizza the writer had prepared. His pizza *wasn't so much a circle* (this refers back to the requirement that pizzas be prepared as perfect circles in the first paragraph) *as an early map of the world* (presumably something without a regular shape) **(3c)**. Francesco then picked it up on his *paddle* (an implement on which pizzas are placed and then put into the oven) and threw it *disdainfully* (with contempt or great disapproval) into the oven to destroy it **(3a)**. The reference to it burning on a *funeral pyre* (a pile of wood on which dead bodies are burnt as part of funeral ceremonies in certain religions) echoes the reference to it being *cremated* in the first paragraph.
In the paragraph after the gap, the writer goes on to talk about the art of pizza-making. He says that pizzas have to be prepared in the correct shape **(2a)** and says that doing this was causing him *grief* (a lot of trouble) **(2c)**.

28 D: In the paragraph before the gap, the writer has told us that pizza-making is *an art* (something requiring skill and special ability) and that there is a *procedure* for shaping pizzas before they are cooked **(1c)**, which was causing him trouble **(1d)**.
In the first sentence of D, *it* refers to the procedure. The writer then describes Francesco carrying out the procedure to show the writer how to do it **(3d)**, beginning with what has already been prepared and put into the fridge, and then going on to the first thing that is done with this **(3b)**.
The paragraph after the gap continues the description of Francesco carrying out the procedure to show the writer what to do **(2b)**. *From here* means 'after this stage of the procedure' (after it was *mixed with a small handful of polenta*). The writer then describes each stage of the procedure for preparing the dough for a pizza **(2c)**.

29 H: In the paragraph before the gap, Francesco completed the preparation of a pizza from the dough with the right shape – *a perfect circle* **(1d)** – and the writer describes how he did this **(1a)**.
At the beginning of H, the writer says that it was now his turn to try to achieve *the same result* that Francesco had achieved **(3c)** – a pizza with the right shape. The rest of H describes the writer beginning to attempt to do the same as Francesco had done **(3b)** and problems he encountered doing so.
In the paragraph after the gap, the writer continues his description of his own effort to do what Francesco had done. He explains what you are supposed to do to create a pizza with the right shape **(2d)**, how you can easily go wrong by pressing too much **(2a)** and what happened as a result of him making this mistake.

30 A: In the paragraph before the gap, we have been told that, while trying to prepare the dough into the right shape, the writer could not resist the temptation to press *everything in sight* **(1b)** and that pressing in the wrong places resulted in *thick edges and a thin centre* **(1d)**.
The first phrase in A *To put those things right* refers back to the two things that were wrong with what the writer produced – it had thick edges and it had a thin centre **(3a)**. At the end of A, the writer says that he *did some twirling* (twisted or turned the dough around and around) and that as a result *flour showered everywhere* (flour flew around in the air and onto the ground) – something which might well have made the writer look foolish **(3b)**.
After the gap, we learn that the writer attracted the attention of some customers, which means that obviously the preparation and cooking of pizzas in this restaurant was carried out in a place where the customers could see it being done **(2d)**. The writer realized this to his *horror*, which means that he was not at all happy that people could see him doing badly **(2c)**.

31 E: In the paragraph before the gap, we have been told that the writer became the focus of some customers' attention **(1a)** and that he didn't like this because he reacted with *horror* when he realized that they were watching him prepare a pizza **(1d)**.
The first sentence of E (*Clearly, the stage was all mine.*) refers to the fact that the writer realized that people were watching him and that he was the centre of attention as he tried to do the right thing but failed **(3c)**. E continues with a description of his attempt to make a pizza properly. The reference to feeling *more and more eyes on him* means that he felt that more people were now watching him in addition to those he mentions in the paragraph before the gap. In the last sentence, the writer says that something terrible then happened **(3b)**.
In the paragraph after the gap, we learn what *the worst thing* was – a hole appeared in the writer's pizza – and that he felt *crestfallen* (extremely disappointed) and *defeated* as a result **(2a)**. We also learn that this pizza was destroyed by Francesco in the same way that the first one had been **(2b)**.

32 G: In the paragraph before the gap, we have been told that the writer's second attempt was also a disaster **(1a)** and that it had to be destroyed like the first one **(1d)**.
In G, *as it did so* in the first sentence refers back to *go up in flames* immediately before the gap and means 'as it went up in flames' or 'as it burnt'. The writer was naturally *baffled and embarrassed* by his second attempt having to be destroyed **(3d)**. However, he felt that he was *onto something* (making some progress) and his next attempt was more successful. He realized *where I had gone wrong* before and so was very careful when he reached that stage again. His efforts now to prepare the pizza correctly *began to work* **(3a)**.
At the beginning of the paragraph after the gap, Francesco noticed that what he was doing was beginning to work – that he was doing it properly – and that is why he *applauded* (showed approval by clapping his hands together) **(2d)**. The writer was so pleased with his comparative success that he wanted to tell the little girl that he could make pizzas. Francesco then decided that the writer's pizza was good enough for them to put toppings on **(2a)**.

33 C: In the paragraph before the gap, we have been told that the writer had made a pizza base that was good enough for toppings to be put on **(1a)**, that he was pleased about this **(1c)** and that they then put the toppings on.
In C, *Having done that* means 'having *put on a thin smear* (a layer, roughly applied) *of tomato sauce and some mozzarella.*' *It* in *it was time to get it on to the paddle* is the pizza, now ready to be cooked. The writer then *headed for* (went towards) the oven **(3d)** to put the pizza in to cook **(3c)**.
After the gap, *When I got there* means 'When I reached the oven' (*there* refers back to the oven at the end of C). The writer reached the oven and Francesco told him where in the oven the best place to cook a pizza is **(2b)**. He then put the pizza he had made into it, and watched it cooking so that it could be eaten rather than being burnt because it was no good, which is what had happened to his previous efforts **(2c)**.

The paragraph which does not fit into any of these gaps is B.

p97–98 PAPER 1 PART FOUR

Two marks per question (Total: 14)

The Chess Player

34 A: The writer says that David R. Norwood *will be the first to admit* that he is *one of the hottest properties* (one of the most popular people, one of the people who is in the greatest demand) *on the international chess circuit* (the chess tournaments around the world featuring the best players). Normally, the phrase 'the first to admit something' is followed by faults or mistakes that someone is willing to admit to, but here the writer is being ironic, because it is followed by a claim to be important. The writer is therefore implying that David R. Norwood likes to say how good and important he is and to praise himself.
B: The writer knows David R. Norwood's name because he gives him a business card with his name on it. The writer tells us what the card says but he does not comment on that and it could be that many chess players have business cards. He describes him as a *boy wonder* (an exceptionally successful and talented young man) and uses the phrase *all of 19*, to emphasize how young he is to be a top chess player, so he does emphasize how young he is, but he does not make a particular point about the business card.
C: The writer describes the pub champion as looking like a *bum* (a very untidy, lazy or dirty person who has no

particular home and moves from place to place), with untidy hair, a big beard and his possessions in a *white polythene bag* (this suggests they were in a shopping bag). He contrasts him with the *kid genius*, who seems to be a fresh and probably smart young man. However, he does not imply at this point that the pub champion is one of the best players or that he is in any way typical of the best chess players.
D: The game is being played on a container for beer that has been turned upside down so that it can be used as a table and the game is clearly taking place in a pub. However, although these are informal surroundings, the writer does not imply that he thinks it is good to see chess being played in such a place rather than in formal surroundings – his description of the surroundings is merely factual.

35 D: In the games, David R. Norwood is *not merely losing*, he is being *taken apart* (defeated easily and completely). The writer says that in the *argot* (words and phrases used only by a particular group of people) of chess players, he is being *'busted'* (this must logically mean 'totally defeated' in the language of chess players). After each game, Speelman sets up the pieces for *the next act of slaughter* (in this context, the next total defeat of his opponent). Speelman is therefore clearly a far better player than Norwood.
A: The writer says that something *funny* (in this context, this means 'strange') happens in the games. This is that Norwood keeps losing heavily. The reason why this is 'funny' is that Norwood usually wins games (we already know that he is a *kid genius* and a *boy wonder*). But he is not losing because they are playing in a pub rather than in formal surroundings or because they are not playing in a real tournament – he is losing because Speelman is much better than him. Therefore the writer believes that Norwood would lose wherever they played.
B: Norwood sometimes says to Speelman that he is *not such a bad player* and the writer says that of course this is a *joke* because Speelman is not simply *not a bad player, he is perhaps the best player in the Western world*. Speelman *laughs* whenever Norwood makes the joke and simply prepares for the next game without saying anything further. Speelman therefore seems to appreciate that Norwood is joking and he certainly does not get offended by the comment. It seems that the games are played in a friendly way and Speelman's reaction is a good-humoured one. There is therefore nothing to suggest that Speelman has a low opinion of Norwood and he says nothing to indicate that he thinks Norwood is a poor player.
C: Norwood does joke occasionally that Speelman is *not such a bad player* but he also *does not seem too worried by this denouement* (the way in which something ends or is resolved, in this case the fact that each game ends with him being heavily defeated). He therefore does not seem embarrassed at losing and the implication is that he expects to lose because he knows Speelman is a much better player than him.

36 B: The writer says that he got the impression that although Speelman told him that he *liked to play with the pieces*, in fact *the pieces enjoyed playing with him*. By this he means that, because of Speelman's approach to the game, the pieces were moved around in ways that they normally weren't by other players. The writer talks as if chess pieces have feelings. He says that when Speelman is playing, he *gives them the time of their life* (he enables them to enjoy themselves thoroughly). Being in a pub, he says, they have probably never experienced *more than the intellectual equivalent of being cooped up in a shed* (because players in the pub are not very clever at chess, the pieces experience only restricted movement, like birds or animals confined in a small building in which they cannot move around much). But when Speelman is playing, he says, they are *roaming free across vast expanses* (they are wandering around freely across large areas, in this case of the board). His point, therefore, is that other people play in a restricted, narrow way, only moving the pieces small distances, whereas Speelman plays in an unrestricted, open way, moving the pieces all over the place.
A: When the writer asked Speelman why he *put up with* (tolerated) *chess jerks* (a slang word meaning 'stupid people') like him, his reply was *instant* (immediate) *and unanswerable* (it could not be argued against because it was clearly true). Speelman seems to have answered his question in a friendly way and the writer does not say anything to indicate that Speelman did not want to talk to him while they were playing.
C: Speelman seems to have enjoyed playing against the writer as much as he enjoyed any other game. The writer says that he got *more bored by losing* than Speelman *did by winning*, which indicates that Speelman continued to enjoy winning each game against the writer and did not start to get bored by this. There is no indication that it was hard for Speelman not to get bored or that he made an effort to keep himself interested.
D: The writer's description of Speelman's style of play seems to be a general one concerning how he always played. There is nothing to indicate that he normally played in a more restricted way if he was playing a serious game or that he was only playing in this way because he wasn't taking the games against the writer seriously.

37 B: His nickname, Spess, is a short form of 'Specimen', which was his original nickname, and the writer says that friends and other chess players called him that because they considered it *descriptively accurate* because of his *rather weird* (strange, not normal or common) *appearance*. A 'specimen' in this context means 'a creature used for scientific research because it is in some way unusual or interesting'. The nickname was therefore used because people thought he looked like a peculiar creature, which is not a very complimentary description of anyone.
A: The nickname is said to be related to his physical appearance, not to any aspect of his personality. Although the nickname refers to his peculiar appearance, it is not said that he was regarded as unfriendly.
C: The nickname originated in a report in a newspaper about a chess tournament he was playing in, but it is not related to the way he plays, it is related to his physical appearance.
D: His nickname was originally 'Specimen' and this was first used as a result of a mistake in a newspaper, when his surname Speelman was *inadvertently* (unintentionally, accidentally) printed as 'Specimen'. This happened not because it was a joke but because it was a mistake – when the writer says *Times sub-editors being Times sub-editors*, he is implying that sub-editors working for that newspaper have a reputation for making mistakes.

38 C: The writer says that Speelman is *only too aware* (extremely aware) of how people might interpret things that he says. Because of that, he wanted to know what the writer was noting when he spoke to him and so while the writer was making notes, he would *stare at* (look keenly at) his pad and try to read his *scribble* (handwriting done very quickly and untidily). The result of this was that, *in an effort to* (trying to) *counter* (respond against) *this awkward* (causing difficulty) *turning of the tables* (reversing of situations, by which the person being investigated seems to be the person doing the investigating), the writer *deliberately* (consciously, intentionally) began to write in *messier and messier* (more and more untidy) *scrawl* (handwriting that is hard to read) so that Speelman would be unable to read what he was writing. As a result, after the interview the writer was unable to read many of the notes he had made. Later, he *surmised* (concluded) that Speelman had *calculated that his scrutiny* (close study) of the writer's notepad *would have this effect* (cause the writer to make notes he would be unable to

read later) and that it was a *deliberate attempt to reduce the number of personal details* about Speelman that he would be able to *decipher* (succeed with difficulty in reading and understanding). Speelman therefore succeeded in his aim of disturbing the writer while he was making notes, so that later he would be unable to read a lot of them and use the information in them in his article.
A: The writer says that Speelman's behaviour while he was making notes happened because of *the chess player in Speelman* (it was natural for someone who was a chess player) and that it was *quite in character with Speelman's way of playing chess* (entirely typical of his playing method), which was *convoluted* (extremely complicated) and involved producing *chaos* rather than taking an ordered, simple approach. He is therefore saying that what Speelman did was typical of his approach to playing chess, but he did it to cause the writer problems, not because he thought the writer was expecting him to do such things.
B: Speelman was not trying to understand the personality of the writer when he looked at his notes, nor was he doing it in order to analyse his style of handwriting. He did it in order to limit the amount of information he could note down that he would be able to read clearly later.
D: Speelman was concerned about how the things he said to people might be interpreted but he didn't stare at the writer's notes while he was making them in order to make sure that the writer would represent what he said accurately, he did it in order to make sure that not many of the writer's notes would be of use to him when he came to write his article.

39 C: When the writer says *Now you get the picture*, he means 'Now you understand the situation, now you appreciate what I mean'. This follows his invitation to the reader to try to do what Speelman does throughout a game of chess, which is to predict the next 25 moves he will make in conjunction with the next 25 moves his opponent will make, making a total of 50 moves ahead that he is constantly predicting while he plays. The writer is implying that the reader would be totally unable to do such a thing because it is far too difficult and he is therefore emphasizing that it is amazing that Speelman can do such a thing in his head.
A: It may be that other chess players can do what Speelman does, but the writer does not say this. The point he is making is that what Speelman keeps in his mind throughout a game is incredible and he is not making a point about chess games in general. Furthermore, he is not emphasizing how complex the games Speelman plays are, he is emphasizing the extent of the mental effort that he personally makes during them.
B: It is true that the writer seems to regard Speelman's style of play as extraordinary – we have learnt previously that he moves the pieces around differently from other people and that his style is based on chaos rather than the simplicity of other players' styles. The writer does say in this paragraph that Speelman's style *makes enormous demands on the exponent's* (the person carrying it out – Speelman's) *nervous system*, which again suggests that he finds it extraordinary. However, Speelman does not seem to find what he does extraordinary, because he says that it is *not too difficult to imagine a position in which one could calculate 25 moves ahead*. In this quote, *one* means 'you' or 'anyone' and so he is saying he thinks it is not something only he can do but something that is fairly easy for anyone to do. So although the phrase *Now you get the picture* is used to emphasize how extraordinary the writer thinks Speelman's way of playing is, it does not refer to Speelman's own view of this.
D: The writer describes Speelman when he plays as *all nervous, twitchy* (with sudden, involuntary movements) *movement*, says that he constantly touches his beard, his glasses and anything else he can reach and says that he will *stand over* (stand next to them while they are sitting, in a way that could make them nervous) his opponent, *nodding his head* (moving it up and down) *as if checking the variations* (in this context, possible future moves made by both him and his opponent). This behaviour may well appear peculiar to others but it is not what *Now you get the picture* refers to and his behaviour is not what the writer is emphasizing here – what is going on in his head is what is emphasized.

40 D: The writer says that Hartston chose the metaphor *quite deliberately* – in order to make a particular point – because he wanted to make it clear that Speelman was *innocent* (not causing offence) and *harmless* (not annoying or upsetting people) and not aggressive or unpleasant like some other chess players. The writer says that *The point is* (the important thing about Speelman, as the description of him as being like a fridge illustrates) that, although he wants to win, he does not dislike his opponent – his aim is that he should win rather than that his opponent should lose. He says that in this way he is completely different from another chess player, who wants to *crush the other guy's ego* (destroy his self-confidence). The writer is therefore saying that a fridge is *an innocent and harmless object* and Speelman has the same characteristics, as illustrated by his attitude to his opponents – he does not want to destroy them and is not unpleasant to them when he beats them.
A: Hartston says that Speelman is like an old fridge with a door that *shuts with a big clunk* (a dull, heavy sound) and that you can't see inside such a fridge but you can see and hear it *whirring* (making a continuous sound caused by engine parts moving around) *and shaking* and you know that something is happening inside it *in an undirected* (disorganized) *sort of way*. His idea is that you don't know exactly what Speelman is thinking when he is playing but you know that thought is going on and that it is rather chaotic. He is not saying that Speelman's style of playing appears different from what it really is in the sense that it is simpler or more complicated than it appears. Furthermore, this aspect is Hartston's description of Speelman and the writer does not say whether he believes this to be appropriate for Speelman or not. He does say that he believes it is appropriate to describe Speelman as being like a fridge but he does not say that it is appropriate because of this aspect of old fridges – it is appropriate because of his attitude towards opponents.
B: It may well be that Speelman's untidy and strange physical appearance contrasts with the sharpness and clarity of his mind when he is playing, but Hartston's comment suggests that Speelman's thought processes are chaotic and he does not suggest that old fridges are scruffy on the outside, he simply says that when you shut the door you cannot see what is going on inside. Moreover, the writer's belief that the fridge is an appropriate image is not based on Hartston's description of old fridges.
C: The writer believes that a fridge is an appropriate image for Speelman because of features of his personality and his attitude, and he does not suggest that these features are not genuine or that Speelman pretends to be *innocent and harmless* when in fact he is not like that. On the contrary, he believes that he really is those things.

PAPER 1:

PART ONE	18 marks
PART TWO	16 marks
PART THREE	14 marks
PART FOUR	14 marks
TOTAL	62 marks

To be converted into a score out of 40 marks.

p99–102 PAPER 2 PART ONE

Task-specific mark schemes

Each answer given marks out of 20

Question 1

Content
Proposal should include:
- list of possible events and when and where they would take place
- details of what events would consist of
- reasons why chosen events would be popular
- how events would be organized

Proposal can include additional ideas of candidate's own.

Range
Language for describing, analysing, hypothesizing and making recommendations. Language for presenting/developing an argument.

Appropriacy of register and format
Register appropriate to situation (member of a committee preparing proposal for colleagues on same committee) and therefore does not have to be very formal. Proposal format, with clear section headings.

Organization and cohesion
Well-structured with clear sections dealing with each different aspect. Within each section, paragraphing where appropriate. Appropriate linking between parts of each section and perhaps the sections themselves.

Target reader
Would understand fully what the writer is recommending and why.

FURTHER PRACTICE AND GUIDANCE (p100–102)

Assessment of sample answer

Content
The proposal covers all of the points listed in the note in the question and is entirely relevant throughout. Events and venues for them are included, and details are given as to what the events would consist of and how they would be organized.

Range
There is some good use of vocabulary and structure, for example *agreed on* and *a great deal* (introduction), *present* and *I am leaving this to the committee to decide* (Town Hall section), *alternate with, take turns with* and *every second day* (Local Theatre section) and *provide you with* (concluding part). The concluding part is particularly well-expressed.

Accuracy
There are one or two mistakes. The phrase *open for the public* in the Town Hall and Arts Academy sections should be *open to the public*. It is not completely clear what is meant by *closely* in the Town Hall section, and in that section, *I suggest to keep* should be *I suggest keeping* ('suggest' is not followed by an infinitive).

Appropriacy of register and format
The register is suitable for a proposal in this context – it is fairly, but not very, formal. The format is entirely appropriate – the proposal itself has a heading, and there is an introduction, followed by separate sections with headings and a conclusion.

Organization and cohesion
The proposal is extremely well-organized. The opening section provides background information and general points concerning the organization of the festival, the three middle sections with headings provide details of events proposed for each of the three venues listed, and the final part successfully concludes the proposal with a suggestion of further action on the part of the writer. There is some excellent linking, for example, the use of the sentence before the three sections with headings, which links the introduction with the specific details to be provided, and the use of *According to* at the beginning of the first sentence of the final part.

Target reader
The reader would be entirely clear what the writer is proposing, what would take place in each venue, what has been agreed so far and how the events might be organized.

Assessment: A good and well-organized proposal.

Mark: 14

p103–106 PAPER 2 PART TWO

Question 2

Content
Article should describe a memorable day, including what led to it, what happened during it and the consequences – good, bad or both – of it.

Range
Language of narration, description and evaluation, and perhaps of analysis and hypothesizing.

Appropriacy of register and format
Register could be formal, informal or neutral but should be consistent throughout. Article format – clearly divided paragraphs, perhaps short ones for impact on reader. Article could have sub-headings.

Organization and cohesion
Clear development of narration, description and comment, starting with the background, moving on to the events and then going on to the writer's views on the consequences of what happened. Appropriate linking within and between paragraphs.

Target reader
Would be interested in following the description of what happened and would understand fully and clearly why it was memorable for the writer and what impact it had.

Question 3

Content
Review should inform the reader about the subject the writer has chosen and compare writer's views on it with those of critics.

Range
Language of narration, description and comparison, as well as language for expressing and supporting views.

Appropriacy of register and format
Register could be formal, informal or neutral but must be consistent throughout. Format should be appropriate for review – description followed by comment and comparison in each paragraph or paragraphs of description, followed by paragraphs of comment and comparison.

Organization and cohesion
Clear development with appropriate paragraphing and linking between description, comment and comparison.

Target reader
Would be informed about the subject chosen for review and would have a clear idea of how critics' comments compare with those of the writer.

Question 4

Content
Letter should describe the candidate's experiences at the hotel and how they reacted at the time, together with suggestions as to how the hotel could be improved.

Range
Language of description and narration, together with language appropriate for expressing opinions, making suggestions and hypothesizing.

Appropriacy of register and format
Formal register, as appropriate for letter of complaint to someone in charge. Formal letter format.

Organization and cohesion
Brief introduction stating reason for writing, clear paragraphing for presenting account of what happened, opinions on these events and suggestions for avoiding repetition of them, with appropriate linking between these elements.

Target reader
Would have a clear picture of what happened, how the writer feels about that, and what the writer is advising the management to do.

FURTHER PRACTICE AND GUIDANCE (p104–106)

Assessment of sample answer

Content
Most of the main points mentioned in the question are covered in the letter, since it describes what happened to the writer in the hotel and the results of this for the writer, and it also includes suggestions to the manager. There is no mention of complaints made to the staff at the time, but this is not a major disadvantage and does not reduce the effectiveness of the letter.

Range
There is some very good use of vocabulary and structure, for example, *made my stay rather complicated and unnecessarily unpleasant* and *of high standard* (first paragraph), *most* (meaning 'extremely') *unpleasant* (second paragraph), *knew nothing about* and *starving* (third paragraph), *omitted* (fourth paragraph), and *I strongly advise you to ... , appalling, endure, steps that have been taken, to avoid such a situation* and *awaited* in the final paragraph, which is excellent. The language used is certainly not too simple, with excellent linking producing some longer sentences that make complex points very well, particularly in the final paragraph. The shorter sentences are used for brief, clear descriptions of what went wrong and are therefore entirely appropriate.

Accuracy
There are a few mistakes. In the first paragraph, *Despite of* is incorrect ('of' should not be there). In the third paragraph *will be delivered* should be *would be delivered* as it refers to a past hope not a future one, and the word order of the final sentence is wrong – it should be *wait for another 45 minutes for my dinner to be ready*.

Appropriacy of register and format
The letter is appropriately formal and appropriately laid out. The tone is entirely suitable, being forceful in the points made and the annoyance expressed but remaining polite throughout.

Organization and cohesion
The letter is extremely well-organized. The opening paragraph gives the appropriate background and explains precisely what the writer's purpose is. The next three paragraphs detail concisely and clearly what happened and why it caused problems for the writer. The final paragraph is excellent, presenting a forceful and very clear view as to what the writer thinks should happen and expects to happen. There is a great deal of excellent linking throughout, for example *Although* (first paragraph), *For some reason* and *Considering* (second paragraph), *Therefore* (third paragraph), *which meant* (fourth paragraph) and *as well as, especially for* and *although* (final paragraph). The only mistake with linking is in the fourth paragraph, where the last two sentences should be linked by *not to mention* rather than beginning another sentence with *Not mentioning*, which is incorrect.

Target reader
The reader would be absolutely clear about what happened, the writer's feelings about it and what the writer expects to happen as a result of the letter. At the beginning, the writer says that three problems will be detailed and each of them is explained very clearly. The fact that the writer does not want money in return, but wants to be informed that action on service has been taken, is very clear at the end.

Assessment: A very well-organized letter with some sophisticated language.

Mark: 15

PAPER 2:

PART ONE	20 marks
PART TWO	20 marks
TOTAL	40 marks

p107 PAPER 3 PART ONE

One mark per question (Total: 15)

Celebrity Crossover

1 **Somewhere:** In the context, this means 'in a place that is'. The writer has said that actors want to be pop stars *and vice versa* (and the other way round, in other words 'and pop stars want to be actors'). He goes on to say that there is a place deep inside our brains in which we all have the desire to be both pop stars and actors.

2 **under:** If you *keep something under control*, you are able to control or deal with it so that others are not aware of it or it does not cause problems. The writer is saying that most people manage to control their desire to be pop stars and actors.

3 **one/former/first:** This refers back to *pop stars and actors* at the end of the first paragraph. The phrase *the one/former/first profession* means 'one of the two professions mentioned' or 'the first of the two professions mentioned'.

4 **except/but:** Both *except* and *but* are followed by *for* to create linking phrases that express the idea of an exception to a statement previously made, or a way in which a statement previously made is not true. The writer has said that being an actor or pop singer does not automatically mean that you can also be the other thing, but then says that there is

one fact that contradicts this and means that being an actor or pop singer can automatically mean that you can also be the other thing.

5 **say:** If someone *never says no to someone,* they always agree with them and they let them do everything they want to do. The writer is saying that because they are surrounded by people who agree with everything they say, actors think they can become pop stars and pop stars think they can become actors, because that is what they want to do and nobody tells them that they can't or shouldn't.

6 **On:** The linking phrase *on the whole* means 'in general' and the writer is generalizing about pop stars and actors.

7 **opposite:** *Someone's opposite number* is a person who is in a similar position to them in another situation or has a similar job to theirs in another organization or, in this case, profession. The writer is saying that pop stars do better when they become actors than actors do when they try to become pop stars.

8 **face:** The phrase *let's face it* means 'we must accept that it is true' or 'we must be honest about this' and is often said before stating a fact that may be unpleasant or difficult for someone to accept. The writer is saying that, although some people might not like to admit or accept it, it is a fact that it doesn't matter if you are a film actor who is no good at acting but it does matter if you try to make a record but cannot sing or play music well.

9 **against:** If something *counts against someone,* it is considered a disadvantage or bad aspect concerning them and has a negative effect on decisions or judgements made about them. The writer is saying that if someone goes into a recording studio to make a record and they cannot sing or play, this is a disadvantage, whereas not being able to act is not a disadvantage if you are a film actor.

10 **sets:** If someone/something *sets an example for someone,* they do something which other people should copy or be influenced by. If someone *sets a bad example for someone,* they do something which it is considered others should not copy or be influenced by. The writer is saying that people who succeed in both professions are not a good example for others to follow because they are exceptions and most people who try to follow them will not succeed in both professions as they have done.

11 **For:** The structure *for every ... , there is/are ...* is used for comparing two things in terms of the relative numbers of them or the proportion of each. The writer is saying that if you analyse all the pop stars and actors who try to succeed in both professions, every time you find one who succeeds you also find *two dozen* (24) who fail – in other words, far more fail than succeed.

12 **how:** The adverb *how* is used before an adjective or adverb to talk about the extent of something. The writer is saying that the people who fail are not aware of the fact that they are not just bad but very bad at the other profession.

13 **Just:** The linking phrase *just as* is used with the meaning 'in exactly the same way as'. The writer is saying that power corrupts people and it is equally true that being famous destroys people's ability to judge what they are doing.

14 **yourself:** If you *make a fool of yourself,* you do something that makes you look foolish or ridiculous to others. The writer is saying that famous people tend not to realize that they are doing this.

15 **If:** *If* is used here to introduce a statement of something that may be true and the second statement in the sentence is the reason why it may be true. The writer is saying that there may be one good aspect connected with actors and singers trying to combine both professions and that is that doing so means that they don't have time to write books. He says in the text as a whole that he doesn't think they should try to combine the two professions but at the end he finds one reason why it might not be such a bad idea – he is implying that their attempts to write books would be even worse than their attempts to combine professions.

p108 PAPER 3 PART TWO

One mark per question (Total: 10)

Captain Webb

16 **undoing:** *Someone's undoing* is the thing that ruins their life or causes them to fail completely. The writer is saying that the fact that Webb refused to give up swimming was disastrous for him in the end.

17 **obscurity:** If you live *in obscurity,* you are not at all famous or well-known. The writer is saying that nobody had heard of Webb until he swam the Channel.

18 **exhaustion:** If you are suffering from *exhaustion,* you are extremely tired and have no strength or energy left. The writer is saying that Webb was extremely tired when he finally arrived on the other side of the Channel.

19 **standstill:** If something *is brought to/comes to/is at a standstill,* it ceases to continue to function and everything connected with it stops. The writer is saying that when Webb made a public appearance in the City of London, no business was done because everyone went to see him.

20 **fearless:** If someone is *fearless,* they are not at all afraid or are not capable of feeling fear. The writer is saying that Webb wasn't usually afraid of anything but he became frightened by all the attention he received.

21 **stardom:** *Stardom* is the situation or status of being very famous as a performer. The writer is saying that being very famous had an enormous effect on Webb, and caused him to make a terrible mistake.

22 **applause:** *Applause* is approval expressed by a crowd or audience by clapping (hitting their hands together). If you *crave something,* you want it desperately. The writer is saying that Webb was extremely keen to receive the praise and admiration of others.

23 **endurance:** *Endurance* is the ability to continue doing or surviving something difficult or unpleasant for a long time without giving up. An *endurance event/contest,* etc is a sports event in which the competitors have to do something (swim, run, cycle, etc) for a very long time. The writer is saying that Webb took part in a swimming event that lasted for six days.

24 **punishing:** If something such as a timetable, schedule or workload is *punishing,* it requires an enormous amount of effort and energy on the part of the person doing it because they have to do a great many things, and it may make the person doing it extremely tired or ill. The writer is saying that Webb's timetable when he went to America was full and that he did too much while he was there.

25 **regardless:** The linking phrase *regardless of* means 'paying no attention to' or 'in spite of'. The writer is saying that Webb ignored advice not to try to swim the Niagara River.

p109–112 PAPER 3 PART THREE

FURTHER PRACTICE AND GUIDANCE (p110–112)

For explanations, see the explanations to the questions in the test, which follow.

Question 26
First sentence: **b** thought / considered
Second sentence: **a** picked
Third sentence: **c** pronounced / found

Question 27
First sentence: **b** once
Second sentence: **c** still
Third sentence: **a** yet

Question 28
First sentence: **b** head
Second sentence: **a** climax
Third sentence: **b** front

Question 29
First sentence: **c** avoid
Second sentence: **b** assist
Third sentence: **a** help

Question 30
First sentence: **c** spell / string
Second sentence: **b** term
Third sentence: **c** run

Question 31
First sentence: **a** striking / marked
Second sentence: **c** sharp / astute / perceptive
Third sentence: **a** tight

p109 PAPER 3 PART THREE (TEST)

Two marks per question (Total: 12)

26 **found:** The way you *find someone/something* is how you consider them or what you think of them as a result of personal experience. The grammatical structure *find + object + adjective* can be used with this meaning. The verbs *thought* and *considered* can also be used in the same structure to describe your opinion or attitude towards someone / something.
If you *find fault with something,* you criticize it when perhaps there is no need to, but you want to criticize and are looking for a reason to do so. The verb *picked* can also be used in the gap to form a phrase with the same meaning.
If someone is *found guilty/not guilty,* the decision of a court of law at the end of a case in which they are accused is that they are guilty / not guilty. To refer to the actual statement made by a judge in court that the person is guilty / not guilty *pronounced* can also be used, meaning 'declared'.

27 **yet:** If you say that something happens *yet again,* you are emphasizing that it has already happened many or too many times and now it has happened once more. *Once again* and *once more* can also be used with the same meaning.
If someone *has yet to do something,* they are expected to do it but they have not done it at this point in time. The phrase *have still to do something* can be used with the same meaning.
As yet means 'so far' or 'until this point of time' and is used for talking about things which have not happened yet but which might happen.

28 **head:** If something such as success or praise *goes to somebody's head,* it makes them arrogant or too self-confident.
If a situation *comes to a head,* it develops or continues until a point is reached when something serious happens as a result. If something *reaches/comes to a climax,* it reaches a point at which it is at its most intense.
If you are *at the head of something,* you are at the front of a line of people or a crowd, or in the leading position in something. The noun *front* could also fill the gap here, with the same meaning.

29 **help:** If you *can't help doing something,* you cannot avoid or resist doing it even if you would prefer not to do it. *Avoid* can be used in the same grammatical structure with the same meaning.
If something *doesn't help,* it doesn't make a bad situation better. *Assist* can be used in the same way, though it is more formal.
If you *help yourself to something,* you take it without asking permission to take it first.

30 **run:** *A run of* something is a continuous, unbroken series of them or a period in which there is a continuous, unbroken series of something. *A string of* can be used with the meaning 'a series of' and *a spell of* can be used with the meaning 'a period of'.
In the long run means 'in the future a long time from now' or 'over a period of time stretching from now until far in the future'. *In the long term* can be used with exactly the same meaning.
If someone is *on the run,* they are trying not to be caught by the police, who are looking for them.

31 **sharp:** *A sharp contrast* between two things is a big, clear difference between them. *A striking contrast* is one that is remarkable, clear and attracts attention. *A marked contrast* is clear and very easy to notice.
If someone is *sharp,* they are clever, quick to realize what is happening and perhaps quick to take advantage of situations. Someone who is *astute* is intelligent with regard to assessing situations and making judgements and decisions, especially to their own advantage. A *perceptive* person is someone who is able to notice things that other people might not notice and who is aware of the reality of situations rather than the way they appear on the surface.
A *sharp bend/curve/corner/turn* is a sudden change of direction in the course of something such as a road or a river. *Tight* can be used to describe the same things, especially to indicate that it is difficult to go safely round them.

p113 PAPER 3 PART FOUR

Two marks per question (Total: 16)

32 **interference** (1 mark)
everything would have gone smoothly (1 mark)
The first part of the third conditional *If + subject + verb* has been transformed into *Without + possessive* and therefore must be completed by a noun to go with the possessive. The noun from *interfere* is *interference.* If something happens without any problems, it *goes smoothly.*

33 **took issue with him about** (1 mark)
how (1 mark)
If you *take issue with someone (about something),* you tell them that you disagree with them or start to argue with them. The phrase *the best way,* in which 'best' is an adjective, has to be transformed into the phrase *how best,* in which 'best' is an adverb.

34 himself to (1 mark)
the possibility of losing (1 mark)
If you *expose yourself to something,* you put yourself in a situation in which you may suffer in some way because you are not protected from something unpleasant or undesirable. *Possibility* is followed by *of + -ing.* It must be preceded by the definite article because the nature of the possibility is defined.

35 was/were deluged with calls (1 mark)
in (1 mark)
If someone is *deluged with something,* they receive so much/many of something that it is hard for them to deal with it all. The verb phrase *responding to* has to be transformed into the noun phrase *in response to.*

36 taken note of my complaints (1 mark)
and would act (1 mark)
If you *take note of something,* you pay attention to it or take notice of it. If you do something that is appropriate in the circumstances you *act accordingly.*

37 costs to a/the minimum (1 mark)
or we'll find (1 mark)
If you *keep something to a/the minimum,* you make sure that there is the smallest amount of it possible. If you *find yourself* in a certain situation, you discover or realize that you are in that situation but you did not deliberately try or expect to get into it.

38 he conducted himself at the conference (1 mark)
(has) resulted (1 mark)
The way that you *conduct yourself* is how you behave. If something *results in something,* it causes it or has it as its result.

39 didn't/did not conform to (1 mark)
what were considered (1 mark)
If something *conforms to something,* it follows or accords with what is expected or demanded. The phrase *the standards that were considered acceptable* has to be transformed into the phrase *what were considered acceptable standards,* with 'what' as the subject.

p114–118 PAPER 3 PART FIVE

Questions 40–43

FURTHER PRACTICE AND GUIDANCE (p116)

For explanations, see the explanations to the questions in the test, which follow.

Question 40:	1 a	2 c	3 b	
Question 41:	1 c	2 c		
Question 42:	1 b	2 d		
Question 43:	1 b	2 a	3 d	4 b

p114–115 PAPER 3 PART FIVE (TEST)

Questions 40–43

Two marks per question (Total: 8)

Answers that are similar to or cover the same points as those given here are acceptable, provided that they are clearly expressed.

40 that it may be true that because people believe classes exist, they do exist, but that this does not tell us to what extent they exist or how important they are
A *trusim* is a statement that is so obviously true that there is no need to make it. The truism the writer is referring to is that 'if people believe that something is true, then it is true'. In this case, what people believe to be true is that classes exist. One indication of this belief is, the writer says, the *commonplace* (often repeated and uninteresting statement) among politicians that the distinctions between different classes are *diminishing* (fading, becoming less strong) or disappearing. This does not prove that there are classes but it proves that people think there are. However, the writer asks, even though people think it is true that classes exist and therefore it is true that they do, *how true* is it that they exist and *how significant* are classes in comparison with other things in society that they believe exist and which affect their lives? In other words, do they exist to any great extent and are they of much importance?

41 there are an enormous number of books in existence/that have been published on the same subject
The writer wonders why she is being so cautious about the subject of class and not dealing directly with it, when there are so many books available in shops (*there are shelves groaning with books* means 'there are so many books on shelves that the shelves are in danger of collapsing under the weight of them') that cover the same subject.

42 it has meant that people have been coming closer financially to those in the upper classes but it has not resulted in much change socially
The writer says that the class system is *alive and well* (very much still in existence and strong) *in people's minds in England.* There has been an enormous change between rich and poor in terms of wealth, so that *Jack* (a name used by the writer presumably to represent ordinary people, or people from the lower classes) is *getting nearer to his master financially* (is no longer so far apart from the people he works for, the upper classes, in terms of how much money he has). In other words, there is no longer such a big gap between the poor in the lower classes and the rich in the upper classes financially. However, she says, *social stratification* (in this context, the division of people into different layers or classes socially) *remains incredibly resistant to change* (is still extremely opposed to change or extremely hard to change). The writer is therefore drawing a distinction between English society in financial terms, where she says there have been enormous changes resulting in fewer class distinctions, and in social terms, where she says little or no change has occurred and the distinctions between classes remain great.

43 people like looking back to the past with a feeling of fondness and in order to express disapproval of injustices that no longer exist and, although they don't like to admit it, they like the idea of society being based on classes of different levels, from high to low
The writer says that *nostalgia excuses everything* (if you are looking back to the past fondly, you can forgive and forget the unpleasant aspects of it). She says that people watching these programmes *click their tongues* (make a noise with their tongues that expresses disapproval) *over the out-dated inequalities* (in reaction to the old-fashioned social injustices which resulted in some people unfairly having worse lives than others) that are shown in them. She says that they *guiltily enjoy* (enjoy, although they are rather ashamed of enjoying) *the sense of hierarchy* (the idea of a system based on some people being of high status and others being of low status) that is evident in these programmes about the past and that this must mean that they have a *hankering after* (a strong desire for) *a social pecking order* (a categorization of people according to how important or

unimportant they are) in the society in which they are living today.

Question 44 Summary

FURTHER PRACTICE AND GUIDANCE (p116–117)

For explanations, see the explanations to the summary in the test, which follow.

1	J	**2**	C	**3**	F	**4**	I
5	A	**6**	L	**7**	D	**8**	H
9	K	**10**	E	**11**	B	**12**	G

The relevant main points are **B, D, F, H, K, L**. The other points deal with various aspects of the subject of class but not with problems associated with analysing it, which is the topic of the summary.

p115 PAPER 3 PART FIVE (TEST)

Question 44 Summary

One mark for each content point included from the following, maximum 4 marks

Note: the letters in brackets at the end of each explanation refer to the relevant sections of the texts highlighted in the Further Practice and Guidance pages.

(i) It is not clear that classes really exist.
The writer says that, although people believe in the existence of classes, and a *pragmatic* (practical, based on an acceptance of reality rather than vague theory) assessment, a lot of evidence suggests that there is a strong *presumption* (belief that something must be true) that classes exist, but this *does not prove that classes actually do exist.* **(B)**

(ii) Class and inequality are not necessarily the same thing.
The writer says that a great many books deal with the question of *gross inequalities* (very clear and very bad ways in which some people are treated unfairly and differently) in society in various different forms but that although it is possible to prove that inequality exists, it is not possible to prove that this is connected with class. This, she says, is the problem that *lies at the heart of* (is the central issue in) *the dialectic between* (the philosophical and academic discussion and examination of the difference between) *the image and the reality of class* (what is thought about class and what it really is). **(D)**

(iii) Statistics on the subject often differ from what people discover elsewhere.
The writer says that some statistics, such as those that result from *national censuses* (official surveys in which governments find out about the population of a country) present conclusions about certain classes and groups in society but *none of these coincides with* (all the groups referred to in the findings differ from) ideas of class that can be found in other places, including *everyday speech* (when people discuss the matter with each other in ordinary conversations). **(F)**

(iv) Some people think it's a subject that is no longer worth paying attention to.
When the writer first thought of writing a book about class, people *drew away from* her *in horror* (reacted by moving backwards in a way that expressed shock and disgust at what she had said), saying that nobody *gives a hoot* (cares at all) about the subject of class any more. She felt that, as a result of the *egalitarian shake-up* (the major change and re-organization involving greater equality between people in society) of recent decades, the subject of class had become *the ultimate obscenity* (something considered the most offensive or disgusting thing possible). **(H)**

(v) Classes are constantly changing and the differences between classes are becoming less distinct.
The writer says that although the class system has *stratification* (division in layers), she found that it constantly formed and re-formed *like coral* (a substance found at the bottom of the sea that is formed from the bones of very small creatures) – in other words, the class system keeps changing **(K)**. She also says that the class system is like a shirt that has *run in the wash* (its colours have dissolved and spread so that they have run into each other as a result of being washed), so that each layer is *blurring into the next one* (is mixing in with the next one so that none of the colours is separate, clear or distinct). In other words, she found that the distinctions between the different classes have become less clear to the point where they are now not clear at all. In addition, she found that *snobbery* (feeling superior to others socially) was at its *fiercest* (strongest) *where one stripe merged with another* (among people who were partly in one class and partly in another). **(L)**

Marks out of 10 are then given for summary skills, based on the following criteria:

- *relevance*
- *accuracy*
- *organization*
- *rephrasing*
- *length*

FURTHER PRACTICE AND GUIDANCE (p118)

Assessment of sample summary

Content points:

1 Most of the relevant points are included. However, the second half of the first sentence and the reference to 'the writer' in the second paragraph are not directly relevant to the task.

(i) This is included, in the first paragraph.
(ii) This is included, in the second sentence of the first paragraph.
(iii) This is not included – there is no reference to statistics.
(iv) This is not included – there is no reference to people not wanting to discuss the issue of class.
(v) This is included, in the majority of the second paragraph.

Content: 3 marks

Summary skills:

2 In the first paragraph, *the* should come before *young generation*, and some linking is required between the two parts of the final sentence.
3 The summary is quite well-organized, flows quite well and is coherent. The language is generally fairly simple, but not too much so. There is some good linking, for example, *although* and *However* in the first paragraph.
4 The points made in the texts have been reworded, with some good language such as *point to* and *their relation to*. In the final sentence, *de-merge* indicates an understanding of what is meant by 'merge' in the second text, even though that word is repeated.
5 The summary is slightly over the maximum word limit, because of the content mentioned in 1 above.

Summary skills: 5 marks

Sample summary total: 8 marks (out of 14)

PAPER 3:

PART ONE	15 marks
PART TWO	10 marks
PART THREE	12 marks
PART FOUR	16 marks
PART FIVE	
Questions 40–43	8 marks
Question 44	14 marks
TOTAL	75 marks

To be converted into a score out of 40 marks.

p119–120 PAPER 4 PART ONE

One mark per question (Total: 8)

1 **A:** The speaker says that British people *never expect their holiday plans to run to schedule* (to happen in the way and according to the timetable that has been planned) and that when things go wrong they *sigh* and say *I knew this would happen* (they are resigned to it rather than angry about it because it doesn't surprise them) and they react *with stoicism* (the ability to experience something unpleasant without reacting strongly or complaining). The problems mentioned are ones which affect people personally rather than only affecting someone else.
B: The speaker says that *administrators are for ever being pressed to disclose their contingency plans* (people are always asking them to reveal what plans they have if their original plans do not happen or work). British people don't expect administrators' plans to succeed and constantly ask them what they're going to do when their plans fail. This is an example of British pessimism but not an example of people believing what they are told.
C: The problems mentioned are presented as real ones that actually happen, rather than potential problems that might happen. They are not examples of things that people pessimistically think may go wrong, they are things that do go wrong and there is no suggestion that the speaker thinks people exaggerate these problems.

2 **B:** The speaker says that British pessimism is a *national trait* (characteristic) that *starts in childhood* and that the character of Eeyore appeals to British children because he is pessimistic. Children relate to him because they, like him, have a *melancholy* (very sad), *phlegmatic* (not reacting strongly or getting angry) *side* (aspect of personality). The speaker is therefore saying British children are pessimistic by nature and that is why they like this character.
A: The speaker says that *irony* (saying the opposite of what you mean with a tone of voice that indicates what you really mean in order to be amusing, or situations which are contrary to expectation and therefore found amusing) is the basis of British humour and that the *prime ingredient* (most important, main element) of irony is pessimism. He is therefore saying that British people like irony but he does not say that this is something that they come to like later in life – in fact, he strongly implies that children also like irony.
C: The speaker says that British humour is *distinctive* (clearly different from other nations' humour) and so he implies that some people might think it strange, but he doesn't say that children themselves think that their own sense of humour is strange.

3 **C:** The speaker says that Ford thinks that *slimming diets* and *regimes of prescription and proscription* (eating plans in which people are told what to eat and what not to eat) will *give way to* (be replaced by) an attitude to food that is *more positive* and focuses on the *pleasures and health benefits of good food*. In other words, Ford believes that there will be a change of emphasis with regard to food – instead of being on what you can't eat, it will be on what it is good to eat.
A: Ford thinks that in the future people will choose food that can *delay the onset* (beginning) *of senility* (a state of mental and physical weakness in old age). He therefore thinks that people will eat things they think will prevent the start of the bad effects of old age, but there is no reference to new things about old age being discovered.
B: Ford thinks that people will choose food that will enable them to *relish* (enjoy) life as much as is possible but the speaker does not say that interest in food in general will increase – it is the attitude to it that will change, not the level of interest.

4 **B:** Ford thinks that we will look back on the snack foods of today in the same way that we look back on the *adulterated* (made into something of poor quality because of the addition of certain substances) *foods* of the past. He thinks that some of today's snack foods contain substances that *could harm a child* and that these will not *be with us in their present form* (they will not exist in the form they have today). People will then regard them as having been as bad as other foods in the past that are now considered unsuitable for people to eat.
A: Ford does distinguish between *junk food* and *snack foods*. He thinks that today's junk food will *disappear* (cease to exist at all) but that snack foods will continue to exist, although not in the form they have today. He doesn't seem to think that snack foods will be considered worse than junk food – since junk food will completely disappear, he implies that the opposite is the case and that junk food will be considered worse than snack foods.
C: He does think that some of today's snack foods are harmful and that in the future people will consider them to have been so, but he does not say or imply that people will exaggerate the extent to which they are harmful.

5 **B:** The speaker says that some fathers today have read about the enormous sums of money that top sportspeople are paid and believe that if their children are successful at sport, this can result in a *lucrative* (producing great wealth, extremely profitable) *economic future*. Such *pushy parents* (parents who are ambitious with regard to their children and constantly try to get success for their children) are not, the speaker says, motivated by *the glow* (feeling of great satisfaction) *of winning* but by the prospect of their children making an extremely large amount of money from sport.
A: The speaker clearly feels that the advice given to mothers in the song he quotes was good advice that has *gone unheeded* (been ignored) *then and now* (and still is ignored). However, he does not say that similar advice – not to be pushy with children of *dubious talent* (it is doubtful that these children have any talent) – has been given to the fathers he is talking about.
C: The speaker says that *the odds on vicarious sporting glory may be long* (the chances of fathers experiencing sporting glory through their children's success are not high, it is unlikely to happen), but he suggests that fathers are aware of this because he says they are *willing to take their chances* (to do something, even though the possibility of success is not high).

6 **A:** The speaker says that some parents have a *potentially damaging obsession* (their desire for their children to succeed is so great that it dominates their thinking and this might be harmful). He says that because of such parents, children *are coerced* (forced as a result of pressure) *into becoming mini-adults* (behaving like adults rather than like the children they are). They become *professionals in all but name* (their lives are like those of professional sportspeople, although they are not actually called professionals). As a result of all this, sport becomes *too serious* for the children. The speaker is therefore warning that because of such parents, children no longer enjoy sport and they are forced to behave in a

way that may be harmful to them.
B: The speaker doesn't suggest that parents should not spend money on their children's sporting activities at all; he says that if they have an obsession about this, it can be *very expensive*.
C: The speaker says there are *plenty of benefits to having active kids* and that it's natural to want your children to do well. He says, however, that *the line between committed support and a potentially damaging obsession is mighty fine* (the first can very easily become the second). He therefore strongly implies that *committed support* is a good thing, which means he believes it is good to support your children enthusiastically in their sporting activities and care about these activities. He is saying that parents should take their children's sporting activities seriously but they should not take them so seriously that they become obsessed.

7 **C:** The speaker says that Edison's *rueful observation* (comment expressing sadness and regret) expresses something that inventors today know to be a fact – that creativity is a *precious commodity* (something that is valuable because it is rare) and that therefore if you have a good idea you will have the experience that someone else will *lay claim to it* (claim that it was their idea). The difference today is that, although the same thing happens that Edison described, because of the existence of patents, you can do something about it when it happens.
A: The speaker says that in the past inventors were *ripped off* (cheated financially) *by the unscrupulous* (people with no moral principles) and that the situation is *not a whole lot* (not much) *better now*, but he does not say or imply that he considers inventors to be naive people. He is critical of the people who cheat them but he does not say that the inventors are themselves partly to blame because they lack experience or trust people too much.
B: The speaker implies that what happens to inventors is totally predictable – if they have a good idea, other people say it was their idea and other people cheat them financially. The change has been that inventors can now take action to make sure that they get *the credit* (that it is recognized that they invented the thing in question) and the money for their inventions.

8 **B:** The speaker says that *the philosophy behind the modern patent* is the same one that existed when patents began – that inventors can *exploit the fruits of* (take advantage of the products of) their *ingenuity* (ability to have clever and original ideas) for a fixed period of time and that in exchange for this they have to teach other people how to produce the thing they invented. The speaker clearly doesn't like this – he says that it has caused a lot of trouble. Because inventors have to *disclose* (reveal) details of their inventions, they have to give other people their *intellectual crown jewels* (most valuable ideas) and tell them what their *marketing strategy* (way of selling products) will be. He therefore believes that the rules concerning patents have always been to the disadvantage of inventors and to the advantage of those to whom they have to give details of their inventions.
A: The speaker does say that the rules are still the same but he clearly opposes the rules governing patents and he is explaining why he objects to them, not explaining why they are still the same as when patents first came into existence.
C: The speaker says that the rules are bad for inventors and so it is likely that some inventors may not wish to obey them, but he doesn't say that any inventors actually break the rules.

p121 PAPER 4 PART TWO

One mark per question (Total: 9)

9 **lead; limestone:** The area which contains the National Stone Centre used to be part of an *upland* (a piece of higher ground) and consist of *tropical lagoons* (a kind of lake) *and small islands*, and *fossils* (the remains of animals and plants) have been found in the *rock face* (surface of rock) there. From *medieval times* (the Middle Ages, approximately AD 1100–1400), *lead* (a metal) *and limestone* (a type of white rock used in construction) have been mined there.

10 **consume/eat:** One *fascinating fact* that visitors to the centre learn is that every person *consumes* (this can mean 'uses' or 'eats') 6 or 7 tonnes of stone each year (1 tonne = 1,000 kilos). The implication is that this seems like a very large and therefore surprising amount. James asks whether this means that we eat stone, and the speaker says that as well as using it in the various ways listed, we also eat it in the sense that it is used in certain products that people eat.

11 **tunnels; tennis courts:** The speaker gives many examples of the use of stone and we are told that it is used in paint, computers and ceiling tiles, in plastics and therefore in cars, ships and planes and in sugar, flour, pharmaceuticals and poultry feed (food given to birds that people eat or whose eggs people eat). The examples given of its use in construction, which accounts for 90% of the stone we use, are tunnels and tennis courts.

12 **teaching resource:** The headmaster said that the centre is a *splendid* (excellent, marvellous) *teaching resource* (thing that is useful for teaching with) because the place enables teachers to teach children *all sorts of skills*, helps children to appreciate how much the world changes, and fits into the *National Curriculum* (programme of what has to be taught in all schools in the country).

13 **Launch Pad:** The speaker says that all of Britain's interactive science and technology centres were *built on the foundation of* (in some way based on the example of) *Launch Pad*, which is part of the Science Museum in London and was the first place of this kind in the country.

14 **roll uphill:** The speaker says that Techniquest has *liquids you can cut* and *bubbles* (balls of liquid that contain air and float in the air) *you can walk in* and *structures that roll uphill* (move up sloping surfaces by turning over and over in the way that balls do).

15 **dentist's chair:** The speaker says that at Techniquest you might see a *granny* (grandmother) or an *eight-year-old* (child) *swivelling around* (turning round and round, revolving), *under discreet supervision* (while being watched in a way that is not very noticeable, by a member of staff, so that they do not come to any harm) *in a specially adapted dentist's chair* (one that has been modified or made suitable for this purpose), in order to experience *the pull of centrifugal force* (the power of a force pulling an object away from the centre around which it is turning).

16 **sound waves:** The speaker says that visitors to Techniquest can *observe how sound waves clash* (act in opposition to each other) *and distort one another* (cause each other to change from their natural sound and have a different sound).

17 **control systems:** The speaker says the *dragon* (a mythical, aggressive animal with wings and claws that breathes out fire and is used as a symbol of Wales, which is where Techniquest is) responds instantly to the fingertip controls that visitors use and that they can see clearly the parts of it that make it respond. This, the speaker says, *may not be a*

formal lesson in control systems, but you cannot fail to learn – in other words, it certainly does teach visitors about control systems, even though this is done in an informal way.

p122–125 PAPER 4 PART THREE

FURTHER PRACTICE AND GUIDANCE (p123–125)

For explanations, see the explanations to the questions in the test, which follow.

Question 18: a, b, e, g, h

Question 19: b, d, e, f

Question 20: b, c, e, f, h

Question 21: a, b, f, g, h

Question 22: a, c, e, g

p122 PAPER 4 PART THREE (TEST)

Note: the letters in brackets refer to the relevant options in the questions in the Further Practice and Guidance pages.

One mark per question (Total: 5)

18 D: Paddy says that readers who enjoy her column *invariably* (always) say that it is *particularly the bad ones* (the reviews that are unfavourable towards the hotels in question) that they like. One reader said that *every other week* (once every two weeks), she used to give a hotelier (hotel owner or manager) *a bashing* (a verbal attack or verbal criticism) but that now *it's a rare treat* (something pleasurable that does not happen often) when she writes a review like that. That reader says *I love it when you lay into* (are fiercely critical of) *a pretentious* (trying to be something better or more sophisticated than it really is) *but bad one* and that although it is helpful when she recommends a good hotel, she should find some *awful ones for entertainment's sake* (in the interests of providing entertainment for the readers). Paddy uses the reader who wrote this letter as an example of readers who like reading her critical reviews and would rather be entertained by them than be told about hotels she recommends, which by implication they may wish to stay in one day. **(e, g, h)**
A: Paddy says that the readers she refers to like reading her criticisms of hotels but she does not say that they tell her that they believe she gets pleasure from criticizing. It is the readers who she says get pleasure from it. **(c)**
B: Paddy says that she always has *high hopes* (is always very optimistic) when she goes into a hotel and thinks *[I] bet this one's going to be good* (I'm certain this hotel will be a good one). However, she says that *you never can tell* (it's impossible to be certain, because appearance and reality may be different from each other) and that hotels that look *idyllic* (beautiful and peaceful and in beautiful surroundings) in a guidebook can be *a terrible letdown* (a very big disappointment). However, she does not say that her attitude has changed because of such disappointments. Moreover, she talks about the response of readers to her reviews, but she does not say that she has become more critical of hotels because readers like reading her reviews which are critical. She presents this as a fact, but does not say that her attitude to hotels has changed so that she can meet their demand for critical reviews. **(a, b, d)**
C: She says that they like reading her comments but she does not say that they have or refer to their own experiences of the hotels she reviews. If she recommends a good hotel, this may be helpful but she does not say that readers contact her to say that they liked a hotel she recommended or disliked one she was critical of. **(f)**

19 B: Paddy says that *hotelkeeping* (running a hotel) has been described as being *akin to* (similar to) *show business* (the entertainment industry that involves artists performing for the public) and that in her favourite hotels, there is always *a leading man or woman* (a hotelier who is like the actor playing the main role in a play or film). She says that these people are often so good that she believes they have *missed their true vocation* (followed the wrong career, because there is another profession that would be ideal for them and which they are naturally suited to: performing). This is what she thinks, she doesn't say that the hotelkeepers she is talking about think this too. **(c, d)**
A: She says that *Such hoteliers* (those who would be good actors) *usually have a sense of humour* and that they respond to what she says about them in her reviews *in a good-humoured way* (in a cheerful, friendly way), even if they don't like what she says. However, she does not say or imply that they have to try hard to behave in this way – indeed, she implies that it comes naturally to them. **(e, g)**
C: She says that she is happy to *slam into* (criticize harshly) pretentious hotels that don't *come up to scratch* (aren't satisfactory or of the standard they should be) but that it is a different matter when the people are nice (she is unhappy when she criticizes a hotel whose owner or manager is a nice person). She says that she still has to write about that hotel but that sometimes doing so *hurts* (she finds it painful because she likes the people). However, she does not say that these hoteliers expect her to be critical of their hotels. What she says is that they react well when she does so. **(a, b, f)**
D: She talks about hoteliers who have responded well to bad reviews she has written about their hotels and says that they are *professionals* (in this context, people who can separate their professional lives from their personal lives) and that many of them *have become friends*. It may be surprising that she and people she has criticized have become friends, but she does not say that the hoteliers in question find it so, nor that she is surprised by it. **(f, h)**

20 C: Paddy says that when she speaks on the phone to people about including their hotels in her book, some of them refer to the fact that she didn't give their hotel a good review. She agrees and then suggests that perhaps they have improved their hotels since she reviewed them and *would like people to know about* the improvements they have made – the implication is that people will know about this if the hoteliers allow their hotels to be included in her book. She says that *Thus encouraged* (encouraged in this way), most of them have allowed their hotels to be included in the book and have also *entered into the spirit* of the book (adopted the same attitude to the book as Paddy has) by telling her interesting stories about things that go on *behind the scenes* (in the background, unknown to the public). In other words, these hotelkeepers have agreed to be included in her book and have given her interesting things to include in it, even though her reviews of them were critical. **(f, h)**
A: She says that if she thinks hotelkeepers might shout at her when she phones them (because her reviews of their hotels were critical) she invents someone called Emily, who is supposed to be her assistant, and Paddy pretends to be Emily. Paddy says that these hotelkeepers refer to the bad reviews *she* gave them when they think they are talking to someone called Emily. This indicates that they do not realize they are actually talking to Paddy and that they believe they are talking to Emily. Therefore, they do believe that she has an assistant called Emily. **(c, d, e)**
B: She asks them to tell her about changes they have made to improve their hotels since she reviewed them and she implies that they do so. However, she does not say that anything she said about their hotels was not true at the time

that she wrote the reviews of them and so she does not refer to any inaccuracies that they could correct. **(a)**
D: She says that she likes their attitude with regard to telling her interesting things she can put into the book but she does not say that she starts to feel that what she originally said about their hotels in her reviews was unfair. She also says that she has a *penchant* for hotels run by the people who own them and that she likes the owners of small hotels and that is why she has enjoyed contacting them concerning her book. However, she does not say that the fact that she likes them and enjoys talking to them has caused her to question whether what she said about their hotels was fair or not. **(b, g, h)**

21 **A:** The hotelkeeper, who presumably thought that he was talking to her non-existent assistant, said that people who have read Paddy's reviews *go to hotels where she's been fawned over* (treated as somebody special and important – the phrase is used to express disapproval of such treatment) but that *they* – the readers – *probably won't be fawned over*. He added that Paddy often goes to hotels that are *almost empty* and so in those hotels *they* (presumably the staff and managers) *have time to fawn over her* – he implied here that other people go to busier hotels where staff don't have time to treat each guest as someone special and important. Paddy comments that being fawned over is in fact *the last thing I want* (she really doesn't want it). **(g, h)**
B: He did discuss what she had said in her review. She says that *To specify the lies* (to give a specific description of the lies he claimed she had told about his hotel in her review), *he pounced on* (he enthusiastically and aggressively reacted to) something she had said about the food at his hotel. **(b, c)**
C: He said that because of what she says in her reviews, a lot of people *cross hotels off their potential list* (decide not to go to hotels they might otherwise have chosen to stay at and in some sense remove them from the list of hotels they would perhaps stay in) – he therefore said that her reviews do influence a lot of people. He did not, however, refer to the amount of influence he thought she believed her articles have, or imply that it is not as great as she thinks. He also did not suggest that people had told him that they had disagreed with what she had written in her reviews and now took no notice of what she said. **(e, f)**
D: He said that, because she had insulted his hotel and lied about it in her article, *there is no way we would help her perpetuate her grievances against the world in a publication* (we – he and others connected with his hotel – would certainly not help her to continue her feeling of bitterness towards the world in general). He therefore refused to allow his hotel to be included in her book because he felt that her review of it was an example of her generally negative attitude and he did not want that attitude to be given further expression in a book. However, there is no reference to his having previously decided or agreed to have his hotel included in her book. Paddy says that she had wanted to include it because she had been *enthusiastic about* the food there and *would have liked to include his hotel in the book* but because he was *so disagreeable* (so unpleasant), his hotel could not be included. She does not, however, say that he had once agreed but had now changed his mind. **(a, d)**

22 **D:** The owner told her that he could not give a description of her to other hotels *because she is fairly nondescript* (if someone or something is 'nondescript', they have no remarkable or interesting features or characteristics to distinguish them). **(b, c)**
A: He said that other hotels asked him for various details about her (presumably so that they would know if she was staying at their hotels and going to write reviews of them) but that *Unfortunately* he couldn't describe her to them. He implied that, since there was nothing remarkable about her when she stayed at his hotel, he hadn't noted what car she drove or what credit card she used. **(a, b, d)**
B: She thinks that one reason why he might have agreed to have his hotel included in the book was that he had remembered that in her review she had said that he resembled a very popular comedian, who was now dead. She implies that he might have been flattered by being compared with a popular person, not that he would have been annoyed by this description. **(g, h)**
C: She says that *when it finally clicked* (when he suddenly realized or understood after some time) that he would not have to pay for his hotel to be included in the book, he decided that he did want it to be included after all. What he had not understood was that being included in the book was free, not why she wanted to include his hotel. **(e, f)**

p126 PAPER 4 PART FOUR

One mark per question (Total: 6)

23 **B:** Helen talks about people on the train answering their mobile phones and *fiddling with* (touching and doing lots of small actions with) their text messages and says that these people *would sooner* (would prefer to) be doing what she's doing, which is reading the paper. She says that these people look *harassed* (under pressure) and so she clearly feels that the fact that these things mean that they can be contacted all the time is a disadvantage for them.
Tony says that it's a good thing that these devices mean that people can be contacted in emergencies but he agrees with Helen that *there are limits* (these things are only an advantage to a certain extent) and says *I turn the thing off sometimes*, meaning that he sometimes decides that he doesn't want to be contactable.

24 **T:** Helen says that she gets *snowed under* (extremely busy, having a lot to deal with) with e-mails and that it's *daft* (silly, ridiculous) that some of these come from people working nearby who could easily come and speak to her rather than sending e-mails. However, she says that some of these e-mails are very *detailed*, which indicates that the people sending them have put careful thought into their content.
Tony says that people *dash off* (produce very quickly or in a hurry) e-mails to him as soon as something *comes up* (happens). He says that these people are *passing the buck* (giving responsibility to someone else rather than accepting it themselves) instead of *working things out for themselves* (solving problems themselves) and that their e-mails contain *question marks and half-thoughts*. He is therefore saying that because people can send e-mails to other people about problems at work, they do not make the effort to think about and solve these problems themselves.

25 **H:** Helen says that technology enables people who are not *real musicians* to make records and that because of this it's *no wonder* (not at all surprising) that pop music is *rubbish these days*. She is therefore implying that it wasn't rubbish in the past.
Tony says that *there's an 'anyone can do it' culture these days*, meaning that people are made to feel that anyone can make a pop record these days because of the technology that is available to them, but he thinks that *there's a lot of good stuff around* (a lot of good records are made).

26 **H:** Helen says that people who have the necessary equipment can watch what a single player is doing in a game and that in her opinion technology like that *adds to* (increases) *the excitement* of watching sport on television.
Tony talks about the use of *replays* in sport on television but he thinks that such things are *daft* (ridiculous, pointless) and that the use of such things *holds the game up* (delays it, prevents it from continuing) *all the time*, and so he does not approve of such things.

27 **H:** Helen says that some features of new technology are created *just* (only) *because some whizzkid* (a very clever young person) *came up with it* (invented it, had the idea for

it). She says that Tony's description of such things – that they are invented simply because they can be invented, not because anyone *actually wants it* – is *nicely put* (very well expressed) and gives as an example of features of modern technology that people don't actually want the things that her computer is capable of but that she would never want to use.
Tony doesn't agree with her that there is no demand for such things. He says that she isn't typical and that there are people who always want to be *up to speed with such things* (always want to follow the most recent developments in technology).

28 B: Helen says that a lot of new technology consists of *gimmicky things* (products created to attract attention and be bought because they are unusual) and that in the future people will think that they *have had their day* (that they are no longer modern or useful). She thinks that people will look back on such things and think they were ridiculous and wonder what use they had.
Tony agrees that there will be features of modern technology that *won't last* (won't continue to exist in the future). He thinks that most of them *are here to stay* (will exist for a long time in the future) but that some will be shown on TV programmes in the future so that people can laugh at them because they are ridiculous.

PAPER 4:	
PART ONE	8 marks
PART TWO	9 marks
PART THREE	5 marks
PART FOUR	6 marks
TOTAL	28 marks

To be converted into a score out of 40 marks.

p127–130 PAPER 5

FURTHER PRACTICE AND GUIDANCE (p129–130)

DESCRIBING MOVEMENT

WALK/RUN
limp: walk with difficulty because one leg is injured or stiff. Also used as a noun (*walk with a limp*).
trot: run slowly
wander: walk around in an area, going from place to place, with no particular purpose or simply to see what is there
sprint: run as fast as possible. Used also for races over short distances.
stagger: walk in a way that suggests you are going to fall, because of being tired, ill, injured, etc
hobble: walk with difficulty because of injury to a foot or feet
totter: walk in an unsteady way
amble: walk slowly because you are not in a hurry
tear: walk or run fast because of being in a hurry
stroll: walk slowly and in a relaxed way, especially when walking for pleasure. Also used as a noun (*go for a stroll*).
dash: walk or run fast because of being in a hurry
hop: move by jumping on one foot
shuffle: walk slowly, without lifting the feet from the ground completely

SHAKE
rock: move slowly and regularly from side to side or backwards and forwards while in a sitting or standing position
shudder: shake suddenly, especially down your back, because of fear, cold, etc
quiver: shake slightly because of feeling nervous, excited, etc
tremble: shake because of fear, illness, etc
shiver: shake because of being cold, ill, etc

HIT
nudge: push or touch someone with your elbow, in order to attract their attention
prod: push someone strongly with one finger, especially as an aggressive act
poke: push someone sharply with one finger to attract their attention or in order to hurt them
punch: hit someone hard with your fist (closed hand) as an act of aggression
dig: push someone strongly in the chest with the elbow to attract their attention, used especially in the phrase *dig someone in the ribs*
thump: hit someone hard in order to hurt them
shove: push someone violently
slap: hit someone hard with an open hand as an act of aggression
whack: hit someone very hard

THROW
sling: throw something to a place with force or carelessly
hurl: throw something violently in a particular direction or throw something a long distance
toss: throw something in a fairly gentle way or carelessly
fling: throw something violently or angrily
chuck: throw (this is an informal word)

DESCRIBING VOCAL SOUNDS

SHOUT
whoop: make a loud noise repeatedly with a high-pitched voice, as a reaction of excitement or great happiness about something that has happened
bellow: shout very loudly
shriek: shout suddenly in a loud, high voice
yell: shout loudly
jeer: shout insults at someone in order to express disapproval or make them look ridiculous
howl: let out a long, loud sound of laughter or pain
holler: shout (used especially in American English)

SPEAK/TALK
mutter: speak quietly in a low voice, making it hard for what you say to be heard
whisper: speak quietly using only breath rather than the full voice, so that what you say is secret and only the person who you want to hear it can hear it
murmur: speak quietly in a low voice
jabber: speak quickly and in an excited way
chatter: talk quickly and for a long period about unimportant things
natter: talk for a long time with someone about social matters, such as gossip. Also often used as a noun in the phrase *have a natter*.
mumble: speak quietly and indistinctly in a low voice, making it hard to be heard or understood
gibber: talk quickly, saying things that don't make sense
drone: speak continuously in a low voice that is boring to listen to. Often used in the phrase *drone on + for + period of time*.
babble: talk too quickly to be understood

LAUGH
Note: all these verbs can also be used as nouns.
giggle: laugh with a high-pitched sound, as children do
roar: laugh loudly. Often used in the phrase *roar with laughter*.
chuckle: laugh quietly or to yourself
snigger: laugh with a low sound in a way that is rude to someone or because you find them or something they have said ridiculous
cackle: laugh with a harsh sound that is considered unpleasant
titter: laugh with high-pitched, short, repeated sounds

SOUND UNHAPPY/COMPLAIN
weep: cry as a result of unhappiness
groan: make an unhappy sound caused by pain, disappointment, disapproval, etc
whinge: complain constantly and unnecessarily in a voice which has a sound that annoys
whimper: make a number of low, weak noises, caused by unhappiness, pain or fear
grumble: complain fairly quietly
whine: complain in a high-pitched voice which annoys
wail: cry loudly in a high-pitched voice
sob: cry continuously with the shoulders moving up and down
moan: make a long, low sound caused by unhappiness or pain, or complain

TOPIC VOCABULARY

OBEYING RULES
enforce: (verb) If someone in authority *enforces a rule/law*, they take action to make sure that it is obeyed.
comply: (verb) If someone *complies with* a rule, they obey it.
conform: (verb) If someone *conforms (with/to something)*, they do what is considered acceptable according to rules or expected standards of behaviour.
observe: (verb) If someone *observes a rule/law*, they obey it.
protocol: (noun) *Protocol* is a system of rules concerning what happens regarding official procedures and occasions.
binding: (adjective) If something that has been agreed between people, such as a contract, is *binding*, they are legally obliged to stick to it and cannot decide not to obey the terms of it.
adhere to: (phrasal verb) If someone *adheres to* something that they are supposed to do, they obey it and act in accordance with it.
etiquette: (noun) *Etiquette* is a set of unofficial rules concerning what is considered correct and polite formal social behaviour or behaviour among a certain group of people.
toe the line: (idiom) If someone *toes the line*, they obey the orders of or express the opinions of those who have authority over them, rather than rebelling.
abide by: (phrasal verb) If someone *abides by* something, they obey or accept a rule or they stick to an agreement they have made.
petty: (adjective) If someone behaves in a *petty* way, they have some authority and insist that other people obey rules which the other people regard as unimportant and unnecessary. If rules are *petty*, they are considered unimportant, unnecessary and annoying.

NOT OBEYING RULES
breach: (noun) If an action is a *breach of* a rule, an agreement, etc, it breaks it.
infringe: (verb) If someone *infringes* a rule / law, they break it.
unruly: (adjective) If people behave in an *unruly* way, they refuse to be controlled by someone in authority and behave badly.
defy: (verb) If someone *defies* someone or something, they refuse to obey them or to do what they are told by someone in authority.
naughty: (adjective) If someone does something *naughty*, they do something considered fairly bad or unacceptable by someone in authority. This word is often used of children.
contravene: (verb) If someone *contravenes* a rule / law, they do something which breaks or is against it.
dissent: (verb / noun) If someone *dissents* or shows *dissent*, they speak or act in disagreement with rules or what they have been told to do.
rebel: (verb / noun) If someone *rebels* or *rebels against* someone or something, they refuse to accept or continue to accept the control of authority or something that they are being forced to do by someone in authority. A *rebel* is someone who behaves in this way.
sin: (verb / noun) If someone *sins* or does something that is a *sin*, they break a religious or moral rule.
cheeky: (adjective) If someone is *cheeky*, they say something which does not show respect for the person in authority that they are talking to, perhaps because they are trying to be amusing.
insubordinate: (adjective) If someone is *insubordinate*, they door say something that disobeys or does not show respect for someone who has authority over them in an organization.

CONVENTIONAL
conservative: (adjective) If someone is *conservative*, they have traditional beliefs and cautious attitudes, and do not like great change.
stick-in-the-mud: (noun) If someone calls someone else *a stick-in-the-mud*, they are criticizing that person for being opposed to change.
middle-of-the-road: (adjective) If someone or something is described as being *middle-of-the-road*, they are considered to be conservative and moderate rather than extreme.
reactionary: (adjective) If someone is described as being *reactionary*, they are being criticized for being opposed to change.

UNCONVENTIONAL
idiosyncratic: (adjective) If someone is *idiosyncratic*, they have attitudes and do things which are individual to them and different from what is considered normal.
unorthodox: (adjective) If something someone does is *unorthodox*, it is different from what is usual or acceptable.
offbeat: (adjective) If something is *offbeat*, it is unconventional and strikingly different from what is common or usual.
eccentric: (adjective) If someone is *eccentric*, they behave differently from most people and are therefore considered slightly strange.

TABLE

1 Noun: **behaviour**
Opposites: **misbehave** (verb) **misbehaviour** (noun)
2 Noun: **conformity** (noun) **conformist** (person)
Opposite: **nonconformist** (person)
3 Verb: **cheek**
Noun: **cheek**
Adverb: **cheekily**
4 Adjective: **defiant**
Noun: **defiance**
Adverb: **defiantly**
5 Adjective: **obedient**
Noun: **obedience**
Adverb: **obediently**
Opposites: **disobey** (verb) **disobedient** (adjective) **disobedience** (noun) **disobediently** (adverb)
6 Adjective: **rebellious**
Noun: **rebellion** (noun) **rebel** (person)
Adverb: **rebelliously**

p127–128 PAPER 5

Marks out of 40 are given for performance in the speaking paper.

TEST 4

p131–132 PAPER 1 PART ONE

Note: all explanations in this part refer to the meaning or use of each option most closely related to the question, not necessarily to the only meaning or use of each option.

One mark per question (Total: 18)

Television Documentaries

1 **C:** If you **get someone to do something**, you cause them to do it by persuading or telling them to do it. The writer is describing his idea for a party game, in which the guests are told to come into the room and guess what the subject of a TV programme is without hearing the sound.
A: If you *have someone do something*, you arrange for them to do it by telling them to do it. (*I'll have my assistant contact you in the very near future.*)
B: If you *sort something into something*, you organize different things by separating them into different groups or categories (*sort papers into categories and then file them away*). If you *sort something out*, you arrange it so that it is neat and tidy or so that various things have been put into appropriate groups or categories. (*I've got to sort out all the documents on my desk.*)
D: If someone *settles somewhere*, they make their home there permanently or become comfortable in that place or position (*settle in a new town/settle on the sofa to watch TV*).
All the options are connected with the idea of arranging people or things or of people or things being in certain places, but only C both fits the meaning in the context and fits grammatically – A could fit but it would have to be followed by the infinitive without 'to'.

2 **B:** If you **have a stab at something/doing something**, you try to do it, although you are not very likely to succeed. The writer is saying that guests have to guess what the programme is about, although they are unlikely to get the right answer.
A: If you *make a bid for something*, you try to get or achieve it. (*By leaving home she was making a bid for independence.*)
C: If you *venture to do something*, you take the risk of doing something that might prove unwise. (*She ventured to argue with him, which resulted in him getting very angry.*)
D: *Speculation* is making a guess without any firm evidence to support it. (*The stories in the media about his future are pure speculation.*)
All the options are connected with the idea of trying to do something, but only B correctly completes the required idiom.

3 **A:** If something is **irrelevant to** something else, it has no connection with it and is therefore not appropriate in the circumstances. The writer is saying that the pictures shown during documentaries have no connection with the subjects of the programmes.
B: If something is *incompatible with* something else, the two things do not match or go together well and are not appropriate together (*actions which are incompatible with the interests of society*).
C: If something is *inconsistent with* something else, the two things differ from each other and are not in agreement. (*Your current plan is inconsistent with what you told me last week.*)
D: If something is *incongruous*, it does not fit in and seems out of place in the circumstances. (*He looked incongruous wearing jeans because everyone else was dressed formally.*)
All the options are connected with the idea of things not fitting together or being appropriate together, but only A is followed by 'to'.

4 **A:** If you **get into a lather** or **are in a lather**, you become very troubled, anxious or agitated. The writer is saying that TV directors panic if they can't think of visual images to put into their programmes.
B: If you *make a fuss*, you become unnecessarily agitated about something and pay too much attention to it and this causes annoyance. (*I wish you wouldn't make such a fuss over a simple arrangement.*)
C: If you do something *without further ado*, you do it without unnecessary complications, trouble or delay. (*He simply got on with the job without further ado.*)
D: If something *causes a stir*, it causes controversy or excitement among other people. (*The scandal caused quite a stir at the time.*)
All the options can be used in phrases connected with the idea of people becoming agitated or excited, but only A correctly completes the required idiom.

5 **B: A small/large, etc proportion of something** is a small/large, etc part of the total of it. **The proportion of one thing to another** is the relative amount of one thing compared with another. (*The proportion of full-time to part-time members of staff is 3:1.*) The writer is saying that the content of most documentaries is more suited to written articles than to TV programmes.
A: *A fraction of something* is a small part of it. (*The ball missed the goal by a fraction of an inch.*)
C: *The ratio of one thing to another* is the relative amount of one thing compared with another (*the ratio of female to male students at a college*).
D: *The bulk of something* is the majority or main part of it. (*The bulk of the company's income comes from one single product.*)
All the options are connected with the idea of the amount of something in relation to the whole of something or in relation to other things, but only B both fits the meaning in the context and can form a collocation with 'large'.

6 **D:** If you do something **at your own pace**, you do it at a speed that is comfortable for you, rather than too quickly. The writer is saying that people can read as quickly or as slowly as they wish when they are reading an article.
A: If you do something *in your own time*, you do it when you are ready to do it, rather than doing it in a hurry because you are under pressure. (*Give me an answer in your own time, I can wait.*)
B: The *flow* of what someone is saying is their continuous, unbroken talking, with logical connections. (*He interrupted my flow and I lost track of what I was saying.*)
C: If something *takes/runs its course*, it proceeds in a way that cannot be changed or stopped and takes an amount of time that cannot be changed. (*We had to wait while the official procedure took/ran its course.*)
All the options are connected with the idea of something happening at a certain speed or over a period of time, but only D both fits the meaning in the context and correctly completes the required collocation – A fits the meaning but the preposition would have to be 'in' not 'at'.

The Rejected Novel

7 **B: Thus far** means 'until now/then', 'so far'. The narrator is saying that at this point in time, his novel had been rejected by four publishers.
A: *As yet* means 'until now/then', 'so far'. (*I applied three weeks ago but as yet I haven't heard anything.*)
C: *Hence* means 'from/after this time' (*The contract expires three weeks hence.*) or 'for this/that reason', 'therefore'. (*Jane and Alan had a big argument some time ago, hence their dislike of each other.*)
D: *By far* means 'by a great amount', 'a great deal' and is used with a comparative or superlative adjective. (*This shop is cheaper by far./It was by far the most embarrassing moment of my life.*)

All the options can complete phrases connected with time or phrases with 'far', but only B correctly completes the linking phrase that fits the meaning in the context.

8 **A:** If something is **done behind someone's back**, it is done secretly so that they do not know about it because they would not like it or approve of it. The narrator says that he thinks his family were secretly laughing about his failure to get his novel published.
B: If something is done *over someone's head*, it is done with someone who is in a higher position of authority than they are. (*He was only a junior manager so I went over his head and complained to a senior manager.*)
C: If something is said *out of earshot*, it cannot be heard by the person mentioned. (*I called to him but he had gone so far away that he was out of earshot and didn't hear me.*)
D: If you say something *to someone's face*, you say it directly to them rather than only saying it to someone else. (*I told him to his face exactly what I thought of him.*)
All the options can complete idioms that include parts of the body, but only A correctly completes the required idiom.

9 **A:** If something is **hard to bear** it is difficult to accept or deal with because it is very unpleasant and affects you personally. The narrator is saying that he found Rhona's sympathetic looks when his novel was returned in poor condition more difficult to deal with than her sister's direct, rude comments.
B: If you *defy someone/something*, you react to them by refusing to do what you have been told to do by someone in authority. (*She defied her parents and went to the nightclub anyway.*)
C: If you *can/can't cope with something*, you are able/unable to deal with something that is causing you problems or putting you under pressure. (*Fiona simply can't cope with her enormous workload at the moment.*)
D: If you *resist something/doing something*, you keep your self-control so that you do not do something which you are very tempted to do. (*I couldn't resist making a joke at that moment, even though I knew it wasn't the right thing to do in the circumstances.*)
All the options are connected with the idea of reacting to things you are faced with, but only A both fits the meaning in the context and fits grammatically – C also fits the meaning but it would have to be followed by 'with' after the gap.

10 **D:** If you **pack in something** or **pack something in**, you give it up or stop doing it. The narrator is saying that Jack thought that he had given up his job in order to become a full-time artist.
A: If you *break off*, you stop talking in the middle of doing so. (*He broke off when the phone rang.*) If you *break something off*, you suddenly end it. For example, a relationship. (*They had a row and broke off their engagement.*)
B: If you *wind something up*, you bring it to an end. (*Let's wind up this meeting now, it's gone on for too long.*) If you *wind up somewhere/doing something*, you are in that place or you do that thing at the end of a series of developments. (*I got lost and wound up on the other side of the city./After a number of temporary jobs, she wound up working in a bookshop.*)
C: If you *pull out of something*, you withdraw from or stop taking part in something. (*We pulled out of the negotiations when it became clear that none of our demands would be met.*)
All the options are phrasal verbs connected with the idea of stopping something or the end of something, but only D correctly completes the phrasal verb that fits the meaning in the context.

11 **C:** If something is **thin on the ground**, there is not much of it or there is less of it than would be desirable. The narrator is saying that not many critical comments had been made about his novel, presumably because publishers hadn't actually read it.
A: If a comment or conversation is *light*, it is meant to be amusing or entertaining rather than serious. (*Keep the conversation light!*)
B: If someone is *shallow*, they show a lack of serious thought or sincerity. (*William is only pretending to have strong emotions about this because in fact he's rather shallow.*)
D: *Scant* means 'very little' or 'not enough'. (*He acted with scant regard for anyone else's feelings.*)
All the options are connected with the idea of 'not much of something' or 'not serious', but only C completes the required idiom.

12 **C:** If something **lies in something**, it can be found there or exists there. The narrator is saying that the people who had made comments about his novel all agreed that the main thing wrong with it was that it didn't have much of a story.
A: How something *stands* is its situation or the circumstances surrounding it. (*How do the negotiations stand at the moment – are you getting near to an agreement?*)
B: If something *revolves around something*, it has it as its main concern or most important aspect. (*Everything he does revolves around his job.*)
D: If something *centres on something*, it has it as its main point or most important aspect. (*The story centres on the experiences of its two main characters.*)
All the options are connected with the aspects of something, but only C both fits the meaning in the context and fits grammatically – B and D would fit the meaning, but only C is followed by 'in' to express the correct meaning.

Loneliness in the City

13 **D:** If you **catch someone's eye**, you try to attract and succeed in attracting their attention. The writer says that lonely people in restaurants try to make some kind of contact with other people who are eating alone.
A: If you *set eyes on someone/something*, you see them and the experience of doing so is in some way important. (*The first time I set eyes on the place, I knew I wanted to live there.*)
B: If you *make eyes at someone*, you look at them in a way that makes it clear that you find them physically attractive. (*Robin and Tina were making eyes at each other throughout the lecture.*)
C: If you *can't take your eyes off someone/something*, you are unable to stop watching them because they are interesting. (*He behaved so strangely that I couldn't take my eyes off him all evening.*)
All the options can complete idioms that include 'eye' or 'eyes', but only D correctly completes the required idiom.

14 **C:** If you **imagine yourself something** or **imagine yourself to be something**, you think that you may be that thing or that it is possible for you to become that thing. The writer is saying that lonely people think that other people may be talking about them.
A: If you *conceive of someone/something as something*, you imagine or form a mental picture of them as that thing in your mind. (*She conceived of herself as a movie star.*)
B: If you *infer something from something*, you believe it to be the case because of the evidence you have or because you think it has been implied. (*I inferred from what my boss said that my job was likely to change.*)
D: If you *fantasize about something*, you think about something that you would like to be the case but which is in fact totally unrealistic. (*He fantasizes about scoring the winning goal in the World Cup final.*)
All the options are connected with the idea of imagining or believing something, but only C both fits the meaning in the context and fits grammatically.

15 **A:** If you **take offence at something**, you get offended by it and it upsets or annoys you. The writer is saying that lonely people get offended by what they think is bad treatment they are given by waiters, although they are not actually being badly treated by them.
B: If you feel *indignation at/over/about something*, you feel angry because of something that has happened which you consider unfair. (*I wanted to express my indignation at the appalling way in which I had been treated.*)

C: *Outrage* is a strong feeling of anger, shock or disgust. (*There was enormous public outrage when the new law was introduced.*)
D: If you regard something as *an insult to you*, you are angry because something that has been said or done is rude to you or indicates that the person who said or did it has no respect for you. (*The pay increase we've been offered is so low that it's an insult.*)
All the options are connected with anger, but only A correctly completes the required fixed phrase.

16 C: If you **stay put**, you remain in the place where you are rather than moving from it. The writer is saying that people who are alone in a restaurant have no reason to remain there after they have finished their meal because they have nobody to talk to.
A: If you *stick around*, you remain or wait in or near a place because something is going to happen there. (*If you stick around for half an hour, I'll be able to give you a lift home.*)
B: If you *hang about/around*, you remain or wait in a place doing nothing in particular. (*The manager kept me hanging around outside his office until he was ready to see me.*)
D: If you ask someone to *hold on*, you are asking them to wait or stop, usually for a short time. (*Hold on – I'll just get a pen so that I can write down your phone number.*)
All the options are connected with staying or waiting in a place, but only C correctly completes the required idiom.

17 B: If you **sigh with relief**, you make an involuntary sound by pushing air out of your mouth because you are suddenly feeling relieved. The writer is saying that lonely people act as if they are involved in a drama when they make a phone call and are relieved when their call is answered, because it is very important to them that they can speak to someone.
A: If you *blow*, you intentionally push air out of your mouth for a particular purpose (*blow out the candles on a birthday cake*).
C: If you *yawn*, you open your mouth wide and breathe both in and out because you are tired or bored. (*He yawned loudly and said he was going to bed.*)
D: If you *snort*, you force air out of your nose in order to express disapproval. (*She snorted when I said I thought she was wrong.*)
All the options are connected with people doing things with their mouth or nose, but only B both fits the meaning in the context and correctly completes the required fixed phrase.

18 B: If you **pester someone to do something**, you ask them over and over again to do it, often with the result that they get annoyed. The writer is saying that if nobody phones a lonely person for a whole day, he thinks that people have plotted to ignore him and repeatedly asks the operator to make sure his phone is working properly, in case the real reason why nobody has phoned is that his phone isn't working.
A: If you *persist in doing something/with something*, you continue to do it, even though you are not succeeding or you are experiencing difficulty or opposition. (*She persisted in trying to get a job in the media, despite the fact that all her applications were rejected./I persisted with the lessons, even though I was doing very badly.*)
C: If you *persevere* or *persevere with something*, you continue trying to do something, even though it is difficult for you. (*If I persevere, I think I'll learn Swedish eventually./I persevered with the treatment and eventually I started to feel better.*)
D: If you *plead with someone to do something*, you ask them to do something you know they probably do not want to do, in a way that makes it clear it is very important to you. (*She pleaded with the parking attendant to let her park there.*)
All the options are connected with continuing to do something or asking for something, but only B both fits the meaning in the context and fits grammatically – D fits the meaning but would have to be followed by 'with' after the gap.

p133–135 PAPER 1 PART TWO

Two marks per question (Total: 16)

The Eleven Plus Exam

19 C: The writer says when he was at school *no consideration was given for talents outside the limited range required by the examining board* (the school system focused only on the abilities required for passing the exams set by the school exam organization). He implies that he felt that he had such talents but that there was no encouragement for him to develop them at school – he considered himself one of the *misfits* (people who do not fit into a system and who are therefore considered strange or inferior) who were given *no incentive* (nothing to encourage them) *to achieve or realize their potential* (to achieve what they were capable of achieving). Instead of being encouraged to develop his abilities, he was *suffocated* (enormously restricted) *by the amount of normality* he was *subjected to* (forced to endure) at school and *force-fed* (forced to study despite not wishing to) *the school syllabus* (everything that it has been decided officially that pupils have to learn at school). He is therefore implying that he believed he had potential he was capable of fulfilling but that the school system prevented him from fulfilling it.
A: He says that the school syllabus was *deemed* (formally considered) *to be the standard* (the thing that was required for everybody) and that a decision had been made that at the age of 11 children would be *segregated* (divided into separate categories that did not mix with each other; in this case presumably on the basis of their results in the exam they all took at the age of 11) *for the rest of their lives*. He says that he didn't like the school syllabus and implies that he disagreed that everyone should have to do it but he does not imply that it was not suited to all the pupils. He implies that he was against the decision to segregate everyone at the age of 11 but he does not imply that no pupils benefited from this – presumably those who were good at studying the school syllabus did benefit. Therefore, although he clearly felt that the school system did not benefit him, he is talking only about its effect on him and he does not imply that it didn't benefit any pupils.
B: He felt that he was one of the *misfits* who were *destined to become* (whose future had been decided with the result that they would become) *factory fodder* (people considered only of use as factory workers rather than valued as human beings), *farm workers or manual workers* (people with low-level jobs, doing physical work) *like my father*. Although he implies that he did not like this idea, he also implies that he felt that this was what would happen to him.
D: He says that complex forms of mathematics were *pushed down my throat* (he was forced to study them but did not wish to) and that he was not allowed to read what he wanted. He says that he could count and read and so he means that he didn't want to learn the kind of maths he was taught or read the kind of books he was given. He therefore didn't like doing what the teachers gave him to do but he does not say that he refused to do these things. In fact, he implies that he did them but didn't like them or see the point of doing them.

20 A: The writer says that he felt a *triumphant explosion* (a sudden, intense feeling of having won in some way) inside his head which resulted from the feeling that he had made his *first statement to the world* (he had done something that would make other people realize something important about him). However, his sense of having in some way won was balanced by the feeling that he was *watching opportunity float away on a piece of paper down the river* (he had caused himself to lose opportunities in life). He felt that his decision not to answer the questions in the exam would *damage* him and he realized that his life was going to be *a battle between me and them* (*them* presumably refers to all teachers and possibly also to all people in authority). He is

therefore saying that, while what he did gave him a feeling of *victory*, he was also aware of what it would mean and the effects it would have on his future.
B: He says that he felt that the exam was testing more than his intelligence, it was testing his *whole being* (everything about him as a person). When he looked at the paper and felt this, he decided not to *play the game their way* (not to conform with what they – the teachers and presumably also authority – were telling him to do) but to *take my own route* (live his life in his own way). He therefore decided to *settle my own fate* (decide what would happen to him in the future himself rather than allow others to decide it from his exam result) by not answering the questions. What he is saying is that he didn't answer the questions because he objected to what he regarded as the purpose of the exam, not because he thought he would do badly at it or that the result would indicate that he was not very clever.
C: He says that he knew what the consequences would be but he does not say that he decided not to answer the questions because he thought this action didn't matter much – on the contrary, he indicates that he felt that his action would have a permanent effect on his life.
D: Although he has already said that he did not like some of the things he had to learn at school, he is not saying that he decided not to answer the questions because he was a rebel at school and so it would be logical for him to be rebellious when it came to the exam. His decision appears to have been one he made suddenly, not because it had any connection with previous behaviour.

A Good Education

21 B: The writer says that all the efforts that his parents made were made *so that we* (their children) *would have better opportunities* and that *they* (his parents) *expected us to grab them* (take those opportunities eagerly) *when they came along* (happened). He says that his father wanted him to *seize* (grab, use with great enthusiasm) *all the opportunities he had missed*. He is saying that while he was at school, his parents had high expectations of him and wanted him to enter one of the *professions they thought that schooling could provide*. He is therefore suggesting that he felt under some pressure to fulfil his parents' expectations of him.
A: He says that the same attitude exists today and will continue to exist for a long time among people of his background – he thinks he will *say the same thing* (that education is the most important thing) to his family and that *over ten generations* in the future, *the same story* (parents wanting their children to get a good education) *will be repeated*. He is therefore suggesting that his parents' attitude is just as common now as it was when he was at school and that he himself is likely to share it.
C: He says that his parents' attitude was *typical* of black families at the time because all black immigrants to Britain saw education as *the key to success* (the most important thing that made success possible). He says that, in view of their experiences, it was *a perfectly natural* (understandable, logical, reasonable) *point of view* (attitude). He is therefore saying that he can understand why they had this attitude but he is not saying or implying that they were the only group of people who thought that education was the most important thing.
D: He says that their attitude was influenced by their own experiences when they came to Britain. They had endured difficulties and done *menial* (low-level, dull and requiring little or no skill) *jobs* and they had done this to make sure that their children *had a better life* than them. However, he does not imply that his parents thought they had made mistakes, he implies that they felt they had done the right thing and that by having a difficult or unpleasant time in Britain they had enabled their children to have more opportunities than they themselves had had.

22 C: The writer says that his parents had jobs that *nobody else would deign to do* (jobs that other people were not willing to do, and considered below their status in society). This means that the jobs they did were considered those that only inferior people would do and so he is saying that his parents, like all black immigrants, were regarded as inferior. Since he clearly respected his parents and what they had done, he is suggesting by his use of this word that he does not like the attitude of people who regarded themselves as superior and would not do the kind of jobs his parents did because they regarded such jobs as beneath them.
A: He says that his parents were *strict with us* but he explains why this was so and says that their attitude was *perfectly natural* in view of his parents' experiences as immigrants. Therefore, although it may not have been pleasant for him that his parents were strict, he is not using the word to imply criticism of them.
B: He says that his parents *scrimped* (lived on little money so as to be able to pay for something) *and scraped* (endured financial difficulty) *and saved* for years so that their children would have a better life. He is therefore using the word to describe the sacrifices that they made for their children. He does not imply that they were wrong to make such sacrifices – in fact he seems to have felt that he should repay them for these sacrifices by getting a good education and he says that he can understand perfectly why they made these sacrifices – so he is not using the word to criticize them in any way.
D: He says that his mother was *totally nonplussed* (completely confused and surprised) by the fact that he was willing to go running *in all weathers* (in bad weather conditions) and do it *for nothing* (without getting paid). She reacted in this way when he told her *'That's how it goes'* ('That's what's involved', 'That's what you have to expect'), which indicated that he didn't mind doing it. He is therefore saying that she couldn't understand why he did it without minding but he is implying that he could understand why she felt like that, not criticizing her for doing so.

A Child of My Time

23 D: The writer says that there were only *hazy* (vague, faint) *intimations* (indications, clues) of what was coming in the 1960s and that she felt at the time that perhaps *there was a bit more to it than* (what was coming was not as simple as) *shuffling around* (sitting, standing or moving with small movements) *smoky clubs*. She says that she was *hellbent on being* (absolutely determined to be) *there when it happened, whatever it was*. What she is saying is that she felt at that time that a more exciting period was going to come and that, although she didn't know what that exciting period would involve, she was determined to be part of it. She implies that that period was the 1960s.
A: She says that the clubs she visited were supposed to be *hip* (part of the latest fashion) and that their names had a *talismanic* (magical) *quality*. She says that when she came to London to go to these clubs, she was *dazzled by* (enormously impressed by because it seemed glamorous) *the scene* (the current social life in a particular place), even though it was *rudimentary* (only basic and not properly developed). She is therefore saying that she was impressed by these clubs and she does not say or imply that any of them were a disappointment to her, even though she says later that she felt that more exciting things would come into being in the future.
B: She implies that she was rather young to go to such clubs but also says that it was typical for teenagers to be *in quest of the forbidden* (searching for things they were not allowed to do). When she was in the clubs she says that she was *alone and unapproachable* (difficult to make contact with because of appearing unfriendly or unwilling to make contact), and *never spoke to anyone*. However, she makes clear that this was her choice – the use of the word

unapproachable means that she did not want people to speak to her and preferred to be alone. She therefore didn't make friends with people there because she didn't want to, not because she was too young to fit in with them.
C: She says that she was *putting together* (assembling, trying to create) *a persona* (an image, a personality that is deliberately presented to other people, rather than someone's real personality), which she was creating *out of a lot of diverse elements* (from a lot of different sources). She therefore makes it clear that she wanted to create a new personality for herself and that she knew exactly what she was doing, rather than that she changed without knowing that she was doing so.

24 A: The writer says that she has *always laid* (made) *my plans secretively and never let anyone in on them* (never revealed them to anyone) and that *more often than not* (usually), doing this has *turned out to be a mistake.* She says that at that time she didn't realize that it was possible to discuss things with people rather than keep them secret and *not lose everything in the process* (not suffer greatly in some way as a result of telling people) and she implies that she has come to realize this since that period in her life. She says that she felt then that if you *confided anything* (told someone a secret on the understanding that they would not tell anyone else), *it would be gone* (your plan would disappear and you would not be able to carry it out for some reason) or the other person would try to prevent you from doing it. She is therefore saying that she learnt that she didn't have to keep all her plans secret and that she could tell other people about them without any bad result for her. However, she says that her previous beliefs were *definitely true of my mother* and that she learnt when she was very young *to conceal* (hide) *my innermost* (most private, deepest) *thoughts from her*. What she is saying therefore is that the idea she later came to realize that she could tell people her plans without this having any bad result did not apply to her mother and that it was certainly not a good idea for her to tell her mother about her plans. She implies that experience of doing so had taught her that this was a bad idea, presumably because her mother had tried to stop her doing what she wanted to.
B: She says that she kept things secret from her mother but she does not say that her mother also kept things secret from other people or imply that being secretive was a characteristic that she had in common with her mother.
C: Since she had *learned very young* to keep her plans secret from her mother, there must have been occasions when she had told her mother what her *innermost thoughts* were and regretted having done so.
D: She did not tell her mother that she had decided to *break away* (leave and become independent) and her mother never *suspected* that she intended to do this. However, this was not because she didn't want to upset her mother, it was because previous experience had taught her that her mother would try to stop her.

The Royal High School

25 C: The writer says that *a market economy developed around this precious information* – boys who thought they had found errors in history texts charged other boys money for telling them about them, and the amount they charged depended on how likely it was that the errors they thought might be errors really were. The writer says that this situation developed *Inevitably*, by which he means that it was totally predictable that it would develop. His point is that if something is of value to someone else, those who have it will want money for it. What he learnt was that the confident boys made money out of the others. He says that the whole situation *was good practice for life, of a kind*, by which he means that what happened at school later proved to be a fact of life. By adding *of a kind*, he implies that he does not really approve of the fact that life is like that.
A: He does not say that he was one of the *Confident boys* who made money out of the others or that the episode caused him to become more competitive in order to be like that. In fact, he implies that he was not one of them.
B: He says that his school days were *a penance* (something to be suffered, like a punishment) and that the attitude of all but one of the teachers was *deplorable* (worthy of the strongest criticism). However, he does not say or imply that he has changed his mind about any of this and now regards his school days in a more favourable way than he used to.
D: The teacher's action led to a *market economy* and this may have caused him problems if he was unable to pay for the errors in the history texts being shown to him by the *Confident boys*. However, he does not say that he was in a worse position with regard to this than anyone else or that it affected him more than others.

26 B: The writer says that the Rector told him *in omniscient tones* (in a way that made him sound as if he knew everything) that he was making a mistake in leaving school so suddenly and that without completing his education, he would only become *a butcher's delivery boy*, which was considered *the ultimate* (greatest) *social disgrace* (thing to be ashamed of). When the writer showed him the letter telling him that he had been accepted into the Civil Service (the government administrative departments in Britain), this *spoiled his day* (ruined it because it stopped him from continuing to feel good). The implication is that, far from being pleased for the writer because he had got a good job, the Rector was unhappy at being shown that he had been wrong to tell the writer that he was being *foolish* in leaving school, because he liked to be right about everything all the time.
A: He says that the Rector was a *very elevated* (of very high status) *person* and implies that perhaps he did not have a great deal of respect for him, but he does not imply that others did not respect him as much as he thought they did.
C: The Rector told him that he was being foolish in leaving school but the writer implies that he was more annoyed than sad. If he had been sad that the writer was leaving, this would mean that he liked the writer, but if this had been true, he would have been pleased to learn of his success in the Civil Service competition, but he was not because it *spoiled his day* when he learnt of this.
D: The writer is not implying that the Rector felt that he was making a mistake in joining the Civil Service, because clearly this was considered a good thing for someone to do. His father had told him to enter the competition and so his father clearly wanted him to join the Civil Service. He is therefore not implying that the Rector disagreed with his father's decision to get him to apply to the Civil Service – what the Rector disagreed with was his decision to leave school because he felt he would not get a good job, but the Rector discovered that this was not the case and that the writer had got a job that the Rector approved of.

p136–137 PAPER 1 PART THREE

Two marks per question (Total: 14)

Rainmaker with his Head in the Clouds

27 H: In the opening paragraph, we learn that Dr Mather tried to make clouds rain and that almost everyone else in the *meteorological community* (people involved in the study of the earth's atmosphere and the weather) advised him not to. We also learn that a film has been made about him. The opening sentence is a play on words – if you 'have your head in the clouds', you have unrealistic aims or ideas, which some people thought was true of Dr Mather, who was also involved in the study of actual clouds.
In H, the phrase *to do so* refers back to the end of the

opening paragraph and means 'to make clouds rain'. As a result of his desire to make clouds rain, he set up a project. A film has been made which shows that various experiments have proved that he was right to think it could be done.
The paragraph after the gap gives some information about what had happened regarding *weather modification* (causing the weather to change) before Dr Mather got involved in it.

28 G: In the paragraph before the gap, we learn that the science of weather modification had *claimed many reputations*, which means that many scientists had lost their good reputations as a result of getting involved in it. We also learn that the idea began in the 1940s and grew after the Second World War.
In G *They* at the beginning refers back to the *efforts* made after the Second World War that are mentioned at the end of the paragraph before the gap. The paragraph then describes efforts to prevent clouds from producing *hail* (frozen rain that falls as little balls of ice) that would damage crops and make them produce rain instead.
In the paragraph after the gap, we are told that the *entire discipline* (the whole field of weather modification) then acquired a bad reputation.

29 A: In the paragraph before the gap, we learn that the science of weather modification got a bad reputation because commercial companies *hijacked the idea* (took it over for their own purposes) and *failed to deliver on their promises* (failed to do what they had promised to do – this must mean they they did not prove that cloud-seeding was possible, as they had promised to). As a result, the process *became the preserve of* (an activity exclusively done by) *crackpots* (crazy people) *and charlatans* (cheats who make false claims about being experts in something in order to make money).
In A, we are told that Dr Mather *refused to be daunted by this image. This image* refers back to the image that people had of weather modification, or cloud-seeding, which was that it was *the preserve of crackpots and charlatans*. Dr Mather was not discouraged by the fact that people had this image of weather modification because *the principle* (the basic idea on which a theory is based) *seemed perfectly plausible* (believable). The rest of the paragraph consists of a detailed explanation of what that principle is with regard to what happens in clouds.
In the paragraph after the gap, this explanation is continued, moving on from what happens in clouds to what scientists believed they could do to change what naturally happens in clouds.

30 C: In the paragraph before the gap, we learn that none of the experiments which were carried out to prove the theory that clouds could be affected by scientists worked. Dr Mather had no success himself in this, and so he was about to *admit defeat* (accept that success was impossible and give up), but then *serendipity* (the ability to make fortunate discoveries completely by chance) *intervened* (entered into the situation and changed it).
In C, we are told what happened when *serendipity intervened*. The *last batch of data* refers back to the *experiments* he made that are mentioned in the paragraph before the gap and means that he collected a last batch of data before giving up these experiments. When he was collecting this, there was an unexpected storm, which he discovered was directly above a *paper mill* (a factory for processing paper).
In the paragraph after the gap, *the place* and *from there* both refer back to the *paper mill* mentioned at the end of C. We learn in this paragraph that Dr Mather thought that the paper mill had caused the storm.

31 F: In the paragraph before the gap, we learn that Dr Mather decided that there was a direct link between the *hygroscopic salts* coming from the paper mill and the storm and that subsequent experiments he conducted proved that rain could be caused by certain substances being put into clouds.
In F, we learn that the scientific community did not believe this *apparent proof* – that clouds could be made to produce rain by putting certain substances into them, as described in the paragraph before the gap. The scientific community remained *sniffy* (contemptuous) and *Foremost among the sceptics* (one of the main people to be extremely doubtful) was Dr Cooper. He saw Dr Mather present *his astonishing claims* – this refers back to his claims concerning the effect of hygroscopic salts on clouds in the paragraph before the gap – at a conference.
At the beginning of the paragraph after the gap, *He* is Dr Cooper and the first sentence means that Dr Cooper was *wary* (cautious, suspicious) when he heard the claims referred to at the end of F. In this paragraph we learn that he was wary because Dr Mather was considered to be *a smooth-talking salesman* (someone who tried to convince others of something that is probably not true by means of speaking persuasively), because scientists don't trust other scientists who are charming and *charismatic* (having great personal charm that makes them have influence over other people because other people are impressed by them), because Dr Mather had been working *in the commercial sector* (this implies that Dr Mather's conclusions might have been influenced by commercial considerations) and because Dr Mather was considered to be a *maverick* (someone in a particular field of work with unconventional views and methods which are often disapproved of). The phrase *On that occasion* refers back to Dr Mather's appearance at the conference, mentioned at the end of F.

32 E: In the paragraph before the gap, we learn that someone considered Dr Mather's results impossible but felt that the statistical evidence for them was *overwhelming* (enormous) and as a result was confused.
In E, the same person (Dr Cooper) goes to South Africa to prove Dr Mather wrong but comes back believing that Dr Mather was *on to something* (had discovered something that could have important consequences). He is now conducting two experiments himself – in Arizona and in Mexico – to *verify* (to confirm, to make sure that they are what they seem) the results so far obtained in South Africa, using a kind of salt.
In the paragraph after the gap, Dr Cooper is speaking about the experiments referred to in E. In the first sentence, *those findings* refers back to *the South African results* in E and *there* refers back to Arizona and Mexico in E. He talks about how significant it would be if his experiments had the same results as those already conducted in South Africa, since this would prove that clouds can be made to produce rain if certain substances are put into them.

33 B: In the paragraph before the gap, we learn that, although it might have been proved that cloud-seeding is possible, scientists must *exercise* (use) *caution* on the matter because it is a subject that is still *mired in* (prevented from making progress because of) *controversy*. Another reason why caution is necessary is that because water is such a *precious resource*, the possibility that it can be produced from making clouds rain puts the subject into the *political arena* (the world of politics).
In B, *such matters* refers back to the controversy surrounding cloud-seeding and the fact that it could become a political issue, both of which are mentioned in the paragraph before the gap. Dr Mather won't be involved in discussing these issues because he died shortly before the film about him had been completed. However, we are told that the film will result in Dr Mather getting the recognition he deserves.
In the paragraph after the gap, we are told why Dr Mather deserves such recognition.

The paragraph which does not fit into any of the gaps is D.

p138–142 PAPER 1 PART FOUR

Comedians

FURTHER PRACTICE AND GUIDANCE (p140–142)

For explanations, see the explanations to the questions in the test, which follow.

Question 34
1 yes, he says that there are familiar stereotypes of professors, lawyers, detectives and reporters in the fifth sentence
2 no, he lists what other people think comedians are like but does not mention how comedians feel about this
3 absent-minded – g, gloomy – h, parsimonious – k, shallow – b, introspective – n, smug – d, amoral – j, venal – f, cynical – l, vulgar – i, arrogant – c, insecure – a, autocratic – e, selfish – m

Question 35
1 yes, in the final sentence of the second paragraph
2 a
3 no, he gives his own opinions on them only
4 yes, in the last but one sentence of the second paragraph

Question 36
1 c
2 humour and jokes
3 no
4 no, only that they don't want it to be known that they wrote it
5 meek, quiet, bashful, discreet, modest, unassuming
6 no

Question 37
1 b
2 ginger and snap
3 b
4 c

Question 38
1 b
2 no
3 yes, he says that some of them are *wits*, that there are *Jokes and jokers* at the top of society and that *Some of our rulers do make us laugh.*
4 no
5 b
6 b

Question 39
1 funnymen, comics, funsters and jesters
2 yes, he says they *administer relief*
3 c
4 b
5 c

Question 40
1 yes, he was considered *a bit of a novelty*
2 *timing*, being *quick-witted* and being able to do *a perfect double-take*
3 no
4 no
5 a and b
6 diverse and singular

p138–139 PAPER 1 PART FOUR (TEST)

Note: the numbers in brackets after each explanation refer to the relevant question in the Further Practice and Guidance pages.

Two marks per question (Total: 14)

34 B: In most of the first paragraph, the writer is asking questions rather than making statements – he is therefore mostly raising possibilities rather than directly stating his own views. With regard to comedians, he wonders what *corny* (repeated so often as to be completely unoriginal) *characteristics ... we attribute to* (people regard as belonging to) them. He then lists a large number of characteristics, all of which are regarded as negative and used when describing people in a disapproving way. **(3)**
A: The writer talks about the familiar stereotypes (generalizations commonly made by people concerning the characteristics of other groups of people) of professors, lawyers, detectives and reporters. In each case, the adjective applied to them reflects a negative view of them and is used for expressing disapproval of someone. He therefore believes that these people have a negative image, as do comedians, and does not suggest that they have a better image than comedians. **(1, 3)**
C: The writer says that people generalize both about comedians and about people in other professions. He says that the stereotypes of people in other professions are *cheaply laughable examples from the world of travesty* (are easy to make, ridiculous descriptions that misrepresent in an exaggerated and unfair way). He also says that the characteristics commonly associated with comedians are true if you read their *superficial stories* (stories that have no depth and do not attempt to present anything serious or thorough) *in the tabloids* (popular newspapers in Britain that are commonly associated with sensational stories and gossip about famous people rather than serious articles). Both of these statements suggest that he may not believe that the characteristics commonly associated with people in certain professions and with comedians are accurate. However, he does not suggest that it's easier to generalize about people in other professions than it is to do so about comedians – he does not make a comparison concerning this, he merely says that generalizations are made about all of them, which may not be accurate. **(1)**
D: The writer does refer to negative judgements being made about comedians. In the first sentence he wonders why anyone would want to *put themselves up for* (willingly present themselves as a candidate for) *disparagement* (being treated as useless, stupid or of little value). He also lists the enormous number of negative characteristics he believes are commonly associated with comedians. However, at no point in the first paragraph does he refer to the feelings of comedians concerning what their image is and how they are commonly regarded. **(2, 3)**

35 B: The writer says that people who prefer or *are drawn to* (attracted to) *anonymity* (being unknown to almost everyone else, not attracting attention) are on an *emotional and intellectual course* (feel and think in a particular way) that is *easily observed but not easily deflected* (easy to see but not easy to change the direction of). The writer is therefore saying that such people have a certain way of thinking which they seldom change from. **(2)**
A: In the final sentence of the paragraph, the writer says that, for people who wear uniforms and prefer anonymity, the idea of performing to an audience and *demanding* (wanting very much) *attention is abhorrent* (disgusting, something intensely disliked). He is therefore saying that they think it is a terrible thing and certainly wouldn't want to do it themselves. However, he does not say that they actually criticize other people who do it. **(1)**
C: The writer suggests in his general tone in the paragraph that he thinks people who want a life of anonymity and wear uniforms have weaknesses of character. However, he

does not refer to their opinions of themselves or imply that they realize they have weaknesses. **(3)**
D: The writer says that if *their egos ache for* (if their idea of themselves means that they have a strong desire for) *recognition and praise*, this desire is something that has to be *contained* (not expressed), *frustrated or satisfied within the rut they occupy* (the boring, routine life they lead). The last phrase here indicates that the writer believes their need for recognition and praise can be satisfied within the life they lead, which includes their working life, since he has already told us that he is talking about people who wear uniforms or *livery* (uniforms with designs that are unique to the particular company they represent). **(4)**

36 A: The writer says in the first line of the paragraph that *comics* (people who perform comedy, comedians) are not to be found among shy people such as *doormats* (people who allow others to treat them badly), *dormice* (extremely shy people), people who are *meek* (timid and willing to let others dominate them), *bashful* (shy) *scholars* (academics), *hermits, anchorites and recluses* (people who live quiet, simple lives, completely apart from all other people, perhaps for religious reasons), people who are *discreet* (not wishing to draw attention to themselves), people who are *modest* (not talking about their own qualities or abilities) and people who choose to live a life of *obscurity* (not being well-known at all) and *seclusion* (being apart from everyone else). However, he says that in this *stratum of society* (among shy people), there is *humour* (the ability to amuse others or to appreciate things that are amusing) and there are *jokes* (formally constructed little stories with endings that are meant to make people laugh). He then gives the example of two people who have an *unassuming* (not wishing to draw attention to yourself) *existence* who write comedy for radio and TV shows. His point therefore is that shy people can't perform comedy but they can write it. **(1, 2, 5)**
B: The writer says that shy people are capable of humour and jokes, because humour can exist in any circumstances, like *lichen* (a plant that grows on rocks, trees or walls) *in Antarctica*. However, he does not refer to how humorous such people think they are and does not say that they are better at humour than they think they are. **(2, 5)**
C: The writer mentions the two *lesser-known comedy writers* as examples of shy people who are capable of humour and jokes but he does not say that they are worried that others may not share their sense of humour. Indeed, they send their material to radio and TV shows, which indicates that they hope that others will find it funny. **(3, 5, 6)**
D: The writer says that the two writers he mentions send *topical jokes* (jokes about matters that are of interest or in the news at the present time) to TV and radio shows and that when they do so, it is *on condition that their real names are not revealed*. This means that they use false names when sending in their material and make it clear to those they send the material to that they do not want their real names to be used. Therefore, they choose not to get any recognition for their material, even if it is considered good enough for inclusion in the TV and radio shows they send it to. **(4, 5, 6)**

37 D: The writer says that the material written by the writers he has mentioned is based on *wordplay, puns and similar equivoques* (all types of humour that involve the clever use of words) and not *aggressive comic observation of life*. He believes that this is because people who live in the *self-effacement* (modesty, not trying to impress) of a *humble life* (people who are not important in society, do not wish to draw attention to themselves and do not talk about their qualities or abilities) also live a life of *sterility* (in this context, lacking imagination or excitement). As a result, it seems *feasible* (possible) to him that before they even begin to decide what is funny, and therefore to write it, their idea of what is funny has been *emasculated* (considerably weakened) because of the life they lead. They have no *ginger and snap* (vigour, liveliness, spirit) in their *daily round* (everyday life) and so their humour is limited to *juggling with language* (rearranging it, in this context in order to use combinations of words in a humorous way). The writer clearly feels that their humour lacks something, from his general tone in describing it, and what it lacks is spirit (energy, liveliness, vigour, aggression) because it is a reflection of the kind of lives they lead and the kind of people they are. **(1, 2, 3, 4)**
A: The writer does not criticize their humour for being similar to or copied from other people's humour, nor does he refer to it being a kind of humour that is very common. **(3c, 4b)**
B: The writer does not say that it is a kind of humour that does not make sense or may not be easily understood by people, even though he does say that it is based on the clever use of words. **(1a, 3a)**
C: The writer does not say that the humour is too simple or not subtle enough – indeed, the fact that it is based on the clever use of words suggests that it may be sophisticated, and it is the fact that it is based entirely on the clever use of words and not on strong emotions or observation of life which he dislikes about it. **(1c)**

38 D: The writer says that in the top *echelons* (levels) of society there is humour, and *wits* (people who say things that are both clever and funny), and that jokes and *jokers* (people who say or do amusing things or play tricks on people) *circulate* (spread throughout) the *loftiest* (highest) level of every advanced society. However, such people feel no *compulsion* (strong urge) to amuse the *hoi-polloi* (ordinary people, as opposed to those at the top of society). Some of them, he says, do make us laugh (in this context, *us* must mean ordinary people) but they don't have to do that for a living. Their comedy is *constricted* (limited and narrow) because *they live a constricted life* (presumably meaning that they only know people from their own level of society) and so they only amuse each other and do not have *the common touch* (the ability to get on well with, and in this context presumably amuse, people from lower levels of society). He is therefore saying that some people from the top of society are capable of comedy but that their comedy is of such a narrow kind that ordinary people would not find it funny and so they could not earn a living as comedians. **(1, 3, 5, 6)**
A: The writer says that people at the top of society do not have a sense of humour that is in common with those from other levels of society, but he does not refer to their opinion of the humour of people at the lower levels of society or suggest that they have a low opinion of those people or their sense of humour. **(1, 2, 6)**
B: Both *wits* and *jokers* are people who deliberately try to amuse others and the writer says that these exist at the top of society. **(3)**
C: The writer says that some people at the top of society *do make us laugh* although he does not make it clear whether he thinks that when they make ordinary people laugh this is intentional or not. He therefore does not directly state that they do not know that other people laugh at them. **(1, 4)**

39 C: The writer wonders whether comics are *called to their vocation* (whether they take up the occupation because they see it as the natural and most suitable thing for them to do). He wonders whether the need of the *mirthless masses* (people who have nothing to laugh about) tends to *summon forth* (bring out or call for) comedians, who are ready to *administer* (provide) *relief as their sole raison d'être* (their only or most important reason for existing). He wonders whether the phrase *a born comedian* (someone who is bound to become a comedian because of their natural ability and qualities) will *do for* (applies to) all comedians or even most of them. And he wonders whether they are, as people like to think, *inescapably driven to expression* (whether they feel an irresistible urge to express themselves through comedy). He therefore wonders whether it is true that even though

most comedians become comedians because that is the natural thing for them to become, whether comedians feel that comedy is their vocation and the reason why they exist, and whether they feel an urge they cannot resist to become comedians. **(1, 2, 4b, 5c)**
A: The writer says that people need comedians because they provide them with relief and that they like to think that comedians become comedians because of some powerful urge they cannot resist but he does not say that people expect too much of comedians. **(1, 2, 4a)**
B: The writer says that perhaps people like to think great comedians are like great painters and composers in the sense that all of them feel a strong urge to become what they become, but he does not compare these people in terms of whether they can be considered great or not. **(1, 3, 5d)**
D: The writer says that comedians are important to the *masses* because they provide them with relief and does imply that they feel it is their role to provide this relief, but he does not refer to wondering whether or not comedians are aware of how important doing so is. **(1, 2, 4c, 5a)**

40 C: The writer says that when he began his career as a comedian, he was *a bit of a novelty* (something new, unusual and interesting, although usually only for a short time) because most comedians were working-class people, not educated, middle-class people like him. But he already sensed that this did not matter and that, although comedians were traditionally working-class, their background did not make them good at *timing* (saying things at exactly the right speed and time to have the maximum comic effect), *quick-witted* (able to think and react quickly) or able to do a *perfect double-take* (a delayed reaction for comic effect). He is therefore saying that these three things, which are concerned with comic technique, are involved in whether a comedian is successful or not, and social background is not. He reinforces this point by saying that, apart from the three facts about comedians he states at the beginning of the paragraph, comedians have no *commonable property* (nothing in common) and are as *diverse* (different from each other) *as fingerprints*. He also adds that they are *singular* (each one is unique). **(1, 2, 5, 6)**
A: Although he came from a different background from that of most comedians, the writer says that he *already sensed the truth* – that coming from a poor background did not mean that someone would have good comic technique. If this was the truth, he clearly believes that his background did not affect whether he was successful or not. **(1, 2, 5)**
B: The writer refers to three elements he believed were involved in good comic performance. He does not imply that he changed his mind about this or say that these concerned common ideas about how to be a good comedian which he found to be false. **(2, 3)**
D: The writer does refer to other comedians and says that most of them shared a common background. However, he does not refer to their attitude towards comedy or to whether there were common beliefs about it – he simply says that most comedians were working-class people. **(4)**

PAPER 1:

PART ONE	18 marks
PART TWO	16 marks
PART THREE	14 marks
PART FOUR	14 marks
TOTAL	62 marks

To be converted into a score out of 40 marks.

p143–146 PAPER 2 PART ONE

Task-specific mark schemes

Each answer is given marks out of 20

Question 1

Content
Essay should cover the points raised in the input – whether the Arts are relevant to most people or only to a small section of society, the question of participation in the Arts and whether or not the Arts are beneficial. Candidates may support or oppose throughout, or mix agreement on certain points with disagreement on others.

Range
Language for expressing and supporting opinions, and language of analysis, evaluation and recommendation.

Appropriacy of register and format
Formal or neutral tone, as appropriate for an essay for a tutor or lecturer.

Organization and cohesion
Clear presentation and development of ideas in paragraphs dealing with each aspect of the input. Appropriate linking within and between paragraphs. Coherent linking of ideas, with no internal contradictions.

Target reader
Would understand the writer's point of view fully and clearly.

FURTHER PRACTICE AND GUIDANCE (p144–146)

Assessment of sample answer

Content
The points raised in the book introduction in the question are covered in the essay. The writer discusses the relevance of the Arts to ordinary people, rather than only to a few people, talks about why people take part in the Arts and deals with the issue of what benefits the Arts have. The writer mixes criticism with regard to some aspects of the topic with positive views with regard to other aspects. However, marks would be lost because the candidate has confused 'art' with 'the Arts'.

Range
There is some very good use of vocabulary and structure, for example the vocabulary used to describe pictures in the second paragraph and the idiom *There are two sides to this coin* there, *express themselves, whatever, in short, obsession* and *what they stand for* (third paragraph), *doing so* and *show it off* (fourth paragraph), *deeper meaning, the issues of their time, colourful* and *dusty* (fifth paragraph), *something to work with, the spirit lifts our whole being, snobby* and *posh* (final paragraph). The use of questions in the first sentence of the essay and in the fifth sentence of the final paragraph is very effective, adding to the lively style of the essay.

Accuracy
There are one or two errors. The use of *mean* is incorrect in the second sentence of the fourth paragraph and that sentence should be something like *For some people, buying art is a very materialistic act ...* . The use of *Though* at the beginning of the fifth paragraph is incorrect – *Though* can only be used if the sentence has a second, contrasting part, which this sentence does not, and so *However*, followed by a comma, would be correct here. In the final paragraph *on an early stage* should be *at an early stage*.

Appropriacy of register and format
The essay has an appropriately formal tone and is suitably paragraphed for an essay. The first sentence, echoing the question, forms an effective and brief introduction.

Organization and cohesion
The essay is very well-organized, with each paragraph dealing with a different aspect and each paragraph flowing well after the paragraph that precedes it. The second paragraph introduces the distinction between artists and the public, the third and fourth paragraphs expand on this, discussing first artists and then the public, the fourth paragraph moves on to talk about the relevance of the Arts in general and the final paragraph moves from that to talk about the benefits of the Arts. There is some very good linking, for example, the use of *on the other hand* in the middle of the first sentence in the fourth paragraph, *For one thing* and *Since* (fifth paragraph), and all of the linking in the very long but very well-controlled final sentence of the essay.

Target reader
The writer's views would be very clearly understood. The reader would be clear as to why the writer sees doing the Arts as selfish and why the writer is critical of some people who buy art, and the reader would be clear as to the writer's views that the Arts teach people about history and benefit people personally.

Assessment: An excellent and well-argued essay, with some sophisticated language. However, the confusion between 'the Arts' and 'art' has affected the mark.

Mark: 16

p147 PAPER 2 PART TWO

Question 2

Content
Report should include:
- brief summary of how survey was conducted
- findings of survey regarding different specific ideas and possibilities for content of weekly magazine supplement
- conclusion summarizing local people's views and preferences regarding possible weekly magazine supplement

Range
Language for analysing, describing and perhaps hypothesizing.

Appropriacy of register and format
Register appropriate to employee/employer relationship – fairly formal. Report format, probably with section headings and perhaps with headings for each possible section of the magazine covered by the survey.

Organization and cohesion
Report should be well-structured, with each aspect of the possible magazine dealt with clearly and results of findings clearly presented. Clear introduction and conclusion, and clear linking of areas of the report throughout.

Target reader
Would understand findings of survey and writer's summary of them fully and clearly.

FURTHER PRACTICE AND GUIDANCE (p148–150)

Assessment of sample answer

Content
The report covers all the aspects mentioned in the question. It includes a description of what the survey involved, the information that was gathered from the survey and conclusions as to what has been discovered with regard to the supplement.

Range
There is some very good use of vocabulary and structure, for example *in which* and *if so* (Research section), *see the point* (Findings section) and *It would appear that, make it worth doing* and the *prefer ... rather than* structure in the Conclusions section. Most of the vocabulary and structures are relatively straightforward, but this is entirely appropriate for a report of this kind.

Accuracy
There are no mistakes in the report.

Appropriacy of register and format
The register is appropriately neutral, since the writer is reporting objectively on factual information. The format is entirely appropriate, with a heading for the report as a whole and clear sections, each with clear section headings.

Organization and cohesion
The report is extremely well-organized in a coherent order, starting with the research that was carried out, moving on to the information gained from it and concluding with a summary of the position, which states the outcome briefly and clearly. The Research section describes clearly what the survey consisted of and how it was carried out, the Findings section explains clearly what ideas proved popular and unpopular and the Conclusions section indicates clearly and briefly how the findings should be interpreted. The linking is appropriate and accurate throughout, and enables the whole report to flow well.

Target reader
The reader would be perfectly clear as to what has been done, what has been discovered and how this should be interpreted. The report totally fulfils the requirements in the question.
Assessment: An excellent report with no errors, that covers everything it should.

Mark: 18

Question 3

Content
Article should cover the points mentioned and, as instructed, consist of a list of what the writer considers to be the good things in life, together with reasons why they are good.

Range
Language for describing, evaluating, expressing and supporting views and perhaps recommending and hypothesizing.

Appropriacy of register and format
Register appropriate for an article of a light-hearted nature – informal – or neutral if the subject is treated as a more serious one. Article format, in this case a series of probably short paragraphs forming a list, perhaps with sub-headings.

Organization and cohesion
List of things considered good in life, accompanied by clear and coherent reasons for choosing them. Article could have brief introduction and/or conclusion intended to have impact on the reader. Appropriate linking between items in the list and between each item and the reason(s) for choosing it.

Target reader
Would understand fully the things chosen for inclusion in the list and why they have been chosen for inclusion in the article.

Question 4

Content
Letter should describe the visit and present a list of aspects of the visit and the place, together with personal experiences and comments relating to those aspects. It should also including recommendations arising from the personal experiences and comments on the visit and the place. Candidates may be enthusiastic about the place or critical of it, or they may combine enthusiasm with criticism.

Range
Language of narration (for the visit and personal experiences), description (of the place), and recommendation, including language for expressing opinions (praise, complaint, etc).

Appropriacy of register and format
Formal letter, as appropriate for a member of the public writing to an official they have not met or spoken to, concerning something the official has authority over. Formal letter format.

Organization and cohesion
Brief introduction, giving clear reason for writing. Clear paragraphing, each paragraph dealing with separate aspects of the trip and the place, followed by comments and, if appropriate, recommendations for action on the part of the recipient. Appropriate linking so that comments and recommendations logically follow descriptions and narration and so that paragraphs together form a coherent whole.

Target reader
Would be completely clear as to what the writer's experiences were, the writer's opinions arising from them and what the writer is recommending.

PAPER 2:

PART ONE	20 marks
PART TWO	20 marks
TOTAL	40 marks

p151 PAPER 3 PART ONE

One mark per question (Total: 15)

The Slow Arrival of the Wheel

1 **everything:** The writer has said that it is nearly impossible to imagine a world without wheels and lists things that have them as examples of the fact that 'everything' has some form of wheel. In this context, by 'everything', he means every kind of machine or device that people use.

2 **Yet/But:** The writer is contrasting two ideas – that wheels are present in so many things and that it was a long time in the history of mankind before the wheel was invented. Other linking words could be used here to express the same contrast, such as *nevertheless* and *however*, but these should be followed by a comma.

3 **without:** In this context *without* means 'not having'. The writer is saying that some civilizations became quite sophisticated even though they did not have the wheel because it had not been invented.

4 **that:** The conjunction *that* is required here to link the subject 'explanation' and verb 'is' with the clause that follows. The writer is saying that the wheel probably wasn't invented earlier because conditions did not suit it.

5 **in:** If someone/something is *in the grip of something*, they are suffering as a result of something powerful which they cannot resist or do anything about. The writer is saying that the last parts of the Ice Age dominated most of the world.

6 **What:** In this sentence *What* is used as the subject, meaning 'the thing(s) that'. The writer is saying that places that were not affected by the Ice Age were affected by other conditions that were unsuitable for the wheel.

7 **from:** If something *evolves from something*, it develops naturally and gradually from it. The writer is saying that the wheel developed from things that Neolithic man did.

8 **by:** The preposition *by* is used here with the meaning 'through the means of' to explain how something is done. The writer is explaining how Neolithic man moved heavy objects.

9 **Such/These/Those:** This refers back to the technique of putting a roller under a heavy load to move it. *Such/These/Those* techniques means 'techniques such as the technique previously mentioned'.

10 **back:** If something *dates back to* a certain time, date or period, it has existed since then or was created then.

11 **Another:** The writer is now beginning to talk about a different technique for moving large, heavy objects from the technique previously mentioned. The gap therefore has to be filled with *Another* rather than *A* because it is the second example of the same thing and not the first mention of a technique for doing something.

12 **with:** The linking phrase *with the result that* means 'and the result is/was ...'. The writer is saying that because the sledge produced grooves (long, narrow cuts in the surface) in the roller, a ratio was developed, which increased the amount by which the roller turned.

13 **and:** The two adjectives are linked with *and* because they provide two distinct and separate pieces of information. The writer is saying that the stage in the development of the wheel that he is going to describe was not only the next stage but it was also the final stage.

14 **this/that:** The linking phrase *in this/that way* is used for linking something that is done with the result of that action. The writer is saying that the wood between the grooves was cut away and that the result of this action was that an axle with a wheel at each end was created.

15 **could:** *Could* here means 'was able to' and *better* is an adverb here. The writer is saying that when the wheel was invented, man was able to able to enjoy travel, speed and movement more than had been possible previously.

p152 PAPER 3 PART TWO

One mark per question (Total: 10)

The Word 'Bogus'

16 **forgeries:** A *forgery* is something that has been created as a copy of something in order to deceive people or as an illegal act. The writer is saying that a 'bogus' was originally a machine for making false coins.

17 **undergone:** If someone/something *undergoes something*, they go through a process which has an effect on them. The writer is saying that the word became an adjective rather than a noun.

18 **misleading:** If something is *misleading*, it creates a false impression or gives people the wrong idea, either

intentionally or unintentionally. The writer is saying that the word was used to describe anything that was intended to deceive people.

19 **linguistic:** *Linguistic* is an adjective meaning 'connected with language' and *linguistic innovation* means the introduction or creation of something new in a language. The writer is saying that computer scientists in America in the 1960s were responsible for the invention of a number of new words.

20 **emergence:** The *emergence of something* is its first appearance in a particular context or its development into something that is known, noticeable or important. The writer is saying that the word started to be used by people in a certain part of America who had attended certain universities.

21 **adoption:** The *adoption of something* is the act of it being used or taken over by someone or a group of people for a purpose. The writer is saying that American teenagers then started using the word with a different meaning.

22 **Interestingly:** An adverb can be used at the beginning of a sentence, followed by a comma, with the meaning *It is/was, etc + adjective + that ...* . In this case, it means 'It is interesting that ... '. The writer is saying it is interesting that there have been no acceptable explanations for the origins of a great many English words.

23 **onlooker:** An *onlooker* is someone who is present when something happens and sees it happen but does not get involved. The writer is referring to someone who saw the police take the machine away.

24 **corruption:** A *corruption of* a word is a word that has come into existence as a result of another word being changed from its original form. The writer is saying that one American theory is that the word is an inaccurate version of someone's name.

25 **Elsewhere:** This means 'in another place or places'. The writer is saying that people in countries other than the US have produced different theories about the origins of the word.

p153 PAPER 3 PART THREE

Two marks per question (Total: 12)

26 **picture:** If you *get/have a mental picture of something*, you are able to imagine it or see it in your mind. The noun *image* would also complete a collocation with the same meaning.
The singular noun *picture* can mean 'the general situation with regard to something'. The adjective *overall* often forms a collocation with *picture* when it has this meaning. The noun *situation* would also fit here, as would other nouns with slightly different meanings, such as *pattern*.
A *picture* on a television screen is an image shown or broadcast on it. This may refer to the quality of what is transmitted, and in this context a *good picture* is one that can be seen clearly. The noun *reception* would also fit here, with exactly the same meaning.

27 **rough:** If you *feel rough*, you do not feel well physically. Numerous other adjectives could fill the gap here with the same or related meanings, such as *ill, unwell*, etc.
The adjective *rough* can mean 'approximate', 'not exact' or 'not carefully or properly planned or considered'. A *rough idea* is one that is not detailed or final. Other adjectives could be used here to form collocations with 'idea' with the same meaning, such as *general, vague*, etc.
If water is *rough*, it is not smooth or calm but is moving around with big waves, strong currents, etc, so that it is difficult, dangerous or unpleasant to go on it in a boat or swim in it. Other adjectives could fit here with the same meaning, such as *choppy, stormy*, etc.

28 **pass:** If a feeling or situation *passes*, it comes to an end or ceases to exist after a period of time. Other verbs could fill the gap here to express the same meaning, such as *go, disappear*, etc.
If you *let something pass*, you allow something you dislike or disapprove of to be said or done, or you tolerate something, without saying or doing anything in response to it and without expressing your dislike or disapproval of it. The verb *go* could also fill the gap to form a collocation with the same meaning.
If you *pass out*, you lose consciousness or faint, because of illness, heat, injury, shock, etc.

29 **light:** If something *comes to light*, it is revealed or it becomes known, when previously it was hidden, secret or unknown.
If you *set light to something*, you cause it to start burning by applying something such as a flame to it. The noun *fire* could also fill the gap to complete a phrase with the same meaning.
The linking phrase *in the light of something* means 'because of something', 'in view of something' or 'taking something into consideration'.

30 **still:** The adverb *still* can be used after a comparative adjective with the meaning 'even' – *worse still = even worse*. The adverb *yet* can be used with the same meaning before a comparative adjective but not after one (*yet worse = even worse = worse still*), so *yet* could not fill the gap here.
The adverb *still* can be used to link two contrasting statements to say that both statements are in fact true, even though the second statement may not seem to follow logically from the first. The use of the word *still* indicates that the second statement is as important as the first. The linking words *however, nevertheless* and *nonetheless* could also fill the gap to express the same meaning.
The adverb *still* can be used with the meaning 'until and including now' to describe a situation or action that is continuing. The adverb *always* could also be used here, with the meaning 'if I want to' or 'at any time'.

31 **packed:** If you *pack something away*, you put it back into the container that it is kept in when it is not being used because it is no longer needed or you have finished using it. Other verbs could fill the gap here with the same meaning, such as *put, stored*, etc.
If you *pack something in*, you give it up or stop doing it as a result of your own choice. The verb *jacked* could also fill the gap here, to form a phrasal verb with the same meaning.
If a place is *packed*, it is so full of people that there is little or no space left and people cannot move around without difficulty. Other adjectives could fill the gap here with the same meaning, such as *jammed, crammed, crowded*, etc.

p154–156 PAPER 3 PART FOUR

FURTHER PRACTICE AND GUIDANCE (p155–156)

For explanations, see the explanations to the questions in the test, which follow.

Question 32: 1 c 2 b

Question 33: 1 b/e 2 a/e

Question 34: 1 a/e 2 a/e

Question 35: 1 d 2 a/e

Question 36: 1 a/e 2 c

Question 37: 1 c 2 e

Question 38: 1 b/e 2 c/e

Question 39: 1 c 2 b

p154 PAPER 3 PART FOUR (TEST)

Two marks per question (Total: 16)

32 the controversy (1 mark)
(that was) caused by (1 mark)
The grammatical structure *Such + to be + noun + that + result = Noun + to be + so + adjective + that + result*. The adjective *controversial* therefore has to be changed into the noun *controversy*, preceded by the definite article *the*, as it is a specific controversy. The second part is passive because *the film* is the subject of the verb *caused*. The part of the relative clause before the verb can be omitted.

33 did he know/realize (1 mark)
what lay/was in store for (1 mark)
Little did he know means 'He had no idea'. The sentence starts with *Little* and so the verb must be inverted in the question form, even though it is not a question. *What lies/is in store for someone* is what is going to happen to them in the future.
The phrase *set store by* in the exercise (2c) does exist and means 'attach importance to'. (*My boss sets great store by punctuality.*)

34 prey on you/your mind (1 mark)
to such an/to such a great/to so great an/to that (1 mark)
If something worries you, especially if it worries you over a period of time so that you cannot forget it, it *preys on you* or *preys on your mind*. The preposition that goes with *extent* is *to*. The phrases *to such an extent, to such a great extent* and, more formally, *to so great an extent* all mean 'so much'. *To that extent* means 'to an extent as great as the one mentioned.'
The phrases *be prey to something* and *fall prey to something* in the exercise (1b and 1d) do exist, and they can both be used with the meaning 'be a victim of'. (*He was naive in business and so he was/fell prey to all sorts of cheats and fraudsters.*)

35 to fame (1 mark)
was/came at the expense (1 mark)
If you *rise to something*, you make upward progress and achieve it. The adjective *famous* has to be changed to the noun *fame*. If something *is/comes at the expense of something*, the fact that it happens results in damage or loss to something else or it is to the disadvantage of something else.
The phrases *meant the expense* (2c) and *led to expense* (2d) could be used in contexts in which 'expense' means 'money spent' or 'a lot of money spent'.

36 did Ray a favour/did a favour for Ray (1 mark)
as a result of/because of/due to (1 mark)
If you *do somebody a favour* or *do a favour for somebody*, you do something that helps them, usually because they ask you to do it, and in this way you are kind to them. The word *which* after the gap refers to 'the fact that I did Ray a favour' and is therefore a substitute for a noun clause. It has to be preceded by a phrase referring to the fact that the favour was the cause of his success or that it resulted in his success. When completed, the second part of the sentence therefore means 'the result of the fact that I did him a favour was that his business became successful' or 'the fact that I did him a favour caused his business to be successful'.
The phrase *in somebody's favour* in the exercise (1b) does exist, meaning 'to somebody's advantage'. (*The decision went in his favour, which pleased him.*) The phrase *find favour with somebody* in the exercise (1c) also exists, and it means 'be approved of or liked by somebody'. (*My proposal found favour with the others at the meeting.*)

37 me waiting (1 mark)
for the best part of (1 mark)
If you *keep somebody/something doing something*, you make them continue to do it, although they may not wish to continue doing it. The phrase *the best part of* means 'almost all of', 'most of', and is often followed by a period of time. The phrase *to the best of* in the exercise (2a) can be used in the phrase *to the best of my ability*, meaning 'as well as I can/could' (*I did the work to the best of my ability.*) and in the phrase *to the best of my knowledge*, meaning 'as far as I know, although I am not completely sure'. (*To the best of my knowledge, George still lives at the same address he had two years ago.*) The phrase *at best* in the exercise (2b) means 'taking the most optimistic or tolerant view'. (*At best, this will prove to have been only a small mistake.*)
The phrase *at the best of times* in the exercise (2c) means 'even when the best circumstances exist'. (*Michael is bad-tempered at the best of times.*) The phrase *with the best of* in the exercise (2d) can be used in the phrase *with the best of intentions*, meaning 'intending only to do good things or to help'. (*I went there with the best of intentions but I only made the situation worse.*)

38 itself (to me) (1 mark)
in/within the near (1 mark)
If a situation *presents itself* or *presents itself to somebody*, it appears or arises without the person concerned having done anything themselves to cause it to happen. The phrase *in/within the near future* means 'soon, not long from now'. The structure *present somebody with something* in the exercise (1c) does exist, meaning either 'give something to somebody' in a rather formal sense (*He was presented with an award.*) or 'cause somebody to be faced with or allowed'. (*The job offer presented me with a problem/opportunity.*)

39 all my good work (1 mark)
(from) going to waste (1 mark)
The grammatical structure required here is *prevent + object (+ from) + -ing*. In this sentence, the object is *all my good work*.
The phrase *go to waste* means 'be wasted', and the verb has to be in the *-ing* form.
The phrase *be a waste* (2a) can be used in phrases such as *be a waste of time, be a waste of energy*, etc. The phrase *lay waste* (2e) means 'destroy a place or area completely'.

p157–159 PAPER 3 PART FIVE

Questions 40–43

Two marks per question (Total: 8)

Answers that are similar to or cover the same points as those given here are acceptable, provided that they are clearly expressed.

40 It has been analysed closely, it has become something with a standard, formal system and set of rules, and it has become part of the way in which big companies establish their individual image.
The writer says that design has been *the subject of systematic and scientific analysis*, that it has been *codified* (arranged into a formal system of rules) *into set* (fixed, standard and always kept to) *procedures* and that it has become *institutionalized* (made into an established practice) *by*

manufacturing corporations (large companies consisting of several different parts) *as part of the overall* (general) *identity* (image) *of the company*.

41 that it is an art because it can make points about life and because it is not only about producing products that may be stupid and lacking in sophistication.
The quote is used to illustrate the point that some people think that design has not been completely institutionalized but is also an art. Sottsass says that design can create a *figurative utopia* (a representation of a perfect world) or a *metaphor about life* (an imaginative image that conveys an idea about life). He says that design is *not restricted to the necessity of giving form to* (not limited to being something that produces) *a more or less stupid product for a more or less sophisticated industry* (the use of the phrase *more or less* implies the view that some products are stupid and that some of the industries that designers work in are not sophisticated).

42 Designers work completely through intuition, whereas engineers combine intuition with testing, and engineers are responsible if the product doesn't work whereas designers are responsible for only certain aspects of the product.
The writer says that designers are *entirely happy with intuitive judgments* (those based on feelings about something rather than on concrete proof), whereas engineers *prefer to test and test* (in order to prove whether what they are doing works or not), even though they *might proceed intuitively* (do things that are based on intuition) as well. Secondly, engineers are *responsible for the structural failure of the product* (it is their fault if the product breaks down because of the way it was built), whereas designers only have a *share of the responsibility*, with regard to such aspects as *the 'human/machine interface'* (how people and machines work together, how a person uses a machine) and areas such as *ergonomics* (people's working conditions, for example how comfortable they are when using certain equipment) *and product semantics* (the kind of language used to describe products).

43 because it can be an advantage in terms of marketing to say that a product originated from a single individual, since people like the idea that products are the work of individuals
The writer says that even though many modern designs are not the *fruits* (results, products) of a single individual's mind, it can be *beneficial from a marketing point of view to play up* (make something seem more important than it really is) *a single designer's name as a signature* (a distinctive, individual quality) *that gives a product a provenance* (an origin) *in the same way that a painter signs his or her canvas.*

Question 44 Summary

One mark for each content point included from the following, maximum 4 marks

(i) making sure their products can be made
In the first paragraph of the first text, the writer says that designers have to make sure that the product they have designed for a client can be made *to the designer's specifications* (the details listed on a document or drawn on a plan as to what something will consist of, how it will be made, etc) so that *each element specified is practicable* (can actually be put into practice or carried out). For this to be possible, the designer has to make sure that the factory where the product is going to be made is capable of making it exactly according to the specifications.

(ii) communicating their intentions
In the first paragraph of the first text, the writer says that, unlike *a single independent craftsperson* (a person using their special skill to make something with their hands), a designer has to communicate his or her intentions to others *for translation into objects* (so that other people can make objects that are as the designer intends them to be) and has to make these intentions *explicit* (clearly expressed) because communication *is at the heart of* (a very important aspect of) design.

(iii) presenting/creating a company's image/ideology
In the second paragraph of the first text, the writer says that designers are concerned with *the way a company looks and presents itself* (its image, how it appears to others) and with *giving a 'family' look to the design of a company's products* (making them similar to each other in such a way that it is clear to other people that they were all made by the same company), and that they *visualize* (imagine, create in their minds) *a company's ideology* (a company's attitudes and beliefs) and then through their *visualizations* (the things that they create through their imaginations), they communicate that ideology to *the world* (in this context, to people in general).

(iv) being just one person among many who produce a product or are responsible for it, rather than the only creator or the person with sole responsibility for it
In the second paragraph of the second text, the writer talks about the *many interpreters* there are in the *continuum* (sequence of stages) between a product being designed and it actually being produced, sold and used. These 'interpreters' include various individuals, specialists and marketing experts who get the product made and *filter out* (remove because unwanted or unnecessary) possible problems with it. They all make a contribution to the process and a designer is just one of these people, even if they *provide an important stylistic signature* (a distinctive quality resulting from their own individual style of design) to the product. A designer is therefore not a *fine artist* (an artist such as a painter or sculptor who is concerned with creating things that appeal to the senses) because a designer is not the sole creator of what is produced, whereas a fine artist is. In the third paragraph of the second text, the writer says that designers of certain objects may be solely responsible for the design of them but that even with such objects, other people may have altered the design so that it can be manufactured more easily.

Marks out of 10 are then given for summary skills, based on the following criteria:

- *relevance*
- *accuracy*
- *organization*
- *rephrasing*
- *length*

FURTHER PRACTICE AND GUIDANCE (p159)

Assessment of sample summary

Content points:

1 Nothing irrelevant is included and most of the relevant points are included. There is some repetition of the first content point.

(i) This is included in the first and second sentences.
(ii) This could be said to be included in all three sentences.
(iii) This is not included.
(iv) This is included in the second and third sentences.

Content: 3 marks

Summary skills:

2 There are no language mistakes.
3 The summary is well-organized and fluent, with very good use of some sophisticated vocabulary and structure, for example the linking phrase *in that*, meaning 'in the sense that', in the second sentence.
4 The summary very successfully rephrases the points made in the two texts.
5 The summary is within the word limit.

Summary skills: 8 marks

Sample summary total: 11 marks (out of 14)

PAPER 3:

PART ONE	15 marks
PART TWO	10 marks
PART THREE	12 marks
PART FOUR	16 marks
PART FIVE	
Questions 40–43	8 marks
Question 44	14 marks
TOTAL	75 marks

To be converted into a score out of 40 marks.

p160–161 PAPER 4 PART ONE

One mark per question (Total: 8)

1 **C:** The speaker says that confidence is an *elusive* (difficult to be precise about) *thing* and that everyone has an idea what they mean when they talk about it. The implication is that different people have different ideas about what it is because it is hard to define it precisely.
A: The speaker mentions one dictionary definition she regards as *not quite right* (not completely accurate) but she does not say that the majority of dictionary definitions of confidence are wrong.
B: The speaker says that *self-assurance* is *more like it* (closer to being an accurate definition of confidence), not that it involves a lot more than just self-assurance.

2 **A:** The speaker uses *We* to mean 'everyone' or 'people in general'. She says that nobody wants to feel inferior to others or be *bullied* by someone else (treated badly by someone who threatens or frightens them) and that we all want to feel that we are equal to others. She says that *of course we all want these things* and since these are signs of confidence, she is saying that everyone wants to have confidence.
B: She says that people don't want to feel inferior and that they want to feel that they are *just as good as* (exactly equal to) other people but she doesn't say that people who lack confidence can gain so much of it that they start to feel superior.
C: She says that wanting confidence and having it are *very different*, which means that for some people it may be very hard to get confidence. However, she says that if we don't have confidence or don't have *an abundance* (a very large amount) of it, we *must set about obtaining more* (we must begin the task of getting more, we must start making an effort to get more). She is therefore saying that people who lack confidence have to start gaining it, and this may be difficult, but she is not saying that it is impossible for some people.

3 **B:** The speaker says that political cartoons are not like *rapier thrusts* (single forward strokes with a sword), they are like missiles with *at least three explosive warheads* (the parts of missiles that explode). He is therefore saying that they get their effect from three different elements and he lists these – they are caricature, the political point being made and the image through which this point is made. The effect achieved by the combination of these three elements is, he says, *formidable* (very powerful).
A: The speaker says that a political cartoon contains an *apparent joke* – something that seems like a joke but is in fact making a serious point – and that this can have a *reverberating, subversive power* (it can have a widespread effect and make people question authority). This is not, however, why they are not 'rapier thrusts' – that is because they contain different elements. Furthermore, he indicates that they are not always meant as a joke, because some caricatures are a *maliciously* (done because of hatred and with the intention of harming) *distorted representation of politicians* (they are drawings of politicians which exaggerate the way they really look).
C: The speaker is not saying that political cartoons can have various aims – their aim is the same, to make a joke that has a serious political point to it, at the expense of politicians. The list of different things he gives is a list of the different ways in which this aim is achieved, not a list of different aims.

4 **A:** The speaker says that a good caricature *does not allow for fine degrees of criticism* (doesn't make it possible for criticism to be complex or not too obvious), that it has an *awful bluntness* (it is direct and honest in a way that may upset some people) and that it cannot *dilute its message* (make its point in a way that is not very forceful). He says that caricature is like being rude to someone *succinctly* (in very few words, very briefly) rather than by saying the same thing to them in a less direct way. He is therefore saying that caricatures can only be forceful and direct, they cannot make points in a complex or subtle way.
B: The speaker says that caricatures work against the image that politicians have of themselves and that they want other people to have of them, and he says that they can reduce a politician's *dignity* (quality which makes people respect them) and therefore their *authority* (quality of being someone with power). However, he does not say that politicians change as a result of this happening to them.
C: The speaker says that many politicians are *flattered* (pleased because they feel they have in some way been paid a compliment) *by the attention* when they are the subject of a political cartoon, and this must also mean when they are the subject of a caricature. Because of this, they ask if they can have the original drawing done by the cartoonist. He is therefore saying that they are pleased to be the subject of caricatures but he doesn't say that they should react in this way. He also says that some politicians are not amused when they are the subject and that it can be *disturbing* to see yourself caricatured, but he does not say that politicians who feel this way should instead by pleased – he seems to find their reaction perfectly natural.

5 **C:** The speaker says that Goldman's *insincerity detector* (his ability to notice that someone is insincere) is working *perhaps too industriously* (too hard). By this he means that Goldman finds insincerity where it does not really exist and criticizes people for insincerity when in fact they are sincere. He says that, in the book, actors *come in for stick* (receive severe criticism) because of their *egos* (because they are selfish and arrogant) and that even when they are being *modest* (not saying how wonderful they are), Goldman thinks they are being insincere. The speaker is saying that this may not be fair.
A: The speaker says that Goldman's previous book contained *splenetic* (very angry) *observations* and this book clearly does too. In this book, Goldman's *principal grouch* (main complaint) is the same as in his previous book (that in the film industry, writers get blame, directors get credit and actors get awards – in other words, writers are unfairly treated). The speaker therefore does not say that the two

books differ in terms of Goldman's opinions – both seem to have the same opinions.
B: The speaker says that Goldman heavily criticizes actors and his references to directors in the index indicate that he heavily criticizes them too, but he does not say that Goldman's comments are confusing, they seem to be very clear. He lists the index references to illustrate how critical Goldman is of directors, not because those references are confusing.

6 **B:** The speaker says that Goldman allows the reader *glimpses* of (only short looks at) his own life and that through these he seems to be a *desk-bound adult in awe of men of action* (someone who spends his life sitting at a desk and feels enormous respect for people who do active things). The implication here is that Goldman feels his work is not admirable in comparison with what these *men of action do*.
A: The speaker doesn't indicate that Goldman finds his job difficult. For example, when he has to write about *pain* (suffering, unhappiness), he approaches that with confidence because it is relatively easy for him. The speaker also says that Goldman may like the pain that is involved in his business. He therefore does not say that Goldman describes his job as more difficult than it really is.
C: The speaker says that an example of the pain of Goldman's business is the *dismaying* (upsetting, discouraging) fact that nobody knows the name of the person who wrote a film, but he thinks that Goldman may like this and that he may enjoy suffering in his job without anyone knowing anything about him. The speaker is therefore saying that Goldman is, like all film writers, unknown to the general public, and he is not saying that he is more widely recognized than he thinks he is.

7 **A:** The speaker says that when he listened to the two records he mentions, he was *enthralled* (enormously interested and entertained) because they did not contain what were simply *arbitrary lists of places* (lists of places chosen for no particular reason), they were *celebrations of America* (expressions of what a wonderful place America was). They therefore communicated the idea that America was a marvellous place.
B: The first record – *Night Train* – was so successful that James Brown made another similar one, which also listed places in America – *Mashed Potatoes USA*. He describes him as *repeating the trick* (producing the same kind of success) with the second record. He is therefore saying that both records were successful but he does not say or imply that this was surprising.
C: The two records were similar to each other, in that they contained lists of the names of places, but the speaker does not say that they were completely different from other records James Brown made.

8 **B:** The speaker says that people growing up in Britain in the 1960s thought that America was *an object of romance* (a romantic place, in the sense that it appealed to the imagination and seemed wonderful) *forged in song* (this image was created by songs). It seemed like a place that should be celebrated. He says that even Americans themselves had this view of it, because for them their own country was *exotic* (attractive and special) and they were excited about living there. He says that they found it an exciting place and so did he when he was growing up in Britain in the 1960s.
A: He says that American songs *hinted at* (suggested) *a vastness* (an enormous place), *a variegated* (very varied) *landscape and a range of experiences* but he does not say that this impression they created was a false one or that it was inaccurate because it was not a complete picture of what America was really like. He does not compare the impression that people got of America through songs with the reality of the place.
C: He says that American songs *described a vista* (in this context, this means 'range') *of possibilities that found no equivalent in British music*, by which he means that the songs suggested that life had much more to offer than British songs did. He lists some of these things (prettier girls, bluer skies, etc), which American songs seemed to create images of and his point is that British songs did not communicate such images of happy lives. He is therefore saying that American songs suggested more images of life than British songs, but he is not saying that British music was more limited than American music – he is not comparing them in terms of the music itself, but in terms of the images suggested by the music.

p162 PAPER 4 PART TWO

One mark per question (Total: 9)

9 **meat importer:** We are told that his father was a *provision dealer* (someone who traded in food and drink) and that he was *a bookkeeper* (a kind of accountant) *and cashier* (person who deals with money received and money paid out) *for a meat importer* (someone who imported meat into the country employed him in these roles).

10 **Self(-)Help:** The book was about the problems inventors had to deal with before they became successful and was written by Samuel Smiles. These days, 'self-help' books are a category of book, in which people are told how to make their lives better, or how to do things themselves so that they do not need other people to do these things for them.

11 **submarine:** He read about someone who invented a *white glaze for earthenware* (surface for pottery) and who failed many times before succeeding with it. Hornby himself wanted to invent something that would *solve the problem of perpetual motion* (continuous movement of something unless it is stopped by an outside force), but he gave that up and started trying to invent a *submarine* (ship that can operate under the surface of water). The submarine he invented did go under the surface of the water on its own, as intended, and travel some distance under the water, also as intended, but *alas* (unfortunately), it did not *re-emerge* (come back up to the surface of the water), as was intended.

12 **interchangeable:** We are told that as Hornby obtained more and more tools, *his ideas turned to interchangeable parts* (he began to think about producing parts which could be exchanged with each other) and which would have *a variety of purposes*. This was the *germ* (the beginning of something, from which it develops) *of the Meccano system*. His idea was that, if the parts were interchangeable, a number of different things could be built using them.

13 **series of holes:** To achieve his aim with the parts, he realized that there would have to be *a standard method of fitting one part to any other part* (something common to all the parts that would make each one fit together with another). What *came to* him (the idea he had) was the *conception* (idea) of parts all *perforated with a series of holes* (with holes made in them) *of the same size and the same distance apart*.

14 **piece of copper:** The first parts he made were *strips* (long, narrow pieces) that he made from *a large piece of copper* (a reddish brown metal). He chose copper because it was soft and easy to work with.

15 **crane:** He worked out the measurements for the strips of metal and made all the other parts required for making different things with (nuts, bolts, angle brackets, axles and wheels) and then eventually he and his sons succeeded in

making a model of a *crane* (a machine with a long arm used for lifting and moving large, heavy objects), which was the first model made with the parts he had invented.

16 **Mechanics Made Easy:** His invention was *originally called Mechanics Made Easy* and marketed by Hornby and his employer operating under the name *Elliott and Hornby*. Later, in 1907, it was given the *trademark* (the registered name of a product) *Meccano* and made by a firm called *Meccano Ltd* (Limited – a word used after the names of private companies in Britain).

17 **E(e)xtension P(p)ack:** Different *Meccano* sets were produced and each set could be converted into *the next larger-sized set* (the set that was one size bigger in the series) *by means of* (by using) *an Extension Pack.*

p163 PAPER 4 PART THREE

One mark per question (Total: 5)

18 **C:** David says that visual planning usually involves putting a designer and a manufacturer together in order to create *an appropriate image for a product*. However, now that it is *the age* (period in history of something being widespread or popular) *of the focus group*, which involves *garnering* (collecting) opinions from small groups of people, *the process has been short-circuited* (a quicker and simpler process has replaced a longer and more complicated one). The process now involves members of the public designing products themselves, rather than designers and manufacturers doing it. During David's session, women were asked to do that and so the session was an example of this new kind of visual planning.
A: He says that the session lasted for three hours and that it was a *brainstorming session* (one in which the people taking part produce and discuss ideas), but he does not say that the sessions he conducts do not normally go on for as long as three hours.
B: He talks about what focus groups are and what they do and says that the use of them *is almost an industry in itself* (they are used so widely that the use of them has almost grown into a distinct and separate area of business), but he does not express his own views about them or compare his personal views on them with other people's views. What he says about them simply describes their function and he does not say that the session shows that he is right about them with regard to any beliefs he has.
D: He says that in the session, the women were asked to *unleash* (release, freely express) *their cleaning foibles* (personal weaknesses or unusual habits), *hates and woes* (things that cause unhappiness). These are all negative aspects and no positive aspects are mentioned.

19 **A:** David says that they filmed shoppers *dithering* (hesitating because of being unsure what to do or what to decide) in supermarkets over washing powders and then the focus group met. He had therefore seen that shoppers were unsure which washing powder to buy when they went shopping before the session took place.
B: He says that the *congested market* (a market in which there are a great many different goods available) *is failing to bloom* (prosper, flourish) *as healthily as manufacturers might wish* (it is not growing as much or being as profitable as they would like). His firm was employed to *arrest* (stop) *this crisis* (serious, problematic situation that requires action). What he is saying, therefore, is that manufacturers were very worried that sales were not increasing as much and that the market was not as profitable as they would like, but he does not say that sales were actually falling.
C: The problem for shoppers is that cleaning products are *a confusing mass* like a *many-headed monster* because they are *cluttered with scientific jargon* (full of technical terms) *and swathed in* (wrapped or enclosed in) *lurid* (brightly coloured but unattractive) *packaging*. As a result, they are often *unintelligible* (impossible to understand). What he knew from research before the session, therefore, was that people were confused by cleaning products, not that they found them dull or uninteresting to look at.
D: He says that people were confused by the *jargon* (technical terms) on cleaning products and couldn't understand it, not that they felt that what was stated on cleaning products was untrue.

20 **D:** David says that one woman told him that she spent *quite some time down that aisle* (quite a long time in the row in a shop in which cleaning products were displayed) and that then *I just grab what I know* (I simply pick up quickly a product I know). This means that after hesitating for a while, she then always buys a product she is familiar with, rather than one she has never bought before.
A: All of the comments he quotes are about difficulties experienced when deciding which product to buy or about aspects of cleaning products the women dislike, but none of the comments expresses the view that the speaker doesn't care which product she buys.
B: One woman says that she doesn't understand the difference between different types of cleaning products (*concentrated and non-concentrated* ones and *biological and non-biological* ones), but this is connected with what they contain and how they work, not with their appearance.
C: One woman says that the products *don't say clearly what they do* and another says that she doesn't want *all this science* (all the scientific terms used on cleaning products). These comments are about not understanding what is stated on products, and do not express a view that what is stated on them is stated with the intention of giving shoppers false information.

21 **A:** What they produced was a visual representation of *how they would want a cleaning product to make them feel* and so it was meant to represent their preferred emotional response to a product rather than a representation of what it did. Their *collages* (pictures made from putting different pieces of paper, cloth, etc together and sticking them on a surface, in this case a board) presented images of *homely comfort* rather than of *germ-busting explosions* – they showed peaceful images of comfortable, peaceful, pleasant homes rather than of products violently attacking dirt that is harmful to people.
B: David is not saying that there were contrasting images in their collages – the images all seem to have been similar and to have been consistent with each other. The colours were *soft* rather than bright, and the *fruit and flowers* were part of the overall image of *homely comfort*.
C: David says that the images they produced were *a dramatic shift from* (were very noticeably different from) *the way these goods are normally presented* and this may well have surprised him but he does not say that it surprised the women themselves or that they had expected to produce different images beforehand.
D: He says that what they produced was different from how cleaning products are normally presented but he does not say that this meant that the images they produced were similar to those involved in the presentation of other types of product.

22 **B:** David says that *the accepted belief* is that people's emotions are not involved much and that they *are on automatic pilot* (doing things that are routine without thinking about them at all, like a plane that is being flown by a computer rather than a person) when they buy cleaning products. He says that his company's research shows that this is not true and that he believes that shoppers' *emotional needs* need to be considered. He says that the session showed him that, *as I suspected* (as I

previously thought was the case), there needs to be *emotion* in the marketing of cleaning goods. He is therefore saying that he thought the *accepted belief* was probably not true and that he concluded from the session that he had been proved right about that.
A: He is not saying that his firm's methods will need to change, but that the methods of those manufacturing and marketing cleaning goods will have to change so that products appeal to people on an emotional level. He also thinks that what his firm discovered through research was proved right in the session, and so he clearly thinks his firm's methods are right as they are.
C: He is saying that there is a general pattern to the buying of cleaning products – people currently do not enjoy buying them, 73% of decisions about which product to buy are made when the customer is actually in the shop rather than before they go there – and that people in general want to feel more involved emotionally when it comes to buying these products. In addition, he does not say that cleaning products differ from other kinds of product or are an exception to what happens with other products – in fact, he implies that people would like them to be more like other products.
D: He says that there is *an opportunity for genuine innovation here*, by which he means that in the work he is doing on cleaning products it is possible that some truly original ideas will result, but he is not saying that these ideas will be required because his beliefs about cleaning products before the session were not absolutely right – he is saying that the method he is using might lead to changes in the way cleaning products are created and marketed. In addition, he says that he already knew from his company's research that the *accepted belief* was wrong, so he didn't learn that he was wrong to share that belief; he didn't share it before the session.

p164–166 PAPER 4 PART FOUR

FURTHER PRACTICE AND GUIDANCE (p165–166)

For explanations, see the explanations to the questions in the test, which follow.

Question 23:	K – a, b, c, f	G – b, d, e, f
Question 24:	K – b, d, e, f	G – a, c
Question 25:	K – b, d	G – a, b, c, d, e, f
Question 26:	K – a, d	G – b, c, d, e, f
Question 27:	K – b, d, f	G – a, c, d, e
Question 28:	K – b, d, e	G – a, c, f

p164 PAPER 4 PART FOUR (TEST)

Note: the letters in brackets refer to the relevant options in the questions in the Further Practice and Guidance pages.

One mark per question (Total: 6)

23 **B:** Graham says that when he joined the police force, he was *amazed* to find that he wasn't *humiliated* (made to feel extremely embarrassed or stupid), *given a hard time* (treated severely or aggressively) or *belittled* (made to feel totally unimportant) by the senior officers, which is what he had expected. On the contrary, he felt *pride* and his *confidence* increased, because taking orders from the officers made him feel that he was *part of a very disciplined team*. He liked this feeling and instead of being *resentful* (angry about unfair treatment), he felt better about himself as an individual. Whereas before that, *left to my own devices* (left alone and not told what to do), he didn't have enough *self-discipline* to *make the most of* (get the maximum advantage from) his abilities, in the *framework* (structure, system) provided by the police force, he felt that he was capable of *shining* (being very good at something). **(b, d, e)**
Karen says that she can understand how what Graham has described is possible. She says that she can understand that for Graham, having to take orders from people in authority all the time was *for your own good* (of benefit to you). She therefore expresses the view that, for some people, having to obey authority all the time can make them feel that they benefit as an individual in some way. **(b)**
Previously, Karen has said that she has always *instinctively* (automatically and not as a result of careful thought) seen authority as *repressive* (controlling people by force against their will and not allowing them freedom). She says that she isn't sure why she has had this negative attitude towards authority but she has had it ever since she was a small child. Graham says that he *used to be like that* (he used to have the same, negative attitude towards authority) but he discovered that this attitude was a *blinkered* (narrow-minded, wrong because of not paying attention to different aspects of something) one and he no longer has it. **(a, c, f)**

24 **K:** Karen says that she now thinks that being a rebel all the time is *taking the easy way out* (making the easy choice, behaving in the way that requires the least effort and involves the fewest problems – the phrase is used to indicate disapproval) and completely *self-centred* (selfish). She now has a *sneaking regard* (a secret, concealed respect) for people who are *in charge* and *have to make decisions* and *take the flak* (receive the criticism that is made of people in their position). She says that it's easy to *stand by and slag off* (to do nothing yourself and criticize severely) people in authority and she disapproves of this. Her attitude has changed because she herself has been in charge of things; she used to *avoid responsibility like the plague* (avoid it because it is extremely unattractive), but now she has been *on the other side of the fence* (in the opposite situation – she means she has been in authority rather than being someone who criticizes authority as she previously used to). Being in authority herself has therefore made her change her attitude towards it and she now understands that it is harder to be in authority than to criticize people who are. **(b, d, e, f)**
Graham says that a *black and white* (seeing something as being entirely one thing or another rather than a mixture of things) attitude to authority as a whole is *childish* (the kind of simple attitude a child might have but an adult should not). He believes that authority is a *necessary fact of life* and that there has to be authority organizing things and making decisions if things are going to *get done*. Since this is true, he thinks that it is *daft* (silly, ridiculous) to regard authority as either completely good or completely bad – it is simply a fact of life and neither totally good nor totally bad as a concept. He does not say that it is easier to be against authority than to be in a position of authority – his point is that it is wrong to be either completely for it or completely against it. **(a, c)**

25 **B:** Karen says that some people do *see it that way* (do regard authority as being either entirely good or entirely bad), and because of this they feel that they either have to *conform* (do what they are told to do or what is expected of them by authority figures) or *rebel* (oppose authority and refuse to do as you are told) all the time. Her point is that such people's attitude towards authority forces them to behave in a certain fixed way. **(b, d)**
Graham says that some people have jobs which require them to conform – they are forced to behave in a certain way at work. However, in his view, there is a *middle course* (an attitude or behaviour that is moderate rather than

extreme) *between the two extremes* (of conforming all the time or rebelling all the time) and people whose jobs require them to conform should allow their *rebellious side* to *come out* (be revealed or expressed) when they are *off duty* (not at work). When he says *myself included,* he means that he is an example of someone who has the right balance between the two extremes because he is required to conform at work but can be rebellious in some way outside work. When he says *Sure* at the beginning of his speech, he is agreeing with Karen that some people feel that they have to either conform or rebel all the time. **(a, b, c, d, e, f)**

26 G: Karen says that *some people don't have that balance* between rebelling and conforming and that they *stick to* (never change from) their normal way of behaving. She says that such people may *secretly wish* to behave differently sometimes. She therefore does refer to extreme behaviour but she does not say that this causes problems for other people. **(a, d)**
Graham agrees that there are people like this and says that people should *express both sides openly* (openly conform sometimes and openly rebel sometimes) – this is *the best thing* in his view and he thinks that people who can do that have the right attitude. He says that if people can't do that, they either rebel all the time and get into trouble, possibly *serious trouble* (presumably by this he means for example because they break the law), or they are the complete opposite and are too *rigid* (strict and unwilling to change ideas or behaviour), *obsessed with petty rules* (too concerned that other people obey small, unimportant rules) *and totally intransigent* (stubborn, unwilling to cooperate with others or listen to other points of view). His view is therefore that people whose extreme behaviour is in the form of rebelling cause problems for themselves and that the opposite kind of extreme behaviour causes problems for other people. **(b, c, d, e, f)**

27 G: Karen says that it's *tricky* (difficult) to be able to continue *treading the path between conformity and rebelliousness* (making sure that you keep balancing the two extremes). She then says that something else *occurs to* her (another thought suddenly comes into her mind as a result of the previous thought she had) and this is that if you learn how to balance the two extremes as a child, you become a better authority figure when you are given authority. She is therefore saying that some people find it easier to balance the two extremes than others and that as a result some people are better at being authority figures than others, but she does not talk about the influence that others may have on them when they are in authority. **(b, d, f)**
When Graham says *For sure,* he is agreeing with Karen's final point in her previous speech – that people who could balance the two extremes as children make better authority figures. He then says that good authority figures use *consultation* – they ask for and pay attention to the views of those affected, including people *below them* (that they have authority over) – before they make decisions, but that after doing that, they take the decision, explain it and then *absolutely stick to it* (not change it at all) and *carry it out firmly* (put it into practice in a strong way, without allowing others to prevent that from happening) *whatever anyone says subsequently* (even if people later say they disagree with the decision). He is therefore saying that once a decision has been made, someone in authority should not be influenced by other people, although they should be before the decision is made. **(a, c, d, e)**

28 K: Karen says that she has *found* (discovered, realized) from her experience of being in charge of exhibitions and other things that if people were allowed to *air* (express) their opinions and believed that the person in authority had *taken those opinions on board* (paid attention to them, been influenced by them), they would *go along with* (accept, cooperate with) decisions they in fact disagreed with. She says that by behaving in this way, she was *'selling'* her decisions to others (persuading them to accept them), despite the fact that they disagreed with them at first. **(b, d, e)**
Graham says that people in authority who do not act in this way are *no good* as authority figures. He says that people who are not good in authority make *sudden, random* (not following any logical system or pattern), *ill thought-out* (not considered properly or carefully enough) *decisions.* He says that they only pretend to consult others but are in fact *autocratic* (they expect to be obeyed all the time and are not interested in what other people think of their actions). For them, consulting others involves only talking to people who they know will agree with them because they don't want the *bother* (trouble, complication) that results from people having different opinions. They regard anyone who disagrees with them as *a threat* (someone who can cause them problems by challenging their authority) or a *'trouble-maker'* (someone who wants to complain and cause arguments because they enjoy doing so). He is therefore saying that people who are not good authority figures do not try to persuade people who disagree with them, they don't ask them for their views and they regard them with suspicion. **(a, c, f)**

PAPER 4:

PART ONE	8 marks
PART TWO	9 marks
PART THREE	5 marks
PART FOUR	6 marks
TOTAL	28 marks

To be converted into a score out of 40 marks.

p167–170 PAPER 5

FURTHER PRACTICE AND GUIDANCE (p169–170)

DESCRIBING PERSONALITY

KIND/PLEASANT
considerate: kind and thoughtful, taking care not to upset others and doing things that are helpful to others
compassionate: feeling sympathy for the suffering of others and wishing to help them
warm: friendly and pleasant
indulgent: allowing someone to have whatever they want
genial: friendly and cheerful, not at all frightening
lenient: tolerant towards someone who has done something wrong and not punishing them severely, when others might do so
tactful: careful in what you say or do so as not to upset anyone
affable: friendly, easy to talk to
mild-mannered: gentle and kind
courteous: polite, having good manners
decent: pleasant and honest
generous: kind in your treatment of others and happy to give them things

FEELING SUPERIOR
pompous: speaking or acting in a way that shows you feel you are very important and much more important than others
arrogant: too self-confident, in a way which others dislike
patronizing: speaking in a way that indicates that you consider yourself superior to those you are talking to and that you consider them stupid
conceited: too self-satisfied, happy in the belief that you are wonderful, in a way that others dislike
smug: too pleased with yourself and too happy in the belief that your own situation is better than other people's, in a way that is disliked

big-headed: having too high an opinion of yourself
snobbish: considering yourself socially superior to others
aloof: unfriendly towards others and not wishing to have a close relationship with them because of considering yourself superior to them
stuck-up: behaving towards others as if you are superior in a way that annoys them
supercilious: showing the attitude that you think you are better than others by being rather rude to them
condescending: treating others in a way that indicates that you think you are superior to them and that you are doing them a favour by dealing with them at all

UNKIND/UNPLEASANT
mean: unkind or unpleasant in what you say or in being unwilling to give things to or share things with people
ruthless: cruel and totally unsympathetic to others because you want to achieve something and do not care who suffers as long as you achieve it
vindictive: doing things in order to get revenge on others or because you want to cause someone you dislike to suffer
spiteful: saying or doing things that are deliberately intended to cause suffering to someone you dislike intensely
petulant: having a tendency to become angry suddenly because something is not the way that you want it to be, with the result that others suffer
ignorant: rude and bad-mannerd
moody: tending to change moods constantly, so that you suddenly become angry or unhappy when previously you were not, in a way that others find it difficult to deal with
narrow-minded: not tolerant of others or willing to listen to or consider their views, when these differ from yours
surly: unfriendly, unpleasant and rude, especially in the way you deal with others

DETERMINED
single-minded: determined to achieve something in particular and concentrating on that entirely, in a way that others admire
tenacious: not giving up an aim or changing a belief, despite difficulty or opposition
resolute: very determined, especially when this involves having courage
obstinate: refusing to change your mind or be influenced by other views, despite attempts to persuade you to do so, in a way that others disapprove of
intransigent: completely certain that you are right and unwilling to listen to opposing views, even if these are reasonable
persistent: refusing to give up, despite failure or opposition
pushy: openly determined to get what you want by persuading others to do things for you, in a way that is disliked
pig-headed: refusing to change your opinion, even though it appears quite possible that you are wrong
tireless: continuing in your efforts to achieve something you are determined to achieve, even though this requires an enormous amount of effort and energy
assertive: showing that you are determined to be listened to or taken seriously, rather than keeping quiet and allowing others to dominate
strong-willed: determined to get what you want and making every effort to get it

DISHONEST
crafty: clever in using deceitful ways to get what you want, rather than doing things openly
cunning: clever at deceiving and tricking people, in a way that is disapproved of
hypocritical: criticizing others for moral reasons while being guilty of the same things yourself
two-faced: deceiving others by pretending to like them when dealing with them but then saying bad things about them to others
scheming: making secret plans to get what you want because other people would disapprove if they knew what you were doing
calculating: clever at planning and doing things that are to your advantage, without other people realizing what you are really doing
devious: being deceitful and dishonest in order to get what you want by indirect means

TOPIC VOCABULARY

TABLE 1

FASHIONS/FASHIONABLE	*UNFASHIONABLE*
in fashion	out of fashion
a craze	dated
a fad	outmoded
all the rage	old hat
in vogue	obsolete
trendy	behind the times
contemporary	antiquated
trendsetting	outdated

TABLE 2

the young/youth
a youth
a youngster
youthful
childish
immature
immaturity
juvenile
infantile
adolescent
adolescence
a kid
a lad
a yob
a lout
a hooligan

grow up
grown up
a grown up
mature
maturity
getting on
middle aged
over the hill
past it
in your dotage
ancient
senile
senior citizen
old age
an old age pensioner
elderly
the elderly

p167–168 PAPER 5

Marks out of 40 are given for performance in the speaking paper.

LISTENING SCRIPTS

TEST 1 PART ONE

You will hear four different extracts. For questions 1–8, choose the answer (A, B or C) which fits best according to what you hear. There are two questions for each extract.

Extract One

WOMAN: Malcolm Gladwell, in his book *The Tipping Point*, has produced a wonderfully off-beat study of that little-understood phenomenon, the social epidemic. His book is organized around the notion of the 'tipping point', the moment when, to put it bluntly, a thing takes off and becomes widespread in a particular society. For fax machines, it happened in 1987; for mobile phones, 1998. Ideas have their tipping points too. The point is that social epidemics usually take us by surprise.

Gladwell makes sense of them by anatomizing them, showing how the spread of ideas or behaviour depends on types whom he christens 'connectors' and 'mavens'. Connectors jump-start the epidemic by virtue of the number of people they know – the book provides a test that allows the reader to work out whether they qualify. Mavens are specialists who possess the power of recommendation. Summarized like this, Gladwell's dissection sounds a bit crude. In fact, *The Tipping Point* is a very subtle piece of work, coming out with ideas – not necessarily his own – that make conventional solutions to social problems seem criminally naive.

Extract Two

MAN: Why am I up here? 400 feet up the side of this crag, wearing a pair of close-fitting, technicolour climbing-trousers. Only another 80 feet to the top. Only? What am I trying to prove? Why is a man who feels dizzy near the edges of sea cliffs and sweats with fear at the top of towers, why exactly is he spending this warm afternoon, the day after his 46th birthday, dangling over a void attached to a long piece of purple-pink string? There is no answer to such fatuous metaphysical questions. Not when your climbing partner has just disappeared from view, for the first time, somewhere far above your head.

This is it, the proverbial moment. Out on my own. Just me, my vertigo and a pair of borrowed rock boots, which are slightly too small, and a great wrinkled slab of ancient geology and a palpitating, sweat-soaked, miraculously heightened sense of existence. I wouldn't be anywhere else. This is also the moment I realize, with a keen pang of guilt, that I completely forgot to check the small print in my life insurance where it states excluded risks. You know, the awesomely dangerous pursuits that men in their 40s are so often drawn to, such as sponsored bungee-jumping and white-water rafting.

Extract Three

WOMAN: Technology changes rapidly: people change slowly. But what will happen when the technology is small enough to be implanted within the body, perhaps directly connected to the brain: will technology supplement the mind? The basic needs of people are fixed by biology: the fundamentals have been with us for thousands of years and are unlikely to change within the next century. These include the necessity for food and shelter, for social relationships, for family bonding, education, sports and entertainment. Cognitive prostheses – as we might call these implants – must build on top of the existing biological substrata.

Consider one type of potential prosthesis: for memory. I once wrote an essay entitled *The Teddy* in which I predicted the development of a toy teddy bear that was given to a child at birth, a bear that could record the child's innermost thoughts, and aid in its development. As the child grew older, the teddy was replaced with more suitable devices – but preserving all the information, eventually being implanted in the brain, the better to allow the person to record all that has ever happened, all that was ever thought. Is this possible? Yes. Is it desirable? Not clear. Our fallible memories are blessings, for if we remembered too much, we would have trouble recalling the important items from amongst the trivia.

Extract Four

FEMALE INTERVIEWER: Writers rarely admit it, William, but they are in quite a comfortable position when they appear as speakers at events at literary festivals, aren't they? They can read from their work, work already done, needing no more than a light dusting on the train to be in shape for the event. Questions asked on the back of such a sampling are gentle and entirely on the author's terms. Or they can branch out, talk about something which will have some interest because of the writer's own proven involvement with that subject. Questions can be tougher here but writers are used to questions. They ask them of themselves every couple of sentences.

WILLIAM: Yes, but the main thing is that it's almost invariably a pleasure to meet readers. A writing life is solitary and mute, and often near to that of a depressive in its conditions. I cannot believe there is a writer who has not at times felt that his or her confidence has dropped open underneath like a trapdoor and suddenly there is nothing to build on and they're left dangling there. Meeting those whose equally solitary experience completes the act begun in hope of contact is a relief and an encouragement, as well as a pleasure.

TEST 1 PART TWO

You will hear someone called Karen Williams talking about her career. For questions 9–17, complete the sentences with a word or short phrase.

KAREN WILLIAMS: I left school with an ambition to work in hotels as a manager in England or maybe abroad. My local college offered a two-year Diploma in Hotel Administration and Tourism. The course involved three periods of work experience as well as modules covering hotel front office, restaurant, housekeeping, business studies and languages.

My first work experience was in the housekeeping department of a hotel. It was hard work and I was only there for two weeks. I learnt all about cleaning rooms, what equipment to use, changing beds and, more importantly, about life in a hotel. For the last two days I worked with the floor housekeeper, planning rotas and checking rooms. The second placement was for four months. I went to work in Germany. Although I had studied the language at college, my language skills improved dramatically. Most of the time I worked in the restaurant and housekeeping. The final work experience of five weeks was in the front office of a hotel, where I learnt all about the switchboard, reservations, porter's desk and cashiers.

I decided to carry on studying and do a Higher National Diploma, or HND, in Hospitality Management. During the summer months between one course and another I worked in a restaurant kitchen. I'd never worked in a kitchen before and it was interesting to see how one worked. Although I decided that I didn't want to be a chef, the experience of seeing what goes on was invaluable.

The two-year HND was very interesting. Some students had come straight from school, some from hotel and catering courses and some had got into the course as a result of their age and experience. We studied a range of subjects, including business studies, hotel management, human resource management and operational techniques. There were also some optional subjects and I took conference and leisure facility management, advanced business and languages. The work experience was very useful, and I had to write a detailed report on 'green issues' in hotels. That was probably the thing I found most difficult on the course, although it certainly gave me a different perspective on things. It was interesting – for example, I reviewed give-aways such as soaps and shampoos as part of the report. I became a student member of the HCIMA, the Hotel and Catering International Management Association, when I started the course and I was able to request information from them. Their magazines often have articles of interest that students can use for assignments. My other source of information was *Caterer and Hotelkeeper*, the weekly magazine.

The college was associated with a university, and so after I completed the HND, I was able to go straight onto the third year of a degree in Hotel and Restaurant Management. I completed that course fairly recently and I've just started work as a junior assistant manager at a London hotel. I love the work there, although sometimes the duty management shifts are a bit of a killer. Usually the hotel is overbooked when I am on duty and so I often end up as the one who has to book out guests. We use a nearby hotel of the same standard and provide transport but it is understandable when a guest gets very irate, arriving after a long journey. My aim is to stay here to gain experience before I move on. Possibilities include hotels within the group or maybe abroad, where I can use my languages. One day I'd like to be a General Manager.

TEST 1 PART THREE

You will hear an interview with someone who consulted a life coach to improve her life. For questions 18–22, choose the answer (A, B, C or D) which fits best according to what you hear.

INTERVIEWER: My next guest is Brigid McConville, a journalist who decided to get herself a life coach. Brigid, what made you do it and what is a life coach?

BRIGID: Well, all was not entirely well with my life. Nothing drastic, I just felt 'stuck' and in need of change, both on the work front – too much to do, too little time – and at home – ditto. I wasn't miserable enough for therapy or counselling. I simply wanted to get a little more from life. Until recently, the options for someone in my situation would have been extremely limited. Now, however, legions of life coaches are out there, ready and waiting to come to the aid of the frustrated and down-at-heart. For about £40 a session, your personal coach will telephone you once a week, and spend half an hour talking to you in an effort to help you sort your life out.

INTERVIEWER: But isn't this just another self-improvement fad? Like all the self-help books and tapes?

BRIGID: Well, I was a bit dubious myself, but I decided to try it. I booked a course with Fiona Harrold, a leading British coach. She identified my anxieties almost immediately. Within half an hour of our first conversation, I found myself agreeing that the first thing I had to tackle was my deeply ambivalent relationship with money. Yes, of course it was rooted in childhood – but what could we actually do about it? Fiona is a passionate advocate of self-belief and with her characteristic verve, she told me I had to carve out a whole new way of thinking about myself. I must see myself as 'a magnet for money', she said. And she told me: 'Consider yourself someone to whom cash flows effortlessly. Why shouldn't you have an easy life, an abundance of pleasure, leisure and luxury – and all without feeling any guilt?'

INTERVIEWER: How did you react to that?

BRIGID: Well, it seemed such a preposterous idea that I laughed out loud down the telephone. But, undeterred by my scepticism, Fiona told me to suspend my disbelief, and gave me a clutch of positive affirmations with which to brainwash myself into readiness for riches. She told me to repeat the following words whenever possible: 'I, Brigid, am now ready to have the ideal life that I deserve.' Doing this, I found, cheered me up no end.

INTERVIEWER: What else did she tell you?

BRIGID: Well, subsequent sessions were more practical. First came the mandatory de-cluttering – she told me to throw out as much unnecessary jumble and rubbish as possible, clearing space for all the goodies to come – once the money started to roll in. Then we began trying to cure my personal finance phobia; I dutifully did my sums, and started saving something, however small, every month. My work also came under close scrutiny, too, as I made up my mind to concentrate on jobs that really interested me. Exactly which issues you tackle during coaching is up to you. According to Fiona, most people want to get organized at home and at work, make the most of their abilities and sort out money problems. She reckons that building up confidence is vital. She really does believe that people are capable of doing anything they want to do, and that all that stands in their way is childhood conditioning.

INTERVIEWER: So what did you get out of it all? And would you recommend it?

BRIGID: Well, coaching makes you get on and do all those things you've put off for so long, because there is the deadline of the next session. If you don't act in time, your coach probably won't want to speak to you. So coaching is hardly a soft option. But for me, it has provided a great boost. There have been no instant miracles, but things are looking up at work and financially, money and I are definitely on better terms. I still have my doubts about the 'me first' approach but, then again, it is a healthy counterbalance to the 'me last' way of thinking I'm used to.

INTERVIEWER: Thanks, Brigid. Now, if you want to find out more about life coaches you can contact this address ...

TEST 1 PART FOUR

You will hear two shop managers, David and Katherine, talking about their jobs. For questions 23–28, decide whether the opinions are expressed by only one of the speakers, or whether the speakers agree. Write D for David, K for Katherine, or B for Both, where they agree.

DAVID: I must say, Katherine, I get a kick out of making the best profit I can. I'm always competing with myself to beat last season's figures. When I'm deciding on the stock range, I have to make sure it's balanced to suit the customers. The customer profile keeps changing – styles, size scales and preferred colours vary constantly – which gives an added dimension to the task.

KATHERINE: Mmm ... I think that knowing what will sell is very instinctive. I have to be prepared to commit myself and take risks. I thrive on the pressure – no two days are the same and I'm always so busy that it's a kind of permanent 'high'. You have to put your whole self into this job – there are no half measures – I love it!

DAVID: There's a lot of responsibility, isn't there? Unless I have a specific job to do, I normally spend most of the day on the shop floor, serving customers, making sure everyone gets a break at the proper time, and generally seeing that everything runs smoothly.

KATHERINE: The way I see it, I'm responsible for the staff, the security of the shop and everything in it. It's my job to make sure that we sell all we possibly can, while keeping the running costs of the place to a minimum. What I don't like is losing staff, especially if I have to terminate their employment. Among other things, it means I was wrong about them.

DAVID: Yeah, but it's all about people, isn't it? I wouldn't have gone into retailing if I didn't enjoy meeting people and feeling good every time a customer decides to buy. And I want success too. The success of my shop depends to some extent on knowing what the customers want. And it also depends on an ability to keep overheads to a minimum, which means tight security, careful checks on all deliveries and invoices, and keeping an accurate record of the movement of goods in and out of the shop.

KATHERINE: I think my success is down to the quality of my team and I'm keen on helping in their development. I recommend individuals for management training courses and follow their progress on those courses and I conduct training on the sales floor when trade is slack.

DAVID: I love the problem-solving aspect, too. A good day for me is when I have a whole lot of problems facing me first thing – for instance, someone hasn't come in, someone else is on holiday or ill, some equipment has broken down, and the electricians are coming to install a new display – and, by the end of the day, I've sorted my way through all the difficulties.

KATHERINE: Mmm, it can get quite hectic, can't it? When the shop is very full and the shelves are emptying fast, you have to make quick decisions about deploying staff. You can't hang around for ten minutes wondering what to do next. And you mustn't let your staff see you falter or hesitate – you must give them immediate answers.

DAVID: I initially thought the staff might find me unapproachable. But luckily, I seem to have a rapport with all my staff, and they tend to come to me with their problems instead of getting resentful or suffering in silence.

KATHERINE: I like that side of things. I suppose I could have made a career behind the scenes, at head office, but I'm interested in the people and the personnel management side of retailing.

DAVID: I find that if you're open with your staff, they will bring you their problems, which often affect how they're working. You find out what areas they like best, try to move them around and encourage them to look beyond what they think are their immediate abilities.

KATHERINE: And then, of course, there are the customers with problems. Most customers simply want help, and some are almost embarrassingly grateful when they get it. A few seem to come into the shop just to complain, and all you can do is stand there and take what they say while they get it out of their systems. They don't really want explanations.

DAVID: Sometimes at the end of a frantic week when you've been working 12 or 14 hours at a stretch, you think about your friends who work from 9am to 5pm. But then you realize that you wouldn't be happy doing their sort of job.

KATHERINE: I know what you mean.

TEST 2 PART ONE

You will hear four different extracts. For questions 1–8, choose the answer (A, B or C) which fits best according to what you hear. There are two questions for each extract.

Extract One

MAN: Standard strategies for negotiation often leave people dissatisfied, worn out, or alienated – and frequently all three. People find themselves in a dilemma. They see two ways to negotiate – soft or hard. Soft negotiators want to avoid personal conflict and so make concessions readily in order to reach agreement. They want an amicable resolution, yet they often end up exploited and feeling bitter. Hard negotiators see any situation as a contest of wills in which the side that takes the more extreme positions and holds out longer fares better. They want to win, yet often end up producing an equally hard response which exhausts them and their resources and harms their relationship with the other side.

There is a third way to negotiate, a way neither hard nor soft, but rather both hard *and* soft. The method of 'principled negotiation' is to decide issues on their merits rather than through a haggling process focused on what each side says it will and won't do. It suggests that you look for mutual gains wherever possible, and that where your interests conflict, you should insist that the result be based on some fair standards independent of the will of either side. The method of 'principled negotiation' employs no tricks and no posturing. It shows you how to obtain what you are entitled to and still be decent.

Extract Two

FEMALE REPORTER: Walking into Roly Curtis's clay-processing shed is to rewind to the Industrial Revolution of the early 19th century. An apparition covered in drying clay dust silences the trundling cog wheels and whirring fan belts to greet you in the gloom. Letting in some light, the burly 56-year-old Roly opens the low wooden swing door at the rear of the red-brick building. The tracks of an old narrow-gauge railway slope away into a meadow thick with hawthorn, primroses and teasels. Like his father and grandfather before him, Curtis winches load after load of hand-dug clay from an open cast pit 400 yards away to supply his pottery. I asked him about the history of the pottery.

ROLY: It was started in 1831. At first, the company was making simple horticultural containers, such as plant pots. It also made domestic ware: baking bowls glazed in cream on the inside with a brown ring around the top, bread crocks, milk jugs and cream 'settling' pans. But the business began to decline. With the advent of the plastic bowl in the late 1950s – a death blow to potteries countrywide – my father, by then nearing retirement, survived by laying off his remaining four staff and by producing more unusual pots. I worked as an industrial chemist until the lure of the clay proved too strong. I was in my early 30s when I took over here and I've been working alone ever since, making mainly horticultural ware.

Extract Three

WOMAN: If people have one dominant image of the great silent comedian Harold Lloyd, it is probably of a bespectacled figure either dangling from a clock, many storeys above the streets of Los Angeles, in 1923's *Safety Last*, or else clutching girders, in the same town, at similar altitude, as in *Never Weaken*, 1921.

He made his screen debut as an extra in 1912, and the following year he met another extra, Hal Roach. The pair created Lonesome Luke, an aggressive figure who, in the year 1916–17, proved a moderate hit. As Lloyd later put it, 'I was quite successful, but not really good.' This changed in 1917, however, when either Lloyd or Roach – history is divided – hit on the idea of making the former don horn-rimmed specs, and reject stylization in favour of normality. Far more than Charlie Chaplin, or even his other chief rival Buster Keaton, Lloyd was now someone with whom audiences could readily identify. For the next ten years, Lloyd could do no wrong. Audiences flocked to see his character save the day through his combination of lateral thinking and preternatural physical prowess. But the double onslaught of cinematic sound and the Depression of the 1930s proved fatal to Lloyd's career. His first talkie, *Welcome Danger* (1929), was a hit, but it was to be his last: he was instinctively a visual performer, and his indomitable optimism was now incongruous.

Extract Four

MAN: We are all living in the past: the idea of 'now' is an illusion. The discovery, reported by a team of scientists, has the bizarre consequence that your brain is collecting information about the future of an event before it puts together what it thinks it saw at the time of the event. Our brains seem to work in a similar way to the slightly delayed broadcast of live TV shows to provide an opportunity for fast editing changes. The delay with which our brains process visual information has now been measured by scientists, providing new insights into how we use vision to make sense of the world.

Human perception of the outside world seems to be delayed by a minimum of 80 thousandths of a second. This is comparative to live television, which can be broadcast after a delay of about three seconds to allow for editing. 'What you think you're seeing at any given moment is actually influenced by events in the near future,' the scientists say in their report. They used a technique called 'the flash-lag phenomenon', which acts as a visual illusion to the brain. They discovered that human brains seem to develop conscious awareness in an 'after-the-fact fashion', analysing information from both before and after an event before committing to a decision about what happened.

TEST 2 PART TWO

You will hear part of a radio programme, in which the history of Ty-Phoo Tipps, a brand of tea that is well-known in Britain, is described. For questions 9–17, complete the sentences with a word or short phrase.

PRESENTER: In 1820, 24-year-old William Sumner took over an old family grocery and druggist's shop at the top of the Bull Ring in Birmingham. Ten years later, William also had a shop in nearby Coleshill and, in 1835, he is listed as a Grocer and Tea Dealer in the *National Commercial Directory*. All the tea sold at that time came from China.

William brought his elder son, John, into the business in 1845. By 1852, William Sumner and Son were listed as tea and coffee dealers, but it would be many years before they could concentrate solely on tea. William later gave the business to his two sons, but in 1863 they decided to go their separate ways and John took premises at 98 High Street, Birmingham.

In Ceylon (now Sri Lanka) a serious disease affected the coffee industry and tea became a prime crop. By 1875, tea from there was being exported to Britain and this was to be important to the Sumners. John Sumner's son, also called John, joined the business and, due to the construction of a railway tunnel, they had to move to 25 and 26 High Street, Birmingham. At the turn of the 20th century, father and son had a flourishing business which now included wines and spirits, as well as groceries. They had six travellers and twenty horses and a range of vans – life was good.

For a long time, Mary, young John's sister, had suffered from indigestion. One day someone sent her a packet of tea which was different from that sold in the family business. Its particles were very small and, whereas large-leaf teas tended to aggravate her problem, this one promised a cure. She decided to try it and to her delight, found that it gave her great relief; she then offered the 'remedy' to other people who suffered from indigestion and they too benefited. Mary told her brother enthusiastically about the tea and asked why Sumner did not sell it. This was the starting point of a great adventure, although when John told a friend, a wholesale tea merchant, of his intention to buy 30 chests of the tea, he said that the public would not buy tea which looked little better than dust. Nevertheless, John went ahead with his purchase, but instead of selling it loose over the counter, he decided to put it in packets and sell it under a brand name.

John set himself three criteria in choosing the name: it must be distinctive and unlike others; it must be one which tripped off the tongue; and it must be one which could be protected by registration. Finally, he came up with the name *Ty-Phoo Tipps* – it had an oriental sound, was alliterative with tea, and whilst the name *Tipps* could not be registered, *Ty-Phoo* could and was. The double 'p' in *Tipps* first occurred as a printer's error, but John decided to stick with this spelling.

The first cardboard packets were filled by girls using scoops, who then weighed them before glueing and sealing them. In the first week of production in 1903, they packed 577 pounds of *Ty-Phoo Tipps*. To encourage customers to buy his new brand, John offered each purchaser of one pound of *Ty-Phoo Tipps* a generous jar of cream. Soon many customers were drinking the new tea. They discovered that, although it was slightly more expensive, it was more economical and its beneficial digestive qualities gave it great appeal. Other traders also wanted to buy the new brand and John founded a wholesale agency. He took a shop in Corporation Street, Birmingham's most important shopping street, and had a row of girls standing inside the window, packing tea for passers-by to see, whilst inside the shop, tea was served with cream and biscuits.

In 1905, John went to Ceylon and brought back 200 chests of tea, mainly the small-leafed variety known as 'fannings'. He drew attention to the fact that his tea came from the edge of the leaf and did not contain the tannin from the fibrous stalk; he also claimed that the leaf-edge tea could produce 80 more cups per pound of tea than the large-leaf tea. From 1906, John Sumner was having his own special *Ty-Phoo* teapots made for sale, and during that year he introduced picture cards, similar to cigarette cards, and inserted them in the packets of tea.

In 1932, John Sumner received a knighthood in recognition of his charitable work. When he died in 1934, each of his 346 employees benefited under his will.

TEST 2 PART THREE

You will hear an interview with someone whose family spent a year living without television. For questions 18–22, choose the answer (A, B, C or D) which fits best according to what you hear.

INTERVIEWER: Miranda Ingram and her family were avid TV watchers until the day when they found themselves without a television. Miranda, how did that come about?

MIRANDA: I would love to be able to say that this was because I flung the set through the sitting room window or sold it, but the truth is that circumstances deprived us. We moved to the middle of nowhere, surrounded by mountains, to an ancient cottage, which had never had a TV point. Unbelievably, perhaps, in the 21st century, our options for getting plugged in were remarkably sparse. We could have spent a fortune laying cables to the nearest village and joining their communal aerial, which sent fuzzy pictures every time it rained – and we're talking Wales here, so rain is not a rare occurrence. And any time strong winds or stray animals knocked it out of kilter, the entire system went down for days. Or we could have got satellite television, but when a satellite technician arrived, he looked round at our mountains and saw not breathtaking natural beauty but obstacles. So neither option seemed worth the trouble.

INTERVIEWER: So, what was it like to be a family without a television?

MIRANDA: Well, we trained ourselves not to look at the TV listings so we wouldn't sigh over what we were missing and started to revel in our moral superiority. 'Did you watch ... ?' people would begin, and we would watch their jaws drop as they wondered what on earth we did, half way up a mountain with two small children and no television. At the risk of sounding unbearably smug, we did indeed read more books, listen to more music, and play more board games. And we sat outside and watched the sun set or merely had an early night. Most significant, however, was simply discovering the untold long, pleasant and potentially fulfilling hours there are in an evening.

INTERVIEWER: Surely, there must have been some downside?

MIRANDA: At times, I must admit, we did feel like cultural oddities. Television enters the language and we didn't know what people meant when they compared someone to an apparently well-known character or when they used what was presumably a catchphrase from a popular programme. And my husband and I are confirmed news junkies, so we really missed the television when it came to big news events. There are certain stories where television pictures tell more than any amount of radio and newsprint. But like any mild addiction, after an initial withdrawal, before long you hardly give it a second thought.

INTERVIEWER: So why, since you were evidently enjoying life without television, did you get connected again?

MIRANDA: Mmm, you may well ask. Well, it was my husband who persevered with the satellite option. Not, I'm convinced, because he missed the broadcasts so much. More because he missed playing with the remote control in the way that men love to. Anyway, I went along with it because I'm certainly not one of those anti-TV types that believes the box to be the source of all modern evil: there are lots of interesting and rewarding programmes for both adults and children, and television is a perfectly good ingredient of a well-rounded life. But its insidiousness lies in its being an easy option – like a ready meal – which seduces you into forgetting the rewards that come from putting a bit more into life. So I must say that when the day arrived for our connection, I was apprehensive, terrified that this thing in the corner would dominate our lives.

INTERVIEWER: So how have things turned out? Are you and the children TV addicts again?

MIRANDA: Well, amazingly, now we have our TV back, the children can take it or leave it. Inadvertently, it seems our year's abstinence must have coincided with their habit-forming years, so it's a habit they don't have. Occasionally they slump, but often they'll switch on for ten minutes before announcing it's 'boring' and rushing off to do something else. I even find myself proposing half an hour's viewing as an activity, but if they suspect it's because I want to sneak off and do something without them, they are very unlikely to agree. We do watch television again, of course we do, but it is no more than an option among others. We even watch rubbish from time to time, but now it's because it's been one of those days when deciding to vegetate is a deliberate choice, not just a habit.

INTERVIEWER: That's interesting. Thanks, Miranda. After the break, we'll be discussing the subject of television and its impact on our lives with ...

TEST 2 PART FOUR

You will hear two people who work together writing scripts for television comedy series, Sara and Vic, talking about collaborating as writers. For questions 23–28, decide whether the opinions are expressed by only one of the speakers, or whether the speakers agree. Write S for Sara, V for Vic, or B for Both, where they agree.

INTERVIEWER: Now, was collaboration a difficult process for you initially? Sara?

SARA: It was fun at first! Then things started to get more and more serious. No, I don't think it was hard at first. Actually, the longer you're in the business the more you tend to believe strongly in your own ideas, which can make the art of compromise a little more difficult at times.

VIC: Because at first you're not sure of yourself, you really *need* somebody. You want their opinion more frequently. As time goes by, you're more at ease, more likely to rely on your own judgement.

INTERVIEWER: What do you see as the advantages of working as a team?

SARA: You get a chance to bounce ideas off each other, and that can be so important, especially in comedy. Sometimes what you think is funny is not at all funny to somebody else, and you kind of need to hear that. You *really* need to hear that, as a matter of fact!

VIC: Sometimes you'd like to take a chance on something, and you may feel it's a little far out. But if you can get someone else's opinion, you can either go ahead with the idea with a bit more confidence, or you can decide the idea won't work and you don't try it at all.

INTERVIEWER: What special qualities do you feel each of you bring to the team?

SARA: We're a lot alike, but I think Vic is more logical. I tend to go too far sometimes, and he'll be there to say, 'Pull back,' and sometimes I need that. But I think back to when we first started, and what was true then is true now: he's a very good story person. He puts things together very well, structures a story so it makes sense. I love dialogue, I just love to talk! But of course you have to have both.

VIC: I feel stronger in story and structure. Sara's great at dialogue, and also at coming up with some really unique ideas.

INTERVIEWER: What do you find to be the disadvantages of being a scriptwriter?

SARA: You can't be married to your work. You'll never get anything done if you are.

VIC: But that's true with any kind of writing, I think. I write plays on my own, and I really value the 'reading' process, where I'm given feedback from other people. Some playwrights get very hurt by criticism, feeling their work is their baby, but they have to accept criticism. Television gets you *very* accustomed to criticism. Rewrites and compromise are a way of life.

INTERVIEWER: What advice do you have for someone who is looking for a writing partner?

SARA: Take the time to really get to know the person before making any commitment. I've seen teams involved in pitched battles, and ...

VIC: Of course, we've seen teams at each other's throats and yet they are still the best of friends ...

SARA: But I would take some time, maybe just try a script or two on a trial basis, see how well it goes. The most important thing is that each member be willing to compromise. If they can't do that, the partnership just won't work.

INTERVIEWER: Do you ever hit times where you feel that one member of the team might be slowing things down, perhaps not pitching in enough?

SARA: I think it all evens out. There might be occasions when I'm having a real hard time, slowing down the process, and there might be times when Vic's having a rough period. It all balances out, and the other person simply pitches in a little more and helps out.

VIC: Or one of us might go out of town, and the other has to finish the outline. It's no big deal, it's just part of being a team. You have to trust each other.

TEST 3 PART ONE

You will hear four different extracts. For questions 1–8, choose the answer (A, B or C) which fits best according to what you hear. There are two questions for each extract.

Extract One

MAN: Pessimism is deeply ingrained in the British psyche. Pessimism is the natural British condition. There's nothing we relish so much as some bad news. Pessimists never expect their holiday plans to run to schedule. When the plane is delayed at the airport, they sigh: 'I *knew* this would happen.' When their bags go missing, they accept the loss with stoicism, reasoning: 'It had to be me.' Our administrators are forever being pressed to disclose their 'contingency plans' and 'Plan B'. Plan A is never expected to succeed.

This national trait starts in childhood with the Christopher Robin stories. Eeyore, the pessimistic donkey who is always certain his tail will fall off, appeals immediately to the young British reader. He connects with our melancholy, phlegmatic side. Irony, on which so much distinctive British humour is based, has pessimism as its prime ingredient. It thinks the worst.

Extract Two

WOMAN: Brian J. Ford, a microbiologist, is the author of a new book, *The Future of Food*, which attempts to present an accurate and balanced picture of how our diet will shape up in the years to come. He predicts that in future food will be selected because of its power to boost the brain, or to delay the onset of senility. We will choose food to enable us to relish life to the fullest extent. Slimming diets, regimes of prescription and proscription, Ford foretells, will give way to a more positive approach that emphasizes the pleasures and health benefits of good food.

Ford reckons that, in general, today's junk food will disappear, as nutrient-rich innovations bring us a diet high in vitamins, minerals and health-giving supplements. Snack foods such as crisps, described as 'puffed-up particles of industrial starch, so rich in salt they could harm a child', will not, he foretells, be with us in their present form two decades hence. He says that we will look back on them as we look back on adulterated foods from a century ago, when flour was expanded with liberal additions of sawdust, lead oxide and powdered chalk.

Extract Three

MAN: 'Don't put your daughter on the stage, Mrs Worthington,' sang Noel Coward. It was a heartfelt plea, but one that's gone unheeded, then and now, by generations of pushy mothers desperate to promote daughters of dubious talent. But an even pushier breed of pushy parents has emerged, spurred on by hopes of fame and fortune for their children, and it's fathers, not mothers, who are at the vanguard. Only now it's floodlights not footlights, trophies not tutus, they are chasing. Admittedly, the odds on vicarious sporting glory may be long, but when the nation reads about the enormous sums paid to the top footballers, tennis players and racing drivers, today's dads are willing to take their chances. A child's sporting success is no longer about the glow of winning; it can lead to an entirely new, and lucrative, economic future.

It may be natural for proud parents to want their offspring to do well, but the line between committed support and potentially damaging obsession is mighty fine. There are, of course, plenty of benefits to having active kids, but when children are coerced into becoming mini-adults – professionals in all but name – sport can become too serious a pastime. Depending on the sport, it can also be very expensive.

Extract Four

MAN: Thomas Edison, the doyen of inventors, said it first: 'No sooner does a fellow succeed in making a good thing, than some other fellows pop up and tell you they did it years ago.' His rueful observation reflects a fact that anyone who has a good idea will run into soon enough: that creativity is such a precious commodity that when even a tiny bit of it appears, people instantly want to lay claim to it. For most of recorded history, having a bright idea was no protection against being ripped off by the unscrupulous. It's not a whole lot better now, but there is something that, in theory at least, makes sure that the credit and the money for the invention go where they are due: patents.

The earliest-known English patent was granted to John of Utynam, a Flemish stained-glass maker in 1449. John received the same privilege as those granted an English patent do to this day: a 20-year monopoly to exploit the fruits of his ingenuity. In return, he was required to teach his process to native Englishmen. That, too, is still part of the philosophy behind the modern patent: that it doesn't just encourage innovation, but also the spread of that innovation. Inventors don't actually have to hold classes to teach everyone else how to make what they've invented, but they do have to disclose how to do it. And what trouble that has caused ever since. For by revealing exactly what you have done and how, you're putting your intellectual jewels right where other people can get them. Not only that, but by stating what is new about your invention, you are revealing your likely marketing strategy.

TEST 3 PART TWO

You will hear a radio report about interactive science and technology centres in Britain. For questions 9–17, complete the sentences with a word or short phrase.

REPORTER: 'It's more interesting than I expected, I shall come here again,' said nine-year-old James Stimson, who'd been enjoying himself at the National Stone Centre in Derbyshire on the day when I went there. He had just seen the fossilized remains of a brachiopod, a prehistoric sea animal that predated the dinosaurs by 120 million years; one of a series of fossils found in a rock face in what, 330 million years ago, was part of the coast of Derbyshire – then comprising tropical lagoons and small islands. The area was part of a huge upland which, from medieval times, has been mined for lead and limestone and now hosts school parties and other groups.

The centre has been created from six worked-out stone quarries. One fascinating fact that visitors to it learn is that we each consume six to seven tonnes of stone a year. James couldn't believe his eyes when he read this on a display board inside the centre's Discovery Building. 'What, we eat stone?' he asked. Well, not exactly. What the display shows is that we use stone in everything from paint to computers to ceiling tiles. 90% of the stone we use is in construction, in everything from tunnels to tennis courts. But stone is also used in plastics, so you will find it in cars, ships and planes. And as it is also used in producing sugar, flour, pharmaceuticals and poultry feed, we all eat a certain amount of stone.

James and some friends in his party moved on to attempt panning 'gems' from mineral fragments; others followed the site's history, ecology and geography trails. I spoke to James' headmaster, Michael Halls of Turnditch Primary School near Derby, who was accompanying the group. He told me that the National Stone Centre is a splendid teaching resource. It helps teachers to teach children all sorts of skills, from observation and looking behind the obvious to hands-on activities, such as dry-stone wall building and making plaster casts of fossils. He told me that it also helps children to appreciate what a changing world we live in. Furthermore, many of the activities there fit perfectly into the National Curriculum, although for the children it's more like an exciting outing than a lesson.

That sums up the philosophy of Britain's 25 or so interactive science and technology centres built on the foundation of Launch Pad, the first interactive gallery at the Science Museum in South Kensington, London, which was opened in 1985. I visited another example. On the site of three disused dry docks in Tiger Bay, Cardiff, Wales, a £7 million temple to science and technology called Techniquest has been built. It houses 160 exhibits and science 'interactives' – experiments which people of all ages can try out for themselves. The complex incorporates a 35-seat planetarium, a 100-seater science theatre, a science shop, workshop and galleries. The success of Techniquest has been based on experiments involving liquids that you can cut, bubbles you can walk inside and structures that roll uphill, and a philosophy against the 'don't touch' exhibits of traditional museums. The centre started from the premise that it wanted to change people's attitudes towards science and technology and the idea is that people of all ages have to use all their senses to discover the fun of finding out about science and technology.

At Techniquest you're as likely to see a granny as an eight-year-old swivelling around, under discreet supervision, in a specially adapted dentist's chair to experience the pull of centrifugal force, or people making odd sounds down a 50-foot-long steel tube to observe how sound waves can clash and distort one another. The favourite exhibition is Puff the Pneumatic Dragon, a huge steel creation in Welsh green and red, whose tongue, wings and claws respond instantly to the fingertip controls of visitors. Puff's 'arteries', the hydraulic tubes and electronic circuits that make him respond, are laid out for all to see. It may not be a formal lesson in control systems, but you cannot fail to learn.

And that is true of all the interactive science and technology centres throughout the country.

TEST 3 PART THREE

You will hear an interview with someone who reviews hotels. For questions 18–22, choose the answer (A, B, C or D) which fits best according to what you hear.

INTERVIEWER: I'm talking to Paddy Burt, who has a weekly hotel review column in a national newspaper and who has just compiled a collection of those reviews for a forthcoming book. Paddy, when you go to a hotel to review it, what's your attitude?

PADDY: I always have high hopes – a 'bet this one's going to be good' feeling. But you never can tell. Hotels that look so idyllic in one of the guides can be a terrible letdown, which is why readers who say they enjoy the column invariably add 'particularly the bad ones'. For example, I recently got this letter from a reader, who says: 'It used to be every other week that you gave some poor hotelier a bashing. Now it's a rare treat to read about one you've been severely critical of, and that's a pity since I love it when you lay into a pretentious but bad one. Of course, it's helpful when you recommend a good hotel, but, for entertainment's sake, do try to find some awful ones, too.'

INTERVIEWER: So are you always aiming to find fault? Are you glad when you find something you can be critical of?

PADDY: I don't have to try. And while I'm always happy to slam into any pretentious hotel that doesn't come up to scratch, it's a different matter when the people are nice and their hotel isn't. I still have to write about it and sometimes it hurts. Hotelkeeping, it has been said, is akin to show business and, in the ones I like best, there is always a leading man or woman who is sometimes so good I think he or she has missed their true vocation. Such hoteliers usually have a sense of humour. They may not like what I have written about them, but will respond in a good-humoured way. They are professionals. Many of them have become friends.

INTERVIEWER: What kind of hotels do you prefer? Is it possible to generalize about that?

PADDY: Well, I admit I have a penchant for owner-run hotels; they're more personal than the chains. With a few exceptions, I like the owners of small hotels. Which is why I've had such fun researching my book of review pieces that have appeared in the newspaper – calling them if they haven't responded to the questionnaire I sent them and either telling them who I am or, if I think they're going to shout at me, pretending to be the assistant I haven't got, Emily. 'She didn't give us a very good review, did she?' some said. Well, no – but maybe they have since made improvements and would like people to know about them? Thus encouraged, the majority of these hoteliers have entered not just into the book but into the spirit and have contributed interesting behind-the-scenes stories.

INTERVIEWER: So some of the hotels you reviewed and wanted to put in the book haven't been included?

PADDY: That's right. There's one, for example, where the owner said – I recorded all the calls – 'After insulting us and lying in her article, there is no way we would help her perpetuate her grievances against the world in a publication.' To specify the lies, he pounced on a remark I had made expressing surprise on being served certain vegetables in his restaurant. 'She doesn't understand proper food,' he said. I was enthusiastic about it actually and, if he wasn't so disagreeable, I would have liked to include his hotel in the book. On and on he went. 'Since her visit, we've noticed that a lot of people read her articles and then cross hotels off their potential list as a result of what she's said. They then go to hotels where she's been fawned over and where they probably won't be fawned over. We've also noticed she prefers staying in hotels that are almost empty because that's when they have time to make a fuss of her.' Actually, being fawned over is the last thing that I want.

INTERVIEWER: So your column can provoke quite a reaction, then?

PADDY: Oh, yes. In fact, the same owner also said, 'After she stayed here, we had four hotels asking for her description. They wanted to know what car she was driving and what credit card she had. Unfortunately, we couldn't give a description because she's fairly nondescript.' But the peculiar thing is that when it finally clicked that being in the book wasn't going to cost him a penny, he said he wanted to be included. Maybe it was because he remembered that I had remarked on his resemblance to a much-loved comedian, sadly now dead. I declined his kind offer.

INTERVIEWER: I can see why. Paddy Burt, thanks for talking to me.

TEST 3 PART FOUR

You will hear two friends, Helen and Tony, discussing various aspects of modern technology in everyday life. For questions 23–28, decide whether the opinions are expressed by only one of the speakers, or whether the speakers agree. Write H for Helen, T for Tony, or B for Both, where they agree.

HELEN: I was on the train the other day and all these people were answering their mobiles and fiddling about with their text messages and, well, I was just reading the paper, and I kind of felt sorry for them. They looked like they'd sooner be doing what I was doing, they looked so harassed.

TONY: Yeah, but it's vital for some people that their offices or members of their family can always get in touch with them, isn't it? I mean, if there's an emergency at home or something like that, and no-one can get hold of them …

HELEN: I know, but there are limits …

TONY: Which is exactly why I turn the thing off sometimes. E-mails can be just as bad.

HELEN: I know. Do you get loads of e-mails at work?

TONY: Yeah, I spend a big chunk of my morning ploughing through them all.

HELEN: Me too. I get really snowed under with them, some of them are really detailed, and half the time they're from people in the next room or even at the next desk. It seems daft. Why don't they just come and talk to me?

TONY: Well, yeah, that would save time sometimes. I get the feeling some people just dash off e-mails to me the moment something comes up. It's passing the buck really. They can do it instead of working things out for themselves. And they're all full of question marks and half-thoughts.

HELEN: Mmm. I was thinking the other day about how things don't get done 'properly' any more. I was watching some group on TV. Nobody seems to play a real instrument in pop music these days, do they? It's all done on computers, they're not real musicians.

TONY: Yeah, there's an 'anyone can do it' culture these days.

HELEN: I know, but if anyone can do it, as long as they've got the technology, regardless of whether they know anything about music or not, no wonder it's all such rubbish these days.

TONY: Well, you might think that. Still, there's a lot of good stuff around, and technology is being used in lots of other ways which are very positive.

HELEN: Yeah, sport on TV, that's something that's making use of it really well. You know, you can press a button on your handset, if you've got the service, and you can follow one particular player around in a football match.

TONY: And there are cameras everywhere, and replays from all angles, and some of the referee's decisions now go to people watching TV replays to make decisions for the referee.

HELEN: I don't mind all that. I think it all adds to the excitement.

TONY: It seems daft to me. Holds the game up all the time.

HELEN: Some of these things, though, you get the feeling that they're just there because some whizzkid came up with it.

TONY: You mean it was invented because it could be invented, not because anyone actually wants it?

HELEN: Nicely put. I mean, there are things I can do on my computer, apparently, that I wouldn't want to do in a million years.

TONY: Yeah, but how typical are you? There are people out there who always want to be up to speed with these things.

HELEN: Sure, but don't you think that in a few years' time a lot of this stuff will be seen as just gimmicky things that have had their day?

TONY: There'll be things that don't last, I guess.

HELEN: We'll look back on some of it and laugh one day. 'Did they really invent that?' we'll say. What for?

TONY: Some of these things will be on one of those 'silly ideas of the past' programmes, no doubt, but the vast majority are here to stay.

HELEN: We'll see.

TEST 4 PART ONE

You will hear four different extracts. For questions 1–8, choose the answer (A, B or C) which fits best according to what you hear. There are two questions for each extract.

Extract One

WOMAN: Most people would admit that they would like to be more confident, more at ease with themselves. So what *is* this elusive thing we call confidence? We all have an idea what we mean when we talk about it. One dictionary describes confidence as 'boldness', but that somehow doesn't seem to be quite right. It isn't boldness we are seeking. Self-assurance seems to be more like it. We want to be able to handle or be comfortable in any situation.

Confidence has a lot to do with our relationships with other people. We don't want to feel inferior to anyone. We don't want to be bullied by anyone. We want to be able to walk into any roomful of people and feel that we *are* just as good as any of them – and know that we *are* just as good as any of them. Perhaps this is all very obvious. Of course we all want these things. Yet wanting and having it is very different. And if not all of us have confidence, if we haven't been born with an abundance of it, we must set about obtaining more.

Extract Two

MAN: Political cartoons are not so much rapier thrusts – which they are often called – as missiles which carry at least three explosive warheads. First, caricature – the humorously, or sometimes maliciously, distorted representation of politicians; second, actual political comment, criticism or stance communicated in the drawing; and third, the vehicle or image chosen to convey the political point. When brought together, the effect can be formidable. The apparent joke can contain a reverberating, subversive power.

The politician at whom the missile is aimed may find the joke less amusing than others – though many are flattered by the attention, and ask for the original. We all have an image of ourselves that we try to maintain, and we work quite hard to get other people to believe in it too. Caricaturists work even harder against this effort. Good caricature has the power to reduce dignity, and therefore authority, and it can be disturbing to see oneself caricatured. In its simplicity, caricature does not allow for fine degrees of criticism. It has an awful bluntness. It cannot dilute its message to say, for example: 'You are behaving like a fool'. It says more succinctly: 'You idiot!' It strikes at the most vulnerable and private side of its targets.

Extract Three

WOMAN: William Goldman, winner of two Oscars for his screenplays, is also widely known for *Adventures in the Screen Trade*, his splenetic observations on the movie business. His latest book, *Which Lie Did I Tell?*, covers his professional heartaches since the last book. Goldman's attitude to Hollywood and his principal grouch remain the same: the screenwriter takes the rap, the director takes the credit, the stars take the awards. Actors' egos come in for stick, and even when they are being modest, Goldman's insincerity detector is working away, perhaps too industriously. For an idea of Goldman's view on directors, you have only to refer to the index, where under 'directors' there are entries for 'fear of', 'as lacking vision', 'media attention to' and 'as screwing things up'.

I would have liked more about Goldman's real, as opposed to film, life. With the glimpses he allows – a lonely child weeping inconsolably on a visit to the theatre, a desk-bound adult in awe of men of action – he suggests that he nurtures his insecurities as a resource. 'I think I have a way with pain,' he writes. 'When I come to that kind of sequence I have a certain confidence ...'. Perhaps he really likes the pain of the business, even the dismaying fact that no one knows who writes the movies. He can suffer anonymously in a trade in which his words might belong in anyone's mouth.

Extract Four

MAN: At the height of his powers in the 1960s, James Brown, the 'Godfather of Soul', styled himself the hardest-working man in show business. Brown, it was claimed, worked 364 days a year, criss-crossing America from gig to gig by bus and train. On a number called *Night Train*, Brown played the role of conductor, shouting out the stops along the way: Miami, Florida; Atlanta, Georgia; Raleigh, North Carolina; Washington, DC, 'oh, and Richmond, Virginia, too'. The song was so successful that he followed it with *Mashed Potatoes USA*, repeating the trick with a new set of names – New York City, Boston, Buffalo, 'going straight down the road, gonna stop at Cleveland, Ohio ...'. Listening to these songs as a teenager, I was enthralled. More than just arbitrary lists of places, they were celebrations of America.

For anyone growing up in Britain in the 1960s, America was an object of romance forged in song, a place where the girls were prettier, the skies bluer, the cars bigger, the action harder and faster and more intoxicating. These songs described a vista of possibilities that found no equivalent in British music. They hinted at a vastness, a variegated landscape and a range of experiences that demanded to be celebrated. Even to the Americans, it seemed, America was exotic. They believed its own mythology, they got excited about just being there; and if they were excited by it, how could I fail to be so?

TEST 4 PART TWO

You will hear part of a radio programme about toys, in which the development of a famous toy called Meccano is described. For questions 9–17, complete the sentences with a word or short phrase.

PRESENTER: Frank Hornby, creator of *Meccano*, was born in Liverpool in 1863. He was one of the seven children of provision dealer John Hornby and his wife, Martha. He married Clare Godfroy in 1887 and they had three children, two boys and a girl. Although Frank worked as a bookkeeper and cashier for a meat importer, and became chief managing clerk, he spent much of his spare time inventing things, a hobby stemming from childhood.

One of the books Frank had been given when a young boy, *Self-Help*, by Samuel Smiles, told the stories of famous inventors, and outlined the difficulties they faced before they reached success. It had a lasting influence on him. The story that fascinated him most was of Plaissy, who invented a white glaze for earthenware, but had many failures on the way. Deciding to be an inventor was one thing; how to set about it was another. He thought he might develop a machine to solve the problem of perpetual motion. Through experiments and study of the principles of mechanics, he learned many skills, but had to abandon the project and turn to other ideas, such as a submarine which, when placed on the water, submerged itself, was propelled for some distance under water, but then, alas, failed to re-emerge. He lacked adequate tools in his small workshop, but was never discouraged.

As he gradually accumulated more tools, his ideas turned to interchangeable parts which could be used for a variety of purposes – here was the germ of the *Meccano* system. After he and his wife Clara had boys of their own, he delighted in making mechanical toys for them. One Christmas Eve, during a long train journey, he thought of his workshop and the problem he had in getting small parts for a crane they were constructing. Later he wrote, 'I felt that what was required were parts that could be applied in different ways to many different models, and that could be adjusted to give a variety of movements by alteration of position, etc. In order to do this it was necessary to devise some standard method of fitting one part to any other part; gradually there came to me the conception of parts all perforated with a series of holes of the same size and at the same distance apart. Such parts, I realized, could be bolted up to a model in different positions and at different angles, and having done their work in one model could be unbolted and applied to another.'

Gradually his ideas clarified, but little did he think that they would change the rest of his life, and result in a hobby that would give hours of pleasure to boys of all ages, in all parts of the world. Enthusiastically, he started to put his ideas into practice, first making strips from a large piece of copper, which was soft and easy to work. He decided that all the strips would be half an inch wide, with equal-sized holes along the centre at half-inch intervals. At first he made a strip two-and-a-half inches long, then a five-and-a-half inch strip and so on, up to twelve-and-a-half inches, which seemed to him an enormous part. The measurements have never been changed since. Similarly, he had to make his own nuts and bolts, and his own angle brackets, axles and wheels – it was a long job, but it was a great day for Frank and his boys when they assembled their first *Meccano* crane. He was so sure his system was good that he consulted a patent agent and obtained an English patent on 9th January 1901; foreign patents followed.

His invention was originally called *Mechanics Made Easy* and was marketed by Hornby and his employer, D. H. Elliott, trading as Elliott & Hornby. The trademark *Meccano* was registered in 1907 and Elliott & Hornby was sold to Meccano Ltd in 1908, Hornby becoming a director. In 1914, Meccano Ltd moved to a purpose-built factory in Liverpool, the company's home until 1979. Over the years, different *Meccano* sets were introduced, each set converting by means of an Extension Pack into the next larger-sized set. Eventually, there were over 300 individual *Meccano* parts.

Hornby Clockwork trains arrived in 1920, electric ones in 1925. Other products followed, including speedboats, aeroplane and car constructor outfits and Dinky Toys, which were launched in 1933. When he died in September 1936, aged 73, Frank Hornby was a millionaire.

TEST 4 PART THREE

You will hear an interview with someone whose work is concerned with the design and marketing of products. For questions 18–22, choose the answer (A, B, C or D) which fits best according to what you hear.

INTERVIEWER: Welcome to the world of visual planning. I'm in the offices of a London design firm, where design consultant David Muir has just finished conducting a session with a group of women on the subject of cleaning products. David, tell me exactly what it is that you've been doing.

DAVID: Yes, well, visual planning usually unites a designer with a manufacturer to construct an appropriate image for a product. But in the age of the focus group, when garnering opinions from members of the public at sessions with small groups is almost an industry in itself, the process has been short-circuited. Today, shoppers are being asked to design the perfect product themselves. In the three-hour brainstorming session I've just done, a dozen housewives and working mothers were asked to unleash their cleaning foibles, hates and woes, and possibly change the way such products are packaged and sold.

INTERVIEWER: Is there anything about cleaning products that poses particular problems when it comes to selling them?

DAVID: Research has exposed the world of soaps, bleaches and powders to be a confusing mass, a 'many-headed monster', so cluttered with scientific jargon and swathed in lurid packaging as to be often unintelligible. Despite enormous annual advertising budgets, the congested market is failing to bloom as healthily as manufacturers might wish. To arrest the crisis, my firm has been called in. Firstly, we filmed shoppers dithering in supermarkets over washing powders. Stage two was the focus group I've just run.

INTERVIEWER: Tell me about what kind of things you did in this session.

DAVID: Well, for example, at the back of the room, scores of products were on display. The women were asked to put them into groups – what we call a 'brand-mapping' exercise – and select any favourites. Many of the brands elicited complaints that they are ugly and confusing. I noted comments like: 'The products don't say clearly what they do', and 'I don't want all this science', and 'I spend quite some time down that aisle. Then I just grab what I know', and 'I don't understand the difference between concentrated and non-concentrated products. Or biological and non-biological.'

INTERVIEWER: So, having got their views, what was the next step?

DAVID. Then I asked them to imagine how they would want a cleaning product to make them feel. I split the women into three groups and got them to tear up magazines and fabric samples, forming giant collages on boards to represent the colours, textures and images of their ideal cleaning goods. And the finished boards – a mass of soft lilacs and mauves, fruit and flowers and images of homely comfort – represented a dramatic shift from the way these goods are normally presented. There are no 'germ-busting' explosions.

INTERVIEWER: So, what have you concluded?

DAVID: I've concluded that, as I suspected, the missing ingredient when it comes to the marketing of cleaning goods is emotion. Research already shows that it is not an enjoyable sector for shoppers. The accepted belief is that when people buy detergents, there is a low emotional involvement, that they are on automatic pilot. But our research shows they want to have more fun, they want products to be about their lifestyle. It is my belief that the visual dimension is vital. Research shows that 73% of purchase decisions are made in the store. But no one is really considering the consumer's emotional needs. That's why in this session, I asked them to express what they feel in a visual sense and create three perfect brands. There's an opportunity for genuine innovation here, to respond to consumers' emotional side. People don't want all this industrial language any more. What we're doing here is extremely radical.

INTERVIEWER: So, a successful session then?

DAVID: Very much so.

INTERVIEWER: OK, now I'd like to move on to another aspect of your work. When it comes to talking to people ...

TEST 4 PART FOUR

You will hear an artist, Karen, and a police officer, Graham, talking about attitudes towards authority. For questions 23–28, decide whether the opinions are expressed by only one of the speakers, or whether the speakers agree. Write K for Karen, G for Graham, or B for Both, where they agree.

KAREN: Graham, I've always, sort of instinctively, seen authority as something repressive. I'm not sure why, I've always been that way, ever since I was a little kid, although I guess I'm changing a bit as I get older.

GRAHAM: I used to be like that but I discovered I'd been very blinkered about authority. When I was a new recruit in the police force, I was expecting to be humiliated by senior officers, and given a hard time – you know, belittled. But I was amazed at the effect that taking orders had on me. Instead of getting resentful, I began to develop a sense of pride in being part of a very disciplined team, all working together. It increased my confidence immeasurably.

KAREN: So you felt that in a sense having authority imposed on you all the time was for your own good. I can see how that might be the case.

GRAHAM: Mmm, left to my own devices I lacked the self-discipline to make the most of what abilities I had to offer, but in that framework I felt more capable of shining.

KAREN: I haven't been in that position of course, but I have noticed a slight shift in my perceptions of what 'authority' means to me over the past couple of years. I guess that's because I've been in positions where I've had to take on certain responsibilities – in the past I used to avoid responsibility like the plague. So now I've been on the other side of the fence and it seems to me that people who are always rebelling against authority are taking the easy way out and being totally self-centred. It's easy to stand by and slag off the people in charge. It's given me a sneaking regard for people who have to make decisions and then take the flak for them.

GRAHAM: Well, in my view, any black and white attitude to 'authority' in general is pretty childish. There has to be some sort of authority if anything's ever going to get done. There has to be some organizing, some decision-making, for anything to happen. So authority is a necessary fact of life and it's daft to see it as a wholly good or wholly bad thing.

KAREN: But some people do see it that way, don't they, and it makes them feel that they have to conform the whole time or rebel the whole time.

GRAHAM: Sure, but of course there's such a thing as a middle course between the two extremes. I mean, there are people – myself included – who are in jobs where they have to conform, but the other side, the rebellious side, can come out when they're off duty, which I think is highly desirable.

KAREN: Mmm, but some people don't have that balance, do they, they're always one thing or the other. Even if they'd secretly like to rebel sometimes, or conform sometimes, they stick to their normal way.

GRAHAM: True, but the best thing is if people can express both sides openly, being conformist when it's necessary and not so conformist at other times. If they can't do that, you get people who are always rebelling and therefore getting into trouble, serious trouble even, or the complete opposite – people who are too rigid, obsessed with petty rules and totally intransigent.

KAREN: It's quite tricky, isn't it? I mean, this business of making sure you keep treading the path between conformity and rebelliousness. But something else occurs to me, presumably if you learn how to do this early in life, as a kid, you make a much better authority figure if you get to a point where you have authority yourself.

GRAHAM: For sure. With people I would categorize as good authority figures, there's a process of consultation before decisions are taken. They gather together all the points of view of the people affected and they pay attention to the opinions of the people below them. And then they make their decision, explaining precisely why they've taken it. After that, they absolutely stick to it and carry it out firmly, whatever anyone says subsequently.

KAREN: I've found, when I've been in charge of exhibitions and things like that, I could get people to go along with what I wanted even if they actually disagreed with it, as long as they felt that they'd had a chance to air their opinions and I'd taken those opinions on board. So to some degree, I was 'selling' them my decision. But a lot of people in authority don't do that, do they?

GRAHAM: No, and such people are no good as authority figures. What they do is, they make sudden, random, ill thought-out decisions, just to remind people they're in charge. And they're autocratic, even if they pretend that they consult others. What they actually do is only talk to people they know will agree with them, they don't want the bother of dealing with differences of opinion. And anyone who does disagree with them, they see as a threat and dismiss as a 'trouble-maker'.

UNIVERSITY of CAMBRIDGE
Local Examinations Syndicate

Candidate Name
If not already printed, write name in CAPITALS and complete the Candidate No. grid (in pencil).

Candidate Signature

Examination Title

Centre

Supervisor:
If the candidate is ABSENT or has WITHDRAWN shade here

Centre No.

Candidate No.

Examination Details

Candidate Answer Sheet CPE Paper 1 Reading

SAMPLE

Instructions

Use a PENCIL (B or HB). Mark ONE letter only for each question.

For example, if you think B is the right answer, mark your answer sheet like this:

0	A	B	C	D

Rub out any answer you wish to change using an eraser.

Part 1

1	A	B	C	D
2	A	B	C	D
3	A	B	C	D
4	A	B	C	D
5	A	B	C	D
6	A	B	C	D
7	A	B	C	D
8	A	B	C	D
9	A	B	C	D
10	A	B	C	D
11	A	B	C	D
12	A	B	C	D
13	A	B	C	D
14	A	B	C	D
15	A	B	C	D
16	A	B	C	D
17	A	B	C	D
18	A	B	C	D

Part 2

19	A	B	C	D
20	A	B	C	D
21	A	B	C	D
22	A	B	C	D
23	A	B	C	D
24	A	B	C	D
25	A	B	C	D
26	A	B	C	D

Part 3

27	A	B	C	D	E	F	G	H
28	A	B	C	D	E	F	G	H
29	A	B	C	D	E	F	G	H
30	A	B	C	D	E	F	G	H
31	A	B	C	D	E	F	G	H
32	A	B	C	D	E	F	G	H
33	A	B	C	D	E	F	G	H

Part 4

34	A	B	C	D
35	A	B	C	D
36	A	B	C	D
37	A	B	C	D
38	A	B	C	D
39	A	B	C	D
40	A	B	C	D

CPE 1 DP479/346

UNIVERSITY of CAMBRIDGE
Local Examinations Syndicate

Candidate Name
If not already printed, write name in CAPITALS and complete the Candidate No. grid (in pencil).

Candidate Signature

Examination Title

Centre

Supervisor:
If the candidate is ABSENT or has WITHDRAWN shade here

Centre No.

Candidate No.

Examination Details

Candidate Answer Sheet CPE Paper 4 Listening

Mark test version (in PENCIL) A B C Special arrangements S H

Instructions

Use a PENCIL (B or HB)

Rub out any answer you wish to change using an eraser.

For Parts 1 and 3:
Mark ONE letter only for each question.
For example, if you think B is the right answer, mark your answer sheet like this:

0	A	B	C

For Part 2:
Write your answer clearly in the space like this:

0 example

For Part 4:
Write ONE letter only, like this:

0 A

Part 1

1	A	B	C
2	A	B	C
3	A	B	C
4	A	B	C
5	A	B	C
6	A	B	C
7	A	B	C
8	A	B	C

Part 2

		Do not write here
9		1 9 0
10		1 10 0
11		1 11 0
12		1 12 0
13		1 13 0
14		1 14 0
15		1 15 0
16		1 16 0
17		1 17 0

Part 3

18	A	B	C	D
19	A	B	C	D
20	A	B	C	D
21	A	B	C	D
22	A	B	C	D

Part 4

		Do not write here
23		1 23 0
24		1 24 0
25		1 25 0
26		1 26 0
27		1 27 0
28		1 28 0

CPE 4 DP440/349

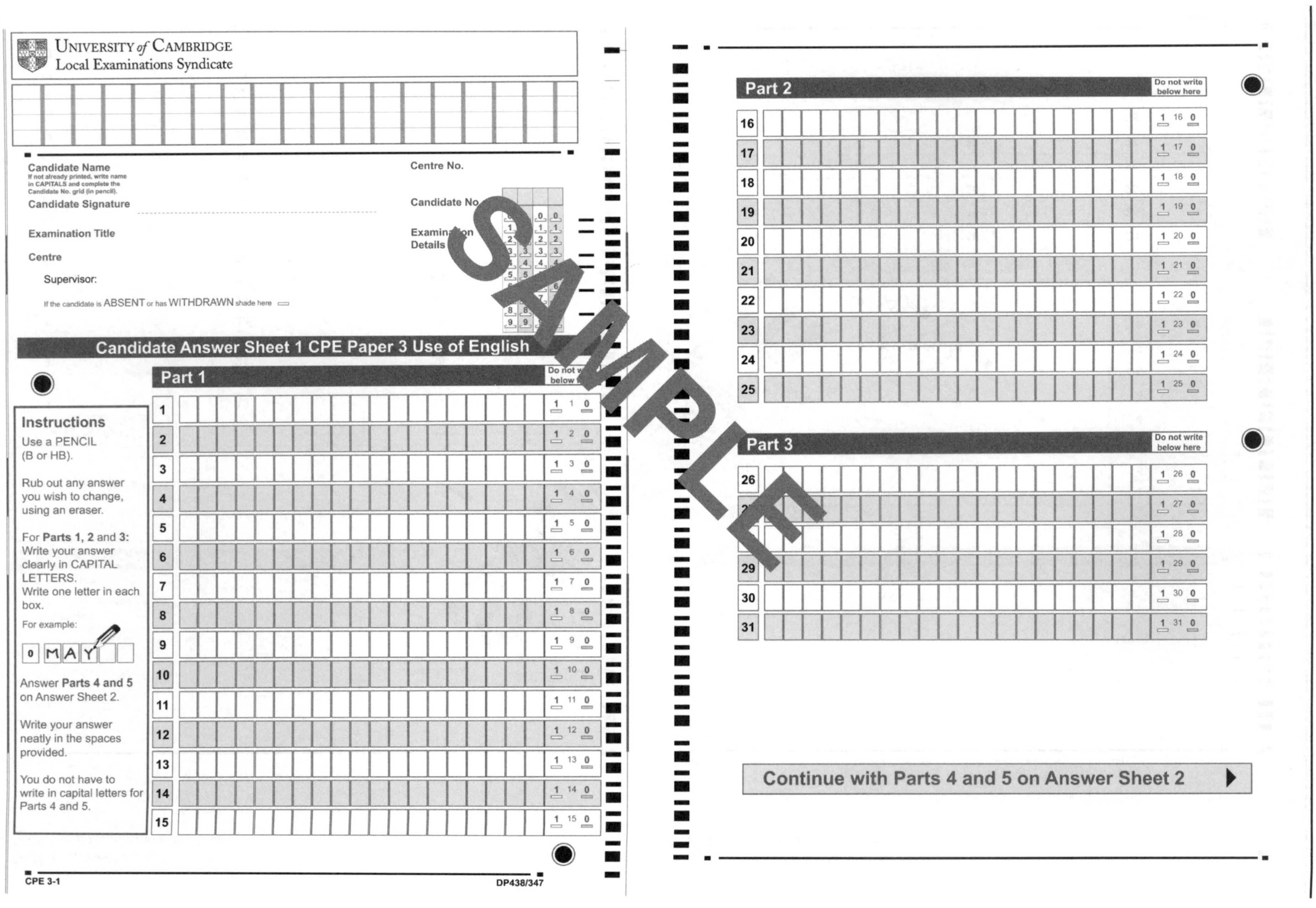

UNIVERSITY of CAMBRIDGE
Local Examinations Syndicate

Candidate Name
If not already printed, write name in CAPITALS and complete the Candidate No. grid (in pencil).

Candidate Signature

Examination Title

Centre

Supervisor:

If the candidate is ABSENT or has WITHDRAWN shade here

Centre No.

Candidate No.

Examination Details

Candidate Answer Sheet 1 CPE Paper 3 Use of English

Instructions

Use a PENCIL (B or HB).

Rub out any answer you wish to change, using an eraser.

For **Parts 1, 2 and 3**: Write your answer clearly in CAPITAL LETTERS.

Write one letter in each box.

For example:

0 M A Y

Answer **Parts 4 and 5** on Answer Sheet 2.

Write your answer neatly in the spaces provided.

You do not have to write in capital letters for Parts 4 and 5.

Part 1

Do not write below here

1 2 3 4 5 6 7 8 9 10 11 12 13 14 15

Part 2

Do not write below here

16 17 18 19 20 21 22 23 24 25

Part 3

Do not write below here

26 27 28 29 30 31

Continue with Parts 4 and 5 on Answer Sheet 2

CPE 3-1

DP438/347

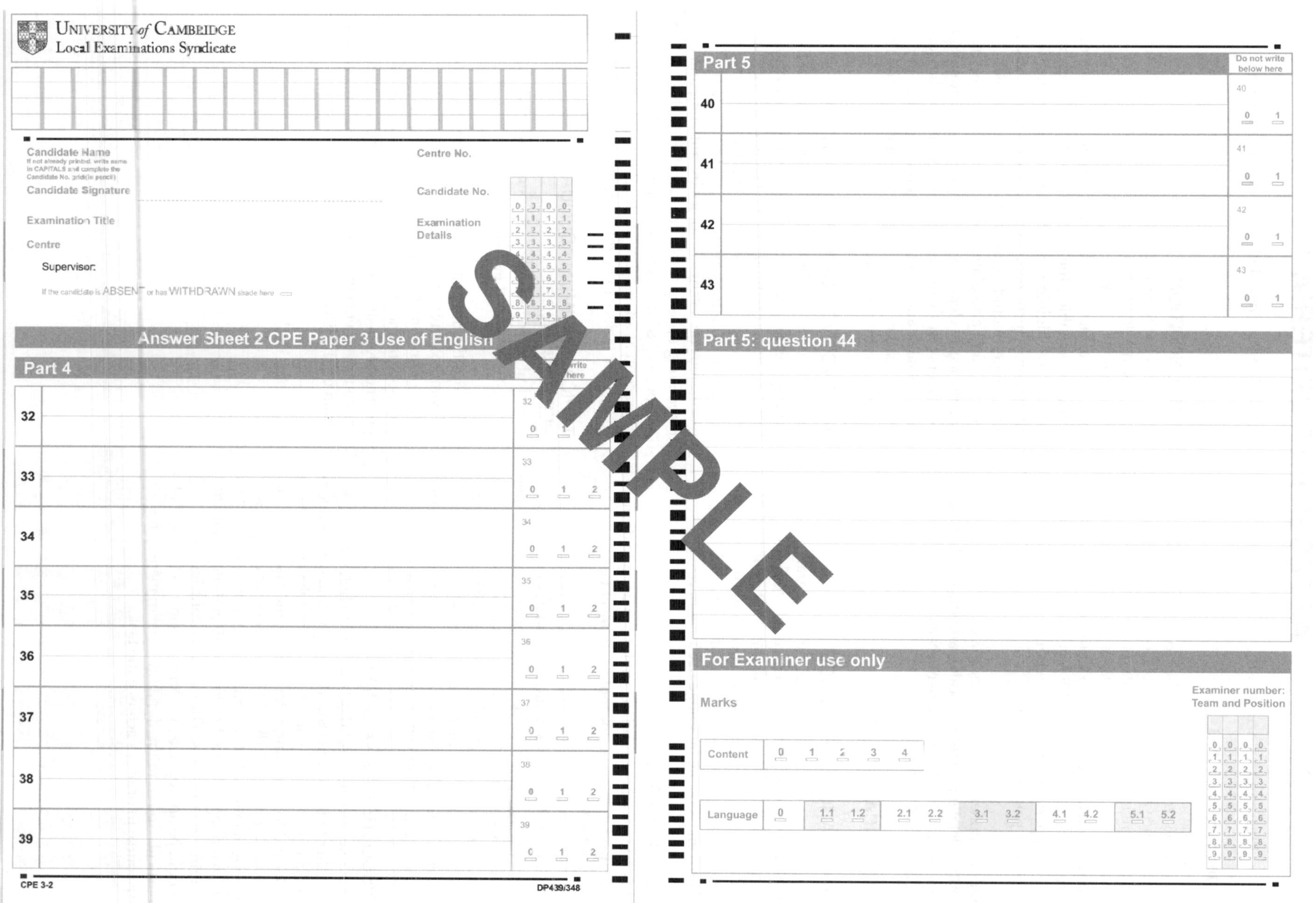

UNIVERSITY of CAMBRIDGE
Local Examinations Syndicate

Candidate Name
If not already printed, write name in CAPITALS and complete the Candidate No. grid (in pencil)

Candidate Signature

Examination Title

Centre

Supervisor:

If the candidate is ABSENT or has WITHDRAWN shade here

Centre No.

Candidate No.

Examination Details

Answer Sheet 2 CPE Paper 3 Use of English

Part 4

		Do not write here
32		0 1 2
33		0 1 2
34		0 1 2
35		0 1 2
36		0 1 2
37		0 1 2
38		0 1 2
39		0 1 2

CPE 3-2

DP439/348

Part 5

		Do not write below here
40		0 1
41		0 1
42		0 1
43		0 1

Part 5: question 44

For Examiner use only

Marks

Content	0	1	2	3	4

Language	0	1.1	1.2	2.1	2.2	3.1	3.2	4.1	4.2	5.1	5.2

Examiner number: Team and Position

ASSESSMENT CRITERIA

Please note: Correct at the time of going to print. Contact UCLES for detailed, up to date information.

Paper 5, SPEAKING

Candidates are assessed on their own individual performance and not in relation to each other, according to the following analytical criteria: Grammatical Resource, Lexical Resource, Discourse Management, Pronunciation and Interactive Communication. These criteria are interpreted at CPE level. Assessment is based on performance in the whole test and not to particular parts of the test.

Both examiners assess the candidates. The assessor applies detailed, analytical scales, and the interlocutor applies the Global Achievement scale, which is based on the analytical scales.

ANALYTICAL SCALES

GRAMMATICAL RESOURCE

This refers to the accurate application of grammatical rules and the effective arrangement of words in utterances. At CPE level a wide range of grammatical forms should be used appropriately and competently. Performance is viewed in terms of the overall effectiveness of the language used.

LEXICAL RESOURCE

This refers to the candidate's ability to use a wide and appropriate range of vocabulary to meet task requirements.

At CPE level the tasks require candidates to express precise meanings, attitudes and opinions and to be able to convey abstract ideas. Although candidates may lack specialised vocabulary when dealing with unfamiliar topics, it should not in general terms be necessary to resort to simplification. Performance is viewed in terms of the overall effectiveness of the language used.

DISCOURSE MANAGEMENT

This refers to the candidate's ability to link utterances together to form coherent monologue and contributions to dialogue. The utterances should be relevant to the tasks and to preceding utterances in the discourse. The discourse produced should be at a level of complexity appropriate to CPE level and the utterances should be arranged logically to develop the themes or arguments required by the tasks. The extent of contributions should be appropriate, i.e. long or short as required at a particular point in the dynamic development of the discourse in order to achieve the task.

PRONUNCIATION

This refers to the candidate's ability to produce easily comprehensible utterances to fulfil the task requirements. At CPE level, acceptable pronunciation should be achieved by the appropriate use of strong and weak syllables, the smooth linking of words and the effective highlighting of information-bearing words. Intonation, which includes the use of a sufficiently wide pitch range, should be used effectively to convey meaning, and articulation of individual sounds should be sufficiently clear for words to be easily understood. Examiners put themselves in the position of the non-EFL specialist and assess the overall impact of the communication and the degree of effort required to understand the candidate.

INTERACTIVE COMMUNICATION

This refers to the ability to take an active part in the development of the discourse, showing sensitivity to turn taking and without undue hesitation. It requires the ability to participate competently in the range of interactive situations in the test and to develop discussions on a range of topics by initiating and responding appropriately. It also refers to the deployment of strategies to maintain and repair interaction at an appropriate level throughout the test so that the tasks can be fulfilled.

TYPICAL MINIMUM ADEQUATE PERFORMANCE

A typical minimum adequate performance at CPE level can be summarised as follows:

Develops the interaction with contributions which are relevant, coherent and of an appropriate length. The range of grammatical forms and vocabulary is appropriate and used with sufficient accuracy and precision to deal with the CPE level tasks. Utterances are conveyed effectively and understood with very little strain on the listener.

Paper 2 GENERAL MARK SCHEME

Note: this mark scheme should be interpreted at CPE level. It should be used in conjunction with a task-specific mark scheme for each question.

Band	Descriptor
5.3 5.2 5.1	Outstanding realisation of the task set: • Sophisticated use of an extensive range of vocabulary, collocation and expression, entirely appropriate to the task set • Effective use of stylistic devices; register and format wholly appropriate • Impressive use of a wide range of structures • Skilfully organised and coherent • Excellent development of topic • Minimal error Impresses the reader and has a very positive effect.
4.3 4.2 4.1	Good realisation of the task set: • Fluent and natural use of a wide range of vocabulary, collocation and expression, successfully meeting the requirements of the task set • Good use of stylistic devices; register and format appropriate • Competent use of a wide range of structures • Well organised and coherent • Good development of topic • Minor and unobtrusive errors Has a positive effect on the reader.
3.3 3.2 3.1	Satisfactory realisation of the task set: • Reasonably fluent and natural use of a range of vocabulary and expression, adequate to the task set • Evidence of stylistic devices; register and format generally appropriate • Adequate range of structures • Clearly organised and generally coherent • Adequate coverage of topic • Some non-impeding errors Achieves the desired effect on the reader.
2.3 2.2 2.1	Inadequate attempt at the task set: • Limited and/or inaccurate range of vocabulary and expression • Little evidence of stylistic devices; some attempt at appropriate register and format • Inadequate range of structures • Some attempt at organisation, but lacks coherence • Inadequate development of topic • A number of errors, which sometimes impede communication Has a negative effect on the reader.
1.3 1.2 1.1	Poor attempt at the task set: • Severely limited and inaccurate range of vocabulary and expression • No evidence of stylistic devices; little or no attempt at appropriate register and format • Lack of structural range • Poorly organised, leading to incoherence • Little relevance to topic, and/or too short • Numerous errors, which distract and often impede communication Has a very negative effect on the reader.
0	Negligible or no attempt at the task set: • Totally incomprehensible due to serious error • Totally irrelevant • Insufficient language to assess (fewer than 20% of the required number of words) • Totally illegible

Please note: Correct at the time of going to print. Contact UCLES for detailed, up to date information.

Paper 3, Part Five SUMMARY MARK SCHEME

Note: this mark scheme should be interpreted at CPE level. A separate mark scheme is used to assess content.

5.2 / 5.1

Outstanding realisation of the task set:
- Totally relevant
- Concise and totally coherent
- Skilfully organised, with effective use of linking devices
- Skilfully re-worded, where appropriate
- Minimal non-impeding errors, probably due to ambition

Clearly informs and requires virtually no effort on the part of the reader.

4.2 / 4.1

Good realisation of the task set:
- Mostly relevant
- Concise and mostly coherent
- Well organised, with good use of linking devices
- Competently re-worded, where appropriate
- Occasional non-impeding errors

Informs and requires minimal or no effort on the part of the reader.

3.2 / 3.1

Satisfactory realisation of the task set:
- Generally relevant, with occasional digression
- Some attempt at concise writing and reasonably coherent
- Adequately organised, with some appropriate use of linking devices
- Adequately re-worded, where appropriate
- Some errors, mostly non-impeding

Adequately informs, though may require some effort on the part of the reader.

2.2 / 2.1

Inadequate attempt at the task set:
- Some irrelevance
- Little attempt at concise writing, so likely to be over-length and incoherent in places OR too short
- Some attempt at organisation, but only limited use of appropriate linking devices and may use inappropriate listing or note format
- Inadequately re-worded and/or inappropriate lifting
- A number of errors, which sometimes impede communication

Partially informs, though requires considerable effort on the part of the reader.

1.2 / 1.1

Poor attempt at the task set:
- Considerable irrelevance
- No attempt at concise writing, so likely to be seriously over-length and seriously incoherent OR far too short
- Poorly organised, with little or no use of appropriate linking devices and/or relies on listing or note format
- Poorly re-worded and/or over-reliance on lifting
- Numerous errors, which distract and impede communication

Fails to inform and requires excessive effort on the part of the reader.

0

Negligible or no attempt at the task set:
- Does not demonstrate summary skills
- Incomprehensible due to serious error
- Totally irrelevant
- Insufficient language to assess (fewer than 15 words)
- Totally illegible

Please note: Correct at the time of going to print. Contact UCLES for detailed, up to date information.